DESIGN LAW

Protecting and Exploiting Rights

Margaret Briffa and Lee Gage

The Law Society

ISBN 1 85328 817 9

Published in 2004 by the Law Society
113 Chancery Lane, London WC2A 1PL

Typeset by J&L Composition, Filey, North Yorkshire
Printed by Antony Rowe Ltd, Chippenham, Wilts

Contents

Acknowledgements

Our thanks to Maija Kontto, Sarah Jeffrey and Lizzie Buckley for their help in collating the appendices. Thanks to Adrienne Wallace and Alex Papakyriacou for their eagle eyes. Thanks also to Patrick Gompertz and Humphry Smith for their continued support. Thanks to everyone at Briffa for bearing with us.

Table of cases

Table of statutes and European legislation

*Page numbers in **bold** type indicate where the legislation is set out in part or in full.*

USA

VIETNAM

EUROPEAN LEGISLATION

INTERNATIONAL LEGISLATION

Table of statutory instruments

*Page numbers in **bold** type indicate where the legislation is set out in part or in full.*

CHAPTER 1

Successfully protecting and exploiting design

INTRODUCTION

Everyone involved in the design industry in the UK will be aware of the danger that their work may be copied, both at home and abroad. With globalisation of trade the need for effective design protection to ensure the success of a design company is all the more great. Design protection as part of intellectual property law is a legal matter. A clear understanding of and intelligent use of the laws available to prevent copying helps design businesses to protect and extract value for the investment they have made in design.

This book is addressed to the non-specialist reader. It is primarily intended for designers, design businesses manufacturers, inventors and non-specialist legal practitioners. This chapter and Chapter 2, History, look at the importance of design and the evolution of the law to the system we have today. Other chapters deal with the specific rights and how they can be applied to assist a designer in the battle to avoid plagiarism. Chapter 7 explores the complementary right of registered trade marks in 3D shapes.

The focus of these first chapters is in the main protection in the European Community. Chapters on protecting designs in the United States and in South-East Asia have also been included. The United States is an important market for designs, and designers need to take appropriate steps to seek protection at the right time. South-East Asia is a place where both copying and manufacturing take place. Accordingly, a chapter which deals with contracting in this region, as well as protection of design will help design businesses formulate a coherent plan.

STYLE OVER SUBSTANCE? WHAT IS DESIGN?

It is a well-known principle of English law that there is no copyright in an idea, but only in the expression of that idea in material form. Under copyright law, there needs to be 'a work' to which rights can attach. Granting rights where there is no such 'work' raises concerns of unfair and unjustifiable restrictions on creativity. This is not a desirable result in a system which recognises that creativity is important enough to protect.

The legal devices by which designs can be protected are a mixture of rights which includes copyright. The principle that there is no legal protection in an idea, only its expression, may translate in design terms to mean that there is no protection in law for style. That is, in order for a design to be capable of protection it must be fixed in material form. This point was tested by two Dutch cases in the 1990s. Although the cases are Dutch and therefore not binding in the UK, they drive home two things. First, they illustrate how blurred the line between idea and expression of idea is. Second, in the absence of a unified system across Europe for the protection and enforcement of rights in design, they give an indication of the difficulties faced by designers in a system where to prevent copying of a design across just Europe they are likely to have to face proceedings in each national court with the prospect of a different result in each one. It is by no means certain that even on similar facts success in one territory follows success in another.

In the first case, the proprietors of Barbie, the well-known 'fashion doll' attempted to prevent Barbie, the product, being copied by the proprietor of the fashion doll Sindy. Following copyright principles, the Court of Appeal found a striking resemblance in the structure of the lower part of the face of the two dolls and the curve between the nose and the forehead. The court found that Barbie was the leading doll and Sindy the doll who wants to be like Barbie; in other words Sindy copies Barbie. Sindy has nothing peculiarly personal or original beside Barbie. In spite of the fact that a continuous flood of imitations may be seen to have eroded the protection of Barbie as an original creation, the judges nonetheless compared the two dolls in detail to determine the extent that Sindy took features from Barbie. On this basis it was found that Sindy was not just directly inspired by Barbie and so followed a certain style but was a copy of a market leader (Hoge Raad, 21 February 1992 [1993] Netherlandse Jurisprudentie 143).

Conversely, in *Decaux* v. *Mediamex* (Hoge Raad, 29 December 1995 [1996] Netherlandse Jurisprudentie 546) the Court of Appeal excluded all elements of 'style' before looking at the question of infringement. In this case Decaux had developed an innovative model for a billboard but the court held that the specific design was an expression of a prevailing trend or fashion. Consequently, copying the main features of such a design was not an infringement.

The judges in the two cases took very different views and it is not possible to say which is correct. One thing that is clear, however, is that in order to protect and exploit design effectively, those creating designs need to appreciate two things: first, that there is a web of legal rights which can be invoked to assist. In the UK, the law protecting designs is a mix of copyright, design, trade mark law, and the common law action for passing off. In other jurisdictions, unfair competition and trade dress may also be invoked. Second, protecting and enforcing rights is an essential strategy in the battle against imitation products.

WHY IS DESIGN IMPORTANT?

Success in business depends on being able to compete effectively. Making a product that people want and producing it efficiently is a start. Where consumers have a choice, however, products need to be designed well in order to sell. The investment in design to achieve just this end is significant whether the company makes products which have not traditionally been particularly inspired, such as vacuum cleaners, or products which are traditionally designed, such as furniture.

Having made the investment in design, innovators look to systems of protection. Where designs have features which are aesthetically pleasing, most countries provide systems of registration to assist the innovator in protecting the investment. The investment in registered rights is however by no means universal. In the UK, around 8,000 applications to register designs are made per year. Only one-tenth of this number of applications (800) are made in Italy, but approximately 96,000 applications are made in Germany. Uptake is clearly patchy and may to date be explained in part by the differences between the various systems of design protection that have existed in Europe historically.

The major question is what impact the introduction of the pan-European filing system will have. As will be explored in this book, the registered Community Design has many advantages to the designer who may otherwise have relied on 15 national copyrights as a bundle of rights.

WHY IS PROTECTING DESIGN IMPORTANT?

Designers are in many senses the instruments of change. They devise and produce new products that take account of social change. Better products mean an improvement in the standard of living.

One-third of companies growing rapidly say design helps make them more competitive. Three-quarters of rapidly growing businesses say design contributes to rising sales (Design Council published statistics: *Design in Business Week* 2002).

There is a deserving argument for encouraging and protecting designers and companies which invest in design from the plagiarist. The development of a marketable design from an original idea involves significant expense and effort. The designer is by definition a risk-taker.

If plagiarists were permitted an unfettered right to copy and thereby avoid the need to invest their own efforts and funds in developing products, they would have an unfair advantage over the original designer.

While this principle is well understood and design law well established, for many designers and companies accessing the protection which the law has laid down is far from simple. Historically, legal redress for designers has been unduly uncertain, costly and slow. It is hoped that the new Community

Design system will go some way to remove or at least significantly reduce these problems.

WHAT IS DESIGN LAW?

Design law refers to the systems by which designs are protected from copying or other unfair use. The available protection and ways in which rights can be enforced are different from country to country and historically were widely divergent even within Europe.

This book focuses on how designs are protected in the UK and Europe as we anticipate that these will be the major markets for readers. However, we have also included chapters on protection in the USA and the systems in South-East Asia to build a bigger picture. The systems in the USA and the countries of South-East Asia again, as in Europe, rely on a bundle of rights and not one unitary system to protect design. The protections available to designers in these territories and the way in which the protection available can be used to strengthen a designer's overall investment in designs is worth noting. Both territories present significant market opportunity for designers. In addition, protection of design by registered rights in South-East Asia can assist greatly as a tool in any enforcement programme in the event of copy products being made in that region. A well-planned design protection strategy will take both these regions into account at an early stage.

In the UK, design is protected by at least six different regimes which may all apply to the same design. These are:

- UK copyright;
- UK unregistered design right;
- UK registered design;
- unregistered Community Design right;
- registered Community Design;
- the law of trade marks as it applies to shapes.

In other European countries the picture is similar, with countries having various systems under which designers can gain protection. Apart from legislation dealing specifically with design, the courts may themselves have bolstered the protections available, for example in the USA through the Law of Trade Dress and in Germany through the Law of Unfair Competition.

The pan-European design system introduced by Council Regulation 6/2000 of 12 December 2001 on Community Designs ((2002) OJ Lo3/1) (referred to as the Regulations) is intended to lessen the impact of some of the inherent inefficiencies of such a fragmented system. It approximates or harmonises most substantive provisions of national design laws. It creates two rights: an unregistered Community Design right which entered into force on 6 March 2002 and a registered Community Design, effective from

December 2002 (with applications accepted 1 April 2003). It is important to note that both these new Community rights coexist with national copyright and other laws which will remain essential in a company's overall design protection and exploitation plan.

The Office for Harmonisation in the Internal Market (Trade Marks and Designs) (OHIM) in Alicante, Spain is responsible for processing applications for registered Community Designs which have been accepted since 1 April 2003.

The details of the new Community system will be explored in this book, as will the various means by which designs can be protected. Compared with 15 different national copyrights systems, a single Community Design offers significant procedural advantage. In addition, while Holland for example, has been prepared to grant cross-border injunctions there is as yet no such thing as a European system of copyright enforcement. The scheme for Community Design sets up Community Design Courts which have jurisdiction to make orders which are enforceable across the whole European Community.

The pan-European design registration system also offers significant advantages over the trade mark system as it applies to protect 3D shapes. The Community Design system is quicker and less burdensome compared with the trade mark system. In particular:

1. Trade marks rights arise from registration following application, while unregistered Community Design right subsists in a design from its first making available to the public within the Community.
2. Trade mark registration is subject to substantive examination and possibly opposition proceedings; registered Community Design is hardly subject to any substantive examination at the registration stage and there is no opportunity for any person to institute opposition proceedings against a design until it is registered.

Chapter 7 contains a more detailed look at the relative advantages and disadvantages of protection under these two parallel systems.

It is too early to say what impact the new pan-European system will have and what the uptake of the new Community registration will be. Businesses that make serious investment in design and that wish to protect and enforce design in the most cost-effective manner may well consider the new Community Design has sufficient advantage to justify investment in Community registrations. If this happens, the registered Community Design may enjoy a popularity which has eluded some national registers of design rights. Indeed, the registered Community Design may turn out to be a highly valuable business tool.

CHAPTER 2

History

INTRODUCTION

The history behind the current system of design protection is the combined history of both copyright and design law. This is because the earliest copyright laws were introduced to protect the interests of printers and protected both literary and artistic works. The idea that copyright was for art while the other more technical and commercial areas of intellectual property were reserved for those with a more technical frame of mind is well embedded. Within this idea there was a distinction to be drawn between articles which could be said to be unique specimens, differing only from works of art in that they have an obvious practical use, such as hand-carved furniture on the one hand and more functional articles which were intended for indefinite multiplication. These ideas, resulting in the relegation of 'design' to second-class citizen status, have had a lasting impact on the relationship between design law and other categories of intellectual property law, including copyright.

HISTORY OF COPYRIGHT LAW

The idea of a right to prevent copying emerges

Copyright is a comparatively modern concept dating from the late fifteenth century. The classical world did not recognise copyright as such although there is evidence that Greek and Roman authors were concerned to be identified as the author of their works and that authorship should be recognised. They did not however enjoy any economic rights, that is the right to prevent copying of their work without permission. The reason for this is that prior to the invention of printing there was little practical need for legal protection of authors with most of the population illiterate and the business of copy-writing being a painstaking task undertaken in the main by monks.

The earliest copyright case on record is an Irish sixth-century case involving St Columba, who while on a visit to the monastery of his former teacher, Abbott Finnian copied the Abbott's psalter. The Abbott demanded the return of the copy and when this was refused, St Columba referred the dispute to the King, who ruled in the Abbott's favour saying 'to every cow her calf and consequently to every book its copy'.

The arrival of the printing press

The invention of the printing press gave rise to a potential new market for books and it is not surprising therefore that the earliest form of copyright protection took the form of printers' licences granted by the Sovereign to regulate the book trade and to protect printers against piracy. The Licensing Act of 1662 established a register of licensed books, which involved a requirement to deposit a copy of the book to be licensed. Deposit was administered by the Stationers' Company which also had powers to seize books suspected of containing material hostile to the church or government. By 1681 the Licensing Act had been repealed and the Stationers' Company had passed a by-law that established rights in ownership for books registered to a number of its members so as to continue regulating the printing trade themselves.

The Statute of Anne

The first Copyright Act passed by Parliament, the Statute of Anne came into force on 10 April 1710. Despite the earlier Licensing Acts, the Statute of Anne is regarded as the foundation on which the concept of modern copyright law is built. The two main principles in the statute were recognition of the author as the person afforded the protection of copyright and the adoption of the principle of a limited term of protection for published works. Copyright in a work subsisted for the lifetime of the author and not beyond.

The Statue of Anne remained in force until it was superseded by the Copyright Act of 1842. It remained unchanged until then, although it was amended from time to time to add to the list of protected works, such as musical and dramatic composition. In addition in this period, further acts of Parliament were passed dealing with other areas of copyright law such as the Engraving Copyright Acts 1734 and 1766, the Printers' Copyright Acts of 1777 and 1836, and the Sculpture Copyright Act of 1814.

The 1842 Act extended the period of literary copyright to include a term of seven years following the death of the author or for a period of 42 years from publication whichever was the longer. In 1833, the Dramatic Copyright Act provided for a public performance right in dramatic works.

Fourteen acts of Parliament dealing with the subject of copyright were passed at various times between 1735 and 1875. The statutes which also impacted on aspects of design law can be seen as attempts to modernise the law and to bring it in line with technological changes which were occurring. There were shifts in methods of production, copying and consumer demand all of which had to be considered as the law developed. In 1875, a Royal

Commission was appointed to enquire into the working of the Copyright Acts. The Commission recommended that the law should be codified and clarified. The Commission also recommended that the government of the day enter into a bilateral copyright agreement with the USA in order to provide for reciprocal protection for British and US authors.

Despite these recommendations, no consolidating statute was passed and it was not until the involvement of the UK in the preparatory work on the Berne Convention (see Appendix C2) that the necessary push for reform eventually came.

The emergence of international convention

Fundamental to the protection of copyright and designs today is the protection which is afforded to 'foreign' designers on the basis of international convention. The cornerstone of this protection is the Berne Convention.

The Conference of Powers held at Berne resulted in the framing of the Berne Convention for the Protection of Literary and Artistic Works which the UK ratified with effect from 1877. The main changes to the existing copyright law were first that registration and deposit in the United Kingdom of foreign works were no longer required. Further British copyright law would be applied to works originating in British possessions. This meant that a work produced in one of the possessions received protection not only in the United Kingdom but in all the rest of them. In the same year an Order in Council was issued under the 1886 Act extending the protection of the Berne Convention to all British dominions.

Despite this step towards an international system, the Berne Convention did not give rise to a comprehensive reform of the law in the United Kingdom at that stage. A number of modifications, including the principle that protection under the Convention should be free from compliance with any formalities and the period of protection for the life of the author plus 50 years thereafter, were not introduced until the Copyright Act 1911, after the conference in Berlin held in 1908.

The Copyright Act 1911 to the Whitford Committee 1974

The Copyright Act 1911 repealed many former statutes on the subject of literary and artistic copyright. The Berne Convention was further revised in 1928 and 1948. Following the Berne Conference of 1951, a further committee was appointed to consider and report on what changes were desirable to the law relating to copyright in literary, musical and artistic works with particular regard to the technical developments and the revised international convention for the protection of literary and artistic works signed in Brussels in June 1948. The changes recommended by the committee are captured within the Copyright Act 1956 which came into force on 1 June 1957.

The 1956 Copyright Act was a complex piece of legislation. Apart from updating the then regime to take account of technological development, the 1956 Act was notable for adding three new forms of entrepreneurial copyright, in films, broadcasts and typographical fonts. The 1956 Act was amended by the Design Copyright Act 1968 (see p. 12).

HISTORY OF DESIGN LAW

Calico Printers' Act 1787 to the Design Registration Act 1839

As stated above, design protection and legislation developed alongside the development of laws relating to copyright.

The first statute to deal with designs was the Calico Printers' Act 1787. This Act gave every person who invented design and printed any new and original pattern on linens, cottons and calicoes, two months' protection. This was extended in 1794 to three months.

By the early eighteenth century there was need of further review to improve the protection afforded to British designs. Britain had the technology to produce goods more cheaply and in greater quantity than other trading nations. British goods were, however, considered to be of poor aesthetic quality. To remedy this, a design school was founded and a museum (now called the V&A) opened. The museum would encourage designers by exhibiting 'good designs'. The legal regime was also tackled. The Calico Printers' Acts were repealed and two new acts were introduced.

The Copyright and Design Act 1839 widened the category of subject matter which was protected under the Calico Printers' Act 1787 to include animal fabrics in addition to the fabrics of vegetable origin previously protected. Protection under this Act, limited to three months, arose automatically on publication of the design. The second Act, the Design Registrations Act 1839, extended the scope of the protection for designs beyond woven fabrics to include all articles of manufacture. It moved protection away from patterns and prints to provide protection for the shape and configuration of any article of manufacture. The Act conferred longer protection for such designs varying according to the nature of the substance to which the design was to be applied, and also provided that protection was only granted if the design was registered. The 1839 Act also introduced a Board of Trade and a registrar appointed by the Board of Trade.

Although these Acts were improvements over the earlier regime, they were repealed and replaced soon after they came into force by the Ornamental Designs Act 1842 and the Utility (or Non Ornamental) Design Act 1843. The 1842 Act consolidated all earlier Acts and further increased the remedies for infringements. The main change introduced by these Acts was to divide design into two separate categories, ornamental design and functional or utility design.

In 1875, the powers and duties of the Board of Trade were transferred to the UK Patent Office. It was perhaps at around this time that the distinction between fine and applied art, the first being more appropriate for copyright protection and the latter for protection as a design, became acute. The Patent Office was aware of the problems that drawing such a theoretical distinction could cause. These concerns were taken up in the Copyright Act 1911 which distinguished designs which were intended 'to be unique' and 'not to be multiplied', which were given full copyright protection, and manufactured mass-produced items, which were to be protected by design law. The 1911 Act was updated by the Registered Designs Act 1949 which was the Act that introduced a registration system for designs. It remains in force today albeit in an amended form. While the intention of the Copyright Act 1911 was to clarify the distinction between artistic and functional or mass-produced design, the current situation as will be explored more fully in this book is that designers can take advantage of both copyright and design law to protect against copying. The boundaries today remain unfixed but workable.

At this point it is more useful to consider copyright and design law together as the histories converge most closely and proceed jointly.

WHITFORD COMMITTEE 1974 TO 1988

Changes initiated by the Whitford Committee

In 1974, the Whitford Committee began the task of reviewing the whole range of copyright and design laws in the UK, including the desirability of retaining a registration system for designs. Legislation did not, however, follow and in the period from 1973 to 1987 the government legislated on an ad hoc basis to deal with such urgent matters as improved remedies against piracy, which had become a problem as a result of new technology facilitating reproduction techniques, and the protection of computer software and cable programmes.

In October 1987, a Bill was introduced into Parliament. The Bill, which was passed as the Copyright, Designs and Patents Act 1988, was not limited to copyright but introduced, among other things, a new design right and amendments to the Registered Designs Act 1949.

The 1988 Act made big changes. Before explaining some of the detailed provisions of the Act, the reason why the unregistered design right (see Chapter 4) was seen as necessary should be put into historical perspective.

In summary, the Copyright Act 1956 gave copyright protection to designs through the provision for 'works of artistic craftsmanship'. Drawings were seen as constituting artistic works and they were broadly defined in the Act to include any 'diagram, map, chart or plan'. Subsequently, by virtue of court ruling, engineering drawings were also included as a class of work capable of protection. By the provisions of the 1956 Act, it was further established that copyright in a drawing could be infringed by 'making an object in three dimensions provided that non experts could see that the three dimensional object was a reproduction of the two dimensional artistic work and that it did not require an expert to identify the relationship'.

In 1962, the Johnston Committee recommended the introduction of a system of design copyright that would have involved the deposit of a representation of the design to be protected, with payment of the appropriate fee but without a search. It recommended that copyright as well as design registration be available for industrial designs with eye appeal, but rejected the idea that either copyright or registered design protection should be available for designs 'dictated solely by function'. The recommendations were well received but were not acted upon on the basis that a major piece of legislation would be required to put the recommendations in place and parliamentary time was not available. Instead, a little-noticed act was passed into law unopposed, the Design Copyright Act 1968, after introduction into Parliament as a private members' Bill.

The Design Copyright Act 1968

The main purpose of the Design Copyright Act 1968 was stated as meeting the needs of industries for which registered design protection was inappropriate. Under the Design Copyright Act 1968, a design in the form of a drawing had initial protection 'irrespective of artistic quality' subject to certain provisos: the design must have sufficient skill and labour expended on it to make it an artistic work; and it must be original in the sense that it is the designer's own work and not a copy of someone else's. The protection meant that the design could not be copied in either two or three dimensions.

The 1968 Act was a great success in that it provided designers with a tool with which to fight plagiarism. In effect, it provided an effective legal remedy to prevent copying in respect of a wide range of products which were not registered or not capable of being registered under the Registered Designs Act 1949.

Anomalies arise

While popular with designers, the 1968 Act dealt with design copyright in a very rough and ready manner and it gave rise to awkward anomalies. For example, protection across a very wide field of design was given, but only if the design originated as a drawing. Registrable designs with 'eye appeal' were protected from copying for 15 years while purely functional designs, which were deliberately excluded from registration because they would impinge on the freedom of competitors, received copyright protection lasting for the creator's life plus 50 years. The protection afforded to purely functional articles as long as they originated in a drawing was unique in the world.

The anomaly that a designer needed to produce a drawing to benefit from the rights afforded by the 1968 Act was problematical for many designers whose products were based on 3D trial-and-error prototypes rather than drawings. It meant that, in order for products which did not start life as a drawing to benefit from copyright protection, they needed to be found to be a 'work of artistic craftsmanship' on which the design of the product was based. The problem is well illustrated by the case of *Merlet* v. *Mothercare* [1986] RPC 115 where Ms Merlet was denied protection on the basis that her baby rain-cosy had started life not as a drawing but as a prototype. On that basis Ms Merlet would need to show that the ultimate product was a work of 'artistic craftsmanship' to qualify for copyright protection. As the rain-cosy had in fact been produced in the first place with the intention of protecting her baby from the rigours of Highland weather, the rain-cosy was found not to qualify for copyright protection.

While designers struggled, like Ms Merlet, to gain adequate protection, the biggest industrial problem to arise and the one which pushed the need for reform sharply forward was with regard to those businesses that produced spare parts for domestic equipment, in particular spare parts for motor cars. Businesses that originated the parts for and on behalf of the motor manufacturers themselves benefited from copyright protection in purely functional design so long as the design originated in a drawing. They argued that any design, however simple, required skill and labour and accordingly, any design warranted copyright protection. All other spare parts manufacturers and suppliers were, under this regime, excluded from the market. They argued that this position was inconsistent with history; the position almost anywhere else in the world; and it was also anti-competitive.

The courts draw the copyright line

The principles were tested in the case of *British Leyland* v. *Armstrong Patents Co.* [1986] RPC 279, [1986] AC 577. In this case, a High Court judge found in favour of a claim for copyright in the exhaust system of a car made by British Leyland. An injunction was granted preventing a spare parts manufacturer from infringing British Leyland's copyright, effectively confirming what was generally believed to be the position, that functional design, so long as originating from a drawing, benefited from full copyright protection, that is the life of the draughtsperson plus 50 years. The decision was upheld by the Court of Appeal in 1984. On further appeal to the House of Lords, the House of Lords saw a direct conflict between copyright in the purely functional exhaust system and the right of car owners to repair their vehicle free from the copyright constraint. The House of Lords decided that a car owner should be free to repair his vehicle, Lord Templeman saying that 'exploitation

13

of copyright law' for purposes for which it was never intended had 'gone far enough'. Lord Templeman saw no reason to confer on manufacturers the right in effect to dictate the terms on which an article sold by them was to be kept in repair and working order. The injunction previously granted was withdrawn.

The practical result of this case is the boundary it set between what was reasonable and justifiable subject matter capable of copyright protection on the one hand and what protection would result in excessive monopoly protection and therefore an unreasonable restraint of trade on the other. This boundary became instrumental in the reform of the copyright law and led to the introduction of an unregistered design right in Part III of the CDPA 1988. The unregistered design right is discussed more fully in Chapter 4. It provides for a reduced term of copyright protection subject to certain conditions. It is a form of copyright which prevents designs that are not 'works of artistic craftsmanship' benefiting from full copyright protection.

Despite this advancement in the UK, the battle with the motor car industry continues to this day as the industry has been heavily involved in the progress of the current European legislation harmonising design protection in Europe. Indeed, due to the controversy regarding this particular industry, the question of protection of spare parts in Europe remains unsettled.

The 1990s

In the 10 years after the 1988 Act came into force, it was amended continuously, mainly to implement EC Directives on the subject of copyright and related rights resulting from the European Commission's programme for the harmonisation of such laws within the European Union.

In 1991 the European Commission published a Green Paper on design protection (IIIF/131/91). The Green Paper expressed the view that the existence of different design laws in different Member States of the EU prevented and distorted competition in the Community. As a remedy, it proposed harmonisation of national laws and Community-wide design protection. There followed a proposed Directive on 23 December 1993 (COM (93) 344 OJ C345) and a proposed regulation on 31 January 1994 (COM (93) 342 OJ C029). The Directive of 1993 proposed the creation of a European Union Design Registry, which would grant design registrations that would be effective throughout the European Union. The progress of the Directive was however extremely slow. One of the main issues which delayed the legislation was a difference of opinion on how spare parts should be dealt with. There was intense lobbying from those with vested interests. Almost five years later the Directive was finally adopted on 13 October 1998 (98/71/EC). Council Regulation 6/2002 to establish the Community Design regime was adopted on 12 December 2001 and published in the Official Journal on 5 January 2002.

The Design Regulation

The new system in Europe, which is explored in full in Chapter 6, creates an entirely new regime for both registered and unregistered designs. It is possible to obtain a registered Community Design, which is directly applicable throughout the European Union. Unlike a Directive, which would give scope for each Member State to provide its own interpretation of the subject matter of a Directive into national law, the Regulation ensures that each Member State benefits from a standard set of rules. The registered Community Design right is obtained by registration at the OHIM at Alicante in Spain. Registered design rights will have a term of 25 years from filing of the application. In addition, an unregistered design right has been created which will be protected for three years from the date on which the design was first made available to the public within the European Union. The provisions relating to the unregistered design right came into effect on 6 March 2002. The provisions relating to the registered right came into effect on 1 April 2003.

The reason given for the two types of right is that a Community Design should as far as possible serve the needs of all sectors of industry of the Community. Some sectors produce large numbers of designs for products which have a short market life where protection without the burden of registration formalities is an advantage. The duration of the protection is of less significance than the ability to enjoy protection for the crucial marketing period. Other industry sectors value the advantages of registration for the greater legal certainty it provides and require the advantage of a longer term of protection corresponding to the predicted market life of the product.

Whereas a registered Community Design will give monopoly rights similar to a patent, the unregistered design right is infringed on proof that copying has taken place. These two rights coexist with national design rights and other national rights such as copyright, national unregistered design rights, trade marks, patent, utility models, typefaces and rights under unfair competition.

The position with respect to spare parts remains unresolved and will no doubt be the impetus for further academic consideration of the copyright-versus-design debate.

CHAPTER 3

Protecting design by copyright

INTRODUCTION

The Copyright, Designs and Patents Act 1988 (CDPA) gives copyright protection to artistic works which includes works of artistic craftsmanship. In so doing, there is limited protection for designs as copyright works so long as they qualify as 'artistic works' and in particular works of artistic craftsmanship.

As will be seen in this chapter, passing the 'works of artistic craftsmanship' hurdle to qualify for copyright protection is not easy. Copyright law however remains very relevant to designers for two reasons. First, surface decoration on a design may be protected as an 'artistic work'. This means for example that a patterned fabric or painting on a dinner plate may be protected by copyright irrespective of any design registration. Second, the UK system provides no definitive answer as to what is and what is not a 'work of artistic craftsmanship'. This means that when designers are faced with a copy product both copyright and design law may be used to help designers protect their market. The ultimate decision in any dispute as to whether a work is protected by copyright, unregistered design right (discussed further in Chapter 4) or registered design right (discussed further in Chapter 5) will be taken by a judge. The best guide we have are the cases which have been decided and these do not provide complete assurance as to what will be considered a 'work of artistic craftsmanship'.

The effect of this is that a designer should be aware that copyright may apply and should take simple practical steps to preserve material which may help in proving the design is a 'work of artistic craftsmanship'. In practice it is common in disputes involving designs, other than purely or largely functional design, for the designer to rely on both copyright and unregistered design right provisions.

Copyright, being a right which arises automatically on creation of a work, is a valuable right. In addition, copyright in an artistic work lasts for the life of the author plus 70 years (see pp. 23–24), whereas the protection given to unregistered design rights and even registered designs is much shorter. Copyright therefore may come into play and indeed may be the only protection available when other rights have expired and for this reason attention should be given to how copyright in a work of artistic craftsmanship may be proved. Ultimately the strength of copyright as a tool for any designer depends on the designer taking simple practical steps to record carefully both the design history before the design is on the market as well as the public reaction to the design once it is launched. Some practical guidance for designers on this topic is included in this chapter.

WHAT IS AN ARTISTIC WORK UNDER THE CDPA 1988?

The relevant provision is s.4(1) CDPA, which defines 'artistic work' as an original work comprising one of the following:

(a) a graphic work, photograph, sculpture or collage;
(b) a work of architecture, being a building or a model for a building; or
(c) a work of artistic craftsmanship.

Copyright in an artistic work depends on originality. This means that the designer did not merely copy the work, but produced it independently by the expenditure of a substantial amount of the designer's own skill, knowledge, labour, taste or judgement. However, the amount of skill and labour which is required to establish copyright is not large and essentially anything suffices as long as it is not insubstantial. Where the subject matter was designs for Lego toy bricks, and those designs simply repeated earlier designs with indications of minor modifications to dimensions and tolerances the drawings did not confer originality such that a separate copyright arose as the variations were not of 'visual significance' (*Interlego* v. *Tyco* [1988] RPC 343 JC). However, if artistic skill is required to make a copy, it seems that that may supply the originality.

Most of the decisions as to what constitutes an 'artistic work' set the minimum level of effort low: a simple drawing of a human hand showing voters where to mark their cross on a voting card (*Kenrick* v. *Lawrence* [1890] 25 QBD 99), the label design for a sweet tin (*Taverner Rutledge* v. *Specters* [1959] RPC 355, CA), the arrangement of a few decorative lines on a parcel label (*Walker* v. *British Picker* [1961] RPC 57). To counter-balance this, as will be seen, the scope of infringement in such cases is narrowly defined.

What is a work of artistic craftsmanship under the CDPA 1988?

The difficulty in making artistic quality an irrelevant test for most artistic works becomes clear when deciding which products may benefit from copyright protection as 'works of artistic craftsmanship'. The provision specifically refers to the quality of being artistic. The House of Lords has indicated that such things as hand-painted tiles, stained-glass windows, wrought-iron gates and certain pieces of furniture might be examples of works of artistic craftsmanship but there is no generally acceptable definition. The leading case is *George Hensher Limited* v. *Restawhile Upholstery (Lancs) Limited* [1976] AC 64 in which five Law Lords took five different approaches to what may amount to a work of artistic craftsmanship. In *Hensher* v. *Restawhile* they all agreed that a flimsy prototype of a mass-produced upholstered chair did not qualify for artistic craftsmanship even if it could be considered a work of 'craftsmanship' in the first place. No complete consensus emerged from the case as to whether only hand-made items qualify (they certainly had a better chance) or whether the question is one of law or fact.

Despite the different approaches taken by the Law Lords, three factors warrant attention in deciding whether a design is a work of 'artistic craftsmanship'.

1. Is it the craftsman's intention to create something artistic that counts, or, rather, is it the perception by the public of artistic quality as to the article?
2. What is the level of artistic aspiration or attainment that must be shown?
3. Is it for the judge to make up his own mind on the question, or is the judge's function to weigh the relative strength of expert and other testimony given to the court?

In respect of the first two questions, the case provides no clear-cut answer. Expert evidence was dismissed as not useful and the ultimate test of whether a design is a work of 'artistic craftsmanship' is one for the judge.

With respect to the first two questions the House of Lords made a number of statements which taken together do not show a unitary approach to defining the phrase 'artistic craftsmanship'. Lord Reid for example held that, 'A work is artistic if it is genuinely admired by a section of the community by reason of the emotional or intellectual satisfaction its appearance gives; that the creator was not consciously concerned to create a work of art is not determinative'. Lord Morris and Viscount Dilhorne held that whether something is artistic or not is a question of fact, to be decided in the light of the evidence and it is pointless to try to expound on the meaning of the word. Conversely, Lord Kilbrandon held that the word 'artistic' is for the court to interpret not witnesses. The true test is whether the creator has been consciously attempting to produce a work of art.

This was the approach applied by *Merlet* v. *Mothercare plc* [1986] RPC 115 to deny protection to Merlet's baby rain-cosy design as a 'work of artistic craftsmanship' where Mothercare had copied the rain-cosy design. The evidence showed that Merlet was more concerned with protecting her baby from the Highland summer weather than with any artistic consideration when she designed the rain-cosy.

Conversely, in *Radley Gowns Limited* v. *Costas Spyrou* [1975] FSR 455 Oliver J. granted an injunction to restrain copying of an Ossie Clarke dress, holding it to be arguable that the original was a work of artistic craftsmanship.

More recently, in the case of *Eduard Rudolph Vermaat & Others* v. *Boncrest Limited* [2000] Ch D, where the issue was whether the design of a patchwork product constituted an 'artistic work' being a work of 'artistic craftsmanship', Evans-Lombe J. held that the samples made by the seamstress were a work of craftsmanship but that the work was not sufficiently artistic so as to be a work of artistic craftsmanship.

Example 1

In 2003 Kathleen designs an armchair which includes her own original patterned textile which she sells to a small specialist designer furnishing store. The shape of the chair is simple and intended to reflect the current popular styles. She dies in 2008. Copyright subsists in the patterned textile until 31 December 2079. Unregistered design right in the shape of the chair (see Chapter 4) expires on 31 December 2013.

Example 2

Same facts as in Example 1 save that the frame of the armchair incorporates a carved pattern and Kathy sells these armchairs to a leading department store. Copyright subsists in the patterned textile until 31 December 2079. Copyright will also subsist to this date in the chair frame if it can be shown the frame is a work of artistic craftsmanship.

While Merlet failed in her battle against Mothercare, this case was decided before the CDPA came into force. Under the CDPA, Merlet may have been able to show infringement of her pattern-cutting as drawings, where artistic quality is not relevant. Further, under the CDPA, unregistered design right protection may have been available to prevent copying of the actual design rather than the pattern-cuttings by Mothercare.

Finally it has been debated whether, in order to qualify as a work of artistic craftsmanship, the craft and the artistry must be united in the same person. The current position is that since the law recognises the concept of joint authorship there is no reason in principle why two persons cannot create a work of artistic craftsmanship, e.g. one to manipulate the material and the other to offer verbal suggestions.

In summary, the difficulty in deciding whether a design is one which merits protection as 'artistic craftsmanship' means that few cases are brought against copyists on this ground alone. Possibly because of the lack of guidance given by the House of Lords' decision in *Hensher* v. *Restawhile* few claims of works of artistic craftsmanship have been raised since that decision. As mentioned in the introduction, however, this category of protection can be used as a tool in a case against a copyist alongside a claim as to infringement of a registered design or an unregistered design right.

Practical guidance

Designers should consider taking the following practical steps to ensure they have the best prospect of success in claiming protection by way of a 'work of artistic craftsmanship':

(a) keep all design drawings and sketches;
(b) keep cuttings and notes relating to the development of the design including all sources of inspiration;
(c) keep notes of any design brief, if it is intended for example that the work should create a design that has genuine artistic appeal as compared to other designs within the same category;
(d) ensure all drawings, notes and sketches are dated and record the creator. Mark material with the international symbol;
(e) keep together with the above a record of all material which assists in dating the design, for example records of exhibition of new designs at trade or other exhibitions or delivery notes from a manufacturer who is making samples;
(f) keep all press reviews favourably profiling the design and all notes or copies of all correspondence with customers' favourable comments on the design;
(g) avoid circulating design drawings, sketches and other preparatory work.

What is infringement of a work of artistic craftsmanship?

Section 16 CDPA states that 'the owner of the copyright in a work' has the exclusive right to do certain things, including to copy the work. Section 16(3) CDPA explains that what is restricted is not only the doing of these things in relation to the work as a whole but also the doing of them in relation to any substantial part of it. In all copyright disputes, where what is in issue is the degree of resemblance of the copyright work and the alleged copy, the key question is whether the alleged infringer has taken a substantial part of what the designer has created.

The test of whether a substantial part has been taken is one of quality and not quantity. This means that it is possible to infringe the copyright in an artistic work by copying a relatively small part if the part that is copied is significant. Another way of looking at the question of whether a substantial part has been copied is to consider the degree of originality the design in question has in the first place. Protection against inexact copying by the copying of a substantial part is most helpful where the original work in question has a high degree of originality.

There are several cases which have attempted in general to define what constitutes a copy of an artistic work. None offers a complete definition and many do not refer directly to works of artistic craftsmanship, as their subject matter is not within this category of work. It is worth reciting them however for guidance on how the court may approach the question of infringement.

In *Hansfstaengl* v. *WH Smith & Sons* [1905] I Ch 159, Kekewich J. suggested that 'to be a copy is that which comes so near the original to suggest the original to the mind of every person seeing it'. This definition however took no account of the independent concept of copying in the sense of derivation. Peterson J. in *McCrum* v. *Eisner* [1917] 87 LJ Ch 99 pointed out that the alleged copy may come near to the original without having been derived from it at all. He therefore offered a definition which presupposed an act of derivation.

Neither of these cases covers the situation where what is taken is an ancillary aspect of the original design but which nevertheless, due to its importance in the design overall, constitutes a substantial part of that design. In *LB (Plastics) Limited* v. *Swish Products Limited* [1979] RPC 611, HL which concerned the copying of a drawing of a knock-down drawer the chief point of difference between the Court of Appeal and the House of Lords was whether the defendants had merely taken the designer's principle of construction and fleshed out that general idea with skill and labour of their own, or had taken the flesh as well. As a general rule, the simpler a drawing of an artistic work, the more closely it will have to be imitated before there can be an infringement. The reason for this is that an inexact imitation of such a work will have to resemble the original at a comparatively higher level of abstraction.

Since the test for infringement is whether the alleged copyist has taken a substantial part of the designer's work, it is no answer to show that the copyist has expended further skill and labour on his or her own work so as to give it original character of its own. However, in a borderline case this circumstance may make a difference. As 'substantiality' is a question of fact and degree the surrounding circumstances may also be relevant. One of the relevant circumstances is for example whether the alleged copy is in competition with the original work (*Weatherby & Sons* v. *International Horse Agency & Exchange Limited* [1910] 2 Ch 297).

These principles were followed in the House of Lords' case of *Designers Guild Limited* v. *Russell Williams (Textiles) Limited* [2000] 1 WLR 2416 in a claim by the Designers Guild that its fabric Ixia had been copied by Russell Williams. The House of Lords held that the Designers Guild's Ixia had been copied as the Russell Williams fabric Marguerite incorporated features that by themselves were not original. Section 16(3) CDPA on the copying of a substantial part of the work came into play where an identifiable part of the whole, but not the whole had been copied and where the copying had been a copying with modifications. This case was an altered-copying case and a useful test to determine whether the altered copy constituted an infringement was whether the infringer incorporated a substantial part of the independent skill, labour and judgement as contributed by the original author in creating the copyright work? The test was based on an underlying principle that a copier was not at liberty to appropriate the benefit of another's skill and labour.

In an altered-copying case, particularly where the finding of copying was dependent on the inferences to be drawn from the extent and the nature of the similarities between the two works, the similarities would usually be determinative not only of the issue of copying but also the issue of substantiality. In altered-copying cases, the difficulty is drawing the line between the permitted borrowing of an idea and the prohibited piracy of the artistic creation of another. In drawing this line the extent and nature of the similarities between the altered copy and the original work must play an important and often determinative role. If the similarities between Marguerite and Ixia were so extensive and of such nature as to justify a finding that, in the absence of acceptable evidence as to independent design of Marguerite, Marguerite was copied from Ixia, it must follow that the Marguerite design incorporated a substantial part of the Ixia design and was an infringement.

HOW LONG DOES COPYRIGHT LAST?

The standard term of copyright protection is life of the creator plus 70 years (Council Directive 93/98/EEC of 29 October 1993; regulations made on 19 December 1995 and which came into force on 1 January 1996; section 12(2) CDPA as substituted by the regulations). The term is calculated from 1 January after the year in which the creator died. For example, if the designer dies on 13 September 2003, copyright expires at midnight on 31 December 2074. There are a number of exceptions. The most relevant to designers are as follows:

1. Where the design is a work of two designers jointly, the standard term is calculated with respect to the last designer to die.
2. Where the design is generated by computer, the first owner is deemed to be the person who made the arrangements for the generation of the work. Copyright protection however expires 50 years from the end of the year in which the computer-generated work was made.
3. Where the design comprises a typographical arrangement, the design itself benefits from the full period of copyright protection as any other drawing. It is not however an infringement of copyright to copy the typeface or design a new typeface based on the old one as the copyright

in respect of typographical arrangements expires 25 years after the end of the year in which the typeface was first published.

4.   Where the design originated in a country which is outside the European Economic Area, the laws of the country of origin apply. This means that if the laws in the country from which the work originates stipulate a term shorter than 70 years, the shorter term applies. This term cannot be longer than the 70 years granted under the CDPA and the regulations. The country of origin of a work is the country of which the designer was a national at the time the work was created. The test is 'was' rather than 'is' because the designer's nationality at the time the designer created the work is the relevant nationality, rather than one which the designer may have acquired at a later date.

COPYRIGHT PROTECTION IN OTHER COUNTRIES

In most cases copyright will be protected overseas automatically in the same way as it is automatically protected in the UK. As discussed in more detail in Chapter 2, the UK is a member of international conventions. In the field of design these are the Berne Convention for the Protection of Literary and Artistic Works, which is administered by the World Intellectual Property Organisation (WIPO) and the Universal Copyright Convention (UCC) administered by the United Nations Educational, Scientific and Cultural Organisation (UNESCO). Copyright material created by UK nationals or residents falling within the scope of one of these conventions is automatically protected in each member country of the convention by the national law of that country.

Western European countries, the USA and Russia are members of the Berne Convention (see Appendix C2 for full list), which does not require designers to mark their work in any way to benefit from copyright protection abroad. However, in order to benefit from automatic protection in other countries arising from the UCC (see www.unesco.com for contracting states information) it is essential that designers mark their work with the international copyright © symbol, followed by their name and the year in which the work was first shown in public. Although it is not a requirement to obtain copyright in countries which are members of the Berne Convention, designers are still best advised to mark their work in this way and to take the other precautions suggested in this chapter (see p. 21). Also, as described in more detail in Chapter 10, in the USA there is an official register of copyright which designers may wish to use when considering exploiting their designs in the USA, although registration is not an essential condition for copyright to subsist in the USA.

Finally, protection overseas can also arise from obligations in the agreement on Trade-Related Terms of Intellectual Property Rights (TRIPS), which forms part of the World Trade Organisation (WTO) Agreement. As with the Berne Convention and the UCC, copyright may be automatically protected in a WTO country. The list of WTO countries can be found on the Internet (http://www.wipo.org).

CHAPTER 4

Unregistered design right

INTRODUCTION

The background leading to the introduction of the unregistered design right was set out in Chapter 2. The right was introduced into law by the CDPA. The relevant provisions are contained in Part III of the CDPA which is reproduced in Appendix A1. This system of design protection coexists with the unregistered Community Design right and is governed by the Act as interpreted by case law. As the UK unregistered design right has a much longer term of protection than the unregistered Community Design right, it is important that designers understand what gives rise to the rights. Once the term of the coexisting unregistered Community Design right expires, the UK unregistered design right may, in the absence of any registered rights which a designer has applied for, be the only right a designer has.

WHAT TYPE OF DESIGN CAN BE PROTECTED?

Original

Unregistered design rights arise in 'original design' comprising 'any aspect of shape or configuration of an article which is not a surface decoration'.

'Original' has the same meaning as in copyright law, meaning 'not copied'. As with copyright, the legal test of what is 'original' is not based on a judgement as to the merit of a design. Nonetheless in establishing whether a design is original it is helpful to ask a designer the questions as set out below.

WHERE DID YOU GET YOUR INSPIRATION FOR THE CURRENT DESIGN?

It is appreciated that designers do not live in a vacuum and that the designs they create are influenced by the sum total of their knowledge and experience. This means it is highly likely that the design does have influences which can be pinpointed. The source of the inspiration should be considered and a comparison made to ensure that the design in question is not a copy of any inspiration material.

HAVE YOU SEEN ANYTHING LIKE THIS BEFORE?

As well as supporting the answer to the question 'Where did you get the inspiration for the current design?' this question ensures that the design in question is not too similar to any previous design of the same designer. The test is that the design must not be slavishly copied from some previous design. It must have involved some skill and labour in reaching its final form in order to benefit from protection. If the design in question does appear similar at first glance, the designer should explain the differences between the two and the work involved in reaching the current design.

DID YOU DESIGN THIS ALONE?

The answer to this question establishes that the design is by a single creator and not joint creators. Joint creation would result in the unregistered design right being owned by more than the creator alone and limits the designer's freedom to exploit or enforce the design on his or her own.

DO YOU HAVE ANY DOCUMENTS WHICH SUPPORT THE ANSWERS YOU HAVE GIVEN?

Any documents which can be collated to support the answers will be useful. In the event that the design is copied, a designer will need this material to establish ownership of the design in question (see example overleaf).

Design documents

The expression of a design may be in a design document or in the actual 3D product itself whichever occurs the earlier. A design document is commonly design drawings but can also be a written description, a prototype, photograph or data sorted on a computer.

External and internal features

The right subsists in any aspect of the design whether the feature is internal or external. As the intention behind the introduction of the unregistered design right was to give protection to technical designs or functional designs, it follows that the unregistered design right subsists even though the design cannot be seen by the purchaser and therefore can have no influence over the purchase decision. In *Farmers Build* v. *Carier* [1996] RPC 461, for example, unregistered design right was found to subsist in various parts and

Example

Celeste is a freelance designer engaged by a company which makes fancy dress clothes for children. In advance of the release of the Disney film The Little Mermaid *the company asked Celeste to design a mermaid costume. Celeste visits the local library and makes sketches from books with pictures of mermaids. She also carries out an online search and is able to see other images of mermaids and well as examples of mermaid costumes for children which are available on the market. Having looked at this material, Celeste decides that the costume she will design will include as its most prominent and unusual feature a forked tail and that the tail would be overlayered in different fabrics to give the impression of movement and waves. She makes various sketches to reach the design she is happy with. Celeste's designs are original in that they are not 'copied' from any previous design. A comparison of Celeste's design with the inspirational or research material shows that Celeste has expended her own skill and labour to reach her design.*

combinations of components that were enclosed in the machinery housing. In *Farmers Build* the influencing factor in any purchase would have been the fact that the Farmers Build design worked, in contrast to other machines on the market and sold for a similar purpose that did not.

The unregistered design right is a flexible tool for any designer. As well as applying to any feature of a design whether internal or external, the unregistered design right can apply to the article both 'as a whole' and also 'to a substantial part'. There are however a number of exceptions.

WHAT TYPE OF DESIGN IS NOT PROTECTED?

Method or principle of construction and 'must-fit', 'must-match' exceptions

The unregistered design right does arise where what is claimed is a method or principle of construction (s.213(3)(a) CDPA 1988). This excludes the process or operation by which the shape is produced as opposed to the shape itself. Further, with respect to the protection given to the shape or configuration, there are two other aspects of a design which are excluded from the unregistered design right. These are design features which:

(a) enable the article to be connected to, or placed around or against another article so that either article may perform its function; or

(b) are dependent upon the appearance of another article of which the article is intended by the designer to form an integral part.

These two exceptions from shape and configuration are commonly known as the 'must-fit', 'must-match' exceptions. They are limited in scope. The first, the must-fit exception, for example does not prevent there being design right in a mobile-telephone carry case except to the extent that the case includes a hole to allow the aerial to protrude from the casing. Once any must-fit exceptions are excluded from unregistered design right protection, the design overall may still qualify.

Example

Ricci designs a compact ladies umbrella with a rectangular handle. When folded flat the umbrella has a rectangular form. The Ricci umbrella also has a distinctive rectangular or 'box-like' case. Ricci has unregistered design rights in both the umbrella itself and the case. A competitor, Georgio copies the umbrella and the case. Ricci sues Georgio. Georgio argues that there is no infringement in the design of the box-like case on the basis that the case is the shape it is to enable it to be placed in or around another article. This defence fails. The design features of Ricci's umbrella were not designed so that the case can perform the function of containing the folding umbrella, but were designed for the purpose of looking attractive and promoting sales. This is in contrast to a car exhaust pipe which has to be exactly shaped to connect mechanically to the car engine.

The second exception, must-match, is thought to have been included to ensure that where a part is added which is integral to the design as a whole, there is no design right infringement by the person supplying that part. In other words, this applies to articles which have to be a particular shape to 'look right'. A common example given is a replacement panel for a car door. The provision that the exception relates to parts of the design which form an 'integral part' is in order to prevent the exception from extending to sets, such as individual articles of a dinner service. This means it is not possible to copy a bowl from a dinner service and claim that the bowl has to be a copy of the 'original' in order for them to fit. The line between what is a design feature which is excluded from protection on the basis that it 'must match' is a test as to whether the feature on which the design is dependent has other features in the design as a whole or not.

Example

Ricci's umbrella when packed flat is a rectangular shape. To complement this feature, Ricci designs a flat rectangular handle of cuboid shape. Georgio copies this feature as well and others. Ricci sues for unregistered design right infringement. In his defence Georgio argues that the rectangular handle is excluded from the design right protection on the basis that the shape of his umbrella is rectangular in order for the handle to 'look right'. He argues that it is likely that a designer of an umbrella which packs to a flat rectangular shape would choose a flat rectangular handle. Indeed a designer of an umbrella that is rectangular when packed flat is constrained to choosing such a shape for the handle. Georgio's argument is misconceived. Although a designer may well choose a rectangular handle in this situation, this is not inevitable. Further, Ricci's claim was not as to rectangular handles on umbrellas generally, but the particular shape of the handle which was a feature of Ricci's umbrella.

The 'commonplace' exception

In addition to the above exceptions, there is an exception from design right for articles which are 'commonplace' in the design field in question (s.213(4) CDPA). The relevant date on which commonplace is judged is the date on which the design is created.

The Act contains no definition of 'commonplace' and its scope is clarified by cases where the meaning of the word has been considered. The expression was considered in the case of *Farmers Build* v. *Carier*. In this case the Court of Appeal decided that the requirement that a design be 'not commonplace' did not import a requirement that the design be new or novel. Rather the court set out the following test to establish whether a design is commonplace:

1. The design must be judged by comparing the design in question with other articles in the same field as at the time of creation.
2. The comparative exercise must be conducted objectively. Evidence from experts in the field should be used to point out the similarities and differences between the design in question and other designs and also to explain the significance of each. The judgement must be one of fact and degree. The closer the similarity of the various designs to each other the more likely that the designs are commonplace especially if there is no causal link such as copying which accounts for the resemblance of the designs to each other. If a number of designers working independently of one another in the same field would produce very similar designs by coincidence, the most likely explanation of the similarities is that there

is only one way of designing that article. In those circumstances the design can reasonably be described as 'commonplace'.

3.   Conversely, if there are aspects of the design which are not found in other designs in the field in question, and those aspects are found in the allegedly copied designs, the court would be entitled to conclude that the designs in question were not commonplace and there would be reason to treat the design as protected from misappropriation under the provisions of the CDPA.

4.   What amounts to the 'same field' when undertaking the above comparisons is narrowly defined. In the *Farmers Build* case the dispute was in respect of a slurry separator. The design field in question was interpreted as the design of slurry separators rather than agricultural machinery generally or an engineering field other than slurry separators. In practical terms what is commonplace in the design field in question should probably be considered through the eyes of those involved in designing products of the type in question.

Showing that the design was made with the specific intention of attracting customers assists a designer in refuting an argument of commonplace. The features used to attract buyers may be diverse, and are not limited to features which make a design more attractive. In *Farmers Build*, for example, the designers wanted to attract buyers by creating a machine which worked and could cope with the type of slurry typical of British farms.

A design which includes a number of features each of which can be said to be 'commonplace' still benefits from unregistered design right protection. The purpose of design right is to prevent a designer seeking to monopolise a design which competitors would be likely to want to adopt without any wrongful motive for doing so. It is intended to strike a balance between giving protection to designs of functional articles and creating a situation where practical problems arise because designers are unduly restricted from using well-known designs (see example overleaf).

Surface decoration

Surface decoration is excluded from unregistered design right protection on the basis that surface decoration is more properly protected by copyright. As explained in Chapter 3, protecting design by copyright is not easy. The designer has to show that the design in question benefits from copyright protection on the basis that it is a work of artistic craftsmanship. The exclusion of surface decoration from protection, however, illustrates the need to consider a claim for copyright alongside any claim for unregistered design right as a design may well include both aspects of shape and configuration and surface decoration. It should also be considered whether the decoration is merely surface decoration or whether it is more properly considered as a

---

Example

Ricci designs an umbrella with a rectangular handle. Georgio copies this handle and claims in his defence to an action for infringement of unregistered design right by Ricci that there are other umbrellas on the market with rectangular handles, therefore a rectangular handle is commonplace and must be excluded from protection. This defence would not succeed. While there were other umbrellas on the market with a rectangular handle it does not follow that the design of such a handle is commonplace. There is in this case considerable scope for detailed design work to be undertaken and for the creation of a handle which has its own qualities of shape or configuration. Ricci designed his handle and the design he created was not an inevitable one. It was not a design which needed to be included in every umbrella featuring a rectangular handle.

---

work of artistic copyright. Further, the availability of registered design protection for all designs which have surface decoration or 'eye appeal' should be borne in mind. As with copyright and unregistered design rights, unregistered and registered design rights can coexist and be used in combination to prevent copy designs.

Surface decoration was considered in *Mark Wilkinson Furniture Ltd* v. *Woodcraft Designs (Radcliffe) Limited* [1998] FSR 63, which concerned the design of certain kitchen units, including various features such as curved quadrant corners between the front and side panels and shallow grooves running down a cornice and on to the quadrant corners. The judge in this case concluded that the expression 'surface decoration' could include both decoration lying on the surface of the article (for example a painted finish) and decorative features of the surface itself (for example beading or engraving). The judge could see no reason to limit the exclusion to features which were 2D, but nor could he see why something which is essentially surface decoration should cease to be such because it also serves a function, such as the decorative beading which also concealed a joint. He held that the v-grooves were surface decoration as on the facts they had been included as a decorative device to highlight the rounded corners. The quadrant corners, on the other hand, were part of the overall shape and configuration of the unit.

The question of what may amount to surface decoration was very recently considered in the case of *Lambretta Clothing Company Limited* v. *Teddy Smith (UK) Limited and Next plc*, 3 June 2003, High Court, Etherton J. (unreported). In this case Lambretta claimed both copyright and unregistered design right infringement in the design of its 'retro-theme vintage track top'. In designing the Lambretta track top the designers used a base sample tracksuit top supplied by Lambretta's manufacturer. The sample track top

33

was a single-colour white garment. The new Lambretta design was recorded in two documents, one featuring a coloured representation of the front of the garment, the other recording an uncoloured representation of the front of the garment and half of the rear. Both documents included written notes relating to the colours and fabrics to be used. One of the most distinctive features of the Lambretta top was the manner in which the navy, white and red colour-ways were applied. Lambretta's claim as to copyright infringement failed. One reason for this failure was that the design was not original as it had been copied from the manufacturer's template design. Having excluded a claim in copyright, the court considered whether unregistered design right applied to the Lambretta garment and decided it did not. The distinctive feature of the design was the colour-ways and colour had to be regarded as surface decoration and not shape and configuration. This decision is being appealed.

PROTECTION IS NOT LIMITED TO FUNCTIONAL FEATURES

The *Lambretta* and *Mark Wilkinson* cases are illustrative of the role that unregistered design right plays with respect to non-functional or technical design. The provisions of the unregistered design right legislation are extremely useful in that they apply equally to machinery as they do to garments. In cases where the design of, for example, a garment does not qualify for copyright, and protection as a work of artistic craftsmanship and registration is impractical as the article has a short shelf life, unregistered design right protection may be the most appropriate protection.

That said, a designer should not necessarily rely on unregistered design right protection and should consider whether registration of a design is worthwhile. For example in the *Lambretta* case the designers were found to have no protection. If Lambretta had, however, registered designs to cover the distinctive colour-ways, it might have succeeded on the basis of the registration.

OWNERSHIP AND QUALIFICATION

As with copyright, the first owner of any unregistered design right is the creator. The exceptions are:

1. Where the designer is an employee, in which case the first owner is the employer.
2. If a design is made under commission for money or money's worth, the commissioner will be the first owner. Whether a design is made under commission is a question of fact in each case. Money's worth could

include for example an agreement between a commissioner and a manufacturer that the manufacturer once would be granted a contract to make the article to a particular design the specification of which is agreed upon.

Qualifying individuals are citizens, subjects or habitual residents of the UK, other Member States of the EU, the colonies and like territories to which the rights are extended which are countries which must accord reciprocal protection to British designs. These countries are specified by Order under s.256 CDPA. Qualifying persons are qualifying individuals together with corporate bodies incorporated in, or carrying out substantial business in, such a country.

If there is no qualification according to these rules, qualification may arise from first marketing of the article by a qualifying person with exclusive marketing rights in the UK, its extended territories or the EC.

Where the design is created by the collaboration of two or more designers but the contribution of each is not distinct from the others, at least one of the designers has to be a qualifying person for the purposes of the CDPA. Where the work is generated by a computer, the qualifying person is the person who inputs the information which results in the computer-generated work.

Where a design does not qualify for unregistered design right protection by reference to any of the above, then it may still qualify if the first-marketing provisions of the Act are complied with. In that case the qualifying person is the person who first markets the design. Marketing of a design for the purpose of the Act means an article being sold or let for hire.

Although the person who markets the articles must have exclusive marketing rights in the UK, it is not necessary for the first marketing to take place in the UK. First marketing may take place in the UK or any other country to which Part III of the Act is extended by virtue of an order made under s.255 or another Member State of the European Union.

At present the countries covered by the Order (The Design Right (Reciprocal Protection) (No. 2) Order 1989) are Anguilla, Bermuda, British Indian Ocean Territory, British Virgin Islands, Cayman Islands, Channel Islands, Falkland Islands, Gibraltar, Hong Kong, Isle of Man, Montserrat, New Zealand, Pitcairn, Henderson, Ducie and Oeno Islands, St Helena and Dependencies, South Georgia and South Sandwich Islands and the Turks and Caicos Islands (see example overleaf).

TERM: LENGTH OF PROTECTION AFFORDED BY THE UNREGISTERED DESIGN RIGHT

The main intent behind the system is to give protection to functional objects and parts against imitation in their early years of exploitation. The term of protection is relatively short in comparison to the protection afforded to

Example 1

Aerofloatie, a company based in the UK which designs kitchen utensils, commissions a Chinese company to design a 'milk frother'. Aerofloatie gives the Chinese company a written brief as to the style features it wishes the design to include and a description of the overall look and feel of the milk frother. The Chinese company uses Chinese designers employed by the company to work on this and their starting point is a hand-held fan which they designed for another company. The Chinese company is not paid for its work but it is agreed that once a design is agreed on it will be given the contract to manufacture the milk frother for sale in the UK market.

In this example of the design, Aerofloatie is the proprietor of the design right. As the commissioner it is the status of Aerofloatie that is important in determining whether the milk frother is a qualifying design.

Example 2

Same facts as above except that Aerofloatie does not agree that the Chinese company will be granted a contract to manufacture the design in the UK market. As the Chinese company is not paid, there is an argument that the instructions to design the product are not enough to establish that Aerofloatie is the proprietor of the unregistered design rights in the milk frother as there is no valuable consideration. Despite the absence of valuable consideration, Aerofloatie launches products made by the Chinese company in the UK market. China is not a country to which reciprocal rights extend. This means that the first marketing of the design in the UK by Aerofloatie is sufficient to fix the design right with Aerofloatie as Aerofloatie is a qualifying person.

Example 3

As in example 2 Aerofloatie is not the first owner of the unregistered design right. Relations between Aerofloatie and the Chinese company break down as a final design cannot be agreed. The Chinese company decides that having invested in the design, and believing the market for milk frothers in the UK to be good, it launches the milk frother in the UK. On this basis the Chinese company is the owner of the design rights by virtue of first marketing in a country covered by the provisions of the CDPA.

Example 4

Same facts as example 3 but the company is based in Hong Kong rather than China. In this example the company in Hong Kong is the proprietor of the unregistered design right as Hong Kong is a qualifying country. The Hong Kong company acquires the right without the need to first launch the product in a qualifying country. The advantage of not having to rely on first launch in a qualifying country is that the Hong Kong company is able to benefit from unregistered design right protection even if before launching in the UK, it had launched the milk frother in another non-qualifying country, such as Australia.

---

copyright works. The shortened term is however consistent with the reason for introducing this type of copyright protection. Unregistered design right expires 15 years after first recording of the design in a design document or the first making of that design, or, if articles to the design are marketed anywhere in the world within the first five years of recording or making, then the period is 10 years from the beginning of this activity – whichever is the shorter period. A 'licence of right' is available in the last five years of the term.

A 'licence of right' is a licence to do anything that would otherwise constitute an infringement of the rights of the unregistered design right owner. Unless agreed between the parties, the terms must be settled by the Comptroller General of Patents.

As per the rights in design, there are rights to authorise others to do things. This means that in relation to a licence for design right, the licensor is able to authorise others to do such things that would otherwise be an infringement of the design rights.

The major term of the licence settled by the comptroller is that of remuneration. This is often a compromise between the parties' maximum demands. A person who is interested in taking a licence of right can apply to the comptroller for the settlement of terms up to a year before the earliest date on which the licence of right can take effect.

Where the identity of the design right owner is not known or discoverable by reasonable enquiry, a prospective licensee may apply to the comptroller for the settlement of the terms of a licence.

The Act prohibits a licensee from applying to goods sold under licence of right any notice that the goods are sold under such licence unless he has the design owner's permission to do so. A licensee who breaches this prohibition does not infringe the design right but does lay himself open to a claim for breach of statutory duty.

INFRINGEMENT

The CDPA provides that the owner of an unregistered design right has certain exclusive rights. A person who does something or authorises another to do something which is within the exclusive right of the design right owner, without the permission of the design right owner, infringes that right.

The exclusive right of the owner is the right to reproduce the design for commercial purposes, either by making the design itself or by making a design document recording the design which enables such designs to be made. Reproduction may be direct or indirect. Whether an intervening act is an act of infringement is not relevant. For example, if a person takes a photograph of another's design at a trade show and reproduces articles made to that design, that is an act of infringement even though the copyright in the photograph would belong to the photographer and not the owner of the design in question.

Primary infringement

Copying a design means making articles the shape or configuration of which are exactly or substantially similar to that design. Making something which functions in the same way but is not of substantially the same shape or configuration would not be an infringement. In *C & H Engineering v. F. Klucznik & Sons Ltd* [1992] FSR 421, it was held that substantiality was an objective test in that whether a design is substantially the same or not is to be tested through the eyes of the person whom the design is intended to attract, that is through the eyes of the intended customer.

Where the design is not visible at the point of purchase because, for example, the design is of internal features, such as was the case in *Farmers Build* v. *Carier*, or where the design is too subtle to be determined by the naked eye, for example with the dimensions of soft contact lenses as in the case of *Ocular Sciences Ltd* v. *Aspect Vision Care Ltd* [1997] RPC 289, then a different test applies. In such a case whether or not there is infringement needs to be assessed by close analysis, for example by taking precise measurements and obtaining the view of an expert in the technology to assist the court on such questions as whether the shape and configuration of the design as copied are significant.

If unregistered design right exists in only part of an article, then it is the design in the equivalent part of the alleged copy that must be considered for the purpose of the infringement. In view of this, the design owner should take care in defining the scope of the unregistered design right in respect of which action is taken and this should be set out at as early a stage as possible, for example in the letter before action. The design right owner should consider aspects of the design which are excluded from protection and restrict his claim to:

- aspects of the design which relate to shape or configuration rather than surface decoration;
- aspects of the design which are not commonplace;
- aspects not excluded by virtue of the 'must-fit', 'must-match' exceptions;
- aspects which have been copied by the alleged infringer.

The ability of an owner of an unregistered design right to tailor his claim to aspects of the design that the alleged infringer is said to have copied, represents a significant advantage to the design owner. The situation with respect to a registered design is quite different, as on applying for a registered design a proprietor must state the aspects of the design in which he seeks a monopoly. It is this pre-existing statement of novelty as shown in the drawings or photographs submitted with the application which the proprietor must rely on and in respect of which infringement will be judged. With registered designs there is little scope for tailoring the claim to what the alleged infringer is actually doing. While the owner of an unregistered design right has a significant advantage here, the practical effect is that a statement of the designer setting out the aspects of the shape and configuration alleged to have been taken as described above assumes a great importance. This was reiterated in *Farmers Build Ltd* v. *Carier Bulk Materials Handling*, where the Court of Appeal confirmed that it is for the design right owner to identify as precisely as possible what he claims to be his original design. The burden is on the design right owner to identify both the original aspect of the shape and configuration of the design and what is original about the design. The evidential burden shifts to the defendant to allege and adduce evidence showing that, although the design is original in the sense that the designer originated it, it is nonetheless commonplace in the design field in question.

It is also an infringement of unregistered design right to reproduce a design for commercial purposes by making a design document recording the design for the purpose of enabling articles to be made to the design. Although it is not necessary that the maker of the design document intends to make the articles himself, the maker of the design document must intend the document to be used for the purpose of making the articles to that design. Again, as with making an article to the design, it is only necessary for the maker of the design document to copy the design substantially for the document to be an infringement.

Secondary infringement

A secondary infringer is a person who without the permission of the design right owner:

- imports into the UK for commercial purposes; or
- has in his possession for commercial purposes; or

- sells, lets for hire or offers to expose for sale or hire, in the course of business

any article he knows or has reason to believe is an infringing article.

In all cases of secondary infringement it must be shown that the alleged infringer 'knows' or 'has reason to believe' that the designs he possesses or is dealing in are infringing designs. This means that where the infringer is a secondary infringer it is appropriate to write to advise the secondary infringer of the design owner's rights. Such knowledge is usually conveyed in a letter before action. It is possible however that this knowledge can be conveyed by a simple letter advising the infringer of the design owner's rights without the threat of legal action and this would avoid any concern regarding the provisions with respect to unlawful threats (see pp.121 and 126). The infringer will be held to have the requisite knowledge after the expiry of a reasonable time within which to check the design right owner's claims.

An article which has been put on the market in the European Community by the unregistered design right owner or with the licence of the design right owner can be sold within the UK by virtue of the application of the principle of exhaustion of right. Such an article cannot be an infringing article. This principle is discussed in more detail in Chapter 9.

An action for infringement

An infringement of design right is actionable by the design right owner.

Making an article to the design will only amount to infringement if it is for commercial purposes. Commercial purposes are defined as being made with a view to being sold or hired in the course of business. It is unclear whether making samples or prototypes with a view to evaluation prior to commercial exploitation is an infringement. In a case of this type, however, there may be evidence that the prototypes are being made with a view to sale or hire, in which event it may be justified to commence a pre-emptive action.

Exclusion from copyright infringement where design right infringement is claimed

To prevent an act from being an infringement of both copyright and design right, s.236 CDPA provides that it is not an infringement of design right in the design to do anything which is an infringement of copyright in that work.

An act can constitute an infringement of copyright or design right but not both. Where the alleged primary infringement of design right takes the form of making articles substantially to that design, the exclusion created by s.236 can have no impact as the provisions of s.51 CDPA are intended to restrict cases in which the manufacture of an article can constitute an infringement of copyright. Section 51 CDPA provides that it is not an infringement of any copyright in a design document to copy the shape or configuration of that article made to that design. This means that unless the allegedly infringing article is itself a work of artistic craftsmanship, its manufacture cannot constitute a copyright infringement and the design owner has the right to sue for design right infringement.

Where the primary infringement constitutes making a design document recording the design for the purpose of enabling articles to the design to be made, the exclusion under s.236 is more significant. In this case copyright continues to subsist in drawings and it continues to be an infringement of copyright in the drawing to copy that work directly or indirectly, for example into the form of drawing stored in a computer file or into another drawing. In this situation s.236 of the Act precludes an action for design right infringement in respect of those rights.

This principle is illustrated in the *Lambretta* case (unreported, 23 May 2003, Ch.D). In that case Lambretta claimed that it was the owner of artistic and literary copyright in specification drawings and that these rights had been infringed by Teddy Smith and Next by copying those documents and selling such copies to the public. Counsel for Teddy Smith submitted that even if Lambretta did own the copyright in the specification documents, these were 'design documents' for the purposes of s.51 CDPA. As such, they precluded Lambretta from claiming relief for infringement of copyright. Counsel for Lambretta argued that s.51 CDPA should be interpreted in a 'purposive manner' looking at the background to the introduction of the unregistered design right (see Chapter 2). He argued that the intention of Parliament was to protect designs which, prior to the CDPA 1988, had been protected by copyright, but to do so by bringing them within the ambit of unregistered design right provisions. On this footing, s.51 CPDA is intended to achieve no more than marking the demarcation between design right and copyright, so as to provide, in effect, that, if unregistered design right applies, infringement of copyright cannot be alleged. The judge rejected this submission and concluded that the words of s.51 should be given their natural and ordinary meaning. It was wrong to apply a 'purposive approach' where the words in the CDPA were clear. Accordingly, s.51 applied in this case to prevent Lambretta claiming copyright infringement in respect of its garments.

THREATS OF ACTION

The proprietor of a design in which unregistered design right subsists may not make groundless threats of court proceedings. In such circumstances, the recipient of such threats will be entitled to bring an action for a declaration of non-infringement and a further declaration that the threats were groundless. The action for groundless threats does not apply where the allegation is made against those that are manufacturing the article in question or where the business threatened is importing the articles alleged to infringe. As the provisions against threats are capable of turning the tables on a designer who would want to be in control of any action to prevent copying of a design, letters to a suspected copyist should be carefully considered and worded. A designer should be sure that he can provide title to design by production of dated documents and also that he recite the circumstances in which the designs are alleged to have been copied.

In some circumstances the unregistered design right owner may wish to write to the alleged infringer to advise the infringer of his rights and to detail what the alleged infringer has done wrong. These letters often include a suggestion for a commercial solution, failing which the design right owner may wish to take further action. Such letters are often successful in resolving the dispute. Further, such a letter may be desirable to ensure, for example, that a secondary infringer has the necessary knowledge to found a claim or to minimise the scope for the infringer being able to claim innocence and so limit the damages payable to the design right owner following proof of infringement.

An action for 'threats' may be brought by the person to whom the letter is addressed or by any other person who is aggrieved by such a letter. For example a manufacturer may bring an action in respect of a letter written to a customer. The only requirement to found such an action is that the recipient (or the person aggrieved by the letter) understands from the letter that there is a threat to sue and a successful action entitles the person so aggrieved to claim an injunction to prevent further threats and damage for any loss caused by the threat. It is an absolute defence for the design right owner to show that the threats were justified. This can be done by the design right owner issuing and successfully concluding proceedings in respect of the alleged infringements. It is possible that a threatening letter intended by the writer to do no more than bring an alleged infringer to the negotiating table can have the opposite effect and provoke the recipient of the letter into issuing an action for 'threats'. Subject to what is said below, a design owner needs to be careful, and obtaining legal advice on this issue would be prudent.

A design right owner who has gathered all the pertinent information required to found an action for unregistered design right infringement, and who is confident of his rights should not be deterred by the threats provisions from pursuing his rights, or doing what is necessary to give an alleged infringer notice of his claims. It is possible to avoid a threats action: by avoiding the 'threat', that is by simply notifying an alleged infringer of the design rights or by issuing proceedings without writing a letter before action. Both these routes however appear to fly in the face of the proper approach to dispute resolution, in that they do not give the alleged infringer the information he or she needs prior to the issue of a claim on which to assess his position and avoid the issue of proceedings if that is so desired.

Threats do not have to be in writing to be actionable. The same rules apply where the 'threat' is made orally.

REMEDIES FOR INFRINGEMENT

The remedies available to a design right owner for infringement are the same as remedies for copyright infringement. The design right owner is entitled to ask the court for an injunction, damages, accounts of profit or otherwise and delivery-up of offending articles.

Injunction

Although an injunction is available in respect of unregistered design right infringement in the same way as it is available for infringement of copyright or registered design, there are two situations where an injunction is not available. First, the court has no power to grant an injunction in the case of a secondary infringement where the defendant shows that the offending article was innocently obtained by him or a predecessor in title. Second, the court has no power to grant an injunction where licences of right are available either through the Comptroller because the design is in the last five years of the term or by the Competition Commission under the provisions of the Competition Act 1998.

In order to avoid an injunction in these situations the alleged infringer must agree to take a licence on such terms as may be settled by the Comptroller, Competition Commission or as agreed with the owner. An actual undertaking to take a licence must be given. It is not enough for the alleged infringer to state that he will take a licence if he loses an infringement action.

Damages

A design right owner successful in an action has the right to seek normal damages for loss. The court has the power to award additional damages for flagrancy depending on the circumstances of the case. In the case of an action brought by a design right owner who has licensed the designs in question the terms of the licence agreement made previously become relevant. The court is entitled to take into account the terms of the licence between the design right owner and the licensee in determining any damages to be paid.

Delivery-up

In conjunction with an application for an injunction, it is common for the design owner to ask for an order for delivery-up. There is statutory power to order delivery-up of two categories of article in design right cases. The design right owner may apply for an order that any person with infringing articles in his or her possession, custody or control deliver up such articles. A similar order is available against anyone who has in his possession, custody or control of anything specifically designed or adapted for making such articles. This means that the things to be delivered up need not be the infringing items themselves but could be for example design documents or special machinery for making moulds. In asking for such delivery-up the burden is on the design right owner to show which items in the possession, custody or control of the infringer can only be held for infringing purposes. Conversely, it is not necessary to show that such items are held for commercial purposes.

Forfeiture, destruction or disposal

The design right owner may ask the court for an order that the infringing designs are forfeited to the design owner to be otherwise dealt with. An order may include an order for destruction of infringing designs by either the design right owner or the alleged infringer. The question of destruction of tooling used to make infringing designs is more difficult. It is unlikely that tooling which can be shown to have a non-infringing use would be the subject of an order for destruction. In making orders for forfeiture and destruction, generally the court is obliged to consider what other remedies are available to the design right owner to compensate him for his loss and to protect his interests.

Account of profits

In most cases a design owner successful in a claim may elect for an account of profits instead of damages. As with damages, where the proceedings relate wholly or partly to an infringement in respect of a design in which the design right owner and an exclusive licensee have concurrent rights of action, the court will apportion profits between them in the ratio it considers just.

Innocent infringers

An innocent infringer's liability is limited or extinguished. The extent to which a defence of 'innocence' assists those claiming it depends on whether the infringer is a primary or secondary infringer. If a primary infringer can show that at the time of the infringement he did not know and had no reason to believe that design right subsisted, the claimant is not entitled to damages but only an account of the infringer's profits.

A secondary infringer who is able to establish that the infringing article was innocently acquired by him or by a predecessor in title can only be liable to the claimant in damages, which must not exceed a reasonable royalty.

Again the secondary infringer or the predecessor in title is treated as innocent if the person who acquired it did not know or have reason to believe that the article was an infringing article.

The fact that a secondary infringer who is himself not innocent can rely on the innocence of a predecessor in title means that the design right owner should collate as much information as possible about the chain of supply and advise those in the chain of his rights.

A design owner's right to recover damages may also be restricted where the design right is in the last five years of its term. In these circumstances, a person alleged to infringe a design can limit the damages payable by undertaking at any time prior to final order to take a licence on such terms as may be agreed between the parties or as settled by the Comptroller General of Patents. In these circumstances, damages are limited to double the amount that would have been payable by the defendant had he or she been operating under the terms of the licence so agreed or settled. This limitation on damages does not apply where the infringement consists of importation from a country which is not a member of the European Union.

PRACTICALITIES

Unregistered design right relies on the person claiming the right to show evidence of title. To this end, records should be kept of all product development design work. A system for marking documents with the creator's name, the date and a drawing number should be devised. In addition, all material which indicates the inspirational sources or influences should be collated if possible. A note should be made as to what the designer hopes to achieve in creating a design: is the purpose to create something that appeals to buyers, or to make something that works?

Once a design is ready for market, a designer should consider whether the design or any aspect of the design would benefit from registered design protection. The relevant considerations would be the value which a designer could hope to extract from a design by relying on registered rights in addition to unregistered rights. Obtaining registered design protection rather than relying on unregistered rights may be particularly useful to a designer who is intending to create an income stream for his designs through licensing (see Chapter 8).

CHAPTER 5

Registered designs

INTRODUCTION

Like copyright and unregistered design right, registered design's primary function is to prevent third parties from appropriating the look of an original design. It exists alongside copyright and unregistered design right, and all these rights may coexist in any design. This chapter looks at the Registered Designs Act 1949 (the 1949 Act) and explains the requirements for registered designs under this legislation. We then consider the improvements that have been made to the UK registered design regime following the recent introduction of the Registered Designs Regulations of 2001 (SI 2001/3949; see Appendix B1). Finally, we discuss the practical steps that practitioners should take, including useful strategies to register designs and how to police and enforce them. Examples of application forms to assist designers and practitioners in making registered design applications are included within the chapter.

Although the registered design right is a right which prevents others from unfairly taking the look of an article, the fact that it is a registered system means that it has features in common with the patent system as well as the copyright system. One of these similarities is the requirement of novelty, described below (see p. 86). Another feature in common with the patent system, which is most relevant when it comes to enforcement of design right, is that the protection granted is a monopoly protection. This monopoly right means that infringement will be proved against a third party who markets a design that is substantially similar to a registered design whether or not he actually copied it. By contrast, the enforcement of copyright depends upon proof of actual copying of the work by the infringer.

THE REGISTERED DESIGNS ACT 1949

The 1949 Act as amended by the CDPA can be found in Schedule 4 to the CDPA. The Registered Designs Regulations 2001 (the new Regulations) are self-contained. The 1949 Act remains the underlying statute governing the regime in the UK, and because practitioners may deal with designs that were registered prior to the introduction of the new Regulations, this chapter examines the 1949 Act in some detail.

What can be registered?

Section 1 of the 1949 Act defines a registered design as being:

- any feature of shape, configuration, pattern or ornament;
- applied to an article by any industrial process;
- which has appeal to and is judged by the eye (so-called 'eye appeal').

For an article to have 'eye appeal' it must have had 'something which catches the eye and in this sense appeals to the eye' (Lord Pearson, *Amp Inc* v. *Utilux Limited* [1972] RPC 103). In essence the design must have had some kind of decorative or ornamental appearance in order for it to be capable of being registered as a design.

In addition, the design must be new. This means that it must not be the same as a design previously registered and that it must not have been published/disclosed in the UK prior to the application date.

Prior to the new Regulations, which are discussed more fully in this chapter, the application for a registered design was based very much on prevailing patent law (and patent law which is still in force). The requirement of non-disclosure was paramount and was a way in which an application could easily be defeated. Therefore when dealing with registered designs under the old regime under the 1949 Act, it is important that a practitioner verifies that the registration complies with the points outlined above so that the quality of the registration can be properly determined.

Registered design, patent and trade mark protection compared

This is discussed more fully in Chapter 7.

PATENT

The very best form of intellectual property protection a patent is granted for 20 years to *inventions* that are:

- new;
- not 'obvious' in that they are a leap forward from the prior art;

- capable of industrial application;
- not disclosed at the date of application unless protected by confidentiality agreement (non-disclosure agreement – NDA).

Each patent is a monopoly right in the particular invention. Because a patent is concerned with the way in which a design functions, it protects inventions. It does not protect mere surface designs or the shape of an object unless the shape and the use of the shape has a 'technical effect' in that the result of the interaction with the shape produces a result that complies with the tests above.

TRADE MARK

Trade marks are available to words, pictures, signs, objects, colours, tunes and, in some circumstances aromas, that:

- have distinctive character;
- are not descriptive;
- are a 'badge of origin' in respect of goods and services to which they relate;
- are not the same/similar as previously registered trade marks registered in respect of the same/similar goods and/or services.

Trade marks are renewable every five years indefinitely; in practice many companies rebrand every 5–10 years and in doing so, must submit a fresh application rather than renewing their existing mark.

COEXISTENCE

Each of the different forms of protection can exist in the same item at the same time, affording the owner different types of protection in the same article and thereby protecting different aspects of the same article (see example overleaf).

It is always useful to consider all three types of protection when considering each of the different types of registered designs. As the example overleaf shows, the same product may attract different types of protection and one aspect of that product may be capable of protection by more than one type of registered right. For the owner of such a design to be properly protected, he must be made aware of all the forms of protection that are available and the advantages and disadvantages of each. For example, a registered trade mark might be preferable to a registered design if the intended life of the design is more than 25 years, given that a trade mark can exist indefinitely whereas the life of a design is limited to 25 years. However, if the product's lifetime is intended to be short, the registered design would be preferable for the same reason. This is explored in some detail in Chapter 7.

Example

Brusk and Sons manufacture toothbrushes and have done for many years. They create a revolutionary product that cleans the teeth in just one minute in a new way never seen before using air. To capitalise on the invention and differentiate it in the marketplace, they decide to give the brush a distinctive shape. They also settle on the brand name 'Mistral' for the new brush because it is light and quick. They create an advertising campaign that uses the slogan 'Breeze Easy'.

The forms of registered protection available to Brusk and Sons are:

- *patent for the new technology (the way in which it functions);*
- *registered design for the shape of the product (the way it appears in ordinary use);*
- *trade mark protection for the shape of the product (its distinctive shape acting as a badge of origin for the product), for the word 'Mistral' and for the slogan 'Breeze Easy'.*

Having looked in brief at the principal differences between the various forms of registrable rights, we will now turn in depth to United Kingdom registered design. We will look at the situation prior to and then following the introduction of the new Regulations.

What was a design under the 1949 Act?

To qualify as a design under the 1949 Act the design could have been a:

- 2D pattern (such as a lace or a wallpaper pattern);
- 3D shape (such as a teapot).

Two-dimensional designs, when applied to numerous articles (for example the pattern on a dinner service) were only protected in respect of each article if they were the subject of separate, individual registrations. This was costly and was a barrier to the registration of many designs which were employed in respect of sets of articles. A practical consequence of this is that, for designs registered under the 1949 Act, a check should be made as to which items were included for the registration. This is particularly relevant when, as a practitioner, you are enforcing the design registration on behalf of a client. If the 2D design is registered in respect of a teapot, and a third party applies the pattern to a plate, the infringement cannot be prosecuted using the registered design. In that case, the client must use copyright laws (see Chapter 3) to pursue the infringer.

Altering the design

Designs which were altered in a very minor way were not capable of being registered as a separate design if they were too similar to the original design. It was not uncommon at the expiration of the registration period for a design to be altered in a minor way and a new application submitted in an attempt to extend the period of protection for the article/pattern in question. For such a design to be capable of registration in its own right, the later design had to be substantially different from the earlier design. A useful guide is as follows:

- Is the second design similar to the first?
- Are the similarities substantial?
- Would the second design be considered an infringement of the first were they created by different people?

If the answer to the second two questions is 'yes' then the later design is not capable of being registered in its own right. If the owner of the design has ceased to market the earlier design in favour of the latter while the former is still within the protection period, the owner may not be able to enforce the registration.

Example

Annie registered the design of her children's toy, a painted wooden cat. When the registration period for her design expired she attempted to register a second toy. The toy had a different colour of collar to the first and was made of plastic, being cheaper to produce. The shape of the cat remained the same as did the remaining colours used for the fur and the eyes. Annie applied for a new registration based on the changes that she made. The application was rejected on the grounds that the new registration was not sufficiently different from the earlier one.

The requirement for novelty was also much stricter under the 1949 Act. To qualify as a registered design, the design needed to go beyond what was merely original in the copyright sense. Rather than straightforward originality, a designer was required to show a 'difference of form or character which is a departure from previous designs and which is, therefore, of some significance or substance'. In other words, there was a kinship with patents analysis in that there must have a been a leap forward from the prior art, in this case, current designs.

Example

Re Nicholas' Application [1974] RPC 645

In this instance, an application to register a design for a stack of miniature tablets in a tube was refused because, although it was original, it lacked a distinctive quality, i.e. although the design itself was an original work, the concept of tablets stacking in a tube was not. The comment was made that sweets have commonly been sold as tablets stacked in a tube for the best part of the twentieth century and earlier.

The registered design protection was also only available to those designs capable of industrial application. Therefore a one-off piece such as a sculpture or a work of art could not be registered as a design. Furthermore, s.6(5) of the 1949 Act went on to say that where there had been industrial exploitation of a design with the applicant's permission, registration of the design would not be granted.

Example

Sarah wishes to manufacture her distinctive cutlery that she designed in order to attract new work to her design practice. She locates a manufacturer in Sheffield who is willing to make it for her and to help with her marketing. In the process of creating the range, several prototypes are made and the design is tweaked to take into account the manufacturing process. Once the finished articles are ready, Sarah approaches her lawyer to register the design. Unfortunately, because she has had the articles manufactured by an industrial manufacturer in the absence of a confidentiality agreement, she may not register them as designs. In the event that she goes ahead, a competitor may apply to have her registrations revoked on the grounds that they have been exploited industrially.

Also excluded were those designs whose shape was dictated solely by the function of the article.

Duration

As now, the registered design was registrable for up to five, five-year periods (a maximum of 25 years), based on the registration date and not the application date. Should registrants forget to renew a period, they had a grace period of six months in which to do so, and that period was backdated to the actual renewal date so that no unfair extension of time was granted.

Where, contrary to s.6(5) of the 1949 Act, a design registration was secured in respect of a design previously industrially exploited, and copyright in that design expired prior to the registered design, the registration expired at the same time as the copyright. Thus, while the registered design was intended to grant a monopoly right, it would not be granted at the expense of copyright law.

The 1949 Act treated designs as a hybrid of copyright and patent law. The principles surrounding secrecy and non-publication were clearly based on the principles applying to patent law. In the circumstances, designs registered under the 1949 regime had to comply with stricter tests than under the new regime.

Compulsory licence

This is dealt with more fully in Chapter 8, but the compulsory licence system should be considered here in brief. At any time after the first five years of registration, a third party could apply to the Comptroller of Patents, Designs and Trade Marks for a compulsory UK licence on the grounds that the design was not being exploited in the UK. A licence would then be granted to such an extent as could be considered reasonable. The owner of the design would receive such royalty for the exploitation of the design as would be considered reasonable in the particular circumstances or industry and the third party would get the opportunity to market the design. To prevent a compulsory licence from being granted, the owner of the design in question would have to show that he had a bona fide intention of exploiting the design to the extent that he had carried out preliminary acts sufficient to indicate this bona fide intention. These acts could include a manufacturing agreement, manufacturing of the design (prior to marketing) or other contractual arrangements.

THE NEW REGULATIONS AND THE NEW REGISTERED DESIGN REGIME

In only providing protection to designs which were not disclosed and novel, the regime under the 1949 Act was inflexible and uncommercial. It did not allow designers the flexibility to decide whether a design had commercial value or whether they might exploit it in the future before applying to register it. The requirement for 'eye appeal' excluded designs which were very plain in appearance, and the need to make separate applications for all articles bearing a design was expensive. In addition, there was no protection for designs which were not applied industrially. The new Regulations were intended to surmount these problems and are successful in doing so.

The current UK regime for registered designs has its basis in the European Design Directive. The key features of the new regime as compared with the 1949 Act are that there is no longer a requirement for 'eye appeal'. Further, the design need not be applied to only one article and thus one registration can be exploited in many different ways. Finally, there is no longer a requirement of industrial application. Thus, one-off pieces such as artworks and sculpture can be registered under the revised regime.

What is registrable?

To be capable of registration as a design, designs must:

- be novel;
- have individual character; and
- not be excluded under the 1949 Act or the new Regulations.

Novelty

There is no longer a requirement of 'eye appeal' as required under the 1949 Act. Thus, as long as a design is original and is not identical to one previously made available to the public, it will be registrable. Similarly, a 'new' design cannot be based substantially on an existing or expired registration.

Example 1

Jonathan is a self-employed sculptor specialising in figurative pieces. He creates a work which is the image of his neighbour, Ursula, who commissioned the piece. The piece is a one-off image carved from marble and Jonathan hopes to use it in the promotion of his work to attract new commissions. As a result, he seeks to register it as a design. The work is registrable under the new regime due to its original nature. Under the 1949 Act registration of this design would not have been possible because the design was not 'industrially applied'.

Example 2

Ursula is pleased with the work and re-commissions Jonathan. This time she asks for a plain cylinder with a small amount of textual detail, to stand in her window. Jonathan provides Ursula with the piece and is pleased with its appearance in the setting of the window. Again, he decides to register the piece because he intends to use the design in his marketing materials. Although the piece is very plain and would very likely have been rejected under the 1949 Act for reason of lack of eye appeal, the piece may be registered under the new Regulations.

INDIVIDUAL CHARACTER

In assessing individual character, the overall impression of the design applied for must produce on an informed user an impression that differs from that of a previously available product. The degree of freedom of the designer in producing the design is taken into account when assessing individual character (s.1B(4)). A useful test to apply is that of *déjà vu*, i.e. the feeling of having seen the product elsewhere. However, within the new Regulations, no guidance is given as to who the informed user might be, although one might consider him to be a person 'skilled in the art' as with patent applications. We submit that the informed user will need to be someone who has day-to-day dealings with the product concerned so that he is able to use his above-average knowledge to form a conclusion of originality. This person might also be the type of expert witness used to determine issues of 'commonplace' design in unregistered design right cases.

Example

Sarah designs a range of crockery bearing stars arranged in a pattern. She is pleased with the results and registers the patterns as a design. Subsequent to the registration, her solicitor receives a letter from the offices of a well-known designer, Amara, who uses stars as her signature. You ask Sarah how she came to design the stars and in the particular arrangement that she chose. She mentions that she was inspired by the night sky on holiday in Greece. However, on further questioning she says that she recalls having seen Amara's design when she worked in a major department store which stocked the Amara line. On this basis, although there was no deliberate intention to copy Amara's work, Sarah's work does produce a feeling of déjà vu and, given her experience of working in close proximity to the designer's work, an inference of copying could be drawn, although it is by no means definite. The parties consider using an expert witness to settle the matter out of court.

Section 1B (8) of the 1949 Act, as amended by the new Regulations deals with designs that are part of complex products. These designs qualify for individual character only if the component part remains visible during normal use of the product and where the design of that part itself has new and individual character.

Example

Michael and Dawn market hand-held electric whisks to the catering indus-try. As part of a marketing drive, they register their design which was created by an employee of the company. The design is very successful. After two years of successful trading, they decide to update their design. In order to better distinguish their product, they ask the designer to create a distinctively shaped 'on/off' switch and also to make the head of the whisk distinctive. The design otherwise remains the same. To protect the updated design, both the new switch and the new head are registered separately as designs at the Designs Registry.

Excluded designs

Section 1C of the 1949 Act deals with the exceptions. Designs which have a 'technical function', i.e. those that are dictated solely by their function, are not capable of registration. In other words, a design which lacks any freedom of design will not be capable of being registered. So, a nut which must fit a particular bolt already in existence could not attract registered design pro-tection. By contrast, simple designs (which lack the 1949 Act requirement of 'eye appeal') may be registered even though they are very simple in appear-ance. This is a huge improvement over the 1949 Act and is certainly of benefit to those designers whose style is minimalist or who design everyday products such as household items (cutlery, light switches and radiators being good examples).

Who may register?

Section 2 provides that three categories of person may make the application:

- the creator/author;
- the commissioner;
- the employer.

For the avoidance of doubt, where the applicant is a commissioner of the design or an employer of the designer, the necessary assignments/employment contracts should be checked to ascertain ownership. The first owner of a design is the designer unless it is created by a designer employed to design in which case the design belongs to the employer. Designs may be assigned from a first owner to another proprietor. Assignments have to be in writing and signed by the person assigning the right.

Priority

When considering in which countries to protect a design outside the UK, it is not necessary to make all applications at once. This is because under international convention, a priority period within which to make further applications is granted to a designer.

In essence, priority is a system of backdating later applications once an initial application has been made, as long as the later applications are made within the prescribed period. This means that a designer can file in a second (or multiple) country, backdating to the date of filing in the first country. A priority period of up to six months can be claimed for registered designs if they have previously been registered in a Locarno Convention country. The list of convention countries can be found on the website (http://www.wipo.org). This means that once an application is made in the UK (for example) all subsequent applications in convention countries will be backdated to the date of the UK filing, as long as the subsequent application(s) are filed within six months of the UK filing date.

In order to claim priority, when the later application(s) are filed in the relevant jurisdiction, the applicant needs to file a certified copy of the UK application as proof of the earlier right claimed, together representations of the design as registered in the UK. Note that for priority to bite, the design must be identical to the earlier UK registration. The certified copy of the registration documents must be filed with the registry within three months of making an application for priority. In the event that they are not filed in time, the application for priority will fail and the application will be given the actual date of filing of the new application.

Note that the same rules apply if priority is claimed in the UK based on an earlier filing in another jurisdiction. Also, note that in either case if priority is being claimed in a country that has different official language from the country of the earlier application, the certified copies will need to be certifed translations.

Note that the copies of the representation of the design must be clearly discernible. To that end, if a designer submits photographs of the design with the original application, the copies produced by the relevant Designs Registry may not adequately reflect the design as claimed and for intricate designs it may be useful to submit drawings along with photographs. Certainly the practitioner ought to retain the images as submitted so that he has a record of the images as filed.

Note that in order to claim priority at Community level, a designer must have registered the design within the previous six months; the relevant date on which to base the claim for priority is the registration date, which is the same as the application date in the UK. If that date is missed, it may still be possible to register the design depending on the date on which the design was first marketed, but this is in the ordinary way of registering a design rather than making any claim of priority.

Example 1

Agatha first marketed her handbag design in December 2001 at a trade fair. The response is positive and for the following year she continues to market the design, gaining interest with larger retailers until she obtains a contract with a major high street retailer in November 2002. She decides to register her design and does so in December 2002. With the introduction of the registered Community Design in April 2003, Agatha makes an application for 1 April 2003 and uses her priority period to backdate her Community Design application to December 2002.

Example 2

Brian designs shoes. He first marketed his designs in September 2001 by putting on a show at his workshop. Over the course of the following 12 months, he ascertains that one design in particular is the most popular. He decides that this is to be his signature piece and he registers it at the UK Designs Registry in September 2002. Unfortunately he is not able to take advantage of the new registered Community Design, given that he is unable to claim priority because he has first marketed the design more than 12 months prior to the earliest Community Design application.

Example 3

Brian has a second design which he first marketed in May 2002 and which he registered in September 2002. Although he is unable to claim priority and backdate his Community Design application, because he has first marketed his design within 12 months, he can apply for registration at Community level. In this example, Brian is able to rely on the provisions relating to the 12-month grace period to secure protection.

PRIORITY TIMELINES

Note: the Australian jurisdiction is used as an example but it could in fact be any foreign jurisdiction.

Scenario 1

Australian application 1 January 2003	Australian registration 1 January 2003		
Product first marketed in Australia		UK application made by 1 June 2003	UK registration dated 1 January 2003 based on Australian registration
		UK application made by 1 June 2003 but incorrect documentation submitted and out of time	UK registration dated 1 June 2003 once the rectifications have been made outside of period of priority claim

Scenario 2

Product first marketed 1 January 2003 in the UK	UK application made 1 June 2003	UK registration granted 1 June 2003		
			Community Design application 1 December 2003 claiming priority	Community Design registration granted and dated 1 June 2003 based on UK registration

Scenario 3

Product first marketed 1 January 2003	UK application made 1 March 2003	UK registration granted and dated 1 March 2003		
			Community Design application made 1 November 2003	Community Design registration dated 1 November 2003
				No claim of priority can be made because outside six months' period but within first 12 months' marketing

Scenario 4

Product first marketed 1 January 2003				
	Application made 1 September 2003	Registration granted 1 September 2003		
			Community application made 1 April 2004	Community application *refused* on grounds that no priority can be claimed (seven months) and outside the 12 months' grace period of first marketing

What type of design may be registered?

A design can be a 3D object such as a chair, a 2D textile or even part of an object such as the handle of a teacup. As long as the design qualifies under the new Regulations, it is capable of registration.

Complex products

Section 7(A)(5) of the Act, as amended by the new Regulations, says that it is not an infringement of the design in a complex product (as defined in s.1B(8)) to repair a complex product. So it would not be an offence to repair the windscreen of a car where the windscreen was a registered design as part of a complex product (a car).

Disclosure to the public

The applicant can show a design to the public up to 12 months prior to the filing date. This is a huge improvement on the old regime under the 1949 Act and allows an applicant to gauge market opinion of a design prior to filing – the design can be shown at trade shows or degree shows, for example. This grace period is useful to designers who have a range of designs on show but who are unsure if they are each equally marketable. Designers will therefore need to keep careful records of when they first showed the design applied for, although this is usually straightforward.

Registered design protection starts from the date of first registration of the design and not of first showing, so that if a design application is opposed on grounds of lack of originality prior to grant of registration, the applicant will have to rely on copyright law to prove originality.

Term of registration

Each period of registration lasts for five years, up to a maximum of 25 years (five, five-year periods). Renewal can be granted up to six months after the renewal date in exceptional circumstances. After the renewal period, a designer who wishes to revive a registration must have a compelling reason for the Registry to grant such a renewal. Each case will turn on the facts, but a typical example is where, for example, the design has been the subject of a copyright infringement allegation and the allegation has been successfully defended or settled.

The Designs Registry search

The Designs Registry does not carry out design searches for novelty and there-fore it is useful to inspect the Register prior to submitting an application.

The process is laborious and the system is based on a system of classification by 'type' of design, the Locarno categories which can make searching difficult. Added to which, the quality of images is dependent on the images submitted by each applicant which vary from sharp digital images to hazy line drawings (particularly when viewed online).

It should also be borne in mind that for certain designs the search process is more difficult:

- Wallpaper and lace designs are not available for inspection for a period of two years (lace three years) from the grant of the registration certificate.
- Only paper copies of non-textile designs from January 1991 onwards and textile designs from August 1989 onwards are held by the Registry.

It is possible to ask the Designs Registry to carry out a formal novelty search, on submission of the relevant form and a fee. The time taken for the results of that search will depend on the number of designs submitted in the category of the requested Locarno categories.

If you are a practitioner, it is recommended that you establish the ownership of a proposed registered design by questioning the designer or applicant in the same manner as you would for a copyright infringement case. A thorough practitioner will obtain the design history, that is the circumstances surrounding the creation of the design applied for. He should also ask the designer or applicant if they have seen anything similar. If any information is provided that throws doubt on the novelty of the design, the application should not be made or the applicant should be made aware that a challenge to the validity of the design could be made once the design is registered.

Note that the Registrar will refuse the application if the Registrar is aware that the design lacks novelty.

Deferment of publication

Under the Act as amended by the new Regulations, it is possible to defer publication of a design for a period of 12 months. After that period it is possible to defer publication by a further three months on payment of a fee.

Deferment is a useful strategy in a number of situations, notably:

- Where a designer is looking to steal a march on competitors and keep a design secret prior to launch.
- Where a designer wishes to source production for the design without letting competitors know.
- Where novelty is questioned by the Registry but where the applicant believes that he can prove their orginality.

- Where a patent application has been made alongside the application for design registration and there is a concern that disclosure of any aspect of the design application may prejudice the patent application.

As a matter of course, where a designer is also making a patent application, deferment should be considered. Note that the deferment of publication means that registration will not be granted until after the design has been published. Practically speaking, therefore, owners will find it difficult to enforce the design prior to publication because they will have to show that an alleged infringer actually copied the design and, given that it has not been published, this will necessarily fall to the copyright infringement test as explained in Chapter 3, even though the date of registration will be the date of publication.

The normal time taken for an application to reach registration is six to eight weeks depending on the workload of the Registry.

Modifications

If the design is modified so that it can be considered to be a new design, a new application should be made. The design must possess the same characteristics of novelty and individual character as the subject of the original application; it is therefore useful to apply a copyright analysis by breaking the design down into its key elements to compare the old with the new. If the new contains altered key elements of design then it can be registered as a modified design. If the changes are so small as to render the new design substantially the same as the earlier design, then the later design will not be granted protection at the Registry.

This should be explained to an owner who wishes to rely on an application that has not yet been published.

The current application forms appear in Appendix E. They are completed as though they are original applications.

A useful flowchart is as follows:

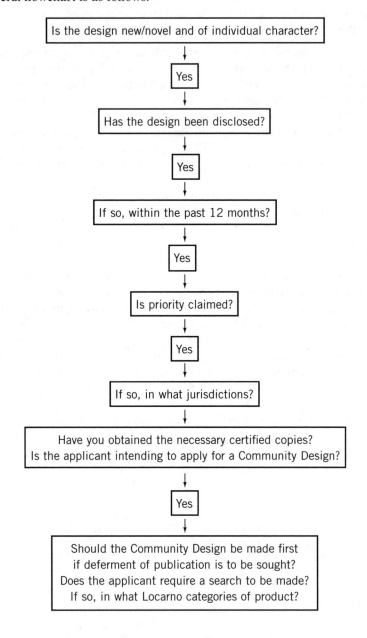

Strategy

A portfolio of registered designs is very useful, particularly where they are intended to be marketed for up to 25 years. Applicants should consider which markets they intend to move into and a diary should be kept so that the priority periods are never missed (particularly where the products have been marketed ahead of a registration being applied for). Also, the 12-month grace period is very useful to assess the marketability of a product ahead of registration but this has a necessary knock-on effect if the priority period is missed. Therefore, extra caution should be taken once the application is deferred for six months or more from the date of first marketing.

What to register?

Examine each product and how it works. If there is a distinctive handle or lock to a range of products, consider whether this ought to be registered on its own instead of/as well as the whole piece itself. Consider also whether distinctive elements of a design are likely to be rolled out to be added to other products in order to create a range of products. If that is the case, then certainly an application ought to be made to register that part of the design.

Marking the product/packaging/stands at shows

As soon as an application number is granted it ought to be used. If possible, put it on the product itself but at the very least it must appear on the packaging and on stands when showing/exhibiting the product. Once the registration number is granted, this must appear on the product as 'UK Reg. Des. No. 123456'. This is crucial in terms of putting third parties on notice in relation to damages claimed for infringement (discussed more fully at Chapter 9).

Claim priority wherever possible

If priority can be claimed, it ought to be. By backdating the application (and therefore the registration) via the mechanism of priority, the owner obtains up to six months' protection ahead of the product launch, which could be crucial in preventing a rival from marketing a similar product.

Watch the registrations

Remind owners two months before the end of the priority period to renew any registrations. At the same time check that they are still marketing the product as registered. If there is a difference between the product as registered and as marketed, query whether a new application or applications ought to be made.

Conclusion

The new regime for registered designs offers designers a more flexible tool with which to protect and exploit designs. Many of the restrictions imposed by the 1949 Act have been removed and, as a result, far wider and less expensive protection is given to designs.

CHAPTER 6

Community Design

INTRODUCTION

On 1 April 2003, the Community Design regime came into force as part of the harmonisation process of intellectual property law throughout the European Union. Practitioners will be familiar with the Community Trade Mark which allows one application to be sufficient for the whole of the European Union. There has been a standardised unregistered design law since 2002 and the Community Design regime will complete the process. This chapter explains the various regulations and the application process itself, and the advantages to clients seeking to protect their designs throughout the European Union.

THE REGULATIONS

Commission Regulation 2245/2002 (see Appendix L) governing the registration and protection of Community Designs implements Council Regulation 6/2002 of 12 December 2001 on Community Designs (see Appendix K), which created a Community-wide registration system and set the foundations for the requirements of a Community Design, including the application, appeal and invalidation procedures. Registrations are effected by application to the Office for Harmonisation in the Internal Market (OHIM). Council Regulation 6/2002, which in turn flows from Directive 98/71/EC (see Appendix J), has as its object the harmonisation of the requirements for, and the effect of, registered design protection in EC Member States. It became law in the United Kingdom by incorporation in December 2001. Commission Regulation 2245/2002 of 21 October 2002 contains the practical steps that must be taken in order to make a Community Design application; these are the regulations which a practitioner will use more often, day to day.

These provisions came into being as a result of rationalisation registrable intellectual property rights throughout the EU. Although reference was made to the applicable laws of the Member States at the time, in fact, the Directive is based on those provisions of national law that were thought to have the most effect on the functioning of the internal market. As such, both the Directive and the regulations are framed with a clear purpose in mind: to facilitate intra-Community trade.

What is clear is that the registered Community Design is intended to be regarded in the context of being just one of a bundle of rights that an individual might hold in any one object, be those rights copyright, unregistered design right, trade marks or patents. In the same way as registered designs operate at national level, a registered Community Design cannot and should not replace other forms of intellectual property law protection.

THE COMMUNITY DESIGN IN PRINCIPLE

Many of the principles discussed in Chapter 5 (on UK registered design) are relevant here because the national registered design process flows from the same Directive. Nevertheless, in order to put the practice of the Community Design in context, we will revisit those principles here.

SCOPE OF THE REGISTRATION

The registered Community Design is available only in respect of those designs that are visible on the object itself. It will not, therefore, be available for any design that is purely an internal feature of an object (which is readily visible only upon dismantling or opening it). As in the UK registered design regime, protection is only available for 2D and 3D objects that possess *novelty* and *individual character*. We shall look at the definition contained in the Directive, but suffice it to say that the design in question must differ substantially from any design that is currently in the public domain. If in doubt, a useful exercise is to apply a straightforward copyright infringement test: is the later design a substantial copy of an earlier design? The viewpoint of the informed user will almost always assist in determining whether the later design is an infringement. According to the Regulations, a design which may not be registered is one that has features which differ only in immaterial details to the earlier design.

Individual character (Council Regulation 6/2002, Article 6) is determined by the freedom that the designer had in creating the product/design. Here, freedom means artistic freedom, so a question to ask all designers when they seek to make a registered Community Design application is whether they designed particular features for particular reasons. It can then quickly be determined which features are a necessary shape (and are therefore incapable of registration because their shape is dictated by their function) and which are a 'free' shape and therefore can be registered.

The Community Design system is a mechanism designed to promote trade throughout the EU and, as such, registrations will not be granted to designs that are purely functional, i.e. where the shape or configuration of the design is dictated solely by its function. This is much more likely to be of relevance to 3D designs and, if in doubt, always ask the applicant why he or she has given the design its particular shape. However, this principle does not mean that they are not capable of protection per se, and indeed UK unregistered design law will assist applicants in protecting them.

Example

Maya has designed a holder for toothpaste for the German market. She wishes to register it as a registered Community Design because she anticipates it being very popular and she thinks that it will be copied. The design is quite plain. Maya explains how she came to design the piece: she simply measured a toothpaste tube so that the design had to take the shape in order to house the tube efficiently. Her design may not be registered by reason of its form following its function, i.e. that it necessarily took its particular shape in order to house the toothpaste tube.

While the requirement for aesthetic character (so-called 'eye-appeal', as discussed in Chapter 5) has been removed so that even the most mundane of designs can now be registered (in a bid to encourage commercial exploitation of designs), designs which are dictacted soled by their function (so-called 'must-fit, must-match' designs), cannot be registered under the Community Design regime.

COMPLEX PARTS

The Community is open to discussion of how best to protect component parts of complex products (complex parts). At present they cannot be protected by registration; however, the preamble to the Directive suggests that the issue is open to debate and indeed Article 14 of the Directive, which relates to component parts, is a transitional provision. What is unclear is whether the repairing of complex products by replicating (and thereby infringing) a Community Design that is a component part, ought to be allowed and to what extent. Certainly this is a policy issue, where intellectual property rights and promotion of commerce collide. Perhaps one way of dealing with this situation is where the parts in question are essential for the functioning of the product as a whole, they may be reproduced. Where a part is non-essential, a registered Community Design could protect it in the normal way. Certainly this would strike a balance between consumer choice and the protection of intellectual property.

Given that this is an area of uncertainty at the time of writing, applicants ought to be made aware that obtaining a registered Community Design in respect of such complex parts might not be as valuable as at first it seems.

Note that where the part is necessary for the functioning of a design, it is not an offence to replicate that portion that is necessary for the functioning of the design. However, given that the wording of the Article remains unclear, the applicant ought to be cautioned that a successful registration may well be open to challenge by a third party.

WHAT IS A DESIGN?

Article 3 of the Regulations clearly states what will be considered a design. The Community Design protection may apply to any design:

- whether 2D or 3D;
- which is either the whole or which is a part of a product;
- which is visible externally.

Given that a registered Community Design has direct effect in each Member State, a prior registration for a same or substantially similar design at national level will take precedence over the later Community application. It is prohibitively expensive for designers to search the Designs Registries of each country, but they ought to be made aware that the Community application is subject to earlier registrations not just at Community level but at national level of every EEA (European Economic Area) country.

Article 19 of Regulations grants a monopoly right to the owner of the design, namely:

- the exclusive right to prevent any third party from using the design without consent if he had produced an unauthorised copy;
- the right to prevent any unauthorised copiers from making, offering for sale, putting on the market, importing, exporting, stocking or using any product in which the design is incorporated or to which it is applied.

Article 4 of the Regulations requires a design to be:

- new;
- have individual character;
- not have been previously disclosed unless within the grace period of 12 months.

Article 4 of the Regulations also has specific provisions which cover complex parts and these are discussed fully (see p. 69).

Please note that individual character and novelty are assessed in comparison to other designs and not in isolation; there is no per se test of either novelty and/or individual character and there is no requirement of aesthetic quality as there used to be under the UK's Registered Designs Act 1949. Thus, even the more mundane types of designs are capable of registration assuming that they comply with the Article 4 provisions.

GRACE PERIOD

Perhaps one of the most useful provisions of the registered Community Design, and one which has already been implemented at national level, is the 12 months' grace period. A designer can test the market in order to assess the popularity and therefore the likelihood of commercial success of any product ahead of registration.

The 12-month period runs from the date on which the design is first shown to the public and the registration must occur within 12 months of that date.

If a designer wishes to show his design to developers he should ask third parties to sign a confidentiality agreement or non-disclosure agreement (NDA) so that the date of first disclosure is not considered to be the development meeting. Furthermore, if in doubt, the applicant should avoid showing the work in public if the design is unlikely to proceed to registration within 12 months of its first being shown. This is true of UK registered design as well. There is an example of an NDA provided in Appendix H.

Example

It is January and Sunita has created a new textile pattern but is unsure of the best material on which to print it. She enters into negotiations with various textile manufacturers to decide which is the best material for her pattern. Before the negotiations begin she makes sure that each company signs an NDA. Discussions are still ongoing in June and she decides not to show her work at a trade fair. By November, she has decided to go with KottonTech, and she therefore shows her design in December. Depending on its success, she has a year from December in which to register her design as a registered Community Design.

Note: the type of material will not affect the registration of the 2D pattern.

PRIORITY

As with UK registered design, a registered Community Design application can be backdated by up to six months based on an earlier application made at national level. So, if an application were made on 1 April 2003 at the UK Registry, a Community application made any time thereafter up to 1 October 2003 would have a filing date of 1 April 2003. Once the six-month period has expired, there is no priority period, so that an application filed on 2 October 2003 would have a filing date of 2 October 2003.

This was described in full in Chapter 5, but we repeat the timeline tables here for ease of reference.

Priority timelines

Note: the Australian jurisdiction is used as an example but it could in fact be any foreign jurisdiction.

Scenario 1

Australian application 1 January 2003	Australian registration 1 January 2003		
Product first marketed in Australia		UK application made by 1 June 2003	UK registration dated 1 January 2003 based on Australian registration
		UK application made by 1 June 2003 but payment not submitted in time	UK registration dated 1 June 2003 once the rectifications have been made outside of period of priority claim

Scenario 2

Product first marketed 1 January 2003 in the UK	UK application made 1 June 2003	UK registration granted 1 June 2003		
			Community Design application 1 December 2003 claiming priority	Community Design registration granted and dated 1 June 2003 based on UK registration

Scenario 3

Product first marketed 1 January 2003	UK application made 1 March 2003	UK registration granted and dated 1 March 2003		
			Community Design application made 1 November 2003	Community Design registration dated 1 November 2003
				No claim of priority can be made because outside six months' period but within first 12 months' marketing

Scenario 4

Product first marketed 1 January 2003				
	Application made 1 September 2003	Registration granted 1 September 2003		
			Community application made 1 April 2004	Community application *refused* on grounds that no priority can be claimed (seven months) and outside the 12 months' grace period of first marketing

DEFERMENT OF PUBLICATION

In certain circumstances, the applicant may wish to make an application but defer publication of the design. It is always useful to ascertain the applicant's intended use of the product and further when the applicant intends to bring the product to market. For example, if a product is still in development but the applicant is certain of its commercial viability and therefore that it is likely to be copied, publication of the application (together with the design drawings) can be deferred by up to 30 months. This should also be considered where there is, or there is the potential for, a patent application. Once the design is disclosed, a patent application for that design will fail and it is therefore vital that where both a registered Community Design and a UK registered design are being applied for at the same time, secrecy is maintained. Please note that there is a sample NDA provided in Appendix H which will assist the applicant. Also remember that an NDA must be signed *before* negotiations begin.

However, before proceeding with an application for deferment, it should be determined whether the applicant has a previous application in another jurisdiction. For example, should an application have been published in the United Kingdom then the deferment of publication at Community level has no practical benefit. Furthermore, if the applicant has a design at the application stage for registration both in the United Kingdom and the Community simultaneously, the publication deferment period can only be a maximum of 15 months since this is the maximum permissible under English law.

The deferment period is useful in situations where the applicant is keen not to reveal the nature of a design to rivals in the marketplace or where the same design is the subject of a patent application and the publication of the design would defeat the patent application. It is therefore imperative that in all circumstances the applicant confirms whether he intends to apply, or has applied, for a patent and in which jurisdictions.

COMPLEX PRODUCTS VS MODULAR DESIGNS

The distinction between complex products and modular designs is important in order to avoid valuable registrations being missed. A design which is solely dictated by its function is one which must take on a particular shape and size; where the designer has no freedom in creating it. So, a wheel nut of a particular make of car would fall within this definition and there has been much case law at national level on this issue, more particularly discussed in Chapter 5.

By contrast, modular designs are for products that can be assembled or connected in a variety of ways. The key difference with these types of products is that, although they fit together, they need not fit together in a particular way and therefore the parts need not be of a particular size. Modular furniture would be a perfect example of items which can fit together in one or more ways, but the design of the pieces is not dictated by a pre-existing product or part.

Example 1

Janine runs a design company designing furniture. She designs a series of modular furniture. The range consists of a number of seats which can (but need not) interlock to form seating units that can seat as many people as the space available for the units. The units are bought by retail customers who typically purchase a maximum of four seats for an ordinary house.

Miguel runs a wine bar and likes Janine's designs. He orders 14 units to be interlinked along one wall of his bar.

In both cases the design is protected by the initial registration of the individual units.

> ### Example 2
>
> *Miguel is pleased with the result and asks Janine to make bar stools to fit in between metal bars that he had specially commissioned for his wine bar, a bespoke design. Janine's design must allow the stools to interconnect with the bar in order that they remain upright.*
>
> *Janine's designs have to take a specific form. Although she could choose the materials for the seat and the base, the dimensions and the overall shape of the stools are dictated by the recess in the bar. Janine cannot therefore apply for a registered Community Design in respect of the stools because their form is dictated by their function.*

A car part, for example, offers no room for originality of design since the part to which it connects determines the part's form and therefore its function. Another way of looking at the issue of modularity is to ask: did the product necessarily have to take the overall shape in the first place? With modular systems of furniture very often the answer is 'no' unless they form part of a larger system, or where, as in the second example above, they had to fit a specific space and there was no originality of design. Consider, therefore, whether the applicant was bound to create the shape in a certain way, or whether the designer had freedom in determining the design; in other words, designs that are capable of registration are 'clean sheet' designs.

PERIOD OF REGISTRATION

The registered Community Design, like the UK registered design, lasts for periods of five years, renewable up to a maximum of 25 years. Once the 25-year period has expired, the owner of the design will have to rely on copyright to protect its design (assuming that the design is within copyright: see Chapter 3).

RIGHT OF DESIGNER(S) TO BE CITED

The Regulations provide that a designer, whether acting alone or as part of a team, has the right to have his name cited in the application. Should a team of designers be responsible for the design, then all of them should be cited.

PRIOR USE

Where a third party has been using the design prior to registration, that prior use will take precedence over the application. Goodwill in the design will accrue to the third-party user assuming:

- that such use has been in good faith; or
- where the preparations for use had been taken to such a point by the third party that such use would have naturally occurred had the applicant not made the registered Community Design application.

Example

Michael and Robert went to design school together. One of their areas of study was lighting. Both were ceramicists and used ceramics in their work. It was always acknowledged that they had a similar style, although they created their work independently of each other.

A year later Michael creates a range of disc lights which he sells to individuals, clubs and pubs in the north of England.

Two years later Robert creates a disc light and seeks a registered Community Design because there is a lot of interest in his work. Michael speaks to the OHIM to protect his idea because there is a lot of interest in his work too. Searching the Community Designs Register, Michael sees Robert's application. Robert's design is almost identical to Michael's, who is anxious to prevent Robert's application from proceeding. If it were to go through, it would prevent Michael from continuing his profitable business.

Robert may not obtain a monopoly right in the design and Michael's objection is successful on ground of prior use. Both designs may coexist given that neither is a copy of the other and there is therefore no infringement of copyright in either work.

GROUNDS FOR INVALIDITY

Article 25 of the Regulations sets out the grounds for invalidity (see Appendix K). As noted above, it is good practice to find out from designers the circumstances under which they created the design. For example, if they were an employee at the time of creation, it will belong to the employer and as such a registered Community Design application by the employee will technically be infringing the (ex-)employer's intellectual property in the design.

Similarly, the designer may have collaborated on the work; again, a registration in a single name will infringe any copyright that is owned jointly, in absence of express permission to do so.

THE PRACTICALITIES OF FILING AN APPLICATION

Title IV of the Regulations together with Commission Regulation 2245/2002 (see Appendix L) deal with the practicalities of filing an application at the OHIM in Alicante, Spain (see Appendix F).

Although the draft Regulations 2445/2002 make provision for filing at the Member State's national register (so that an application for a registered Community Design could be filed at the UK Patent Office, for example), we submit that, as with the Community Trade Mark, the more sensible option is to file the application at the OHIM direct and to pay the fees there. This avoids there being any need to chase the local office to ensure that it processes the application with the OHIM within time.

BASIC CONDITIONS FOR A SUCCESSFUL APPLICATION

Before the application is made you should ensure that the design and the application comply with the following:

- The correct form (available at http://www.ohim.eu.int) is used and a request for application is made (including the names and addresses and contact numbers for the legal representatives and the applicant). An example is set out in Appendix F.
- A description or example of the design is enclosed describing the product itself and not its brand name. For example, you would say 'Modular Seating' and not 'Star Seat' if that were its brand name.
- Representations should be enclosed which are suitable for publication. Typically these will be images of different angles of the design. It is in the applicant's interest to represent the design as accurately as possible since the design *as registered* is the one that will be enforced. If the design is 3D the usual method is to take views from the front, back, each side, top bottom and a ¾ view to show perspective. The typical number is six, given that the sides of an object are often identical, but fewer are required if the design is 2D.
- The class to which the design belongs based on the Locarno classifications must be included. These can be found on the OHIM website and cover all types of objects capable of registration. The class should be included on the application as indicated on the form in Appendix F.

- The citation of the designer/design team involved in its creation should be included.
- The application will always be subject to payment of the relevant fee at the same time as the application is lodged (Commission Regulation 2245/2002, Article 6). However, if the fee is not paid at the same time, it must be paid within one month of the application having been made. This said, it is good practice to pay the fee with the application and therefore a practitioner should collect the fee on account, ahead of making the application. If an application for deferment is made, then a deferment fee is paid initially and a publication fee is levied at the appropriate time prior to publication.
- If priority is claimed, the details of the prior registration on which priority is based must be included in the application by lodging certified copies of the registration in the relevant jurisdiction (Commission Regulation 2245/2002, Article 8). If the applicant wishes to claim priority after the application has been filed, he will need to file the application within one month of the registered Community Design application having been made.

MULTIPLE APPLICATIONS

Occasionally a designer may wish to register several designs at once. Under the UK system, each would require a separate registration and they could not be registered as a series unless the designs were sold together, for example as a dining set, or where they are part of the same item.

In contrast, Article 2 of Commission Regulation 2245/2002 provides for registrations of several designs at once regardless of whether they are sold together or separately, provided the items belong to the same class of Locarno classification. The classifications can be found at www.ohim.eu.inst and they break the product down, for example from 'furniture' to 'rocking chair' so that the numbered code e.g. 01.01 signifies that the first number is the type of good and the second number is the actual good itself.

Article 3(1) of Commission Regulation 2245/2002 provides that an application will not proceed to registration unless it is classified according to Locarno.

Fees

The fees for multiple applications are levied on a sliding scale and are more particularly described on the OHIM website (as above). Please note that where the application contains goods of differing Locarno types they will be separated into different applications and an uplift in fees will be payable at the prevailing rate.

REPRESENTATIONS

Article 4 of Commission Regulation 2245/2002 concerns representations. Representations should each be made on a single sheet of A4 unless the application is filed electronically, in a format to be determined by the OHIM (undecided at the time of writing); one imagines pdf images or similar programs will be acceptable.

A maximum of seven views of each design should be supplied so that they provide a clear and discernible understanding of the design. Should more than seven views of the image be provided, the additional ones will be disregarded by the OHIM and therefore it is crucial that the first seven views clearly identify the design for which application for registration is made.

Specimens of the product for which application for registration is made can be filed but they must be submitted to the OHIM at the same time as the application is filed. For example, an actual print or door handle can be sent to the OHIM. Bulky or perishable designs will not be accepted, so that a bed or a lollypop design would not be accepted. Should the design be the subject of a deferred application, the submission of a specimen is encouraged by the OHIM.

The quality of the design submitted should be carefully considered. For example, if the design is a repeating pattern, the design should show the full extent of the pattern before it repeats so that it is clear from the representation how the design appears in full.

PERFECTING THE APPLICATION

Should the design application be deficient in any way, the application must be perfected within two months of the application being filed, otherwise the application will lapse. Therefore it is crucial to make sure that any imperfections are dealt with speedily and it is recommended that a diary is kept so that applications are perfected within time.

INFRINGEMENTS

Infringements of the design may be prosecuted in any jurisdiction that is a member of the EEA where infringments are taking place. However, owners of the designs should take note that if the matter is heard at national level, the court may only award damages for loss suffered in that jurisdiction. The location of the hearing will be determined by the extent (geographically) to which the damage has been suffered and the likelihood of recovery of those damages. Finally, and in the usual way, the cost of any such action will have to be borne in mind.

The owner of the registration will have to balance the prospects of success against the cost in each jurisdiction. Given that the monopoly right may be enforced against anyone who markets a design that is the same/similar to the one registered, the law in each jurisdiction ought to differ only slightly. However, the application of that law will vary between countries and owners must obtain advice from a practitioner qualified in the relevant jurisdiction(s).

An alternative way for the owner of a design to enforce rights arises where it becomes apparent that a design that has been entered on the Register ought not to have been, by reason of an earlier design or where the design is an infringement of an earlier work protected by copyright/unregistered design and where evidence of copying can be substantiated. This will turn on the facts of each case, but in these circumstances an application may be made for a declaration of invalidity by the examiner.

Details from all parties with knowledge and/or experience of the design process and/or the act of infringement will be taken by the practitioner and submitted along with the application for a declaration of invalidity. The relevant fee must also be enclosed.

Articles 28–37 of Commision Regulation 2245/2002 deal with such applications and appeals made against them. In brief, as is customary in such instances, the successful party in the application may recover the application fees. Articles 42–8 of Commision Regulation 2245/2002 deal with hearings and while it is beyond the scope of this book to examine the proceedings in detail, it is worth noting that a hearing may be had at either national or Community level and, in either case, the hearing officer has the power to make awards of costs in favour of the successful party.

UNREGISTERED COMMUNITY DESIGN

Directive 98/71/EC on the legal protection of designs introduces Community-wide unregistered design right which can be enforced at either national level or anywhere in the EEA an infringement takes place. As with the registered Community Design, any successful action relates to that particular jurisdiction so that an award of damages and an injunction granted in Germany will only be capable of enforcement there, not Community wide.

The regime is the same as in the UK (see Chapter 4) with the key exception that the protection applies to the appearance of the whole or part of a product which may be the configuration of elements or parts of a product, or the decoration that appears on the shape. This is very different from the UK unregistered design right which does not recognise surface decoration of any sort.

Those items not capable of protection are:

- features that are solely dictated by their function;
- features that require interconnection but not including modular systems (such as furniture);
- component parts of complex products. This allows the consumer a choice in the market when repairing a radio, for example, and is a profitable balance between the protection of intellectual property rights and the furtherance of commercial freedom. However, we add a note of caution (as mentioned earlier in this chapter): it remains to be seen how this will work in practice.

To be capable of protection the unregistered design must have individual character in accordance with the analysis discussed at the start of this chapter in relation to registered Community Designs.

The period of protection is just three years (unlike the UK where it is 15 years), from the end of the first calendar year in which the protection starts. The protection starts not with the making of the design/creation of the design document embodying the design, but rather when the product is made available in the EU.

CONCLUSION

The Community Design puts registered designs on an almost equal footing with the Community Trade Mark system. Having a Community-wide system means that those rights can be enforced anywhere in the EU/EEA that an infringement takes place. What remains to be seen is how the Community Design functions. At the time of writing there have been applications but nothing further, so it is still difficult to understand the relationship between the national and Community Registers and how subsequent applications (such as those for a declaration of invalidity) will be enforced. The Locarno system of classifying designs by type certainly assists the registration process and as Community Design becomes commonplace, the system of searching, application and enforcement will be made easier. The only foreseeable difficulty is that, given that there are so many classes of goods, it will be a very time-consuming process.

Unregistered designs have also grown up with the unregistered Community Design giving owners a short-lived but useful tool in the enforcement of designs that embody design right. Certainly much will be written in both areas once they become established and decisions are made by the OHIM and the national courts.

CHAPTER 7

3D trade marks, registered designs and patents

INTRODUCTION

In previous chapters we have considered the protection that is available for unregistered design and how that overlaps with copyright law. To recap, in general, the law seeks to avoid any overlap between the two, although often both rights will coexist in respect of the same design.

In this chapter the nature of and the relationship between 3D trade marks and designs is considered, in particular the following:

- The relative benefits of each system of protection.
- The purpose that a designer wishes to make of the intended shape, if any, and the influence this has on which type of protection may be most appropriate.
- The public policy arguments against extending protection by registering a shape as a trade mark once its protection as a design has expired.
- Useful pointers in deciding whether a shape is best protected as a trade mark, a registered design or both.
- The relationship between patents and other forms of protection, namely registered rights (trade marks, registered designs and patents) and copyright.

WHAT IS A TRADE MARK?

A trade mark is any sign which is capable of distinguishing the goods and/or services of one trader from those of another. Under UK law, a trade mark can be a word, a logo, a shape, a picture, a 3D object or any combination of these.

To be capable of trade mark registration, a trade mark must:

- be distinctive for the goods or services for which registration is applied;
- not be contrary to public policy, deceptive or be contrary to law;
- not be identical or similar to a previous mark for the same goods or services.

It therefore follows that as long as a shape conforms with these requirements, it can be registered if it is also a 'sign' s defined in s.1 of the Trade Marks Act 1994 in that it refers solely to a 'sign'.

Example

Coca-Cola Trade Mark Applications [1986] 2 All ER 274 (A decision under the 1938 Trade Marks Act)

The Coca-Cola company filed an application to register its distinctive bottle shape as a trade mark. The application was refused by the Registrar on the grounds that the company was attempting to register the 'thing itself' as a trade mark rather than a badge of origin distinct from the thing (in this case the drink). Both the Registrar and the court interpreted the 1938 Act as requiring that the mark be something distinct from the thing marketed. The House of Lords also had public policy concerns; it was reluctant to set a precedent which granted the applicant a monopoly in containers. The 1994 Act changed this approach, clearly stating that shapes (as well as smells, designs, letters, words, devices and 'jingles') are registrable assuming the tests in the 1994 Act (as outlined above) are fulfilled. Coca-Cola was able to proceed successfully to register its distinctively shaped bottle.

Section 3(2) Trade Marks Act 1994 provides for the refusal of registration of signs as trade marks which consist exclusively of:

- the shape which results from the nature of the goods themselves; or
- the shape of the goods which is necessary to obtain a technical result; or
- the shape which gives substantial value to the goods.

Example

Philips Electronics NV v. Remington Consumer Products C-299/99

This case went all the way to the European Court. Since 1985, Philips had held a trade mark for the image of the head of its three-headed electric shaver. The registration protected the 3D-shape of the three rotary heads arranged within an equilateral triangle. Philips had always used the mark together with the word 'Philishave', and for this reason Jacob J. referred to the image mark as 'limping' because it needed the support of the word when used. In his opinion, it lacked distinctiveness per se when considered in isolation from the qualifying word 'Philishave' which was a necessary part of the mark as registered.

Remington began to produce an electric shaver with three rotary heads, forming an equilateral triangle bearing the company name 'Remington'. Philips claimed that this was an infringement of its trade mark. In reply, Remington sought to have the Philips mark revoked on the grounds that it was invalid for the following reasons:

- *that it lacked distinctive character (s.3(1) of the 1994 Act);*
- *that the design resulted from the nature of the goods themselves; and*
- *that it was necessary to achieve a technical result.*

Jacob J. found that the design of the goods was necessary to achieve the desired technical result and therefore that the mark was invalid. In other words, the form of the mark followed the function of the three-headed razor. The House of Lords overturned the decision, disagreeing with Jacob J.'s analysis of the mark. It was held that the design did not automatically flow from the product itself. An appeal was made to the European Court of Justice which found for Remington in that the mark was necessarily shaped as an equilateral triangle in order to achieve the desired technical result and therefore lacked the required distinctiveness. Effectively the configuration of the three heads within an equilateral triangle was the only way in which a three-headed razor could achieve the desired result: that of a close shave.

This case has limited the trade mark protection available to shapes and has placed the emphasis on a shape registration as a badge of origin.

If we compare the Registered Designs Regulations 2001 (SI 2001/3949) (see Chapter 5), these prevent registrations for designs that are solely dictated by their function. Although the shape was necessary to achieve the desired technical function, it was not (arguably) dictated solely by the function since it could have taken an isosceles triangle (as Philips demonstrated in its first instance evidence). Thus the shape may well have been protected by registered design. Of course, the battle for trade mark protection was a practical one. Registered designs last only for up to 25 years whereas a trade mark can last indefinitely assuming that its use complies with the Act. However, a consideration to bear in mind is that, in these circumstances, a shape can be used to steal a march on competitors if registered as a design. It has the same effect as a patent: that of a monopoly right.

PATENT PROTECTION

For a patent to be capable of protection it must be an invention:

- capable of industrial application;
- that is new;
- that has not previously been disclosed; and
- that is a leap forward in the prior art (i.e. not obvious).

Patents last for 20 years and are available in the UK for inventions that fulfil the requirements set out above.

Example 1

Husband and wife team Alberto and Maria Vargas have designed a range of stacking furniture that they would like to protect. The furniture must take a particular form in order for it to stack. The system is based on an interlocking 'socket' and 'plug' which the Vargases designed themselves. Although they are using it just for furniture, they believe that it could be applied to other areas of their work, and have never seen anything like it.

They have not shown the 'socket' and 'plug' to anyone and are convinced that it could be mass-produced.

They approach a solicitor for advice and she recommends that they consult a patent attorney to see if they can protect it that way. The patent attorney makes the application to protect the invention. Once the patent application has been filed, they apply to register the seat shape as a design. In making both applications, the Vargases have succeeded in protecting the function and form of their design.

Note: The patent would be drafted so that the 'socket' and 'plug' could be used in relation to other items. The best form of patent protection allows flexibility of use. The Vargases mark their product Pat. Pending and Reg. Des. No. 12345678.

HOW ARE DESIGNS AND TRADE MARKS SIMILAR?

As with registered designs and registered Community Designs, where the shape is dictated by the function of the product, the design may not be registered as a trademark. The law of trademark goes further, however, and a trademark that is descriptive of the product (for example, using a stylised version of the word 'coffee' for a coffee product) will not be registered. Rather, the shape must be suggestive of the goods (for example, a stylised picture of a coffee bean for the same product) in order to be registered as a trademark. This is a stricter test than for registered designs.

Shape and function

The limitations of trade mark protection for shapes were not clearly defined in the *Philips* case. It is possible to have both types of protection for the same shape; there is nothing in law to prevent such layered protection. To complicate matters, each can be protected at national or Community level. Therefore, depending on the use of the shape, a client may seek more than one form of protection. The courts are reluctant, however, to extend registered design protection to trade mark protection merely because the design registration has expired and cannot be renewed.

Example 2

The Vargases become celebrated for their work and it becomes synonymous with their design practice. In order to capitalise on this national recognition, they decide to package it in a box which is a fusion of an 'egg' and a 'cube'. In order to prevent others from copying their packaging, they register it as a design and as a trade mark. Both registrations are accepted at the Registry and run concurrently. The packaging is a badge of origin according to the Trade Marks Act 1994 and as it is not dictated solely by its function, is capable of being a registered design.

Furthermore, the trade mark is a less clear arena for the protection of shapes, where a shape is a combination of elements. For example, the 3D mark could have more than one sign which in combination produce the distinctive character necessary for registration. So a colour, a shape and a particular font or typeface in combination could be a registered trade mark. By contrast, each element of that mark is capable of registration as a design, so that the colour, the shape and any 2D surface decoration can be registered separately.

Shape and distinctiveness

Returning to the exclusions under the Act, it is clear that public policy is more at work in trade marks than in the registered design system. Trade marks must necessarily concern themselves with avoiding generic signs in a way that designs need not do. As a 'badge of origin' a trade mark must necessarily be distinctive. By contrast, a registered design need only be original. It need not even have 'eye appeal'. There is, therefore, more flexibility within the registered design system.

For example a decision in 1998 to refuse Application No. 2006389 by Wickes plc to register a shape as a trade mark was made on the basis that the application, consisting of a 'three-dimensional booklet which was substantially square in format', lacked distinctive character. As an application for registered design it is likely to be have been refused too, on grounds of lack of originality, although it would have been possible to register as a design any original surface decoration or any key features of the booklet such as a flap, which may have had the desired commercial effect in preventing a competitor from producing a similar marketing tool. It is essential to ascertain the applicant's use of the shape and desired result before deciding what type of application to make. So if the cover of the booklet were to show a certain shape (say a wave) and if that wave were made up of two colours (say, blue and green) the design could be registered as a blue and green wave. In order to protect the particular use of colour for the wave, the Pantone number of each colour should be cited in the application. However, the applicant should bear in mind that if colour is claimed in the application, the design is only protected where the colour is used in conjunction with (in this instance) the wave. Again the applicant should be probed as to how he will use the mark. For example, if the mark will be used with many different colours, it will be of no use to register one colour variation and a black and white version ought to be used instead.

Example

Jeryl Lynn [1999] FSR 491

This case indicates that there is nothing wrong in one design having multi-layered intellectual property right protection in the same article. The crux of analysing whether the article is so entitled is to decide, from a trade mark point of view, whether the article/product is capable of distinguishing the goods and/or services of one trade mark owner from those of another.

It should be borne in mind that an applicant cannot claim priority of registered design when making a trade mark application or vice versa. Although it is possible to have different types of intellectual property protection in the same article, they are not interchangeable in that the rights granted under one type of protection have no relevance when making an application or invoking another type of protection. They should be considered in the alternative. (For more on this, see Chapter 9.)

TRADE MARK OR DESIGN PROTECTION?

The Dualit Application No. 2023946, which was also refused, raises an interesting distinction between registered designs and trade marks. In order to succeed with its application, the company had to demonstrate that the shape of its toasters had acquired distinctive character through use. It had to show that the consumers (rather than trade resellers) would associate the shape of its toasters with the company in order to get trade mark protection. Owing to flawed survey evidence, the manufacturer was unable to show that a significant proportion of those interviewed associated the shape with Dualit. The decision was appealed and upheld on the grounds that the shape of the toaster added value to the product per se and as such it lacked a distinctive quality. By contrast, a registered design would, assuming that the applicant had complied with the provisions of the 1949 Act and the Regulations, have succeeded, which would have given Dualit the commercial protection sought for up to 25 years.

The benefits of design registration over a trade mark

What is clear is that logos, devices or shapes that were once thought of as only being capable of trade mark registration, can in fact be registered as either UK or registered Community Designs as well.

Registration can give protection for all goods within a particular filing, so can be cost-effectively applied to a range of goods which, although not part of a series, are nevertheless put together to create a unified look. Thus, a chair may have a distinctive shape and be registered as a trade mark, but if sold as part of a dining set with other chairs and a table, the whole set can be a registered design.

Another benefit is that the distinctive character required under the Trade Marks Act may flow from the monopoly protection offered by design registration, which prevents others from copying the design. A shape which lacks distinctiveness in years 1–5 may acquire distinctiveness through exclusive use by year 6 and so become capable of trade mark registration. This is an example of design law paving the way for a trademark.

The benefits of trade mark protection

When considering primary infringement one must distinguish between the different types of right available to the applicant. A trade mark will be infringed if:

- An identical or similar mark is used for identical goods.
- An identical or similar mark is used for identical or similar goods where there is a likelihood of confusion on the part of the public. This includes a likelihood of association with the registered trade mark.
- Where an identical or similar mark is used for dissimilar goods but where the mark has a reputation within the territory, and where the mark will be associated with the dissimilar goods.

Registered designs are infringed only where someone does an act that is the exclusive preserve of the registered owner (or licensee). Such an act can only be reproducing the design in substantially the same form as that registered, i.e. it must be a substantially similar design.

It is clear, therefore that a trade mark affords the owner a more far-reaching protection than a registered design.

One should also consider that where a design is registered under the 1949 Act, or where that design is protected as an unregistered design, and the right expires, the following scenario could ensue.

Example 1

Sally registered the design of her building bricks as a design. After 25 years, the registration expired. Because it had expired, a number of competitors adopted a similar design and method of attachment as Sally's building bricks. She then sought to apply for a trade mark. Owing to the widespread use of the type of brick, her mark was refused for reason of lack of distinctive character. The shape had become generic among manufacturers and marketers of building bricks. Had Sally and Sally alone used the shape, it would have retained its distinctive character. Her undoing was that she allowed it to become a generic shape within her industry.

Sally ought to have properly policed the use of her design and made sure that, rather than it becoming generic in her industry, it retained its distinctive character. She could have done this by means of an enforcement paragraph in her licences (see Chapter 9).

Example 2

During the period in which the design right and/or registered design is in force, Sally decides to license her design to a well-known manufacturer of children's toys. As well as the general provisions contained in the licence, Sally must ensure that the design number and/or the trade mark symbol® is used. This deters would-be infringers and also makes it clear that, rather than a generic product, hers is a product specific to no one but her.

(See Interlego AG's Trade Mark [1998] RPC 69)

Trade marks are a more specific right and as such the protection afforded to owners is, in theory at least, as long as the person seeks to renew the mark. A trade mark could also be used in conjunction with a feature that is not capable of design registration, for example, a brick that smells of perfume. It could not be registered as a design, since a design cannot be a smell or words (unless the words are using a font particularly claimed or it is a design using letters).

However, in the application made by Procter and Gamble (reported in 1998 RPC 710) the hearing officer gave some useful guidance on the registrability of 3D trade marks saying a shape must be immediately identifiable as 'different' and therefore 'memorable'.

If the shape was *purely* functional or if it had a *purely* decorative or aesthetic purpose, it would be unlikely to be capable of performing the essential function of a trade mark, namely that of distinguishing one good/service from another.

The key here is that the shape will be associated with a particular good or service if it is registered as a trade mark but where it is registered as a design it can be applied to any number of products or services with just one protection. Furthermore, that more generalist protection can be used as a testing bed for a possible future trade mark application. By contrast, the trade mark is very specific but as such it can give a longer protection (assuming that it is renewed where available).

IS THE BOUNDARY BETWEEN DESIGN LAW AND TRADE MARK LAW CLEAR?

In short, it is. Although at times the different types of protection can exist simultaneously in the same article, they are intended to complement rather than compete with one another. Remember that in neither case is the *function* of the piece protected but rather its distinctiveness and its appearance. It is useful to note that passing off may well apply to an unregistered trade mark which has acquired a distinctive character and that it refers to the origin of goods without being descriptive of it.

Example

Reckitt & Coleman Products Limited v. Borden Inc. [1990] RPC 341

This is the famous Jif Lemon case. Lord Jauncey stated that a trader could obtain protection for the 'get-up' (i.e the look, colours and shape) of a mark whose shape and/or colour alluded to the contents of the article. He went on to say that the trader who imitated such an article ought to go to lengths to prevent the public from becoming confused into believing that the products of the second trader were the products of the first.

There is no apparent reason why the rights deriving from design law and trade mark law may not apply to in the same article. The two regimes are naturally separate and, as such, are not intended to influence each other. Dual protection serves different purposes depending on the circumstances of infringement and, as is more fully explored in Chapter 8, the protection regimes are often argued in the alternative when a claim is launched. What ought to be borne in mind are the commercial considerations of the client. Does he seek monopoly protection indefinitely or for a limited period of time? For how long is he likely to market the article? These are the primary considerations in assessing the type of protection that is most relevant to the applicant.

In considering the above, the following are useful pointers:

- the life cycle of similar products in the range/portfolio;
- is the article a 'stand-alone' product or is it intended to complement the range?
- the way in which the applicant works: with signature pieces, or with a series of distinctive designs based on a similar principle;
- whether, and to whom, the designer intends to license the product for manufacture.

Of interest are those designs that contain a functional element but which are ultimately a distinct design. An example would be the grille of a motor vehicle: although it contains the purely functional struts of the grille itself, its overall shape is distinctive of the brand (e.g. Mercedes, BMW, Volvo, and so on) and one immediately associates it with the relevant company. The grille shape is capable of being registered as a trade mark (because its form is not the only shape to perform the technical function; it could be a completely different shape) and as a design because again, the form is not dictated *solely* by its function.

In determining whether a design with a functional element is capable of registered protection, the effect of that functional element on the article when taken as a whole should be considered. For example, were the grilles of such motor manufacturers a plain square shape, so as not to be distinctive, the mark would more than likely be refused since to have a square grille is not distinctive of any one car manufacturer. The same is true, for example, of the shape of tennis-racquet heads designed to hit a ball, but taking a certain shape so as to distinguish them in the marketplace and thereby being of distinctive character.

Protection	Registered	Burden of proof?	Term	Applies to?	Type of right granted	Infringement	Remedies
Trade mark	yes	With alleged infringer	Indefinite. Renewable every 10 years	Words, images, smells, shapes and jingles	To stop same/similar mark on same/similar goods. Also special provisions for famous marks	Use of same/similar marks on same/similar goods or dissimilar goods for famous marks	Damages, destruction, delivery-up, injunction
Registered designs	yes	With alleged infringer	25 years. Renewable every 5 years	2D and 3D designs	Monopoly	Monopoly right. A substantially similar design is marketed	Damages, destruction, delivery-up, injunction
Copyright	no	With owner of copyright work	70 years from end of year in which author dies	Original literary, dramatic and artistic works	Negative right	To prevent others from copying the original work	Damages, destruction, delivery-up, injunction
Patent	yes	With owner of patent	20 years	New, not obvious undisclosed industrial designs	Monopoly right	Invention conforms to claims as drafted in the patent	Damages, destruction, delivery-up, injunction
Unregistered design	no	With owner of unregistered design	Community: 3 years UK: 15 years	2D and 3D designs but not to surface decoration or colour	Negative right	The making of a design substantially similar to the whole design or part thereof	Damages, destruction, delivery-up, injunction

CONCLUSION

What is clear is that registered design offers applicants a cost-effective way of testing the market or to acquire distinctiveness in the provision of goods/services without costly trade mark applications. Particularly following the ECJ decision in *Philips* v. *Remington*, design rights may be more suited to 3D shapes in the shorter term and should certainly be used as a means to pave the way for future trade mark registrations.

Trade mark protection is more difficult to obtain; because the protection is indefinite, it is the best type of monopoly right to have. Furthermore, 3D shapes can allude to their contents and still be capable of protection. They can also contain a functional element or elements and still be capable of protection.

What is clear is that the different types of intellectual property protection available for shapes are intended to coexist. The different types of protection should therefore be considered as a series of weapons in an armoury of pro-tection rather than a set of interchangeable rights. Depending on the needs of the applicant, each type of protection should be considered on its merits and in relation to the shape/article in question.

While the totality of the intellectual property protection afforded in respect of 3D shapes is not entirely clear, the law is intended to be used according to the specific needs and use of the owner. Each design must be analysed according to its intended life and use before the ideal method(s) of protection can be selected and implemented.

CHAPTER 8

Exploitation of design and competition law

INTRODUCTION

This chapter has four areas of focus:

- The requirements for effective assignment of designs.
- The circumstances in which licences are compulsory.
- The common provisions in any licence.
- The competition law provisions that apply in such circumstances.

ASSIGNMENT

Assignments (outright transfer of ownership, i.e sale) of designs can take place in a number of circumstances. Two common examples are:

- Where a business has acquired the assets of an individual or body corporate, such as the sale of the shares or assets of a company. In this case an assignment is usually contained within the sale documentation.
- Where a company or other person engages the services of a freelancer and wishes to acquire all work carried out as part of a particular project (for example packaging design). In this case the assignment is usually contained within an engagement letter containing the terms and conditions on which the parties do business together.

Licensing is very often the main way in which the owner of a registered (or unregistered) design is able to receive an income over a longer period of time from his design. Licence agreements are used freely in the design industry as design-driven companies seek to expand their business by using the market strength of a larger concern to make and/or distribute their designs. This chapter sets out the crucial clauses in any design licence. It also discusses the different clauses that arise in different circumstances. After each topic, an example clause typical of many such agreements is given.

What is an assignment?

An assignment is an outright unfettered transfer of the ownership of the design(s) in question. As with any other type of property, intellectual property may be bought and sold. Until recently, stamp duty was payable on such transfers of ownership but this has been abolished by the Chancellor of the Exchequer. Like any contract, for an assignment to be valid in law there must be consideration paid in exchange for the right that is to be acquired, which as with any other piece of property, must be money or money's worth.

Given that assignments vary widely from deal to deal, an example of an assignment has not been provided, but we concentrate on the key areas that should be considered when drawing up an assignment.

Assignment of a registered design

The subject of the assignment must be clear. With a registered design that task is made easier by using the registration number (and the Locarno classification if it is a registered Community Design). For the absolute avoidance of doubt, a copy of the certificate, together with the images of the design should be annexed to the agreement, and all other information that appears on the Register.

Next, verify that the parties to the agreement are correct and check that the party which purports to assign the right appears on the Register as the proprietor. If that party has taken an assignment of the design, make sure that a copy of that assignment is annexed to the assignment document and that a warranty in terms of ownership of the design is included in the assignment.

While not making it a formal requirement, the Patent Office does recommend that all assignments are registered with it and it is certainly best practice to do so. By contrast, Article 28 of the Regulations (see Appendix K) provides that any transfer (and indeed licence) of a design must be registered and it must be made in the form specified on the OHIM website (www.ohim.eu.inst). In the event that the transfer is not registered, it will not be valid, which will mean the purchaser will not be able to deal in or enforce the newly acquired design.

Therefore if the assignment of a registered Community Design has taken place and has not subsequently been registered with OHIM the purported owner will not have taken the assignment as intended and it will not have legal validity.

Next, verify that the design registration is still in force. There is a design fee which is payable each five years up to a maximum of 25 years. A quick check of the relevant jurisdiction's online database (www.patent.gov, www.ohim.eu.inst) provides an up-to-date report of the status of the design in question.

Finally, verify the circumstances in which the design was created. If a company is purporting to assign a design and that design was in fact created by a freelancer, the company will need to take an assignment of the design from the freelancer in order to have rights to assign under the agreement. At Appendix I there is an example of a freelancer agreement which covers this point.

If acting for the purchaser, a practitioner should obtain a warranty as to the originality of the design and furthermore the seller should indemnify the purchaser in this regard, so that in the event of the purchaser being success-fully sued by a third party for reason of infringement, the purchaser can recoup any losses from the seller.

Assignments of unregistered design

The points to bear in mind for assignments of unregistered design are broadly similar to those set out above for registered design but with the requirement of extra diligence given that there is no register on which the ownership of a design can be checked.

As well as commercial considerations such as the value of the right, the assignment should clearly express the subject matter of the agreement. The only way to do that adequately is to annex the first design document to the agreement itself or a copy of the original if the original cannot be located. If the first design document cannot be located, the purchaser should make reasonable enquiries of the seller as to its whereabouts, given that it is a vital document where the rights have to be enforced against a third party.

The draftsperson should use as much description as possible in order to be clear as to what is being transferred. If in doubt, annex more rather than less detail to the assignment document. Remember, there is no formal way of checking the history and details of an unregistered design so it is very much the responsibility of the practitioner to identify the subject of the assignment adequately and clearly.

The commercial value of a design will need to be ascertained by reference to its worth in the particular context of the relevant industry. There are com-panies and individuals which specialise in the valuation of intangible prop-erty. A useful body to contact in these circumstances is the Institute of International Licensing Practitioners (IILP), who can put you in touch with someone with the relevant experience. However, bear in mind that this is a very specialist area and therefore the fees for valuing such a right are unlikely to suit every pocket.

Any assignment should be phrased so that the transfer takes place at the date of the agreement. Again, obtain copies of any previous assignments so that you can ascertain the exact nature of the rights that are purported to be assigned.

Avoid confirmatory assignments which refer to an assignment having already taken place and which are unclear or do not specifically refer to the design in question. In the case of the compulsory registration of licences, a record is kept at the Patent Office.

LICENCES

Compulsory licences

The points mentioned in brief above in respect of the assignment are equally true for the licence. Under the new design regime there is no longer a provision for a compulsory licence but where a designer is dealing with designs registered under the 1949 Act compulsory licences are still a possibility. Further, according to s.247 CDPA, licences of right in respect of unregistered design right still apply and can be granted in such circumstances where the owner has not exploited the design commercially after the first period of registration. The third party seeking to apply for the licence will have to show that the owner of the design in question has no intention of exploiting that design and that they themselves are in a position to exploit the design for commercial gain. (See Appendix G for an example of a more comprehensive design licence, which is provided in addition to the sample licence clauses given throughout this chapter.)

The reasoning behind the compulsory licence is that a registered design is a monopoly right and it necessarily prevents others from creating a similar design and therefore it will not be granted 'defensively', i.e. without any intention to exploit it but to prevent others with a legitimate interest in the same/similar area of design from being able to exploit the fruits of the designer's labour.

In such circumstances, the matter will usually be heard at a formal hearing and the design owner need only show a genuine intention to exploit in order to defeat the application made for a compulsory licence. The licence granted will be for as long as the life of the design, i.e. up to 25 years from the date of grant. This principle applies equally to registered designs and to unregistered design right (see example overleaf).

Voluntary licences

In order to make money from designs, owners of designs will often license their designs to a manufacturing or retailing company that is able to get their design to market. Before drawing up a licence, the draughtsperson should

---

Example

Company A has designed a particular garage door hinge. Company B is aware of the hinge but is also aware that Company A does not market the hinge commercially. Company B believes that the hinge could revolutionise the market and that it is a very useful way in which it can steal a march on its competitors. It approaches Company A, which refuses to license the unregistered design right in the hinge mechanism. Company B then applies to the Comptroller for a licence of right. Together with its application it submits a licence in order that the Comptroller will approve the clauses of the agreement.

Company B was concerned that due to Company A's reticence to license the design, the drawings necessary to manufacture the product will not be disclosed by Company A. Therefore it requested that the Comptroller order Company A to disclose all its material ahead of the hearing, so that the Comptroller could reasonably assess whether Company A had in fact provided sufficient material to enable Company B to manufacture the hinge. Furthermore, at the hearing the Comptroller listened to the arguments of both parties.

Company A attempted to demonstrate that it had a very real intention of marketing the hinge but that the delay was due to the personal circumstances of its founder and principal shareholder who was extremely ill and was therefore unable to give the company the guidance that it required.

While the Comptroller had every sympathy for the circumstances surrounding Company A's delay, he felt that, nevertheless, such circumstances should not prevent Company B from exploiting the commercial potential from the design in question. Therefore, he granted the licence, in accordance with the terms drawn and ordered Company A to provide the necessary drawings so that they could be annexed to the licence itself.

---

ascertain the reasons for entering into the licence so that the particular focus of the licence is clear. It will vary from licence to licence. For example, one owner may have a desire to move into a geographical area where it is logistically and financially impossible for him to go it alone. Or it might be the case that a designer wishes to move up market where she lacks the necessary contacts and/or brand to penetrate a premium market. Licensing for the purposes of manufacture is very common in the field of design. These are just three examples, but, whatever the reason, the owner's focus must be borne in mind at all times.

What follows are examples of typical clauses in non-compulsory licences, with alternatives where necessary. We have also provided hints on drafting where necessary.

Parties

Each party should be clearly identified and very precise language used. When referring to a limited company, quote the full company name as it appears on the relevant jurisdiction's register. If in doubt, ask for a copy of the incorporation certificate. Always quote the registered company number so that in the event of a change of name, the company remains identifiable. If the party is a partnership, say so:

(1) Michael John Raymond Smith and Katherine Suzanne Jones of 1 The Avenue, London W1 3HP trading together as Magick Momentz (a partnership) ('the Licensor')

and

(2) The Really Fair Manufacturing Company Limited (Co. regn. no. 1234567) a company incorporated under the laws of England and Wales and whose registered office is situated at 4 High Street, Anytown, Anyshire A12 B34 ('the Licensee')

In other words, include as much information as possible in order to ensure that the parties are clearly identifiable without any likelihood of confusion.

Recitals

As with any other commercial agreement, this clause sets the scene for the relationship and should accurately reflect the situation that has caused the parties to enter into the licence:

Background:

(a) The Licensor produces knitwear patterns for ladieswear and menswear;
(b) The Licensee produces high-quality knitwear garments;
(c) The Licensee has expertise in manufacturing knitwear and wishes to take a licence of the Licensor's knitwear patterns for eight (8) fashion seasons as specified in this Agreement.

Occasionally the recitals will need to be altered and this can be done straightforwardly ahead of the agreement being signed. Using the example above, the deal might change to six fashion seasons and they should be altered accordingly.

Grant

This is the operative clause, so it must be unequivocal and absolutely clear. Put this clause as the first of the main agreement because all clauses flow from it:

> In consideration of the sums paid or payable in accordance with the terms of this Agreement, the Licensor grants the Licensee an exclusive licence to manufacture, sell, reproduce and distribute the Designs in order to produce the Licensed Product.

If the designs were being licensed solely for the purposes of manufacture (ie. without marketing), the wording would be altered to:

> The Licensor grants the Licensee an exclusive licence to manufacture the Designs in order to produce the Licensed Product.

Be clear with the definitions and distinguish between the designs and licensed product in the definitions in the normal way:

> 'Designs' means the knitwear designs created by the Licensor in accordance with this Agreement.

Within the agreement the Licensed Product will be more particularly defined:

> 'Licensed Product' means jumpers, cardigans, jackets, tank-tops and other similar garments produced in wool, silk or a blend of the two yarns and according to the Designs.

This helps to limit the scope of the licence and to determine precisely how the designs may be used. For example, the licensor may have entered into a similar relationship with a manufacturer of accessories (scarves, hats and gloves) and it will therefore want to ensure that there is no overlap for two reasons: legally, because they might breach any exclusivity that is given; and commercially because they will not want their designs used by different manufacturers and in different fabrics.

For example, if the same design is available in silk at £100 and in nylon at £20, the more expensive items will lose their cachet and thus income to the licensor could be severely reduced. Be clear on this point when acting for the manufacturer. Make sure that the agreement clarifies the exact nature of the product that can be produced under the terms of the agreement and check with the manufacturer to make sure that it conforms with their expectations.

Finally, make sure that you have granted a licence of all intellectual property that is required for the manufacturing or other intended use to take place. For example, there might also be copyright works and/or trade marks that need to be licensed in order for the deal to proceed as intended.

Exclusivity

The type of licence granted will depend on whether the licensor wishes there to be competition in the marketplace, or, rather, where the licensee expects to be the only operator in a particular market. This depends very much on the deal that is struck between the parties.

There are advantages and disadvantages to each. For example, the exclusive licence helps to maintain premium designs since they are necessarily being produced only by one licensee. On the other hand, this becomes the licensor's only route to market and if exclusivity is included it should be balanced with a high minimum sales clause (see p. 107).

In the alternative, a non-exclusive licence would allow many players to compete in the marketplace which creates more than one route to market for the owner of the design. However, this must be balanced with the intended market for the product. For example if the product is intended to be a premium product, a non-exclusive licence will defeat this object since it will naturally gain mass-market appeal.

Scope

Of key interest to licensees is the extent of the rights that they are granted. For example, in some instances no right to sub-licence will be granted, usually where the licensee has agreed that it will manufacture and distribute the product that is the subject of the licence. In other circumstances, perhaps where the design is licensed to an agent, it will need to be made clear that that agent will have to sub-licence to manufacturers since agents typically are not in a position to make the products themselves. The licensor should make sure that it has final approval of the sub-licences:

> The Licensee may enter into sub-licences with third parties only for the purposes of manufacturing the Licensed Product. Such sub-licences shall take the form substantially of this Agreement.

> The Licensor shall approve all sub-licences entered into by the Licensee pursuant to the clause above.

Example

Jackie has designed a range of crockery and has sold it to a well-known high street retailer. Following the negotiation with the retailer, it was agreed that a sub-licence would be granted in the licence to enable the retailer to have the goods manufactured. Initially the high street retailer was going to use a factory in the Far East. Jackie was concerned on hearing this because the last time that her work was manufactured in the Far East, cheap copies were found on sale in the local tourist market. Jackie is an award-winning ceramicist at the top of her field. As such, she insisted that the crockery be manufactured in the UK, and sold for a slightly higher price to take into account higher labour costs. The high street retailer agreed.

Territory

Exclusivity and territory together determine the value of the licence and the value of subsequent licences since they will be granted according to the initial licence. This is a key clause in any licence.

Furthermore, a draughtsperson needs to be very careful to define the territory. 'Europe' or 'North America' or 'Asia' each mean very different things to different people. Add a schedule listing the countries for clarity.

The rights granted under this Agreement are restricted to the Territory as set out in the Second Schedule.

Definitions

'Territory' means the country or countries more particularly described in the Second Schedule.

Second Schedule

United States of America and its dependent territories
The West Indies and Caribbean Islands
Canada
Mexico

If the licence is intended to be global, simply insert 'the world' in the document at the appropriate point.

Note that the choice of territory will depend very much on the type of product, its likely success in different markets and the intended term of the licence.

Option

Occasionally a licence will include an option clause. This states that the licensee shall have a right of first refusal to take a further licence at the end of the agreement. Proceed with caution. If the relationship is fruitful this is a useful tool, but, if not, it could be a disaster. In any event, by the expiration of the agreement, one or both of the parties is often keen to renegotiate the entire relationship.

Example

Sandra and Jocelyn created a series of characters which they have registered as designs in the UK and Europe and as design patents in the USA. The characters are household pets that will be used to teach children how to count, spell and learn generally about the world.

They grant a publisher the right to use the characters in books and merchandise in the USA and the UK. In each case, they agreed to license the characters for six specific book titles, each containing at least one of the characters. In the UK the designers want to enter into a licence with a UK-based global marketing company, License It, which seeks to exploit the characters by merchandising and making a film. However, on closer inspection of the licence, the designers had already given the publisher the rights to publish books based on the first three films produced based on the characters. The deal with License It was therefore put on ice.

When drawing up a licence for owners of registered designs, it is therefore important to review all existing licences, whether they are for copyright or for design right/registered design so that you can ascertain whether the rights which the designers purport to license can in fact be licensed. Also, it is a useful exercise when taking over a designer's portfolio of licences so that you are aware of the agreements that he has entered into. This proves to be a particularly useful exercise where the designer's agreements have been drawn up by more than one firm.

Term

Again, this must be absolutely clear. The term should be set based upon the knowledge of the parties of each other. For example, if they have a long history of successful dealing, a five-year agreement would not be out of the question. However, if the parties are contracting for the first time, a one-year agreement is more suitable:

> This Agreement shall come into force from the date of this Agreement and shall continue for a period of 12 calendar months subject to earlier termination provided for in this Agreement.

Inspection of the books and of the factory

Often products will be made in the Far East because of the cheap costs of labour and materials there. In these circumstances, the designer should ensure that he or his agent has a right to inspect the factory. In the case of foreign-based factories, a foreign agent is extremely useful.

> The Licensor shall upon reasonable notice have the right to inspect or to instruct his Agent to inspect the factory(ies) in which the Licensed Product is being manufactured.

Similarly, in order to ensure that the royalties are accurate and more particularly where the royalty payments do not seem to be accurate, the designer should be able to inspect the relevant accounts or, as is more common, to instruct an accountant to inspect the relevant accounts.

Quality

Be sure that, if the design is aimed at the high end of the market, the design will not be sold cheaply or made from poor quality materials. For example, if your client imagines that his product will appear on sale in Harvey Nichols, ensure that the licensee does not intend to market the product in Pound Stores. In the sample clause on p101 defining Licensed Product, the material was specified but the not the quality of the material, so do not confuse the two. Particular industries have standardised methods of assessing quality so that an agreement for jewellery designs would refer to the number of carats in relation to gold. Find out from the parties if there is commonly understood language that can be used.

Furthermore, rather than relying on phrases such as 'reasonable' or 'satisfactory' quality to determine the quality of the goods sold, the manufacturer should provide the Licensor with a prototype and that prototype should be the benchmark of the quality of the goods, once it has been signed off by the Licensor.

Example

Having graduated from the College of Footwear design, Mike has had a lot of interest in his graduation show. The main interest has been shown in his design for thigh-high crocodile skin boots. He is approached by many of the established design houses but eventually decides to do a deal with a small independent UK-based company. In order to protect his design, Mike registers it in the UK. He enters into a licence with the manufacturer. The clause in the licence in relation to quality reads 'Licensee shall manufacture the Product [the boot] to a satisfactory quality'.

Mike had intended his boot to be sold in boutiques and top department stores. The manufacturer was not aware of Mike's intention. It made the boot well, but using materials that Mike would have rejected had he known that they were to be used because they were not suitable for his intended market.

Mike contacted the manufacturer about the problem. The manufacturer is adamant that it has fulfilled the quality clause, having produced boots that are of a satisfactory quality. Mike wishes to reject the goods but is unable to because the goods can be sold, though not at the high end of the market as he intended.

In practice it is rare that such a misunderstanding would arise but this example highlights what can go wrong if the quality is determined by use of vague phrases. However, the wording in the clause below means that the licensor retains control at all times. Furthermore, given that our example is premium knitwear, we have clearly identified the stores that are considered competitors, which further defines quality.

> The Licensee warrants that the Licensed Products shall conform to the highest possible quality standards approved by the Licensor and they shall certainly not be of a lower standard than goods generally sold to those companies that appear in Schedule Three.

Schedule Three
  Bloomingtons
  Mallards
  Don Gianni
  Akko Mokito

These next two clauses protect the licensor in relation to reimbursements made to wholesalers or retailers and they also allow him a get-out if the quality falls below the agreed standard on a regular basis.

In the event that items of Licensed Product are returned for reason of inferior quality, the Licensee shall be wholly responsible for reimbursing to Licensor any sums that are paid by the Licensor.

In the event that quality does not reach the agreed standard for three consecutively delivered batches of Licensed Product, the Licensor may terminate this Agreement by giving the Licensee three months' notice in writing.

It is possible to go further and include the following clause:

Approval of Designs and Samples

(i)   The Licensee hereby agrees that the Licensor shall have the right of final approval of the appearance, quality, design and materials used comprising the Licensed Product.

(ii)   Before commencing this Agreement, the Licensee shall provide to the Licensor accurate and true samples of the Licensed Product.

(iii)   Once the samples have been approved by Licensor, this Agreement shall be entered into by the parties.

(iv)   The Licensor shall provide to the Licensee at least four different designs suitable for the appropriate season of at least four different items of Licensed

Season	Garments	Due Date
Autumn/Winter 2003	Licensed Product	April 2003
Spring/Summer 2004	Licensed Product	November 2003
[repeat for duration of agreement]		

Product on the following basis:

In this way both parties are clear what is expected of them and when.

Royalty and minimums

The payment provisions, which include both the sum of the royalty and the payment procedure, need to be clear. The percentage is often expressed as a percentage of a selling price which could be the ex-factory selling price to the licensee or the licensee's wholesale price. Another common arrangement is a fixed sum on each unit of product sold. In all cases the licence should state any exclusions from payment of a royalty, for example in respect of samples sent to retailers. The licence should also state when payment is due.

> The Licensee shall, each and every six months from the commencement date of this Agreement ('the Royalty Period') pay to the Licensor 10 per cent (10%) of the gross income to the Licensee in respect of the Licensed Product.

The royalty rate will vary between industries. Typically for furniture the rate is a 2–5 per cent royalty and famous brands can go above 10 per cent, although 7–10 per cent is a good rule of thumb when deciding on an appropriate figure. Also, note that receiving a royalty based on gross sales income is slightly optimistic. In most cases the royalty will be based on the net figure and as such the licensor needs to be clear on the deductions that will be made. For example: what are 'reasonable business expenses'? It is always best to clarify them by agreeing between the parties and drawing up an agreed list or definition.

Always include a minimum in the royalty clause. Designers should consider what they are prepared to accept from the deal and may price this on the basis of the time and effort it has taken to reach the point at which they are able to license the designs. The licensor may also be mindful of whether the income from the licence is the main income of the licensor or the second (or even third) income. The licence should express the minimum royalties payable in a given period.

> The Licensee shall pay to the Licensor each Licence Period the minimum amount of £10,000 sterling exclusive of taxes and other prevailing payments levied.

Make sure that it is clear as to the amount that the licensor can expect to receive. For example, specify who will pay taxes and other such deductible sums.

In the example of the knitwear company, the designers are providing the designs so that the following clause would be appropriate in addition to those already examined:

> For each design supplied by the Licensor to the Licensee under the terms of this Agreement, the Licensee will pay to the Licensor the sum of £500 + VAT within 30 days of its receipt.

This ensures that the licensor is able to pay its day-to-day expenses, particularly where it engages freelancers to create the designs.

The licensors should also bear in mind exactly what it is that they intend to license and for how long. They should also make enquiries in their industry about the licensee in question and find out if it has taken similar licences in the past and what the previous licensors' experiences were (see example overleaf).

Rival products and infringements

The licensee should agree not to market similar products, rival products or infringements particularly where an exclusive licence is granted by the

---

Example

Stephen has produced a design for a mixed-media coffee table. He is approached at his graduation show by a furniture manufacturer. The manufacturer asks Stephen for a licence of the design and offers him a 2 per cent royalty based on his net sales. This is the first interest that Stephen has ever had in his designs and he is naturally very excited. However, it soon transpires that this manufacturer has approached many of Stephen's contemporaries and his tutor advises him that the royalty figure that he has been offered is unusually low.

Stephen decides to progress the deal, since it is the only offer that he has received. Stephen quickly realises that the manufacturer has not fully explained what is meant by net sales. What are the legitimate expenses that the manufacturer may deduct? Plus, by putting his ear to the ground, Stephen quickly discovers that this manufacturer has a history of promising much and delivering little to new designers but he also manages to sell a lot of pieces. When confronted, the manufacturer becomes extremely hostile. Stephen decides not to enter into the deal.

---

licensor. Remember, this is the licensor's only route to market. Also, they should report immediately to the licensor any infringements that may come to light. Furthermore, the licensor should retain the right to bring an action against infringers since in the main they are the ones most interested in protecting their designs and therefore their goodwill and reputation:

> The Licensee shall not manufacture any infringing products. In the event that Licensee wishes to manufacture competing or rival products, it shall obtain the express consent of the Licensor. In the event that such consent is refused, the Licensee may not manufacture such products.

> Licensee shall notify the Licensor in writing within 48 hours of it becoming aware of any infringing products or of it becoming aware of products that it suspects might be infringing.

The above clauses are particularly valuable if the manufacturer is based abroad, since without an agent with his ear to the ground, the person best placed to report on the situation is the manufacturer. In any event, this clause should be included not least because it means there is an additional 'guard dog' patrolling the parameters of the licensor's intellectual property.

The benefit to the designer of a non-compete clause is that the licensee remains focused on selling the designer's work and not someone else's, the licensor wants to guarantee that the licensee is putting every effort into getting his product to market. Furthermore, in order to establish their particular product in the marketplace, designers will not want it to become confused with other products which are similar in nature and are receiving a similar type of marketing push.

Sometimes licensees will not agree such clauses, particularly if they regularly market a range of products or if they are used to marketing a portfolio of similar products aimed at different segments of a market. Remember, just as the licensor seeks to protect its intellectual property, the licensee seeks to protect its commercial viability. In this instance, the licensor should obtain a compromise clause worded as follows:

> The Licensee shall not market products that are similar to or that compete with the Licensed Product, either directly or indirectly without first notifying the Licensor.

With this clause, the designer will be able to determine what the licensee markets and will also be able to keep its design discrete. This can be all important if the licensor has avoided licensing the product to a manufacturer or licensee who markets a portfolio of products very similar to the licensed product.

Technical assistance and ownership of amendments

Very often in order to make the product, the licensee will need the assistance of the licensor, particularly where the design is complex or is a completely new product. The licensor should consider how much technical assistance it is prepared to give the licensee. The amount will depend on the availability of the designer and the amount of assistance that the licensee estimates it will require.

The ownership of any amendments that result from the assistance should be decided. Note also that in the manufacturing process, very often small changes will be made to the design. The licence should ensure that the licensor retains ownership of the designs.

> The Licensor shall give to the Licensee all reasonable technical assistance of whatever nature such is reasonably required by the Licensee upon reasonable notice.

> In the event that the Licensee makes any change, addition, improvement, manipulation or any such other alteration to the Design [or Intellectual Property if there is more than one type being licensed] all such additions, improvements, manipulations and any such other alterations shall belong to the Licensor.

Product insurance

When entering into a licence agreement, the licensor should make enquiry of the licensee as to the level of product liability insurance that the licensee has. All products on the market must have product liability insurance to ensure against the risk that a consumer suffers harm as a result of using the product. As a licence often covers many countries, it is also important that consideration is given to the level of insurance in each country. Some countries, the USA being a prime example, generate many more lawsuits than others. In addition to product liability insurance, the designer should establish the terms of their own professional indemnity insurance and to what extent the designer can give warranties against harm to a consumer resulting from defective design.

> The Licensee shall maintain product liability insurance to cover any one claim up to a maximum value of [£XXX] million and the Licensee shall provide to the Licensor if so requested a copy of the policy document.

Termination

You should aim to allow your client to terminate for as many reasons as are practicable and reasonable under the terms of the licence. The designer will want to be able to have as much control over the licence as possible and be able to bring the relationship to an end in the event that the minimum royalty is not reached, that the quality does not consistently meet the agreed standard or where the product is not reaching the required market in sufficient numbers.

Also, there must be some protection for the licensee. If the designs are not up to the required standard or if they are not delivered on time it could jeopardise the licensee's ability to meet forward orders and as such termination of the agreement may be the only solution to allow the manufacturer to continue to honour agreements that it has with retailers and/or wholesalers.

> Both the Licensee and the Licensor shall be entitled to terminate this Agreement in the event that:
>
> (i) the other Party is in breach of any clause of this Agreement and having been given written notice of the same, has failed to remedy that breach within thirty (30) days, and:
> (ii) where the other Party becomes bankrupt, insolvent, enters into liquidation, enters into an agreement with its creditors or otherwise ceases to trade.

Once termination has been effected, the parties must deal with the aftermath. Situations to take into account are sell-off of existing stock and the designs that have been provided under the agreement:

111

Upon termination of this Agreement:

(i)   the Licensee shall cease to manufacture, sell, market or otherwise distribute the Licensed Product save where it has commenced an order for the Licensed Product. In such circumstances the Licensee shall be entitled to sell the same and complete the order within six months of the date of termination.
(ii)   the Licensee shall return to the Licensor within 48 hours all designs, drawings, documentation and all such other designs that it has in its possession.
(iii) the Licensee shall pay all outstanding royalty payments in full.

Note that there may be other clauses to add depending on the specific nature of the agreement between parties in other scenarios; however, these are the most common clauses to include on termination.

Warranties

There are certain minimum warranties that the licensee will require to ensure that it is not vulnerable to claims by third parties:

The Licensor hereby WARRANTS that all Designs supplied under this Agreement are its original work and that they do not infringe the intellectual property of any third party.

The Licensor hereby agrees to indemnify and hold harmless the Licensee in the event that any such claim is made against the Licensee in respect of infringement of intellectual property rights referred to above.

The Licensor hereby WARRANTS that it shall at its own expense maintain all intellectual property rights that are registered wheresoever in the world at the date of this Agreement, for the duration of this Agreement.

It is imperative that the licensor maintains all registered rights. This will be particularly important where the registration of the design comes up for renewal during the licence period or where there is an option to extend the licence which would take the licence into a new period of registration.

The Licensor will enforce all registered rights that are the subject of this Agreement in the event that they are infringed by a third party.

This is crucial because the licensee will want to know that the subject of the agreement is adequately protected and policed but that they themselves will not be obliged to bring that action as (exclusive) licensee.

As a 'for the avoidance of doubt' clause, the following is advised so that it is quite clear that the licensee acquires no rights beyond those in the licence:

For the avoidance of doubt, the Licensee shall acquire no rights in the Licensed Product or in the Design of whatever nature and all rights, goodwill and all other benefits in the Licensed Product and the Design shall accrue to the Licensor.

This is particularly necessary where the design is branded with someone else's trade mark, so that the two rights are kept completely separate and that the design does not become submerged into the brand.

Confidentiality

There is often a requirement that the details of the licence be kept confidential. The reason is that it can distort the market and it can also cause problems for a licensee who does various deals with licensors depending on the marketability of the respective designs.

Furthermore, the designer will want his design to be kept confidential and particularly if the application of the design to a product or product requires know-how on the part of the designer.

The Licensee and the Licensor shall keep confidential the contents and existence of this Agreement. This clause shall remain in force between the parties beyond the termination of this Agreement.

Boiler plate clauses

These are the standard clauses that one finds in any commercial agreement and which are self-explanatory:

1. No waiver (whether express or implied) by either party of any breach by the other party of any of its obligations under this Agreement shall be deemed to constitute a waiver or consent to any subsequent or continuing breach by such party of any such obligations.
2. Unless otherwise stated every notice and other communication given under this Agreement shall be sent by first-class post addressed to the other party at the address above. Notice shall be deemed given two clear business days after posting.
3. In the event of a party failing to perform any obligation under this Agreement (save the making of any payment due under or pursuant to this Agreement) as a result of strike, lock-out or other labour difficulties, fire, flood, act of God, embargo, act of war, regulation or restriction of government or law or any other occurrence of circumstance beyond the reasonable control of the party, that party shall not be liable in damages or otherwise for failure to perform that obligation and such failure shall not be a ground for terminating this Agreement.

4. Any and all information, data, sketches or drawings or any other material ('Confidential Information') that may be obtained by either party from any source as a result of this Agreement shall be considered strictly confidential. Furthermore, unless either party has given consent, neither party may at any time during this Agreement or at any time afterwards disclose such Confidential Information to any third party.

5. The Licensee shall, at its own expense, comply with all relevant local legal requirements in relation to the Licensed Product and in particular those relating to the storage, labelling, marketing and distribution of the Licensed Product in the Territory.

6. This Agreement may not be varied or modified unless made in writing and executed under seal on behalf of both parties.

7. This Agreement is to be governed by the laws of England and the parties submit to the non-exclusive jurisdiction of the English courts.

SUMMARY

An assignment can be a way to net some money where the designer does not want to monitor and police the relationship with a licensee. A licence, however, offers the licensor greater freedom because it brings him a steady income while enabling his product to reach markets that the designer cannot reach alone. A licence should always be amended to take into account the specifics of the deal in question.

COMPETITION LAW AND DESIGN LAW

The exercise of design rights and in particular the licensing of them, operates in direct contrast to competition law both in the UK and at Community level. On the one hand, design law is about the protection of rights which must necessarily only be exploited by a limited number of people. On the other hand, competition law exists to promote freedom in commercial dealings and to prevent just the type of monopoly situation that is created by an exclusive licence.

The Competition Act 1998

Agreements which have as their object or effect, the distortion of competition in the UK and any abuse of a dominant position in the UK are prohibited by the Competition Act 1998.

For guidance, Articles 81 and 82 of the EC Treaty need to be considered.

Article 81(1) prohibits any agreement that has as its object or effect the prevention, restriction or distortion of competition within the Common Market. Article 82 prohibits any abuse of a dominant position within the whole or a substantial part of the Common Market.

Both may apply to a licence but it is also arguable that most agreements are intended to foster competition since without the licence the product is unlikely to be manufactured.

These provisions must be balanced against Article 295 of the EC Treaty of Rome 1957 (amended) which states:

> This treaty shall in no way prejudice the rules in Member States governing the system of property ownership.

So that we can see the crux of the matter is how the right is exploited and not how it is owned per se.

Articles 28 and 29 of the EC Treaty prohibit the use of a national right as a means to prevent the free circulation of goods and/or services within the European Economic Area (EEA); again these Articles must be balanced against Article 295 so that the owner of a design right (whether unregistered or registered) should be the first person to have the right to put the product into circulation within the EEA. Once those products are in circulation the owner has *exhausted his rights* to prevent the free circulation of goods so that he may not continue to seek to control their movement. This is the *exhaustion of rights* principle. The principle is applied regularly to trade marks and there seems little to suggest that it should not apply in the same way to designs given that they are subject to similar legal principles of ownership and of exploitation (see example overleaf). Indeed, reference is made to this principle in the Regulations.

The owner of design rights can still prevent them from being infringed in the country in question by enforcing his registered right. Under the new regime, he could invoke the unregistered Community Design right where no registration has been obtained.

Article 81 EC Treaty and licences

As mentioned above, Article 81 prohibits agreements that have as their intention or their effect the distortion, etc. of the market. (In the event that the European Commission were to find against a licence on this basis, it can fine both parties up to 10 per cent of their total global turnover.) If the licence appears likely to have such an effect either party can apply to the European Commission for a specific exemption according to Article 81(3) which requires that they submit full details of the arrangement including the various economic activities (turnover, profit, sales, similar relationships with similar organisations) of the parties to the licence.

Example

Sarah owns a UK registered design in a distinctive print used on handbags. She has licensed the design to a retailer in the UK who sells the designs in a shop in the Trafford Centre in Manchester. Sarah also has registered designs in Germany and France because the design proved popular there. It has come to Sarah's notice that people are buying the bags in the UK and reselling them in France and Germany where they are cheaper than the store-bought products in both countries.

The licensees in both countries are furious because they are unable to sell the bags at a profit. They have both contacted Sarah and demanded that she do something to prevent the sales from continuing.

Sarah approaches you to help her enforce her registered designs in France and Germany to prevent the goods bought in the UK being resold in France and Germany.

The Competition Rules of the EC Treaty prevent Sarah from being able to enforce her design. Once the product is sold, her rights are exhausted. Under the principles of the free movement of goods and free competition, the German and French resellers are entitled to resell anywhere within the EEA. That the local retailers are unable to make a profit cannot be prevented. There is an obvious benefit to the French and German consumer that the UK-sourced bags are available more cheaply.

Such an arrangement will be granted an exemption on the basis that it can be justified because it:

- promotes economic progress;
- promotes technical progress;
- is beneficial to consumers.

Usually an agreement will fall under the third exemption. In any event it is a rare occurrence to have to apply to the European Commission.

Article 82 and licences

This Article prevents the abuse of a dominant position and those activities that have an adverse effect on intra-Community trade. There is no exemption as there is under Article 81 and the fine for falling foul of this Article is the same, up to 10 per cent of total global turnover of both parties to the agreement. Article 82 is designed to catch the activities of both multiple parties acting in concert and the activities of a dominant single player and as such it is easier to fall foul of this Article.

WHAT IS A DOMINANT POSITION?

A dominant position means one in relation to the relevant product market and within a substantial part of the EEA. Therefore this will not apply to most clients, and will only ensnare very large clients or those that are particularly specialist. The 'substantial part' can be a country or it can be an economic region and each case is very much decided on the particular facts and merits.

Dominance itself will depend on the particular facts of the market in which the client operates. If, for example, all remaining players in a market hold 5 per cent or less of the relevant product market, 30 per cent would certainly be dominant. If there are a number of players with 15–20 per cent, the 30 per cent is unlikely to be considered dominant. A useful question is: What percentage is a barrier to entry?

ABUSE

Once dominance has been established the position must be shown to be abused for it to fall foul of Article 82. Such abuse could be the simple ownership of a design if it could be shown to the European Commission that the design in question was an essential product that was needed by more than just the owner.

Since each case will turn on the particular facts it is difficult to provide examples of each of the scenarios discussed above but a useful illustration is *RTE & ITP* v. *Commission* [1995] 4 CMLR 718, otherwise known as *Magill*. In this case it was decided that ownership of the television listings and the refusal to license them was an abuse of a dominant position since they gave the owner a monopoly over the information which they could exploit, and which was essential information required by others.

SUMMARY

Most agreements will not fall foul of either Article, but it is prudent to have an eye on the provisions when drafting a licence and considering the subject matter of the licence. Also the *exhaustion of rights* principle of Article 81 can be a useful defence as occasionally an action will be launched against a defendant who has acted within the spirit of free trade of the EC Treaty. It also serves to advise claimants who believe that they have a claim against a third party, when in fact that party is merely taking advantage of the free trade within the EEA to his advantage.

CHAPTER 9

Enforcement

INTRODUCTION

This chapter looks at how to prevent others from infringing design rights and, in the event of infringement, what the right-holder should do. It examines the 1949 Act, the Regulations and the Community provisions with respect to both registered and unregistered design rights. Finally we consider trade dress, passing off and damages.

WHAT CONSTITUTES INFRINGEMENT?

Registered design

The CDPA 1988 made some changes to the Registered Designs Act 1949 and these are found in Schedule 4 to the Act. The main changes have already been explored (see Chapter 5) and these are the extension of the period of design protection from 15 to 25 years and the so-called 'must-fit, must-match' exceptions.

Ownership of a registered design gives a right-holder the exclusive or monopoly right to do certain acts. The owner can prevent a third party from making or selling the registered design, or importing it for sale, hire or use for a trade or business. He can also prevent a third party from selling, hiring or offering for sale to the public an article which is made to (or substantially to) the design which has been registered.

Under the 1988 amendments, exclusive licensees of designs (unlike exclusive licensees of patents, copyright and trade marks) do not have the automatic right to sue for infringement: *Isaac Oren* v. *Red Box Toy Factory* [1999] FSR 785. Therefore, if the exclusive licensee requires a right to sue, it should be expressed in the licence (see Chapter 8). The Designs Register being a public document, the offence of infringement is one of strict liability so that the owner need not show that the infringer must have known that he was infringing.

Under the old system, design registration was restricted to one article to which the design was applied. If it was applied to numerous articles, the design would have to be registered for each article. For example, to protect a range of crockery with a distinctive pattern, each item of the set would need to be registered. *Best Products Limited* v. *Woolworth & Co. Limited* [1964] RPC 215 demonstrates this point succinctly. The registration was a design for a kettle with an 'audible alarm'. The infringing copy applied the design to a kettle *without* a whistling mechanism. Because the registered right related only to an 'audible alarm' kettle, it was held that, despite being a copy of the registered design the product was not an infringement because it was not a whistling kettle. The test for copying was interpreted by the courts strictly. In addition, an infringement need not be the finished article as a single article. For example, it could be a kit of component parts, where the components, once assembled, are an infringement of the design as registered.

The old regime required 'application by industrial process'; therefore if a design were copied by hand rather than by machine on a large scale there would be no infringement. Thus, if a potter were to make in his studio a replica of the registered design of a Royal Doulton pattern, it would not be considered an infringement for the purposes of the 1949 Act. The courts also used to apply what is known as the 'squeeze' argument. By looking at the prior art (other designs in existence at the time the design was registered), the courts set a benchmark as to how different a registered design would need to be before it could be considered a substantially new design. In other words, the courts assessed how substantially different the registered design was. If deemed substantially *different* it would not be considered an infringement of the prior art. This was only a shorthand way of assessing the law but was useful in determining the strength of the registered right and what the right sought to protect. If there was only a small difference between the registered right and the prior art, the registered right had limited scope.

REMEDIES AND DEFENCES UNDER THE 1949 ACT

There are no specific remedies under the 1949 Act and as such the civil court remedies are used in the normal way. One thing to note is that defendants who could show that they did not know and did not have reason to believe that the design in suit was registered, might not have damages awarded against them. The owner of the registered design is under a duty to mark the product with the number and the words 'registered' or 'registered design'. Thus, if the infringer is not put on notice, it will affect the damages available to the owner of the registered design. In any event, it is good business practice to mark products that are registered because it deters would-be infringers.

In the event that injunctive proceedings are launched by a registered design holder, the defendant can apply for a compulsory licence as a means of defence (see p. 98). In such circumstances, any damages awarded are capped at double the licence fees that would have been paid from the date of the first infringement to the date of the licence being granted. This is a useful mechanism for the alleged infringer who has sought to exploit the design through legitimate negotiations but whose requests to do so have been spurned by the design owner.

LETTERS BEFORE ACTION

It is not an offence to notify a potential infringer of the design registration and the remedies available to the client. A well-worded letter would read:

> We believe you are manufacturing a product which infringes our client's Registered Design No. 1234567. We have advised our client that the remedies available to it are:
>
> Interim injunction pending a final hearing;
> Final injunction;
> Delivery-up/destruction;
> Damages.

The above paragraph would appear as part of a letter before action which must be written prior to the issue of a claim. The letter before action sets out the claimant's claim and usually (but not always) invites the alleged infringer to settle the matter prior to the issue of proceedings. In the event that an offer to settle the matter is made and that offer is less than the full amount of damages that would be claimed were an action to be commenced, the letter must be clearly marked *'without prejudice save as to costs'*. This means that the letter will not reduce the claim (that the claimant is entitled to make the full claim in the event that a settlement is not reached) and it allows the claimant to claim his costs in making the offer in the event that it is rejected and proceedings are launched against the defendant.

Each letter before action is different and there is no formal way of drafting one. However, a typical format for setting one out is as follows:

1. **Background**
   Set the story and explain who the claimant is and what he/she does.

2. **Claim**
   Set out the claim referring to sections of the relevant Act/Directive where necessary.

3. **Nature of infringement**
   Detail the nature of the infringement and precisely why the alleged infringement is an infringement of registered design right. Include information here from which copying can be inferred if you have no direct evidence.

4. **Remedies**
   Set out the remedies as you have advised your client and explain the consequences to the defendant if your client were to be successful.

5. **Time Limit**

Set a deadline of 7–14 days for a reply.

6. **Undertakings**

Set out everything that your client requires of the defendant in order to settle the matter and draft it in the form of an agreement letter so that the alleged infringer can sign it and return by the deadline and resolve the matter as swiftly as possible

7. **Annexes**

Attach photographs of the original design and the infringement. Include copies of any receipts if the infringing product was purchased and notes of any telephone calls/other relevant information.

Therefore, if a threats action is to be successful, it should be brought as soon after the threat is made as it is practicably possible.

THREATS

Groundless threats to issue proceedings in respect of a design infringement are actionable according to s.26 of the 1949 Act. Where a threat to issue proceedings in respect of an infringement is made and the alleged infringement transpires not to be an infringement, or where no proceedings are issued, the person who was threatened can obtain from the court a declaration that the threats lacked justification and that there was no infringement of the registered design. This is a useful tool as a counter-claim, particularly where the alleged infringer restricts/withdraws from sale a product as result of the threat to sue having been made. However, where the allegation is made in relation to the importation or the manufacture of an infringing product, the threats provisions does not apply.

Example

Carflow Products (UK) Limited v Linwood Securities (Birmingham) Limited & Others (including Argos) [1988] FSR 691

In this case, the plaintiff issued a threats letter to the defendant in respect of an allegedly infringing product. The defendant counterclaimed for losses which occurred as a result of the threats, namely that Argos cancelled all of its orders for the product.

The counterclaim was struck out because it was found that, while a threats letter had indeed been sent to Argos, the retailer did not withdraw the

---

> *products from sale or cancel orders until after the claim had been issued against them. The court held that by the time the action had been commenced, the threats were no longer relevant and only of historical interest. In other words, by commencing the action, the plaintiff had acted upon the threat and Argos was in fact responding not to the threat but to the action.*

CRIMINAL PENALTIES

It is an offence to mark as registered a product which has never been registered or the registration for which has expired. Entering or conspiring to enter false entries on the register as an individual or an officer of a company are also criminal offences. In all cases the offences are punishable by a fine or in extreme cases by imprisonment.

UNREGISTERED DESIGN RIGHT

Primary infringement of an unregistered design right pursuant to the 1949 Act is committed if a person infringes the owner's monopoly right to make articles to the design or copies design documents which enable articles to that design to be made for commercial purposes. This is therefore a commercial requirement.

Primary infringement

The making of an article that is identical or that is substantially similar to the design is an infringement if it is made without the consent of the design owner. As with copyright protection, the copying of a design may be direct or indirect and it has no bearing on the issue of infringement whether the intervening acts are considered to be infringements or not.

Given that unregistered design right may be claimed in respect of the shape or the configuration of all or of part of an article, an allegedly infringing design need only copy a part of a design to be considered an infringement of the original, assuming that the tests for infringement are fulfilled. In order to properly particularise the claim, the claimant must specify the part of the article in respect of which the infringement is claimed. This was explored in *C & H Engineering* v. *F. Klucznik & Sons Limited* [1992] FSR 421.

This case dealt with pig fenders. The plaintiff claimed unregistered design rights in the whole pig fender. The court examined the two products in the whole, and found that the defendant's pig fender had sloping sides which rendered it sufficiently different so as not to be an infringement of the plaintiff's design.

However, one part of the product, a roll bar, was identical in both pig fenders. Had the plaintiff claimed unregistered design rights in just that part of the product, he would have been successful in his claim.

Example 1

Janice designs girls' clothes at home and makes them on her sewing machine. The range is called Fantastical Fruits because the garments are often heavily embroidered and they are cut to resemble fruit. Having exhibited her garments at shows up and down the country, she is dismayed to note that a major retailer, KidzFun!, is selling a similar range of clothing. In particular, she has noticed that her design rights in her 'Rain Berry' garment, which she created in 2000 have been infringed. Although hers is a smock and the retailer is selling a coat, the hood of both garments is identical, being stitched and cut to create the shape of a berry. The way in which the hood attaches to the body of the garment is also identical. Janice shows her lawyer both garments. Her lawyer writes a letter before action citing the hood as the infringing part of the garment. She also cites the configuration of the stitches, its overall shape and the way in which it attaches to the body of the garment as being her unregistered design right.

Secondary infringement

A third party will be guilty of secondary infringement where he has imported, possessed, sold, hired or offered for sale or hire an infringing article knowing or having reasons to know that the article was an infringement. As with primary infringement, there must be a commercial purpose to the activity on the part of the third party.

Note that there must be some knowledge on the part of the infringer. Often the party marketing or selling the infringement is one or two links away in the supply chain from the primary infringer and so proving knowledge can be quite difficult. It is therefore of paramount importance to show that there is a causal link between the unregistered design and the infringement. For example, you should find out how many shows the work has been shown at and where they were; whether the infringer is known to attend certain shows or to visit certain fairs and whether samples of the work have been sent to the infringer. In absence of any actual evidence of copying, this information helps to suggest that the infringer has seen the original design and copied it. The claimant will need to show a judge enough evidence from which an inference of copying can be drawn in any direct evidence of copying. This is explored in the example overleaf.

Example 2

Janice cannot be sure that the retailer copied her designs. She has no definite link with them. However, having done some background research she is able to ascertain that their head of merchandising, Tamara Twinkle, was present at all the shows at which Janice showed her work. Furthermore, she knows that the supplier is Kidz Klothez and that they were exhibiting at same shows at which Janice showed her work and in particular the 'Rain Berry' design. Both organisations (the retailer and the manufacturer) having been at the shows, it is reasonable to infer that they have copied Janice's design.

REMEDIES AND DEFENCES

These are the same as for copyright infringement and are: to bring a civil action for delivery-up/destruction and/or damages and/or a criminal prosecution by the local Trading Standards body.

Section 239 CDPA provides that in response, a defendant can apply to take a licence of right for the design on terms as agreed between the parties or as determined by the Comptroller.

The courts have applied s.239 strictly. Created with the intention of resolving commercial disputes, it is only to be used where the defendant has a real intention of exploiting the design, as well as the capability of doing so.

Example

Dyrlund Smith AS v. *Tuberville Smith Limited [1988] FSR 774*

In this case, the defendant was merely a shelf company and as such would not be able to comply with the terms of the licence of right if granted. In addition, the defendant was only prepared to give an undertaking to take the licence in the event that it lost at trial.

The court felt that the s.239 should be used by a defendant only to avoid an injunction where it was capable of properly fulfilling the terms of the licence of right. In this case, it was felt by the court that any offer to enter into a licence of right ought to be unequivocal and made solely on the basis that a defendant sought to avoid an injunction rather than allowing him to hedge his bets by waiting to see the outcome of the case.

HEADS OF CLAIM

Note that according to s.236 CDPA where copyright and unregistered design right subsist in the same article, infringement of copyright in the work will not automatically be infringement of unregistered design right in the same article. Therefore the two should be considered as alternative heads of claim and be argued in the alternative. It is likely that if copyright in an article is claimed it will be as a 'work of artistic craftsmanship' (see Chapter 3). In order to claim infringement of unregistered design right, it must be found that there is no copyright infringement. In the event that none is found, the claim for unregistered design right will be reconsidered on its merits as explained above.

When drafting a claim it is therefore, good practice to plead, wherever possible, copyright infringement and unregistered design right in the alternative, so that in the event that one head of claim fails, the other can be argued successfully.

GROUNDLESS THREATS

As discussed above in respect of registered design, the threats provisions exist in respect of unregistered design right as well (s.253 CDPA). If the recipient of the threats can demonstrate that the threats are groundless, he can be granted an injunction against the continuation of such threats, and where the threats cause damage (such as the loss of profit for a withdrawn product as result of having received the threat) he will be entitled to damages.

SEMICONDUCTOR TOPOGRAPHY DESIGN RIGHTS

In 1987, a very specific type of design right protection was introduced for electronic circuits. The main regulations in this area are the Semiconductor Products (Protection of Topography) Regulations 1987 (SI 1987/1497) which were designed to implement the relevant EC Directive No. 87/54/EEC and the Design Right (Semiconductor Topographies) Regulations 1989 (SI 1989/1100). The 1989 Regulations have been the subject of numerous amendments.

These regulations make it clear that semiconductor design will generally follow the law relating to unregistered design rights, except that the protection is extended to *layers* of the semiconductor itself. This change was required due to the nature of the product; unregistered design rights do not give protection to surface decoration and those layers were, arguably, surface decoration.

In brief the person enforcing the rights must be a rights holder in the UK or a qualifying country, and the infringement must have taken place within the UK. The rights last for 10 years from the end of the calendar year in which the product was first made available anywhere in the world.

There are some exceptions to the provisions on copying in relation to unregistered design rights in that a copy of a semiconductor may be made for private study in order understand how it works. It is also a permitted act to manufacture a non-infringing product that will work *in situ* based on the analysis of the original. This is to facilitate the teaching process; without the ability to make copies of the chips and to analyse their composition, the industry would not have developed.

THE NEW REGULATIONS 2001

The above provisions remain in force in relation to registered designs with the exception of the compulsory licence. For designs that are registrable under these regulations there is no longer the possibility of claiming a compulsory licence as a method of defending an infringement injunction. Rather the defendant can apply to have the design cancelled and declared invalid by the registrar according to s.11 of the CPDA (1988) as amended by the Regulations. In the event that proceedings have been issued, the defendant may ask the court to consider the question of validity and, if necessary, cite prior art in its defence which means that right-holder has no claim to the registered design.

Note that a lack of knowledge is not a defence to the act of copying in relation to registered designs, but can merely limit the amount of damages that are awarded.

THE COMMUNITY DESIGN

Unregistered design

Infringement of unregistered design at Community level applies to any copying which is done for commercial purposes and not merely teaching or academic purposes. (There is an unfettered right to make limited private copies of the article).

There is no provision for the grant of compulsory licences to defendants in an action for copying. This advantage is for unregistered design rights holders prosecuting claims for infringement.

Registered design

The registered Community Design is like the UK registered design with the exception of licences. For licences to have validity they must be registered at the OHIM and they should be registered within three months of the licence being completed. Certainly if the licence is an exclusive one it should be registered so that the exclusive licensee may sue in respect of the design in question. Similarly, if a sub-licence has been granted, that too may be registered but only by the licensee who has already registered its licence in the usual way (Article 25 of the Commission Regulation 2245/2002) in the first place.

As with the UK design regime, where the product has the number and the words 'registered Community Design' on it or its usual packaging, the infringer will have no defence to an allegation of copying. The test according to Directive 98/71/EC is that the infringing design must differ only in 'immaterial details' (Article 4). What this tells us is that, as under the UK registered design regime, the infringement must be substantially similar to the design as registered for it to be considered an infringement by the courts.

Community Design infringement actions are heard by the national court or tribunal in the state in which the infringement took place. In the case of multiple jurisdictions, it is up to the claimant to decide the best place to sue the defendant and he should also consider the costs involved.

PASSING OFF AND TRADE DRESS

Just as goodwill can attach to a company, it can also attach to the appearance or the 'get-up' of a particular design. Where a designer has a signature design or designs, the goodwill associated with the owner is in fact attached to the specific design.

In the event a third party copies another's design or where that third party uses a similar form of packaging and/or configures a product in the same way, there is a potential to bring an action in passing off assuming that the following tests are met.

Establish goodwill in the earlier (original) design

While one need not show a specific amount of goodwill in the design, one needs to show sufficient goodwill. Such goodwill can arise from advertising, sales or the widespread availability of the product. Furthermore, the court will need to be satisfied that the goodwill attaches to the *product* rather than a brand used, so that the so-called relevant public (the target market for the product) associates the design of the product with its owner/marketer rather than any trade mark used. It can be difficult to demonstrate such goodwill, particularly where the design bears the brand name or trade mark of the seller.

Establish confusion between and/or deception regarding, the original design and the alleged infringement

Where there is a similar design on the market, the next step is to show that the relevant public is confused and/or deceived when confronted by the alleged infringement into believing that it originates from the owner of the original design.

To show that there has been confusion, the claimant will have to take survey evidence from members of the public. The phrasing of the questions asked in relation to both products must be carefully drafted. If the questions invite the respondent to consider the products in ways in which they would not ordinarily do when buying the product, the evidence will be poorly looked upon. The questions will depend on the specific nature of the alleged infringement and, where necessary, respondents should be available to give oral testimony if the matter proceeds to trial.

Establish that the confusion and/or deception cause damage to the original design

There must be damage in order to make an action cost-effective, and to fulfil the final part of the test. Such loss could be loss of sales or even loss of contracts. For example, loss could be caused to the owner/marketeer of the original design if, on seeing a design on sale in Shop A, Shop B, who wishes to sell the original design, cancels its order.

Passing off should be added to a claim only where the circumstances are right and the practitioner should consider this carefully before a claim is started, to avoid the claimant incurring unnecessary costs.

HOW TO PROCEED

The action brought will depend on the damage that has been suffered and the urgency of the need to prevent the infringement. To obtain an interim injunction in the UK (a temporary court order preventing (usually) the defendant from continuing to deal in the product or otherwise sell or market it), the claimant will need to show that the balance of convenience lies with him. In other words, the claimant must convince the court that the granting of an injunction will benefit him more than it will cause harm to the defendant. Note that the injunction is awarded pending the outcome of a trial, so that in the event that the claimant were to be awarded an injunction but then proceeds to lose the action, he should consider that the defendant had been restrained from marketing its product for a period of time – typically six months. Depending on the defendant, this could result in a very high figure of damages and certainly has the potential to wipe out a small claimant business.

As mentioned above, claims can be argued in the alternative, but the likelihood of success in each head of claim must be properly assessed before the claim is launched. In the event that the claimant is successful in some and not all of the heads of claim, the court will not award damages and costs in relation to those heads of claim that he loses, i.e. the costs of the defendant will be deducted from the overall sum awarded in successfully defending those heads.

In practice, smaller disputes do tend to be settled, either in correspondence or at a meeting. However, there are occasions on which a settlement cannot be reached, or at least not without having to launch a claim. The claimant needs to have a clear goal when commencing proceedings. Is it to recoup damage, or to get an infringing product off the market for good (a final injunction)? Whatever the goal, litigation, especially in the High Court, is time-consuming and expensive.

Similarly, when acting for the defendant establish his goal. Is it the intention to defend successfully the action to continue trading or is to escape proceedings having incurred as little costs as possible? Knowing the defendant's aim will make it easier to know which procedural steps to take. Whenever necessary, seek the advice of a litigator and/or counsel.

Act fast

As soon as the infringement comes to light, the claimant must act quickly in instructing a legal representative. The legal representative should then send a letter before action (information permitting) to the alleged infringer within two or three days of first being instructed on the matter. It will typically take longer to gather the necessary information when acting for the defendant given that there will be specific facts to which a response will be required. Note that it is worth spending time on the response because it is the best way of fending off a potential action and avoiding proceedings being commenced altogether.

Gather evidence

Whether acting for the claimant or for the defendant, you should gather the evidence that you need as quickly as possible as follows:

CLAIMANT

1. Details of right claimed. If registered, a copy of the certificate (ensure that the registration is still in force). If unregistered, the original design document or at least a copy of it.
2. Details of who made the design and the circumstances at the time of creation. Was he in employment or freelance?
3. Verify that the design as marketed reflects the design as registered.
4. An example of the infringement and where it was obtained. If you can, find out where the infringing item has been on sale (i.e., in how many shops) and for how long. Always keep a copy of the till receipt. Buy further items throughout the dispute as evidence of their continued offering for sale to the public.
5. Find out if there is any correlation between the two designs in terms of personnel, place or time. Find out if the claimant ever sent the design to the defendant as a sample, or if the claimant showed his work at a fair which the defendant attended.
6. Invite the designer to list as many similarities between the two pieces as he/she is able.
7. Is this the first time an alleged infringement has been brought to the defendant's notice? If not, repeat the earlier allegation together with the new in the letter before action.

DEFENDANT

1. Obtain details of creation of the alleged infringement. Find out the circumstances in which it was designed.
2. Speak directly to the designer of the alleged infringement if possible. Ask him about his inspiration for the design.
3. Prepare a list of differences between the original design and the alleged infringement with the help of the designer of the alleged infringement. This is especially relevant if the claim relates to a registered design.
4. Ask the designer to comment specifically on the allegations of copying. Was the designer present at the relevant show or fair? Was the designer employed at the material time when a sample was sent to the defendant?
5. Obtain evidence of other similar designs on the market to establish whether the design in question is part of a larger trend. For example, at the time of writing there is a trend in stripes and many different objects exist which are decorated in stripes. This helps to support an assertion of original creation.
6. If the allegation is made in relation to a registered design, examine the strength of the registration by requesting further details such as the date of first showing to the public and the claimant's relationship to the creator of the design.

BURDEN OF PROOF

Unregistered design

It is worth remembering that it is for the claimant to show that copying has taken place or at least to present a sufficient matrix of facts from which such inference of copying may be drawn. The defendant need only show that he has created the design independently to defeat such an allegation. Useful facts to support the claimant's arguments would be a catalogue of similar infringements, or evidence that the designer of the infringement had had a copy of the claimant's design in his possession prior to creating the design or was previously involved with the claimant. Each case will turn on its individual facts but these questions should be asked of the claimant/defendant in every case to avoid costs building up or to create a robust defence.

Registered design

Registered designs are entered on a publicly available registry and, as such, it is incumbent on a designer of a new product to be aware of the registered product. Defendants should note that, contrary to the unregistered design regime, independent creation will not be a defence if the claimant can show that he has been marketing the product properly marked with the registered design number. However, if you are acting for the defendant, you will seek to show that there are significant differences between the two designs since, unlike unregistered design rights, the registered design infringement must be a substantial copy and taken as whole. A claimant may choose to rely on unregistered design right if just a part of a design is infringed; he will have to also show evidence of inference of copying.

DAMAGES

The damages that can be sought will depend on the circumstances surrounding the infringement and can also depend on the specific actions of the defendant. It is open to the successful claimant to elect his preferred method of calculating damages and this will depend on the numbers of infringing products sold and the costs involved. For example, additional damages are awarded for 'flagrancy' where a defendant continues to infringe the claimant's design right after he has been put on notice of the infringement by the claimant.

Account of profits

According to this method the defendant must give to the claimant all the profit that it has made in selling the infringing product. This can be difficult to ascertain not least where there are differences of opinion as to what are legitimate business costs, since these will not form part of the profit costs. If the defendant has made a loss, for example, or where he has apparently not made much money the claimant may elect to use a different method of calculation. The claimant should bear in mind (as should the defendant) that where the profit costs are disputed, the claimant may ask an accountant to verify the figures supplied. This is often done by forensic accountants who are expert in analysing the necessary costs of business as distinct from profit. This is a lengthy and expensive course of action. In the event that the claimant is right to pursue the course of action, i.e. because the accounts subsequently turn out to be an inaccurate reflection of the true profit, the costs of the forensic examination will be borne by the defendant. However, if the forensic examination yields nothing new, the costs will be borne by the claimant. Therefore, he should have very good reason for instructing forensic accountants.

An account of profits is a good method for payment of damages at the high end of the market, where few products are sold but with a large profit. It can also be a good method of calculation at the bottom end of the market where, although the profit margin is small, the number of products sold is great and the profit figure is high. However, it often proves unsatisfactory in the middle of the market where the product is neither sold in volume nor at a high price.

The rule in *Gerber Garment Technology Inc.* v. *Lectra Systems Ltd* [1997] RPC 443

Although this is a decision relating to patents, the principles of damages calculation apply to designs. Here the rule is simply that a royalty payment will be made by the defendant to the successful claimant for every example of the infringing product that was **made** (as opposed to every example that was **sold**). The rationale here is that, had the defendant sought a licence from the claimant, this is what the defendant would reasonably have paid the claimant for the right to reproduce the design in suit. However, you must take note of what is usual in the particular industry in which the claimant operates so that a big brand or fashion designer is likely to be able to recoup 10 per cent per item made, whereas a furniture designer will only realistically be able to recover 2–4 per cent.

The next question is a percentage 'of what'? The percentages can be based on anything from net sales to gross sales costs and will depend on the particular industry norm. A claimant will want to reclaim as much as possible (naturally) and therefore will be inclined to claim a percentage based on gross sales. The defendant, on the other hand, will argue that a percentage of net sales is the norm.

Certainly by the disclosure stage the defendant will have confirmed the precise number of products made to the design and consequently claimants will be able to calculate which is the better route to go down to maximise their damages.

Loss of profits and growth

Basing a claim on lost profit is often the safest method of calculating damages since the information available to the claimant can be easily verified and the claimant does not have to rely on the defendant for the provision of figures and supporting information.

The claimant must be able to show his actual losses that are caused as a direct result of the infringing product being marketed at the material time. Furthermore, if the claimant can show that a loss in growth of income to the company is caused directly by the defendant's actions this should be factored into the claim. If you are acting for the defendant you will seek to limit such damages as much as you are able; one way to do so will be to claim that the loss of growth was due to other factors such as an increase in competition generally or a change in marketing/management at the claimant's company.

SUMMARY

The type of action and remedy sought will depend on a number of factors: the claimant's loss (damage), his willingness to litigate, the likelihood of success, and the identity of the alleged infringer. Wherever possible, a settlement with the defendant should be attempted to avoid time-consuming and costly court proceedings.

CHAPTER 10

Design protection in the USA

INTRODUCTION

Designs are protected in the USA through a number of laws as in Europe, including copyright law, design registration (known as 'design patents'), trade mark law and the law of trade dress. As in Europe, these forms of protection are not mutually exclusive and may coexist in respect of a design.

A design patent covers new and original designs having aesthetic ornamentation. To obtain a design patent, the design must be an article of manufacture which is ornamental, non-functional and non-obvious. Novelty, the property of being new, is usually determined from the standpoint of an 'ordinary observer' in comparison with earlier designs, known as 'prior art'. A design which is dictated solely by functional considerations is not protectable.

Trade dress actions for infringement of designs are possible in the USA. While trade dress once referred to the manner in which the product was 'dressed up' to go to market with a label, package display card and similar packaging elements, the concept has taken on a more expansive meaning and includes the design and appearance of a product as well as the container and all elements which make up the total visual image by which the product is presented to customers. Trade dress endures so long as the dress is being used in commerce and it identifies the source of the product.

Copyright protects original works of authorship embodied in a tangible medium of expression. As in Europe it arises automatically on creation of the work, and works published in the USA are eligible for copyright protection. There is a system of copyright registration with the Library of Congress which confers certain advantages on the copyright owner.

Trade marks are defined in the Lanham Act as any word, name, symbol or device or any combination thereof. One of the earliest and best-known examples of a registered shape is the shape of the Coca-Cola bottle. To register a shape mark the designer must demonstrate distinctiveness by establishing either that: (a) the mark is 'inherently distinctive'; or (b) the mark has acquired distinctiveness through use. The requirement is essentially that the customer associates the shape with a single source; like the shape of the Coca-Cola bottle clearly identifies the source as the Coca-Cola Company. In addition to proving distinctiveness, an applicant may be required to prove the product shape (configuration) is not functional, as in not essential to the use or purpose of the article.

The US market is potentially a valuable one and for this reason designers should consider protection available in the USA when formulating an overall design strategy. In particular it is important to consider protection at an early stage in order for a designer to establish relevant deadlines by which to make corresponding design patent or trade mark filings. The deadlines are particularly important when considering design patents where acquiring the right rests entirely on making a filing within the appropriate time period. For example as explained below an application to register a design patent in the USA can claim priority from a UK or Community registered design application or other filing so long as it is made within six months of the filing date of the application from which priority is claimed.

An example of how this may work to a designer's advantage is given below in the section on design patents (p. 144). Although planning and recording relevant deadlines to avoid missing the opportunity to obtain protection is seen by some designers as an unnecessary chore, the system does provide flexibility to the designer and an opportunity to spread the costs of protection as the market for the product develops.

PROTECTION BY COPYRIGHT

The law is set out in the main in the Copyright Act 1976. Copyright is granted to authors of original works which includes 'pictorial, graphic and sculptural works' and to useful articles. Pictorial, graphic and sculptural works may be 2D or 3D works of fine, graphic and applied art. Protected works include:

> advertisements, commercial prompts and labels;
> artificial flowers and plants;
> artwork applied to clothing or other useful articles;
> bumper stickers, decal stickers;
> cartography works such as maps, globes and relief models;
> cartoons;
> comic strips;
> dolls, toys;
> drawings, paintings, murals;
> enamel works;
> fabric floor and wallcovering designs;
> games, puzzles;
> greeting cards, postcards, stationery;
> holograms, computer and laser artwork;
> jewellery designs;

models;
mosaics;
needlework and craft kits;
original prints, such as engraving, silk screen prints;
patterns for sewing, knitting, needlework;
photographs, photomontage;
posters;
record jacket art work or photographs;
relief prints;
reproductions such as lithographs;
sculpture, such as carvings, ceramics, figurines, moulds, relief sculptures;
stained-glass design;
stencils, cut-outs;
technical drawings, architectural drawings or plans, blueprints, diagrams, mechanical drawings;
weaving designs and tapestries.

A useful article is an article which has some useful function and which is not merely decorative. Examples include clothing, furniture, dinnerware and light fixtures.

Copyright does not protect the mechanical or utilitarian aspects of such works of craftsmanship. It may however protect any aspects of the work which are pictorial, graphic or sculptural where these can be identified separately from the functional aspects of the object. Useful designs may therefore have both copyrightable and non-copyrightable features.

Obtaining copyright

Copyright is secured automatically on creation of the work. A work is created when it is fixed in some material form.

Published works are eligible for copyright protection in the USA if certain conditions are met. These include:

1. Where on the date of first publication, one or more authors is a national or domiciled in the USA, or is a national, domiciled in or a sovereign authority of a treaty party. A treaty party is a country or intergovernmental organisation other than the USA that is a party to an international agreement.
2. The work is first published in the USA or in a foreign nation if on that date of first publication, that country is a treaty party.

When is a work published?

Publication is defined as the distribution of copies of a work to the public for sale or other transfer of ownership or by rental lease or lending. The offering to distribute copies for purposes of further distribution or public display constitutes publication. A display of a work in itself does not constitute publication.

Indeed any dissemination in which the material object does not change hands is not a publication no matter how many people are exposed to the work.

Publication is an important concept in US copyright law for a number of reasons. In particular, works which are published in the USA are subject to mandatory deposit with the Library of Congress. A single deposit can be made to satisfy both the deposit requirement for the Library of Congress and the registration requirements.

In general the copyright owner has a legal obligation to deposit at the Copyright Office in the Library of Congress within three months of publication in the USA two copies of the work for the use of the Library of Congress. Failure to make the deposit can result in fines and other penalties, but does not affect copyright protection.

Certain categories of works are exempt entirely from the mandatory deposit requirements and the obligations are reduced for certain other categories. Mandatory deposit also applies to foreign works at the point that they are published in the USA through the distribution of copies that are either imported or are part of an 'American edition'.

The law envisages that deposit will be made voluntarily to satisfy this requirement. The Library of Congress has the power to make a written demand for the required deposit at any time after publication. If the required deposit is not then made within three months of the demand, the person or organisation obliged to make the deposit is liable to a fine of not more than $250 for each work plus the retail price of the copies. If there is a wilful failure to comply with such a demand, a fine of up to $2,500 may be incurred.

Because many deposits are not suitable for addition to the Library of Congress collections or for use in the national libraries programmes, the Copyright Office has issued regulations that exempt certain categories of works from the mandatory deposit requirements, or which reduce the number of copies from two to one in certain circumstances.

Who can claim copyright?

The copyright in the work of authorship becomes the property of the author who created the work. Where the author is employed to design, the employer and not the employee is considered to be the author.

Depending on the subject matter of the work, a work created further to a commission will belong to the commissioner and not the creator. The categories of work which may fall under this heading and which are of interest to designers include a contribution to a collective work and a compilation.

Copyright in each separate contribution to a collective work is however distinct from copyright in the collective work as a whole and vests initially with the creator of the contribution.

In addition, the parties can agree in writing that the work to be created under the commission is work for hire and that the copyright rests with the commissioner and not the creator.

The authors of a joint work are co-owners of the copyright in the work, unless there is agreement to the contrary.

Term of copyright

Works created (fixed in tangible form for the first time) on or after 1 January 1978 are automatically protected for a term enduring for the life of the author and 70 years after the author's death. Joint works of copyright are protected for a term which endures for a period of 70 years from the death of the last surviving author. Anonymous and pseudonymous works of design are not common, but where they exist they are protected for 95 years from publication or 120 years from creation, whichever is the shorter. Where an author's identity can be established from the records at the Copyright Office, the work is not an anonymous or pseudonymous work.

Works created prior to 1 January 1978 but not published until after that date will be subject to the same rules as works created after 1 January 1978.

Works created before and published before 1 January 1978 benefited from copyright for 28 years from the date of creation and the term could be renewed in the last year of the original term by a further 28 years. The Copyright Act 1976 extended the renewal term from 28 to 47 years and legislation enacted in October 1998 (Public law 105-298) further extended the renewal term of copyrights still subsisting on that date by an additional 20 years, providing for a renewal term of 67 years and a total term of protection of 95 years.

COPYRIGHT REGISTRATION

Copyright registration is a legal formality intended to record the fact of a particular copyright. Registration can be made pre- or post-publication of the work. Registration is not a condition of copyright protection except that the proprietor of copyright of US origin must register a work before filing a copyright infringement action in a US court. Registration is encouraged and a registration may be made at any time within the life of the copyright.

Registration confers a number of advantages to the copyright owner. These include:

1. Establishing a public record of the copyright.
2. If registration is made before or within five years of publication, registration will establish prima facie evidence in court of the validity of the copyright and the facts stated in the registration certificate.
3. Where registration is made within three months of publication of the work or prior to the infringement of the copyright, statutory damages and attorney's fees will be available to the copyright owner in court actions. Remedies for infringement in respect of copyright works not registered within this time frame are limited to actual damages and profits.
4. Registration allows the copyright owner to record the registration with the US Customs Service for protection against the importation of infringing copies.

Copyright registration procedure

Copyright owners can register their works by submitting the following material to:

Library of Congress at US Copyright Office
101 Independence Avenue SE
Washington, DC 20559-6000

1. A completed application form.
2. A non-returnable deposit of the work to be registered, generally one complete copy of the work if unpublished, two complete copies of the best edition of the work if the work was first published in the USA.
3. A non-refundable filing fee of $30 for each application.

A 'complete copy' of an unpublished work is a copy which includes all the copyrightable material of the work being registered. The 'best edition' is the edition published in the US at any date before the date of deposit at the Copyright Office.

Where the work to be registered includes sculpture, toys, jewellery, fabric or textiles attached to or part of a 3D work, the Copyright Office requires the deposit of 'identifying material' instead of copies of the 3D works. Identifying material generally consists of a 2D reproduction of the work, which may be photographs, drawings or transparencies that show the complete copyrightable content of the work.

The Copyright Office issues detailed guidelines for the submission of material to it which should be checked with the Office prior to submission.

RIGHTS OF THE COPYRIGHT OWNER

The copyright owner has the exclusive right to do and to authorise others to do acts which would otherwise constitute an infringement of the copyright owner's rights. In respect of designs the important rights are:

- to reproduce the work in any material form;
- to distribute copies of the work to the public by sale or other transfer of ownership by rental, lease or lending;
- to display the copyrighted work publicly.

In addition certain authors of works of visual art have the right to have work credited to them and the right of integrity to prevent derogatory treatment of their work.

It is illegal for anyone to violate the rights provided to the copyright owner.

Defences to copyright infringement

It is a defence to an infringement action that the act complained of amounts to 'fair use'. Further, compulsory licences may be granted in certain circumstances by the Copyright Office on payment of specified royalties and in compliance with statutory conditions.

DEALING IN COPYRIGHT

As intangible property, copyright may be conveyed by operation of law or left in a will as personal property.

The copyright owner may transfer the whole or any subdivision of his exclusive rights. To be valid, transfers must be in writing and signed by the owner of the rights being transferred. Non-exclusive licences are not required to be in writing.

The law does not require that the transfer of ownership of copyright is recorded at the Copyright Office. Recording the transfer at the Copyright Office does however provide certain advantages and may be required to validate the transfer against third parties.

A 'transfer of ownership' is an assignment, grant of an exclusive licence or any other change in the ownership of any or all of the exclusive rights in the copyright whether or not it is limited in time, place or effect.

No special forms for documents are necessary for recording a transfer at the Copyright Office. The Copyright Office does not attempt to judge the legal sufficiency of any document, by simply recording the document. Recording the transfer may be without legal effect unless the remitter has prepared the document in a way that satisfies applicable legal requirements.

It is possible that the Copyright Office would not reject a transfer that has not been signed by the copyright owner or otherwise notarised in accordance the rules.

There are a number of advantages to recording transfers in this way:

- Recording a transfer may establish priorities between a conflicting transfer or a non-exclusive licence.
- Recording a transfer establishes a public record of the contents of the transfer document.
- By recording a transfer the owner gives 'constructive notice', meaning that members of the public are deemed to have knowledge of the facts stated in the document and cannot claim otherwise as long as the work to which the document relates is registered and the document specifically identifies the work to which it pertains by reference to the registration.

NOTICE OF COPYRIGHT

Copyright notices are not required under US law. Notice was required under the 1976 Act, but this requirement was removed when the USA adhered to the Berne Convention, effective 1 March 1989.

Despite the fact that a notice is not required, it is beneficial to include a copyright notice on designs as it informs the public that the work is protected by copyright, and identifies the copyright owners and the year of first publication. An example of notice is ©2003 Inkpen Designs.

There is also an advantage in the event of infringement of the copyright. Where a notice has been applied to the copyright work the infringer cannot claim innocence in mitigation of actual or statutory damages. The notice should be fixed to the copyright work in such a way as to 'give reasonable notice of the claim to copyright'.

The notice should contain *all* the following elements:

- The symbol © (the letter 'C' in a circle), or the word 'Copyright';
- the year of first publication of the work;
- the name of the copyright owner.

It is useful to include a copyright notice on unpublished works that leave the control of the copyright owner. In this event the appropriate notice is 'unpublished copyright work ©2003 Inkpen Design'.

DESIGN PATENTS

The design consists of the visual ornamental characteristics embodied in or applied to an article of manufacture. As design is manifested in its appearance, the subject matter of a design patent application may relate to:

- the configuration or shape of an article;
- to the surface ornamentation applied to an article; or
- to a combination of surface design and ornamentation.

A design for an article of manufacture that is dictated primarily by function of the article and lacks ornamentation cannot be registered as a design patent.

A design for surface ornamentation is inseparable from the article to which it is applied and cannot exist alone.

Design patents may be granted to any person who has invented a new, original and ornamental design for an article of manufacture. A design protects only the appearance of an article and not its structural or utilitarian features.

An ornamental design may be embodied in an entire article or only a portion of an article, or may be ornamentation applied to an article.

A design patent application may only have a single claim. This means that designs which are distinct must be filed in separate applications. Designs are independent if there is no apparent link between two objects. For example the designs of a chair and a desk (not joined together) are independent articles and must be claimed in separate applications. Designs are distinct if they have different shapes and appearances even though they are related articles. For example two table lamps which have the same shape but different surface ornamentation which creates distinct appearances must be claimed in separate applications. However, modified forms of a single design concept may be filed in one application. For example the table lamps with only minimal configuration differences may be filed in one application.

Priority for a design registry filing in another country can be claimed in the USA and as mentioned (see p. 36) the priority period in which a filing elsewhere can be extended to the USA relying on the first filing date is a useful tool for designers (see example overleaf).

Practicalities and cost of design patent filings

It is not necessary to employ the services of a patent attorney in the USA and it is possible for designers to make their own filings and deal with the US Patent and Trade Mark Office (USPTO) direct. That said, there is no guarantee that the filing made by a designer with little experience of the requirements and process will cover the design it is intended to. Further, there are detailed requirements relating to the form of the drawings submitted to the USPTO. Photographs may be accepted but only after approval of the photographs by the USPTO as to their form following the submission of a petition to the USPTO. Photographs will be acceptable if they clearly define the design which it is intended to protect. The time required to make the petition and obtaining approval needs to be considered by a designer in calculating when to put a design patent filing in motion.

Example

Jake designs a range of light fittings in the spring of 2003 and exhibits them at an exhibition in London on 9 July 2003. The designs attract favourable reviews. A French company with European-wide manufacturing and distribution capability expresses an interest in taking a licence from Jake for the European Community. Jake and the French company correspond regarding a potential deal but by September nothing has been agreed. Jake decides to continue to sell by himself. He struggles to meet demand and continues to exhibit at shows. On 1 July 2004 he makes an application for a registered Community Design, calculating 9 July 2003 as the date on which the designs were first shown in public. In August 2004 Jake is approached by a US lighting company, which expresses an interest in manufacturing and marketing the design in the USA. Negotiations progress well. On the basis that concluding the US licence looks likely, Jake applies for a design patent in the USA for the designs as shown in the registered Community Design application on 3 December 2004, claiming a priority date of 1 July 2004. By taking these steps, Jake has effectively secured registered design protection in the European Community and the USA. In so doing, Jake has increased both the prospect of securing successful licence deals and the potential income which may flow from them.

Whether drawings or photographs, the views submitted with any application should include front rear right and left views. Perspective views although not required may also be submitted to show clearly the shape of 3D designs. If photographs have been used in a national application and no line drawings are available for filing within the priority period, it is possible to file photographs to secure a filing date and then to lodge drawings later in order to fix the filing date. The USPTO is not keen on photographs for design patent applications and using photographs carries the risk that the filing is limited, for example, with colour photographs, to the colours shown in the photographs. Alternatively there may be a limitation in that the design as disclosed is deemed to include background extraneous material not intended by the designer to be part of the design.

The current cost of a design patent application in the USA is $330 per application and typical attorney fees range between $375 and $590 per application. As well as confirming initial filing fees, a designer should establish with an attorney the further costs which may be involved in the filing.

WHAT AMOUNTS TO AN INFRINGEMENT?

Design patents

It is an infringement of a design patent to make use, offer for sale or sell a product as disclosed in a design patent throughout the USA or to import such a product into the USA. A person who actively and knowingly encourages or assists another person to infringe is also liable as an infringer.

It is a defence to a claim for design patent infringement that the design differs from the design as disclosed in the design patent or that the design patent is invalid. Invalidity can be claimed on the basis that the design patent is improper subject matter for registration or that the design patent lacks novelty on the basis of other designs on the market as at the priority date of the design patent.

Copyright

To succeed in an action for copyright infringement, a designer must show both that the designer is the proprietor of the design in question and also that there has been copying. As in the UK, designs which come to market after the time at which a designer puts his designs on the market and which are independently conceived and developed cannot be attacked on the basis of copyright. The ability of the alleged copyist to have had access to the copyright work allegedly infringed is sufficient as evidence that copying may have taken place. Contributory infringement is also a possible claim against a person, firm or company who, with knowledge of the infringing activity, induces, causes or materially contributes to the infringing conduct of another.

Trade dress

As trade dress actions are based on unregistered rights, enforcement of trade dress depends on showing that the designs in question are inherently distinctive or alternatively that they have acquired distinctiveness through use. The infringement standard is likelihood of confusion, mistake or deception as to the origin of the goods or services among the relevant public. Owners of designs claiming protection by way of trade dress must also be able to prove ownership of the relevant designs.

INFRINGEMENT PROCEEDINGS IN THE USA

Intellectual property owners may seek preliminary injunctions that order the alleged infringer to cease the infringing activity. Preliminary injunctions are available where the court decides that:

- there is a reasonable likelihood of success on the merits;
- irreparable harm will occur if injunctive relief is not granted;
- the threatened harm to the intellectual property owners outweighs the harm the injunction will cause to the alleged infringer; and
- the grant of such a preliminary injunction will serve the public interest.

The proprietor seeking the injunction is usually required to post a bond to compensate the accused infringer for any damages suffered after the grant of a preliminary injunction if the injunction is ultimately dissolved.

The ultimate decision is a matter of equity and is within the discretion of the trial court.

With respect to trade mark and copyright cases, irreparable injury is presumed when the party seeking the injunction has demonstrated likelihood of success on the merits.

Permanent injunctions may be granted at trial.

Temporary restraining orders can be obtained under Federal Rule of Civil Procedure and are most common near the beginning of a case. Such orders may be granted without notice and expire after a maximum of 10 days. As with preliminary injunctions, a bond must usually be posted by the party seeking the injunction.

Owners of intellectual property are also entitled to monetary relief to restore the designer, whose work has been taken, to the financial position he or she would have enjoyed if the infringer had not violated the proprietor's exclusive rights. Courts are also able to order the impoundment and destruction of goods. Attorney fees and costs are at the court's discretion.

SUMMARY

Designers with their sights on the US market should make careful records of when designs were first shown in public or applications were made to register the designs. In addition, to secure the advantages of copyright protection, and even in the absence of applying for a design patent, a designer should consider registration prior to launching designs in the US market.

CHAPTER 11

Design protection in South-East Asia

INTRODUCTION

When considering a worldwide design protection strategy, the significant role that South-East Asian countries play in manufacturing cannot be ignored. It is common for a company to seek to manufacture consumer products in this territory, due to the significant costs advantages. That said, manufacturing in this region does have drawbacks. A designer who appreciates what these may be and takes steps to ensure that so far as possible risks of manufacturing abroad are avoided, will find that the prospects of a successful relationship are much greater. In addition to setting up manufacturing in this region, as discussed in Chapter 8, a designer may wish to enter into a licence for the exploitation of designs in countries in this region. In this case it is also important to ensure that the terms of the licence agreement take into account the risks posed.

In this chapter we note what special considerations a designer should bear in mind when entering into a manufacturing or licence agreement with persons or companies in this region. Also included is a summary of the protection for designs available in each country. A designer who has his designs manufactured in this region, or a designer who is licensing his design in this region, should consider putting basic protection in place. Such protections may then be used as a tool in the event that the design is copied either by the company which is meant to be manufacturing on his behalf or by any other person. Indeed, whether or not a designer has decided to manufacture or license his designs in this region, this region is responsible for a significant amount of copy and counterfeit products. Strictly speaking, counterfeit product is product made by a business with which the design owner has no connection. Product which is made or put into circulation by a business which has a connection with the design owner is known as unauthorised product. Unauthorised product can be overruns, or B-grade product. In some cases it may be product made specifically by a manufacturer with the intention of supplying third parties with large quantities of product. In the battle against either counterfeit or unauthorised product, obtaining design protection in countries in this region is a useful tool and should be considered as part of any designer's strategy to preserve the integrity and value in his products.

CONTRACTING

Specific areas of the contract which require special consideration are as set out below.

Quality control

The agreement should provide for designs to be made to the agreed quality, usually by reference to an agreed sample. The designer should keep a copy of the sample and check consignments regularly to ensure that the products meet the required standards. The agreement should provide that there should be no deviation from the sample including no substitution of materials. Technical products manufactured in the region may still need to acquire the relevant certification marks for sale in Europe.

Factory inspection

The designer should consider including the right to appoint a local agent to carry out inspections of the factory where designs are being made to ascertain compliance with the contract. Such an agent may be a useful link where the designer is unable to visit the factory on a regular basis. Such an agent should also be given the right to ensure that, following termination of the agreement by the licensor, any stock which the licensee may sell within the 'sell-off' period is actually sold and the licensee holds no copyright material of the licensor.

Inspection of books

A local agent can again help with the inspection of books which will be a right that the licensor has under the contract. It is also worth considering whether the licensor should provide for electronic transfer of files by e-mail so that the licensor can access the information without the need to rely on a foreign agent unless there appears to be a problem with the licensee's accounting or reporting.

Back-door product

The agreement should be explicit about the ban on selling or otherwise disposing of seconds in the local market. Such activity devalues the original design.

Quality

Ensuring quality of products in a long-distance relationship is difficult enough. The task becomes more difficult if a manufacturer or licensee is able to subcontract to others. While a good agent may be able to police such a situation, it is advisable that the agreement bans subcontracting by your manufacturer to ensure that the design owner retains control over the manufacturing process and can enforce the terms of the agreement.

Royalties and minimum

The designer should consider whether a proportion of the royalties should be paid in advance to reduce the risk of the licensee failing to make payments. Credit references should be checked and if possible references from other designers using the factory should be obtained. A designer may ask which other licences the company holds or which other companies the factory manufactures product for.

Choice of law

A UK designer will tend to favour the law of England and Wales as being the applicable law as well as providing that any disputes arising be pursued in the courts of England and Wales. This may be a good strategy where, for example, the goods are being manufactured in Malaysia or Hong Kong or any other jurisdiction where international conventions allow the enforcement of a UK judgment in the country of manufacture. It may not be a sensible strategy where manufacture is taking place in a country which does not recognise the judgment of a UK court unless the manufacturing company has assets which could be proceeded against in the UK, which is unlikely.

Design ownership

As discussed in Chapter 4, there is risk in certain circumstances that a manufacturer in, for example, China may be able to be the first owner of unregistered design right. In order to minimise the prospect of such a claim, the agreement should clearly set out the designs to be manufactured and the title to the designs. Although a manufacturer will not necessarily generate any further rights in manufacturing a product to a designer's specification, it is possible that rights are generated. Most commonly a manufacturer will make design changes if it makes the manufacturing process easier (and hence cheaper). A designer should ensure that the agreement provides that rights in any changes made by the manufacturer belong to the designer.

DESIGN PROTECTION IN CHINA

China is a signatory to various international treaties and conventions including the Paris Convention, the Berne Convention, the Madrid Agreement and the Universal Copyright Convention and the Patent Co-operation Treaty. There is also a set of laws covering patents, copyrights, trade marks and licensing all of which can come into play in a strategy to help to prevent copying of designs in China. They are: The Patent Law (1985, amended 1993) under which design registration is possible, The Trade Mark Law (1983, amended 1993), The Copyright Law (1991) and the Unfair Competition Law (1993). China has undertaken to revise intellectual property law to bring its laws in line with the World Trade Organisation's TRIPS protocol.

Registered designs or design patents

Design patents may generally be granted to foreign nationals on government agreement or by international treaty. In addition an applicant may claim priority in accordance with the Paris Convention, allowing filing in China 30 months after filing in the applicant's home territory. Applications are made to the Patent Office.

Design patents are granted on 'any new design of the shape, colour, pattern, or any combination thereof of an object, creating an aesthetic feeling and suitable for industrial application'.

Design patents are granted on a first-to-apply basis. Applications must be made through a patent agent designated to work for foreigners and must be made in Chinese. A design patent will not be granted if:

(a) before the date of filing (or the priority date for a Paris Convention application) the same or a similar design was published anywhere in the world or publicly put to use in China;

(b) a design patent has been granted for the same or a similar new design which was filed earlier than the current application;

(c) the design is obvious to people familiar with the relevant field.

There is no substantive review of the application. Despite this processing, a design patent may take several months to obtain. A design patent lasts for 10 years from the filing date.

A design patent is suspended if challenged by a third party.

A pending application or registered design patent may be assigned to another party. The assignment must be registered with the Patent Office and takes effect as of the date of registration. If the assignee is a foreign party, the assignment is subject to approval of relevant authorities. Granted design patents may also be licensed to other parties. A written contract must be recorded within three months in order to protect against penalties from the Patent Office.

Copyright

Chinese copyright law protects copyright including fine art for 50 years plus the life of the author, or in employment situations 50 years from first publication. In China, copyright can belong to employees rather than the employer and it may therefore be advisable to sign licence agreements with any employees in China who may have design input.

Copyright protection in China is comparatively poor as the authority which oversees the drawing up of copyright legislation, the National Copyright Administration of China, is less capable and less proactive than other intellectual property administration organisations. Most lawyers will look for a 'trade mark angle' to take action against copyright infringers.

What is infringement?

Any person who without the consent of the registered designer or copyright holder manufactures, uses, promises to sell, sells or imports an article made to the design infringes the right of the proprietor of the design patent or copyright. Unauthorised use constitutes infringement unless otherwise provided by law.

Action against infringers

In all but the more serious counterfeiting cases where a letter may simply cause a factory to close and open elsewhere to avoid detection, a raid of the premises may be organised to catch the infringers 'red-handed'. It is worth pointing out to the company concerned that it is breaking the law and that you will take further action against it if it does not stop the activity.

If this fails, there are three other options, administrative action, customs seizure and legal proceedings.

ADMINISTRATIVE ACTION

A design patent holder may ask the Patent Office to impose administrative penalties on an infringer or may bring a civil law suit against the infringer. The limitation period for design patent actions is two years from the date on which the proprietor of the design patent knew or should have known of the infringement.

Damages awarded to the proprietor of a registered design are calculated on the illegal profit of the infringer, actual loss of the right owner or on multiples of appropriate royalties.

Administrative actions are the most popular and cheaper way of dealing with intellectual property infringement problems. Many courts will not hear cases that have been handled previously by administrative means, so proceeding subsequently to court is not always an option. Careful planning is therefore essential.

To commence an administrative action, evidence should be taken to the appropriate authority (in the case of design patents the Patent Office) who will then decide whether or not to raid the premises of the alleged infringer. The Patent Office may decline to do so if legal action has already been commenced or for reasons of local protectionism. If the Patent Office does take action, raids of premises can be extremely effective in combating copying and, in the case of a small copying operation, may be sufficient to deal with the immediate problem. Copy products may be seized and destroyed. With larger-scale copying operations, however, many rights-holders find that the authorities are unable or unwilling to follow up effectively and fines are not substantial enough to be a real deterrent. Lack of coordination between the various administrative bodies also makes effective and long-term solutions to the problems difficult.

CUSTOMS

Regulations introduced in 1995 allow Customs to stop counterfeit goods from entering and leaving the country. Design patent owners who could benefit from this procedure should register their rights with Customs and provide information on when copy goods are likely to be entering and leaving China and the details of the importer/exporter. Customs require a bond equal to the value of the shipment to be lodged with Customs when a shipment of goods is seized. Customs may hold goods for three weeks. The importer/exporter is given one week to object and Customs hold the goods for a further two weeks pending their decision as to whether or not the goods are an infringement. Infringing goods are either destroyed or sold. Customs will deduct the cost of storage of the goods before repaying the bond. Where Customs decide the goods are not an infringement, the bond may be forfeited.

LEGAL ACTION

Legal action is normally recommended over administrative action when the case is complex or involves large sums of money. Courts may charge fees and require large bonds to be posted in case of non-guilty verdicts.

Civil proceedings are pursued through the local People's Court and must be filed through a Chinese lawyer. Many larger cities have intellectual property tribunals in the intermediate courts, which will handle intellectual property cases involving foreign companies.

Criminal proceedings may be brought by the Public Prosecutor and the case for criminal prosecution must be presented by a Chinese lawyer. The maximum penalty is a seven-year jail sentence and fines calculated as a multiple of turnover.

Summary

While there are clearly provisions which assist designers in protecting and enforcing rights in China, the laws themselves are not the greatest challenge. The main problem that intellectual property owners face is poor enforcement of the law. The effectiveness of action and the willingness of the authorities to take action varies depending on the problem. While the authorities may take action on infringers of registered trade marks effectively, copyright is a poorly protected area. Local protectionism exists in many areas and the various administrative authorities may not be willing to work together. Further, many government officials in China and the police force have yet to be convinced that intellectual property infringement is wrong. All these factors conspire to make design protection in China a challenge.

Despite this, protection in this region should not be ignored. Central authorities involved in intellectual property legislation are aware of the problems and some are being addressed. Ease of enforcement will improve as Chinese companies come to appreciate the growing value of their own intellectual property portfolios and lobby for change from within. It is important to investigate all the different ways in which you can protect your designs through registration and to make sure that you complete registrations fully and properly in accordance with the relevant regulations. Although registration can be expensive, it is the best insurance against copy problems which may arise.

It is also important to watch the market and to be aware of possible infringement. This can be as simple as checking shops to look for copy products or simply staying alive to what is happening in your field of design so you notice any suspicious developments. It is possible to hire investigators to check the marketplace for you. Finally let your embassy and trade association know of any problems so that they can take the opportunity to help you.

DESIGN PROTECTION IN HONG KONG

Registered designs

Designs can be registered for a wide variety of products. Registered designs are granted in respect of the appearance of the product. Applications are made to the Hong Kong Patent Office and can be made by the proprietor or an agent. An address in Hong Kong for service of documents is required, as is a statement of novelty in both English and Chinese.

Only new designs are registrable and designs need to be kept confidential until an application to register the design is made. There is a limited exception for designs which have been exhibited at official international exhibitions registered under the 1928 Convention on International Exhibitions. These are rarely held and none have been held in Hong Kong. For information on whether an exhibition is a Convention exhibition contact: International Exhibition Bureau, 56 Avenue Victor Hugo, 75783 Paris Cedex 16, France.

If an application is properly filed, a certificate of registration will be issued within three months of filing.

Registered design protection lasts for five years from the date of filing the application and is renewable for periods of five years, subject to payment of the renewal fees, up to a maximum of 25 years.

Registering a design in Hong Kong gives protection in Hong Kong only. To have protection outside Hong Kong registration should be made in every country in which protection is sought.

Under the Paris Convention for the Protection of Industrial Property of 20th March 1883, an application in Hong Kong can give the applicant priority for any subsequent application to register a design within six months in certain other countries and territories.

Registered design owners have the right to prevent others from manufacturing, importing, using, selling or hiring the design product. A registered design owner or an exclusive licensee in his own name can bring civil proceedings for infringement committed after the date on which the design certificate was issued.

Copyright protection

Copyright protection for articles produced from a designer's original design drawings subsists side by side with registered design protection. Protection under copyright law is for 15 years from first marketing of the article.

Copyright protection depends on copying, in that it is not possible to take action for copyright infringement where another person independently produces a similar design.

Trade marks

A new Trade Marks Ordinance entered into force on 4 April 2003. The law of trade marks is based largely but not entirely on the UK's Trade Marks Act 1994. The meaning of trade mark has been broadened to allow for registration of 3D shapes. However, there is nothing to suggest that Hong Kong is preparing to join the Madrid agreement.

REGISTERED DESIGNS IN SINGAPORE

A law effective from 13 November 2000 replaces the former system under which designs registered in the UK were deemed to extend to Singapore.

Designs which are registrable are those relating to shape, configuration pattern or ornament applied to an article by an industrial process. Protection does not extend to shape or configuration dictated solely by function or to features which are necessary to fit with or match another article with which the article in question is intended to form an integrated whole.

To be registrable a design must be new and differ in more than immaterial differences or features from designs commonly used in the trade. Designs registered in other countries will not be considered new. Except for designs for certain textiles and wall coverings, applicants will be required to submit a statement of novelty pointing out how their design differs from prior designs. Designs for which protection is obtained by filing will initially be registered for a period of five years, which is capable of extension for two further periods of 15 years.

Under the transitional provisions, all designs registered and in force in the UK prior to 13 November 2000 are deemed to remain in force in Singapore until next due for renewal. At that point a separate renewal must be effected in Singapore if Singapore protection is to continue. Further, any such design can benefit for a period up to 25 years from application in the UK.

REGISTERED DESIGNS IN MALAYSIA

These are currently protected by the extension of three English statutes:

- The United Kingdom Designs (Protection) Act 1949 (Revised 1978) for West Malaysia;
- The United Kingdom Designs (Protection) Ordinance Chapter 152 for Sabah; and
- The Designs (United Kingdom) Ordinance Chapter 59 for Sarawak.

By these provisions, the registered proprietor of a design registration in the UK under the Registered Designs Act 1949 has the same rights and privileges as though the registration in the UK had been issued with an extension to Malaysia. The effect of this is that Malaysian residents and others who desire design protection in Malaysia must therefore obtain a registration in the UK before they can obtain protection in Malaysia.

REGISTERED DESIGNS IN INDONESIA

It has been possible to register designs in Indonesia since the law of Industrial Designs which came into effect on 29 December 2000.

Designs which give aesthetic impression are capable of registration and this includes such features as the shape, configuration, composition, lines and colour, or a combination of all these features, whether in 2D or 3D form.

A design must be capable of industrial application to be registered and there is a worldwide novelty requirement. Subject to a check on the formalities, applications are published and subject to a three-month opposition period. Only applications which are opposed are examined. Priority claims may be made within six months of the first application in the Paris convention country.

Civil and criminal remedies are available for unauthorised use, manufacture, sale, importation, export or distribution of goods protected by a registered design.

REGISTERED DESIGNS IN KOREA

To be registrable, a design needs to be the 'shape, pattern or colour of an article or a combination thereof which creates an aesthetic feeling through the sense of sight'. A registrable design is also required to have novelty. A design which has been publicly known in Korea or any other country prior to the filing of an application will lack novelty. A design must also be capable of industrial application to qualify as a registrable design. The scope of the design right is decided on the basis of the statement in the application and the design as represented in the drawings in the application.

Korean design law has been amended with effect from 1 July 2001 to permit protection for parts of an article as well as the whole of the article. Additionally, protection will be possible in a single application for sets of articles, for example those constituting a suite of furniture.

The design right gives the owner of the design right the exclusive right to exploit commercially the registered design for a period of up to 10 years from the date of the registration.

REGISTERED DESIGNS IN THAILAND

Design patents are available under the Thai Patent Act.

Designs are registrable if they are capable of industrial application and have a form or composition of lines or colour which give a special appearance or pattern.

There is a worldwide novelty requirement, though priority claims can be made within six months of application in the Paris convention country or member of the World Trade Organisation. The term of protection is 10 years from the date of filing.

Applications are subject to preliminary examination as to formalities then publication. There is a three-month opposition period followed by substantive examination.

Civil and criminal remedies are available for unauthorised manufacturing, use, sale, offer for sale, importation or distribution of goods protected by a registered design.

REGISTERED DESIGNS IN VIETNAM

Design patents are granted under Decree no. 63/CP of 24 October 1996 on industrial property as amended by Decree no. 06/2001/nd-CP of 1 February 2001.

Designs are registrable if the appearance of the product in terms of contours, 3D form or colour, or a combination of these elements is novel worldwide. Priority claims can be made within six months of first application in the Paris convention country.

The term of a design patent is five years and may be extended twice for periods of five years, giving a maximum of 15 years' protection.

An application for a design patent is subject to a three-month formality examination and if accepted is published within two months of this period. Substantive examination takes nine months from the date on which the application is accepted as to formalities. Applications may be opposed following publication and within the substantive examination period.

Civil and criminal sanctions are available to counter unauthorised trading in copy designs. Administrative remedies are also possible.

APPENDIX A1

Part III CDPA 1988

PART III

Design Right

CHAPTER I

Design right in original designs

Introductory

213.—(1) Design right is a property right which subsists in accordance with this Part in an original design. Design right.

(2) In this Part 'design' means the design of any aspect of the shape or configuration (whether internal or external) of the whole or part of an article.

(3) Design right does not subsist in –

    (a)   a method or principle of construction,
    (b)   features of shape or configuration of an article which –
        (i)   enable the article to be connected to, or placed in, around or against, another article so that either article may perform its function, or
        (ii) are dependent upon the appearance of another article of which the article is intended by the designer to form an integral part, or
    (c)   surface decoration.

(4) A design is not 'original' for the purposes of this Part if it is commonplace in the design field in question at the time of its creation.

(5) Design right subsists in a design only if the design qualifies for design right protection by reference to –

    (a)   the designer or the person by whom the design was commissioned or the designer employed (see sections 218 and 219), or
    (b)   the person by whom and country in which articles made to the design were first marketed (see section 220),

or in accordance with any Order under section 221 (power to make further provision with respect to qualification).

(6) Design right does not subsist unless and until the design has been recorded in a design document or an article has been made to the design.

(7) Design right does not subsist in a design which was so recorded, or to which an article was made, before the commencement of this Part.

The designer **214.**—(1) In this Part the 'designer', in relation to a design, means the person who creates it.

(2) In the case of a computer-generated design the person by whom the arrangements necessary for the creation of the design are undertaken shall be taken to be the designer.

Ownership of design right. **215.**—(1) The designer is the first owner of any design right in a design which is not created in pursuance of a commission or in the course of employment.

(2) Where a design is created in pursuance of a commission, the person commissioning the design is the first owner of any design right in it.

(3) Where, in a case not falling within subsection (2) a design is created by an employee in the course of his employment, his employer is the first owner of any design right in the design.

(4) If a design qualifies for design right protection by virtue of section 220 (qualification by reference to first marketing of articles made to the design), the above rules do not apply and the person by whom the articles in question are marketed is the first owner of the design right.

Duration of design right. **216.**—(1) Design right expires –

(a) fifteen years from the end of the calendar year in which the design was first recorded in a design document or an article was first made to the design, whichever first occurred, or

(b) if articles made to the design are made available for sale or hire within five years from the end of that calendar year, ten years from the end of the calendar year in which that first occurred.

(2) The reference in subsection (1) to articles being made available for sale or hire is to their being made so available anywhere in the world by or with the licence of the design right owner.

Qualification for design right protection

Qualifying individuals and qualifying persons. **217.**—(1) In this Part –

'qualifying individual' means a citizen or subject of, or an individual habitually resident in, a qualifying country; and

'qualifying person' means a qualifying individual or a body corporate or other body having legal personality which –

(a) is formed under the law of a part of the United Kingdom or another qualifying country, and

(b) has in any qualifying country a place of business at which substantial business activity is carried on.

(2) References in this Part to a qualifying person include the Crown and the government of any other qualifying country.

(3) In this section 'qualifying country' means –

(a) the United Kingdom,
(b) a country to which this Part extends by virtue of an Order under section 255,
(c) another member State of the European Economic Community, or
(d) to the extent that an Order under section 256 so provides, a country designated under that section as enjoying reciprocal protection.

(4) The reference in the definition of 'qualifying individual' to a person's being a citizen or subject of a qualifying country shall be construed –

(a) in relation to the United Kingdom, as a reference to his being a British citizen, and
(b) n relation to a colony of the United Kingdom, as a reference to his being a British Dependent Territories' citizen by connection with that colony.

(5) In determining for the purpose of the definition of 'qualifying person' whether substantial business activity is carried on at a place of business in any country, no account shall be taken of dealings in goods which are at all material times outside that country.

218.—(1) This section applies to a design which is not created in pursuance of a commission or in the course of employment. *Qualification by reference to designer.*

(2) A design to which this section applies qualifies for design right protection if the designer is a qualifying individual or, in the case of a computer-generated design, a qualifying person.

(3) A joint design to which this section applies qualifies for design right protection if any of the designers is a qualifying individual or, as the case may be, a qualifying person.

(4) Where a joint design qualifies for design right protection under this section, only those designers who are qualifying individuals or qualifying persons are entitled to design right under section 215(1) (first ownership of design right: entitlement of designer).

219.—(1) A design qualifies for design right protection if it is created in pursuance of a commission from, or in the course of employment with, a qualifying person. *Qualification by reference to commissioner or employer.*

(2) In the case of a joint commission or joint employment a design qualifies for design right protection if any of the commissioners or employers is a qualifying person.

(3) Where a design which is jointly commissioned or created in the course of joint employment qualifies for design right protection under this section, only those commissioners or employers who are qualifying persons are entitled to design right under section 215(2) or (3) (first ownership of design right: entitlement of commissioner or employer).

220.—(1) A design which does not qualify for design right protection under section 218 or 219 (qualification by reference to designer, commissioner or employer) qualifies for design right protection if the first marketing of articles made to the design – *Qualification by reference to first marketing.*

(a) is by a qualifying person who is exclusively authorised to put such articles on the market in the United Kingdom, and

(b) takes place in the United Kingdom, another country to which this Part extends by virtue of an Order under section 255, or another member State of the European Economic Community.

(2) If the first marketing of articles made to the design is done jointly by two or more persons, the design qualifies for design right protection if any of those persons meets the requirements specified in subsection (1)(a).

(3) In such a case only the persons who meet those requirements are entitled to design right under section 215(4) (first ownership of design right: entitlement of first marketer of articles made to the design).

(4) In subsection (1)(a) 'exclusively authorised' refers –

(a) to authorisation by the person who would have been first owner of design right as designer, commissioner of the design or employer of the designer if he had been a qualifying person, or by a person lawfully claiming under such a person, and

(b) to exclusivity capable of being enforced by legal proceedings in the United Kingdom.

Power to make further provision as to qualification.

221.—(1) Her Majesty may, with a view to fulfilling an international obligation of the United Kingdom, by Order in Council provide that a design qualifies for design right protection if such requirements as are specified in the Order are met.

(2) An Order may make different provision for different descriptions of design or article; and may make such consequential modifications of the operation of sections 215 (ownership of design right) and sections 218 to 220 (other means of qualification) as appear to Her Majesty to be appropriate.

(3) A statutory instrument containing an Order in Council under this section shall be subject to annulment in pursuance of a resolution of either House of Parliament.

Dealings with design right

Assignment and licences.

222.—(1) Design right is transmissible by assignment, by testamentary disposition or by operation of law, as personal or moveable property.

(2) An assignment or other transmission of design right may be partial, that is, limited so as to apply –

(a) to one or more, but not all, of the things the design right owner has the exclusive right to do;

(b) to part, but not the whole, of the period for which the right is to subsist.

(3) An assignment of design right is not effective unless it is in writing signed by or on behalf of the assignor.

(4) A licence granted by the owner of design right is binding on every successor in title to his interest in the right, except a purchaser in good faith for valuable consideration and without notice (actual or constructive) of the licence or a person deriving title from such a purchaser; and references in this Part to doing anything with, or without, the licence of the design right owner shall be construed accordingly.

223.—(1) Where by an agreement made in relation to future design right, and signed by or on behalf of the prospective owner of the design right, the prospective owner purports to assign the future design right (wholly or partially) to another person, then if, on the right coming into existence, the assignee or another person claiming under him would be entitled as against all other persons to require the right to be vested in him, the right shall vest in him by virtue of this section.

(2) In this section –

'future design right' means design right which will or may come into existence in respect of a future design or class of designs or on the occurrence of a future event; and

'prospective owner' shall be construed accordingly, and includes a person who is prospectively entitled to design right by virtue of such an agreement as is mentioned in subsection (1).

(3) A licence granted by a prospective owner of design right is binding on every successor in title to his interest (or prospective interest) in the right, except a purchaser in good faith for valuable consideration and without notice (actual or constructive) of the licence or a person deriving title from such a purchaser; and references in this Part to doing anything with, or without, the licence of the design right owner shall be construed accordingly.

224. Where a design consisting of a design in which design right subsists is registered under the [1949 c. 88.] Registered Designs Act 1949 and the proprietor of the registered design is also the design right owner, an assignment of the right in the registered design shall be taken to be also an assignment of the design right, unless a contrary intention appears.

225.—(1) In this Part an 'exclusive licence' means a licence in writing signed by or on behalf of the design right owner authorising the licensee to the exclusion of all other persons, including the person granting the licence, to exercise a right which would otherwise be exercisable exclusively by the design right owner.

(2) The licensee under an exclusive licence has the same rights against any successor in title who is bound by the licence as he has against the person granting the licence.

Chapter II

Rights of Design Right Owner and Remedies

Infringement of design right

226.—(1) The owner of design right in a design has the exclusive right to reproduce the design for commercial purposes –

    (a)   by making articles to that design, or

    (b)   by making a design document recording the design for the purpose of enabling such articles to be made.

(2) Reproduction of a design by making articles to the design means copying the design so as to produce articles exactly or substantially to that design, and references in this Part to making articles to a design shall be construed accordingly.

(3) Design right is infringed by a person who without the licence of the design right owner does, or authorises another to do, anything which by virtue of this section is the exclusive right of the design right owner.

(4) For the purposes of this section reproduction may be direct or indirect, and it is immaterial whether any intervening acts themselves infringe the design right.

(5) This section has effect subject to the provisions of Chapter III (exceptions to rights of design right owner).

Secondary infringement: importing or dealing with infringing article.

227.—(1) Design right is infringed by a person who, without the licence of the design right owner –

(a) imports into the United Kingdom for commercial purposes, or
(b) has in his possession for commercial purposes, or
(c) sells, lets for hire, or offers or exposes for sale or hire, in the course of a business,

an article which is, and which he knows or has reason to believe is, an infringing article.

(2) This section has effect subject to the provisions of Chapter III (exceptions to rights of design right owner).

Meaning of 'infringing article'.

228.—(1) In this Part 'infringing article', in relation to a design, shall be construed in accordance with this section.

(2) An article is an infringing article if its making to that design was an infringement of design right in the design.

(3) An article is also an infringing article if –

(a) it has been or is proposed to be imported into the United Kingdom, and

(b) its making to that design in the United Kingdom would have been an infringement of design right in the design or a breach of an exclusive licence agreement relating to the design.

(4) Where it is shown that an article is made to a design in which design right subsists or has subsisted at any time, it shall be presumed until the contrary is proved that the article was made at a time when design right subsisted.

(5) Nothing in subsection (3) shall be construed as applying to an article which may lawfully be imported into the United Kingdom by virtue of any enforceable Community right within the meaning of section 2(1) of the [1972 c. 68.] European Communities Act 1972.

(6) The expression 'infringing article' does not include a design document, notwithstanding that its making was or would have been an infringement of design right.

Remedies for infringement

229.—(1) An infringement of design right is actionable by the design right owner.

(2) In an action for infringement of design right all such relief by way of damages, injunctions, accounts or otherwise is available to the plaintiff as is available in respect of the infringement of any other property right.

(3) The court may in an action for infringement of design right, having regard to all the circumstances and in particular to –

    (a)   the flagrancy of the infringement, and
    (b)   any benefit accruing to the defendant by reason of the infringement,

award such additional damages as the justice of the case may require.

(4) This section has effect subject to section 233 (innocent infringement).

230.—(1) Where a person –

    (a)   has in his possession, custody or control for commercial purposes an infringing article, or
    (b)   has in his possession, custody or control anything specifically designed or adapted for making articles to a particular design, knowing or having reason to believe that it has been or is to be used to make an infringing article,

the owner of the design right in the design in question may apply to the court for an order that the infringing article or other thing be delivered up to him or to such other person as the court may direct.

(2) An application shall not be made after the end of the period specified in the following provisions of this section; and no order shall be made unless the court also makes, or it appears to the court that there are grounds for making, an order under section 231 (order as to disposal of infringing article, &c.).

(3) An application for an order under this section may not be made after the end of the period of six years from the date on which the article or thing in question was made, subject to subsection (4).

(4) If during the whole or any part of that period the design right owner –

    (a)   is under a disability, or
    (b)   is prevented by fraud or concealment from discovering the facts entitling him to apply for an order,

an application may be made at any time before the end of the period of six years from the date on which he ceased to be under a disability or, as the case may be, could with reasonable diligence have discovered those facts.

(5) In subsection (4) 'disability' –

    (a)   in England and Wales, has the same meaning as in the [1980 c. 58.] Limitation Act 1980;
    (b)   in Scotland, means legal disability within the meaning of the [1973 c. 52.] Prescription and Limitation (Scotland) Act 1973;

(c)   in Northern Ireland, has the same meaning as in the [1958 c. 10 (N.I.).] Statute of Limitations (Northern Ireland) 1958.

(6) A person to whom an infringing article or other thing is delivered up in pursuance of an order under this section shall, if an order under section 231 is not made, retain it pending the making of an order, or the decision not to make an order, under that section.

(7) Nothing in this section affects any other power of the court.

Order as to disposal of infringing articles, &c.

231.—(1) An application may be made to the court for an order that an infringing article or other thing delivered up in pursuance of an order under section 230 shall be –

(a)   forfeited to the design right owner, or
(b)   destroyed or otherwise dealt with as the court may think fit,

or for a decision that no such order should be made.

(2) In considering what order (if any) should be made, the court shall consider whether other remedies available in an action for infringement of design right would be adequate to compensate the design right owner and to protect his interests.

(3) Provision shall be made by rules of court as to the service of notice on persons having an interest in the article or other thing, and any such person is entitled –

(a)   to appear in proceedings for an order under this section, whether or not he was served with notice, and
(b)   to appeal against any order made, whether or not he appeared;

and an order shall not take effect until the end of the period within which notice of an appeal may be given or, if before the end of that period notice of appeal is duly given, until the final determination or abandonment of the proceedings on the appeal.

(4) Where there is more than one person interested in an article or other thing, the court shall make such order as it thinks just and may (in particular) direct that the thing be sold, or otherwise dealt with, and the proceeds divided.

(5) If the court decides that no order should be made under this section, the person in whose possession, custody or control the article or other thing was before being delivered up or seized is entitled to its return.

(6) References in this section to a person having an interest in an article or other thing include any person in whose favour an order could be made in respect of it under this section or under section 114 or 204 of this Act or section 58C of the [1938 c. 22.] Trade Marks Act 1938 (which make similar provision in relation to infringement of copyright, rights in performances and trade marks).

Jurisdiction of county court and sheriff court.

232.—(1) In England, Wales and Northern Ireland a county court may entertain proceedings under –

section 230 (order for delivery up of infringing article, &c.),

section 231 (order as to disposal of infringing article, &c.), or

section 235(5) (application by exclusive licensee having concurrent rights),

where the value of the infringing articles and other things in question does not exceed the county court limit for actions in tort.

(2) In Scotland proceedings for an order under any of those provisions may be brought in the sheriff court.

(3) Nothing in this section shall be construed as affecting the jurisdiction of the High Court or, in Scotland, the Court of Session.

233.—(1) Where in an action for infringement of design right brought by virtue of section 226 (primary infringement) it is shown that at the time of the infringement the defendant did not know, and had no reason to believe, that design right subsisted in the design to which the action relates, the plaintiff is not entitled to damages against him, but without prejudice to any other remedy. *Innocent infringement.*

(2) Where in an action for infringement of design right brought by virtue of section 227 (secondary infringement) a defendant shows that the infringing article was innocently acquired by him or a predecessor in title of his, the only remedy available against him in respect of the infringement is damages not exceeding a reasonable royalty in respect of the act complained of.

(3) In subsection (2) 'innocently acquired' means that the person acquiring the article did not know and had no reason to believe that it was an infringing article.

234.—(1) An exclusive licensee has, except against the design right owner, the same rights and remedies in respect of matters occurring after the grant of the licence as if the licence had been an assignment. *Rights and remedies of exclusive licensee.*

(2) His rights and remedies are concurrent with those of the design right owner; and references in the relevant provisions of this Part to the design right owner shall be construed accordingly.

(3) In an action brought by an exclusive licensee by virtue of this section a defendant may avail himself of any defence which would have been available to him if the action had been brought by the design right owner.

235.—(1) Where an action for infringement of design right brought by the design right owner or an exclusive licensee relates (wholly or partly) to an infringement in respect of which they have concurrent rights of action, the design right owner or, as the case may be, the exclusive licensee may not, without the leave of the court, proceed with the action unless the other is either joined as a plaintiff or added as a defendant. *Exercise of concurrent rights.*

(2) A design right owner or exclusive licensee who is added as a defendant in pursuance of subsection (1) is not liable for any costs in the action unless he takes part in the proceedings.

(3) The above provisions do not affect the granting of interlocutory relief on the application of the design right owner or an exclusive licensee.

(4) Where an action for infringement of design right is brought which relates (wholly or partly) to an infringement in respect of which the design right owner and an exclusive licensee have concurrent rights of action –

    (a)   the court shall, in assessing damages, take into account –
           (i)   the terms of the licence, and
          (ii)   any pecuniary remedy already awarded or available to either of them in respect of the infringement;
    (b)   no account of profits shall be directed if an award of damages has been made, or an account of profits has been directed, in favour of the other of them in respect of the infringement; and

(c)   the court shall if an account of profits is directed apportion the profits between them as the court considers just, subject to any agreement between them;

and these provisions apply whether or not the design right owner and the exclusive licensee are both parties to the action.

(5) The design right owner shall notify any exclusive licensee having concurrent rights before applying for an order under section 230 (order for delivery up of infringing article, &c.); and the court may on the application of the licensee make such order under that section as it thinks fit having regard to the terms of the licence.

CHAPTER III

Exceptions to Rights of Design Right Owners

Infringement of copyright

Infringement of copyright.

236. Where copyright subsists in a work which consists of or includes a design in which design right subsists, it is not an infringement of design right in the design to do anything which is an infringement of the copyright in that work.

Availability of licences of right

Licences available in last five years of design right.

237.—(1) Any person is entitled as of right to a licence to do in the last five years of the design right term anything which would otherwise infringe the design right.

(2) The terms of the licence shall, in default of agreement, be settled by the comptroller.

(3) The Secretary of State may if it appears to him necessary in order to –

(a)   comply with an international obligation of the United Kingdom, or

(b)   secure or maintain reciprocal protection for British designs in other countries,

by order exclude from the operation of subsection (1) designs of a description specified in the order or designs applied to articles of a description so specified.

(4) An order shall be made by statutory instrument; and no order shall be made unless a draft of it has been laid before and approved by a resolution of each House of Parliament.

Powers exercisable for protection of the public interest.

238.—(1) Where the matters specified in a report of the Monopolies and Mergers Commission as being those which in the Commission's opinion operate, may be expected to operate or have operated against the public interest include –

(a)   conditions in licences granted by a design right owner restricting the use of the design by the licensee or the right of the design right owner to grant other licences, or

(b)   a refusal of a design right owner to grant licences on reasonable terms, the powers conferred by Part I of Schedule 8 to the [1973 c. 41.] Fair Trading Act 1973 (powers exercisable for purpose of remedying or preventing adverse effects specified in report of Commission) include power to cancel or modify those conditions and, instead or in addition, to provide that licences in respect of the design right shall be available as of right.

(2) The references in sections 56(2) and 73(2) of that Act, and sections 10(2)(b) and 12(5) of the [1980 c. 21.] Competition Act 1980, to the powers specified in that Part of that Schedule shall be construed accordingly.

(3) The terms of a licence available by virtue of this section shall, in default of agreement, be settled by the comptroller.

239.—(1) If in proceedings for infringement of design right in a design in respect of which a licence is available as of right under section 237 or 238 the defendant undertakes to take a licence on such terms as may be agreed or, in default of agreement, settled by the comptroller under that section – *Undertaking to take licence of right in infringement proceedings.*

   (a) no injunction shall be granted against him,

   (b) no order for delivery up shall be made under section 230, and

   (c) the amount recoverable against him by way of damages or on an account of profits shall not exceed double the amount which would have been payable by him as licensee if such a licence on those terms had been granted before the earliest infringement.

(2) An undertaking may be given at any time before final order in the proceedings, without any admission of liability.

(3) Nothing in this section affects the remedies available in respect of an infringement committed before licences of right were available.

Crown use of designs

240.—(1) A government department, or a person authorised in writing by a government department, may without the licence of the design right owner – *Crown use of designs.*

   (a) do anything for the purpose of supplying articles for the services of the Crown, or

   (b) dispose of articles no longer required for the services of the Crown;

and nothing done by virtue of this section infringes the design right.

(2) References in this Part to 'the services of the Crown' are to –

   (a) the defence of the realm,

   (b) foreign defence purposes, and

   (c) health service purposes.

(3) The reference to the supply of articles for 'foreign defence purposes' is to their supply –

   (a) for the defence of a country outside the realm in pursuance of an agreement or arrangement to which the government of that country and Her Majesty's Government in the United Kingdom are parties; or

(b) for use by armed forces operating in pursuance of a resolution of the United Nations or one of its organs.

(4) The reference to the supply of articles for 'health service purposes' are to their supply for the purpose of providing –

(a) pharmaceutical services,
(b) general medical services, or
(c) general dental services,

that is, services of those kinds under Part II of the [1977 c. 49.] National Health Service Act 1977, Part II of the [1978 c. 29.] National Health Service (Scotland) Act 1978 or the corresponding provisions of the law in force in Northern Ireland.

(5) In this Part –

'Crown use', in relation to a design, means the doing of anything by virtue of this section which would otherwise be an infringement of design right in the design; and

'the government department concerned', in relation to such use, means the government department by whom or on whose authority the act was done.

(6) The authority of a government department in respect of Crown use of a design may be given to a person either before or after the use and whether or not he is authorised, directly or indirectly, by the design right owner to do anything in relation to the design.

(7) A person acquiring anything sold in the exercise of powers conferred by this section, and any person claiming under him, may deal with it in the same manner as if the design right were held on behalf of the Crown.

Settlement of terms for Crown use. **241.**—(1) Where Crown use is made of a design, the government department concerned shall –

(a) notify the design right owner as soon as practicable, and
(b) give him such information as to the extent of the use as he may from time to time require,

unless it appears to the department that it would be contrary to the public interest to do so or the identity of the design right owner cannot be ascertained on reasonable inquiry.

(2) Crown use of a design shall be on such terms as, either before or after the use, are agreed between the government department concerned and the design right owner with the approval of the Treasury or, in default of agreement, are determined by the court.

In the application of this subsection to Northern Ireland the reference to the Treasury shall, where the government department referred to in that subsection is a Northern Ireland department, be construed as a reference to the Department of Finance and Personnel.

(3) Where the identity of the design right owner cannot be ascertained on reasonable inquiry, the government department concerned may apply to the court who may order that no royalty or other sum shall be payable in respect of Crown use of the design until the owner agrees terms with the department or refers the matter to the court for determination.

242.—(1) The provisions of any licence, assignment or agreement made between the design right owner (or anyone deriving title from him or from whom he derives title) and any person other than a government department are of no effect in relation to Crown use of a design, or any act incidental to Crown use, so far as they –

   (a)   restrict or regulate anything done in relation to the design, or the use of any model, document or other information relating to it, or

   (b)   provide for the making of payments in respect of, or calculated by reference to such use;

and the copying or issuing to the public of copies of any such model or document in connection with the thing done, or any such use, shall be deemed not to be an infringement of any copyright in the model or document.

(2) Subsection (1) shall not be construed as authorising the disclosure of any such model, document or information in contravention of the licence, assignment or agreement.

(3) Where an exclusive licence is in force in respect of the design –

   (a)   if the licence was granted for royalties –

      (i)   any agreement between the design right owner and a government department under section 241 (settlement of terms for Crown use) requires the consent of the licensee, and

      (ii)   the licensee is entitled to recover from the design right owner such part of the payment for Crown use as may be agreed between them or, in default of agreement, determined by the court;

   (b)   if the licence was granted otherwise than for royalties –

      (i)   section 241 applies in relation to anything done which but for section 240 (Crown use) and subsection (1) above would be an infringement of the rights of the licensee with the substitution for references to the design right owner of references to the licensee, and

      (ii)   section 241 does not apply in relation to anything done by the licensee by virtue of an authority given under section 240.

(4) Where the design right has been assigned to the design right owner in consideration of royalties –

   (a)   section 241 applies in relation to Crown use of the design as if the references to the design right owner included the assignor, and any payment for Crown use shall be divided between them in such proportion as may be agreed or, in default of agreement, determined by the court; and

   (b)   section 241 applies in relation to any act incidental to Crown use as it applies in relation to Crown use of the design.

(5) Where any model, document or other information relating to a design is used in connection with Crown use of the design, or any act incidental to Crown use, section 241 applies to the use of the model, document or other information with the substitution for the references to the design right owner of references to the person entitled to the benefit of any provision of an agreement rendered inoperative by subsection (1) above.

(6) In this section –

'act incidental to Crown use' means anything done for the services of the Crown to the order of a government department by the design right owner in respect of a design;

'payment for Crown use' means such amount as is payable by the government department concerned by virtue of section 241; and

'royalties' includes any benefit determined by reference to the use of the design.

Crown use: compensation for loss of profit.
243.—(1) Where Crown use is made of a design, the government department concerned shall pay –

(a)   to the design right owner, or

(b)   if there is an exclusive licence in force in respect of the design, to the exclusive licensee,

compensation for any loss resulting from his not being awarded a contract to supply the articles made to the design.

(2) Compensation is payable only to the extent that such a contract could have been fulfilled from his existing manufacturing capacity; but is payable notwithstanding the existence of circumstances rendering him ineligible for the award of such a contract.

(3) In determining the loss, regard shall be had to the profit which would have been made on such a contract and to the extent to which any manufacturing capacity was under-used.

(4) No compensation is payable in respect of any failure to secure contracts for the supply of articles made to the design otherwise than for the services of the Crown.

(5) The amount payable shall, if not agreed between the design right owner or licensee and the government department concerned with the approval of the Treasury, be determined by the court on a reference under section 252; and it is in addition to any amount payable under section 241 or 242.

(6) In the application of this section to Northern Ireland, the reference in subsection (5) to the Treasury shall, where the government department concerned is a Northern Ireland department, be construed as a reference to the Department of Finance and Personnel.

Special provision for Crown use during emergency.
244.—(1) During a period of emergency the powers exercisable in relation to a design by virtue of section 240 (Crown use) include power to do any act which would otherwise be an infringement of design right for any purpose which appears to the government department concerned necessary or expedient –

(a)   for the efficient prosecution of any war in which Her Majesty may be engaged;

(b)   for the maintenance of supplies and services essential to the life of the community;

(c)   for securing a sufficiency of supplies and services essential to the well-being of the community;

(d)   for promoting the productivity of industry, commerce and agriculture;

(e)   for fostering and directing exports and reducing imports, or imports of any classes, from all or any countries and for redressing the balance of trade;

(f)   generally for ensuring that the whole resources of the community are available for use, and are used, in a manner best calculated to serve the interests of the community; or

(g)   for assisting the relief of suffering and the restoration and distribution of essential supplies and services in any country outside the United Kingdom which is in grave distress as the result of war.

(2) References in this Part to the services of the Crown include, as respects a period of emergency, those purposes; and references to 'Crown use' include any act which would apart from this section be an infringement of design right.

(3) In this section 'period of emergency' means a period beginning with such date as may be declared by Order in Council to be the beginning, and ending with such date as may be so declared to be the end, of a period of emergency for the purposes of this section.

(4) No Order in Council under this section shall be submitted to Her Majesty unless a draft of it has been laid before and approved by a resolution of each House of Parliament.

General

245.—(1) The Secretary of State may if it appears to him necessary in order to –

(a)   comply with an international obligation of the United Kingdom, or

(b)   secure or maintain reciprocal protection for British designs in other countries,

by order provide that acts of a description specified in the order do not infringe design right.

Power to provide for further exceptions.

(2) An order may make different provision for different descriptions of design or article.

(3) An order shall be made by statutory instrument and no order shall be made unless a draft of it has been laid before and approved by a resolution of each House of Parliament.

CHAPTER IV

Jurisdiction of the Comptroller and the Court

Jurisdiction of the comptroller

246.—(1) A party to a dispute as to any of the following matters may refer the dispute to the comptroller for his decision –

(a)   the subsistence of design right,

(b)   the term of design right, or

(c)   the identity of the person in whom design right first vested;

Jurisdiction to decide matters relating to design right.

and the comptroller's decision on the reference is binding on the parties to the dispute.

(2) No other court or tribunal shall decide any such matter except –

(a)   on a reference or appeal from the comptroller,

(b)   in infringement or other proceedings in which the issue arises incidentally, or

(c)   in proceedings brought with the agreement of the parties or the leave of the comptroller.

(3) The comptroller has jurisdiction to decide any incidental question of fact or law arising in the course of a reference under this section.

247.—(1) A person requiring a licence which is available as of right by virtue of –

    (a)   section 237 (licences available in last five years of design right), or

    (b)   an order under section 238 (licences made available in the public interest),

may apply to the comptroller to settle the terms of the licence.

(2) No application for the settlement of the terms of a licence available by virtue of section 237 may be made earlier than one year before the earliest date on which the licence may take effect under that section.

(3) The terms of a licence settled by the comptroller shall authorise the licensee to do –

    (a)   in the case of licence available by virtue of section 237, everything which would be an infringement of the design right in the absence of a licence;

    (b)   in the case of a licence available by virtue of section 238, everything in respect of which a licence is so available.

(4) In settling the terms of a licence the comptroller shall have regard to such factors as may be prescribed by the Secretary of State by order made by statutory instrument.

(5) No such order shall be made unless a draft of it has been laid before and approved by a resolution of each House of Parliament.

(6) Where the terms of a licence are settled by the comptroller, the licence has effect –

    (a)   in the case of an application in respect of a licence available by virtue of section 237 made before the earliest date on which the licence may take effect under that section, from that date;

    (b)   in any other case, from the date on which the application to the comptroller was made.

248.—(1) This section applies where a person making an application under section 247 (settlement of terms of licence of right) is unable on reasonable inquiry to discover the identity of the design right owner.

(2) The comptroller may in settling the terms of the licence order that the licence shall be free of any obligation as to royalties or other payments.

(3) If such an order is made the design right owner may apply to the comptroller to vary the terms of the licence with effect from the date on which his application is made.

(4) If the terms of a licence are settled by the comptroller and it is subsequently established that a licence was not available as of right, the licensee shall not be liable in damages for, or for an account of profits in respect of, anything done before he was aware of any claim by the design right owner that a licence was not available.

249.—(1) An appeal lies from any decision of the comptroller under section 247 or 248 (settlement of terms of licence of right) to the Appeal Tribunal constituted under section 28 of the [1949 c. 88.] Registered Designs Act 1949.

(2) Section 28 of that Act applies to appeals from the comptroller under this section as it applies to appeals from the registrar under that Act; but rules made under that section may make different provision for appeals under this section.

250.—(1) The Secretary of State may make rules for regulating the procedure to be followed in connection with any proceeding before the comptroller under this Part.

Rules.

(2) Rules may, in particular, make provision –

(a) prescribing forms;

(b) requiring fees to be paid;

(c) authorising the rectification of irregularities of procedure;

(d) regulating the mode of giving evidence and empowering the comptroller to compel the attendance of witnesses and the discovery of and production of documents;

(e) providing for the appointment of advisers to assist the comptroller in proceedings before him;

(f) prescribing time limits for doing anything required to be done (and providing for the alteration of any such limit); and

(g) empowering the comptroller to award costs and to direct how, to what party and from what parties, costs are to be paid.

(3) Rules prescribing fees require the consent of the Treasury.

(4) The remuneration of an adviser appointed to assist the comptroller shall be determined by the Secretary of State with the consent of the Treasury and shall be defrayed out of money provided by Parliament.

(5) Rules shall be made by statutory instrument which shall be subject to annulment in pursuance of a resolution of either House of Parliament.

Jurisdiction of the court

251.—(1) In any proceedings before him under section 246 (reference of matter relating to design right), the comptroller may at any time order the whole proceedings or any question or issue (whether of fact or law) to be referred, on such terms as he may direct, to the High Court or, in Scotland, the Court of Session.

References and appeals on design right matters.

(2) The comptroller shall make such an order if the parties to the proceedings agree that he should do so.

(3) On a reference under this section the court may exercise any power available to the comptroller by virtue of this Part as respects the matter referred to it and, following its determination, may refer any matter back to the comptroller.

(4) An appeal lies from any decision of the comptroller in proceedings before him under section 246 (decisions on matters relating to design right) to the High Court or, in Scotland, the Court of Session.

252.—(1) A dispute as to any matter which falls to be determined by the court in default of agreement under –

Reference of disputes relating to Crown use.

(a) section 241 (settlement of terms for Crown use),

(b) section 242 (rights of third parties in case of Crown use), or

(c) section 243 (Crown use: compensation for loss of profit),

may be referred to the court by any party to the dispute.

(2) In determining a dispute between a government department and any person as to the terms for Crown use of a design the court shall have regard to –

    (a)   any sums which that person or a person from whom he derives title has received or is entitled to receive, directly or indirectly, from any government department in respect of the design; and

    (b)   whether that person or a person from whom he derives title has in the court's opinion without reasonable cause failed to comply with a request of the department for the use of the design on reasonable terms.

(3) One of two or more joint owners of design right may, without the concurrence of the others, refer a dispute to the court under this section, but shall not do so unless the others are made parties; and none of those others is liable for any costs unless he takes part in the proceedings.

(4) Where the consent of an exclusive licensee is required by section 242(3)(a)(i) to the settlement by agreement of the terms for Crown use of a design, a determination by the court of the amount of any payment to be made for such use is of no effect unless the licensee has been notified of the reference and given an opportunity to be heard.

(5) On the reference of a dispute as to the amount recoverable as mentioned in section 242(3)(a)(ii) (right of exclusive licensee to recover part of amount payable to design right owner) the court shall determine what is just having regard to any expenditure incurred by the licensee –

    (a)   in developing the design, or

    (b)   in making payments to the design right owner in consideration of the licence (other than royalties or other payments determined by reference to the use of the design).

(6) In this section 'the court' means –

    (a)   in England and Wales, the High Court or any patents county court having jurisdiction by virtue of an order under section 287 of this Act,

    (b)   in Scotland, the Court of Session, and

    (c)   in Northern Ireland, the High Court.

CHAPTER V

Miscellaneous and General

Miscellaneous

Remedy for groundless threats of infringement proceedings.

253.—(1) Where a person threatens another person with proceedings for infringement of design right, a person aggrieved by the threats may bring an action against him claiming –

    (a)   a declaration to the effect that the threats are unjustifiable;

    (b)   an injunction against the continuance of the threats;

    (c)   damages in respect of any loss which he has sustained by the threats.

(2) If the plaintiff proves that the threats were made and that he is a person aggrieved by them, he is entitled to the relief claimed unless the defendant shows that

the acts in respect of which proceedings were threatened did constitute, or if done would have constituted, an infringement of the design right concerned.

(3) Proceedings may not be brought under this section in respect of a threat to bring proceedings for an infringement alleged to consist of making or importing anything.

(4) Mere notification that a design is protected by design right does not constitute a threat of proceedings for the purposes of this section.

254.—(1) A person who has a licence in respect of a design by virtue of section 237 or 238 (licences of right) shall not, without the consent of the design right owner – Licensee under licence of right not to claim connection with design right owner.

    (a) apply to goods which he is marketing, or proposes to market, in reliance on that licence a trade description indicating that he is the licensee of the design right owner, or

    (b) use any such trade description in an advertisement in relation to such goods.

(2) A contravention of subsection (1) is actionable by the design right owner.

(3) In this section 'trade description', the reference to applying a trade description to goods and 'advertisement' have the same meaning as in the [1968 c. 29.] Trade Descriptions Act 1968.

Extent of operation of this Part

255.—(1) This Part extends to England and Wales, Scotland and Northern Ireland. Countries to which this Part extends.

(2) Her Majesty may by Order in Council direct that this Part shall extend, subject to such exceptions and modifications as may be specified in the Order, to –

    (a) any of the Channel Islands,
    (b) the Isle of Man, or
    (c) any colony.

(3) That power includes power to extend, subject to such exceptions and modifications as may be specified in the Order, any Order in Council made under section 221 (further provision as to qualification for design right protection) or section 256 (countries enjoying reciprocal protection).

(4) The legislature of a country to which this Part has been extended may modify or add to the provisions of this Part, in their operation as part of the law of that country, as the legislature may consider necessary to adapt the provisions to the circumstances of that country; but not so as to deny design right protection in a case where it would otherwise exist.

(5) Where a country to which this Part extends ceases to be a colony of the United Kingdom, it shall continue to be treated as such a country for the purposes of this Part until –

    (a) an Order in Council is made under section 256 designating it as a country enjoying reciprocal protection, or

(b) an Order in Council is made declaring that it shall cease to be so treated by reason of the fact that the provisions of this Part as part of the law of that country have been amended or repealed.

(6) A statutory instrument containing an Order in Council under subsection (5)(b) shall be subject to annulment in pursuance of a resolution of either House of Parliament.

Countries enjoying reciprocal protection.

256.—(1) Her Majesty may, if it appears to Her that the law of a country provides adequate protection for British designs, by Order in Council designate that country as one enjoying reciprocal protection under this Part.

(2) If the law of a country provides adequate protection only for certain classes of British design, or only for designs applied to certain classes of article, any Order designating that country shall contain provision limiting, to a corresponding extent, the protection afforded by this Part in relation to designs connected with that country.

(3) An Order under this section shall be subject to annulment in pursuance of a resolution of either House of Parliament.

Territorial waters and the continental shelf.

257.—(1) For the purposes of this Part the territorial waters of the United Kingdom shall be treated as part of the United Kingdom.

(2) This Part applies to things done in the United Kingdom sector of the continental shelf on a structure or vessel which is present there for purposes directly connected with the exploration of the sea bed or subsoil or the exploitation of their natural resources as it applies to things done in the United Kingdom.

(3) The United Kingdom sector of the continental shelf means the areas designated by order under section 1(7) of the [1964 c. 29.] Continental Shelf Act 1964.

Interpretation

Construction of references to design right owner.

258.—(1) Where different persons are (whether in consequence of a partial assignment or otherwise) entitled to different aspects of design right in a work, the design right owner for any purpose of this Part is the person who is entitled to the right in the respect relevant for that purpose.

(2) Where design right (or any aspect of design right) is owned by more than one person jointly, references in this Part to the design right owner are to all the owners, so that, in particular, any requirement of the licence of the design right owner requires the licence of all of them.

Joint designs.

259.—(1) In this Part a 'joint design' means a design produced by the collaboration of two or more designers in which the contribution of each is not distinct from that of the other or others.

(2) References in this Part to the designer of a design shall, except as otherwise provided, be construed in relation to a joint design as references to all the designers of the design.

Application of provisions to articles in kit form.

260.—(1) The provisions of this Part apply in relation to a kit, that is, a complete or substantially complete set of components intended to be assembled into an article, as they apply in relation to the assembled article.

(2) Subsection (1) does not affect the question whether design right subsists in any aspect of the design of the components of a kit as opposed to the design of the assembled article.

261. The requirement in the following provisions that an instrument be signed by or on behalf of a person is also satisfied in the case of a body corporate by the affixing of its seal –

section 222(3) (assignment of design right),

section 223(1) (assignment of future design right),

section 225(1) (grant of exclusive licence).

262. In the application of this Part to Scotland –

'account of profits' means accounting and payment of profits;

'accounts' means count, reckoning and payment;

'assignment' means assignation;

'costs' means expenses;

'defendant' means defender;

'delivery up' means delivery;

'injunction' means interdict;

'interlocutory relief' means interim remedy; and

'plaintiff' means pursuer.

263.—(1) In this Part –

'British design' means a design which qualifies for design right protection by reason of a connection with the United Kingdom of the designer or the person by whom the design is commissioned or the designer is employed;

'business' includes a trade or profession;

'commission' means a commission for money or money's worth;

'the comptroller' means the Comptroller-General of Patents, Designs and Trade Marks;

'computer-generated', in relation to a design, means that the design is generated by computer in circumstances such that there is no human designer,

'country' includes any territory;

'the Crown' includes the Crown in right of Her Majesty's Government in Northern Ireland;

'design document' means any record of a design, whether in the form of a drawing, a written description, a photograph, data stored in a computer or otherwise;

'employee', 'employment' and 'employer' refer to employment under a contract of service or of apprenticeship;

'government department' includes a Northern Ireland department.

(2) References in this Part to 'marketing', in relation to an article, are to its being sold or let for hire, or offered or exposed for sale or hire, in the course of a business, and related expressions shall be construed accordingly; but no account shall be taken for the purposes of this Part of marketing which is merely colourable and not intended to satisfy the reasonable requirements of the public.

(3) References in this Part to an act being done in relation to an article for 'commercial purposes' are to its being done with a view to the article in question being sold or hired in the course of a business.

Index of defined expressions.

264. The following Table shows provisions defining or otherwise explaining expressions used in this Part (other than provisions defining or explaining an expression used only in the same section) –

account of profits and accounts (in Scotland)	section 262
assignment (in Scotland)	section 262
British designs	section 263(1)
business	section 263(1)
commercial purposes	section 263(3)
commission	section 263(1)
the comptroller	section 263(1)
computer-generated	section 263(1)
costs (in Scotland)	section 262
country	section 263(1)
the Crown	section 263(1)
Crown use	sections 240(5) and 244(2)
defendant (in Scotland)	section 262
delivery up (in Scotland)	section 262
design	section 213(2)
design document	section 263(1)
designer	sections 214 and 259(2)
design right	section 213(1)
design right owner	sections 234(2) and 258
employee, employment and employer	section 263(1)
exclusive licence	section 225(1)
government department	section 263(1)
government department concerned (in relation to Crown use)	section 240(5)
infringing article	section 228
injunction (in Scotland)	section 262

interlocutory relief (in Scotland)	section 262
joint design	section 259(1)
licence (of the design right owner)	sections 222(4), 223(3) and 258
making articles to a design	section 226(2)
marketing (and related expressions)	section 263(2)
original	section 213(4)
plaintiff (in Scotland)	section 262
qualifying individual	section 217(1)
qualifying person	sections 217(1) and (2)
signed	section 261

APPENDIX A2

Part IV CDPA 1988

PART IV

Registered Designs

Amendments of the Registered Designs Act 1949

265.—(1) For section 1 of the [1949 c. 88.] Registered Designs Act 1949 (designs registrable under that Act) substitute – Registrable designs.

'Designs registrable under Act. **1.**—(1) In this Act 'design' means features of shape, configuration, pattern or ornament applied to an article by any industrial process, being features which in the finished article appeal to and are judged by the eye, but does not include –

    (a)   a method or principle of construction, or

    (b)   features of shape or configuration of an article which—(i) are dictated solely by the function which the article has to perform, or (ii) are dependent upon the appearance of another article of which the article is intended by the author of the design to form an integral part.

(2) A design which is new may, upon application by the person claiming to be the proprietor, be registered under this Act in respect of any article, or set of articles, specified in the application.

(3) A design shall not be registered in respect of an article if the appearance of the article is not material, that is, if aesthetic considerations are not normally taken into account to a material extent by persons acquiring or using articles of that description, and would not be so taken into account if the design were to be applied to the article.

(4) A design shall not be regarded as new for the purposes of this Act if it is the same as a design –

    (a)   registered in respect of the same or any other article in pursuance of a prior application, or

    (b)   published in the United Kingdom in respect of the same or any other article before the date of the application,

or if it differs from such a design only in immaterial details or in features which are variants commonly used in the trade.

This subsection has effect subject to the provisions of sections 4, 6 and 16 of this Act.

183

(5) The Secretary of State may by rules provide for excluding from registration under this Act designs for such articles of a primarily literary or artistic character as the Secretary of State thinks fit.'

(2) The above amendment does not apply in relation to applications for registration made before the commencement of this Part; but the provisions of section 266 apply with respect to the right in certain designs registered in pursuance of such an application.

Provisions with respect to certain designs registered in pursuance of application made before commencement.

266.—(1) Where a design is registered under the [1949 c. 88.] Registered Designs Act 1949 in pursuance of an application made after 12th January 1988 and before the commencement of this Part which could not have been registered under section 1 of that Act as substituted by section 265 above –

(a) the right in the registered design expires ten years after the commencement of this Part, if it does not expire earlier in accordance with the 1949 Act, and

(b) any person is, after the commencement of this Part, entitled as of right to a licence to do anything which would otherwise infringe the right in the registered design.

(2) The terms of licence available by virtue of this section shall, in default of agreement, be settled by the registrar of an application by the person requiring the licence; and the terms so settled shall authorise the licensee to do everything which would be an infringement of the right in the registered design in the absence of a licence.

(3) In settling the terms of a licence the registrar shall have regard to such factors as may be prescribed by the Secretary of State by order made by statutory instrument.

No such order shall be made unless a draft of it has been laid before and approved by a resolution of each House of Parliament.

(4) Where the terms of a licence are settled by the registrar, the licence has effect from the date on which the application to the registrar was made.

(5) Section 11B of the 1949 Act (undertaking to take licence of right in infringement proceedings), as inserted by section 270 below, applies where a licence is available as of right under this section, as it applies where a licence is available as of right under section 11A of that Act.

(6) Where a licence is available as of right under this section, a person to whom a licence was granted before the commencement of this Part may apply to the registrar for an order adjusting the terms of that licence.

(7) An appeal lies from any decision of the registrar under this section.

(8) This section shall be construed as one with the [1949 c. 88.] Registered Designs Act 1949.

Authorship and first ownership of designs.

267.—(1) Section 2 of the Registered Designs Act 1949 (proprietorship of designs) is amended as follows.

(2) For subsection (1) substitute –

'(1) The author of a design shall be treated for the purposes of this Act as the original proprietor of the design, subject to the following provisions.

(1A) Where a design is created in pursuance of a commission for money or money's worth, the person commissioning the design shall be treated as the original proprietor of the design.

(1B) Where, in a case not falling within subsection (1A), a design is created by an employee in the course of his employment, his employer shall be treated as the original proprietor of the design.'

(3) After subsection (2) insert –

'(3) In this Act the "author" of a design means the person who creates it.

(4) In the case of a design generated by computer in circumstance such that there is no human author, the person by whom the arrangements necessary for the creation of the design are made shall be taken to be the author.'

(4) The amendments made by this section do not apply in relation to an application for registration made before the commencement of this Part.

268.—(1) For section 7 of the Registered Designs Act 1949 (right given by registration) substitute –

Right given by registration of design.

'Right **7.**—(1) The registration of a design under this Act gives the registered proprietor the exclusive right –

    (a)   to make or import—(i) for sale or hire, or (ii) for use for the purposes of a trade or business, or

    (b)   to sell, hire or offer or expose for sale or hire,

an article in respect of which the design is registered and to which that design or a design not substantially different from it has been applied.

(2) The right in the registered design is infringed by a person who without the licence of the registered proprietor does anything which by virtue of subsection (1) is the exclusive right of the proprietor.

(3) The right in the registered design is also infringed by a person who without the licence of the registered proprietor makes anything for enabling any such article to be made, in the United Kingdom or elsewhere, as mentioned in subsection (1).

(4) The right in the registered design is also infringed by a person who without the licence of the registered proprietor –

    (a)   does anything in relation to a kit that would be an infringement if done in relation to the assembled article (see subsection (1)), or

    (b)   makes anything for enabling a kit to be made or assembled, in the United Kingdom or elsewhere, if the assembled article would be such an article as is mentioned in subsection (1);

and for this purpose a 'kit' means a complete or substantially complete set of components intended to be assembled into an article.

(5) No proceedings shall be taken in respect of an infringement committed before the date on which the certificate of registration of the design under this Act is granted.

(6) The right in a registered design is not infringed by the reproduction of a feature of the design which, by virtue of section 1(1)(b), is left out of account in determining whether the design is registrable.'

(2) The above amendment does not apply in relation to a design registered in pursuance of an application made before the commencement of this Part.

Duration of right in registered design.

269.—(1) For section 8 of the [1949 c. 88.] Registered Designs Act 1949 (period of right) substitute –

'Duration of right in registered design.

8.—(1) The right in a registered design subsists in the first instance for a period of five years from the date of the registration of the design.

(2) The period for which the right subsists may be extended for a second, third, fourth and fifth period of five years, by applying to the registrar for an extension and paying the prescribed renewal fee.

(3) If the first, second, third or fourth period expires without such application and payment being made, the right shall cease to have effect; and the registrar shall, in accordance with rules made by the Secretary of State, notify the proprietor of that fact.

(4) If during the period of six months immediately following the end of that period an application for extension is made and the prescribed renewal fee and any prescribed additional fee is paid, the right shall be treated as if it had never expired, with the result that –

(a) anything done under or in relation to the right during that further period shall be treated as valid,

(b) an act which would have constituted an infringement of the right if it had not expired shall be treated as an infringement, and

(c) an act which would have constituted use of the design for the services of the Crown if the right had not expired shall be treated as such use.

(5) Where it is shown that a registered design –

(a) was at the time it was registered a corresponding design in relation to an artistic work in which copyright subsists, and

(b) by reason of a previous use of that work would not have been registrable but for section 6(4) of this Act (registration despite certain prior applications of design),

the right in the registered design expires when the copyright in that work expires, if that is earlier than the time at which it would otherwise expire, and it may not thereafter be renewed.

(6) The above provisions have effect subject to the proviso to section 4(1) (registration of same design in respect of other articles, &c.).

Restoration of lapsed right in design.

8A.—(1) Where the right in a registered design has expired by reason of a failure to extend, in accordance with section 8(2) or (4), the period for which the right subsists, an application for the restoration of the right in the design may be made to the registrar within the prescribed period.

(2) The application may be made by the person who was the registered proprietor of the design or by any other person who would have been entitled to the right in the design if it had not expired; and where the design was held by

two or more persons jointly, the application may, with the leave of the registrar, be made by one or more of them without joining the others.

(3) Notice of the application shall be published by the registrar in the prescribed manner.

(4) If the registrar is satisfied that the proprietor took reasonable care to see that the period for which the right subsisted was extended in accordance with section 8(2) or (4), he shall, on payment of any unpaid renewal fee and any prescribed additional fee, order the restoration of the right in the design.

(5) The order may be made subject to such conditions as the registrar thinks fit, and if the proprietor of the design does not comply with any condition the registrar may revoke the order and give such consequential directions as he thinks fit.

(6) Rules altering the period prescribed for the purposes of subsection (1) may contain such transitional provisions and savings as appear to the Secretary of State to be necessary or expedient.

8B.—(1)

The effect of an order under section 8A for the restoration of the right in a registered design is as follows.

Effect of order for restoration of right.

(2) Anything done under or in relation to the right during the period between expiry and restoration shall be treated as valid.

(3) Anything done during that period which would have constituted an infringement if the right had not expired shall be treated as an infringement –

(a) if done at a time when it was possible for an application for extension to be made under section 8(4); or

(b) if it was a continuation or repetition of an earlier infringing act.

(4) If, after it was no longer possible for such an application for extension to be made and before publication of notice of the application for restoration, a person –

(a) began in good faith to do an act which would have constituted an infringement of the right in the design if it had not expired, or

(b) made in good faith effective and serious preparations to do such an act,

he has the right to continue to do the act or, as the case may be, to do the act, notwithstanding the restoration of the right in the design; but this does not extend to granting a licence to another person to do the act.

(5) If the act was done, or the preparations were made, in the course of a business, the person entitled to the right conferred by subsection (4) may –

(a) authorise the doing of that act by any partners of his for the time being in that business, and

(b) assign that right, or transmit it on death (or in the case of a body corporate on its dissolution), to any person who acquires that part of the business in the course of which the act was done or the preparations were made.

(6) Where an article is disposed of to another in exercise of the rights conferred by subsection (4) or subsection (5), that other and any person claiming through him may deal with the article in the same way as if it had been disposed of by the registered proprietor of the design.

(7) The above provisions apply in relation to the use of a registered design for the services of the Crown as they apply in relation to infringement of the right in the design.'

(2) The above amendment does not apply in relation to the right in a design registered in pursuance of an application made before the commencement of this Part.

Powers
exercisable
for protec-
tion of the
public
interest.

270. In the [1949 c. 88.] Registered Designs Act 1949 after section 11 insert –

11A.—(1) Where a report of the Monopolies and Mergers Commission has been laid before Parliament containing conclusions to the effect –

    (a) on a monopoly reference, that a monopoly situation exists and facts found by the Commission operate or may be expected to operate against the public interest,

    (b) on a merger reference, that a merger situation qualifying for investigation has been created and the creation of the situation, or particular elements in or consequences of it specified in the report, operate or may be expected to operate against the public interest,

    (c) on a competition reference, that a person was engaged in an anti-competitive practice which operated or may be expected to operate against the public interest, or

    (d) on a reference under section 11 of the Competition Act 1980 (reference of public bodies and certain other persons), that a person is pursuing a course of conduct which operates against the public interest,

the appropriate Minister or Ministers may apply to the registrar to take action under this section.

(2) Before making an application the appropriate Minister or Ministers shall publish, in such a manner as he or they think appropriate, a notice describing the nature of the proposed application and shall consider any representations which may be made within 30 days of such publication by persons whose interests appear to him or them to be affected.

(3) If on an application under this section it appears to the registrar that the matters specified in the Commission's report as being those which in the Commission's opinion operate or operated or may be expected to operate against the public interest include –

    (a) conditions in licences granted in respect of a registered design by its proprietor restricting the use of the design by the licensee or the right of the proprietor to grant other licences, or

    (b) a refusal by the proprietor of a registered design to grant licences on reasonable terms,

he may by order cancel or modify any such condition or may, instead or in addition, make an entry in the register to the effect that licences in respect of the design are to be available as of right.

(4) The terms of a licence available by virtue of this section shall, in default of agreement, be settled by the registrar on an application by the person requiring the licence; and terms so settled shall authorise the licensee to do everything which would be an infringement of the right in the registered design in the absence of a licence.

(5) Where the terms of a licence are settled by the registrar the licence has effect from the date on which the application to him was made.

(6) An appeal lies from any order of the registrar under this section.

(7) In this section 'the appropriate Minister or Ministers' means the Minister or Ministers to whom the report of the Monopolies and Mergers Commission was made.

11B.—(1) If in proceedings for infringement of the right in a registered design in respect of which a licence is available as of right under section 11A of this Act the defendant undertakes to take a licence on such terms as may be agreed or, in default of agreement, settled by the registrar under that section – Undertaking to take licence of right in infringement proceedings.

    (a)   no injunction shall be granted against him, and

    (b)   the amount recoverable against him by way of damages or on an account of profits shall not exceed double the amount which would have been payable by him as licensee if such a licence on those terms had been granted before the earliest infringement.

(2) An undertaking may be given at any time before final order in the proceedings, without any admission of liability.

(3) Nothing in this section affects the remedies available in respect of an infringement committed before licences of right were available.'

271.—(1) In Schedule 1 to the [1949 c. 88.] Registered Designs Act 1949 (Crown use), after paragraph 2 insert – Crown use: compensation for loss of profit.

'Compensation for loss of profit.   **2A.**—(1) Where Crown use is made of a registered design, the government department concerned shall pay –

    (a)   to the registered proprietor, or

    (b)   if there is an exclusive licence in force in respect of the design, to the exclusive licensee,

compensation for any loss resulting from his not being awarded a contract to supply the articles to which the design is applied.

(2) Compensation is payable only to the extent that such a contract could have been fulfilled from his existing manufacturing capacity; but is payable notwithstanding the existence of circumstances rendering him ineligible for the award of such a contract.

(3) In determining the loss, regard shall be had to the profit which would have been made on such a contract and to the extent to which any manufacturing capacity was underused.

(4) No compensation is payable in respect of any failure to secure contracts for the supply of articles to which the design is applied otherwise than for the services of the Crown.

(5) The amount payable under this paragraph shall, if not agreed between the registered proprietor or licensee and the government department concerned with the approval of the Treasury, be determined by the court on a reference under paragraph 3; and it is in addition to any amount payable under paragraph 1 or 2 of this Schedule.

(6) In this paragraph –

'Crown use', in relation to a design, means the doing of anything by virtue of paragraph 1 which would otherwise be an infringement of the right in the design; and

'the government department concerned', in relation to such use, means the government department by whom or on whose authority the act was done.

(2) In paragraph 3 of that Schedule (reference of disputes as to Crown use), for sub-paragraph (1) substitute –

'(1) Any dispute as to –

    (a)   the exercise by a Government department, or a person authorised by a Government department, of the powers conferred by paragraph 1 of this Schedule,

    (b)   terms for the use of a design for the services of the Crown under that paragraph,

    (c)   the right of any person to receive any part of a payment made under paragraph 1(3), or

    (d)   the right of any person to receive a payment under paragraph 2A,

may be referred to the court by either party to the dispute.'

(3) The above amendments apply in relation to any Crown use of a registered design after the commencement of this section, even if the terms for such use were settled before commencement.

Minor and consequential amendments. **272.** The [1949 c. 88.] Registered Designs Act 1949 is further amended in accordance with Schedule 3 which contains minor amendments and amendments consequential upon the provisions of this Act.

Supplementary

Text of Registered Designs Act 1949 as amended. **273.** Schedule 4 contains the text of the Registered Designs Act 1949 as amended.

©Crown copyright 1988

APPENDIX B1

The Registered Designs Regulations 2001 (SI 2001/3949)

STATUTORY INSTRUMENTS

2001 No. 3949

DESIGNS

The Registered Designs Regulations 2001

Made   *8th December 2001*
Coming into force   .   *9th December 2001*

Whereas a draft of the following Regulations has been approved by resolution of each House of Parliament:

Now, therefore, the Secretary of State, being designated[1] for the purposes of section 2(2) of the European Communities Act 1972[2] in relation to measures relating to the legal protection of designs, in exercise of the powers conferred on her by the said section 2(2) hereby makes the following Regulations:

Citation, commencement and extent

1.—(1) These Regulations may be cited as the Registered Designs Regulations 2001 and shall come into force on the day after the day on which they are made.

(2) Subject to paragraph (3), these Regulations extend to England and Wales, Scotland and Northern Ireland.

(3) The amendments made by these Regulations to the Chartered Associations (Protection of Names and Uniforms) Act 1926 do not extend to Northern Ireland.

Designs registrable under the 1949 Act

2. For section 1 of the Registered Designs Act 1949[3] (designs registrable under Act) there shall be substituted –

'Registration of designs.

1.—(1) A design may, subject to the following provisions of this Act, be registered under this Act on the making of an application for registration.

(2) In this Act 'design' means the appearance of the whole or a part of a product resulting from the features of, in particular, the lines, contours, colours, shape, texture or materials of the product or its ornamentation.

(3) In this Act –

'complex product' means a product which is composed of at least two replaceable component parts permitting disassembly and reassembly of the product; and

'product' means any industrial or handicraft item other than a computer program; and, in particular, includes packaging, get-up, graphic symbols, typographic type-faces and parts intended to be assembled into a complex product.

Substantive grounds for refusal of registration.

1A.—(1) The following shall be refused registration under this Act –

    (a)   anything which does not fulfil the requirements of section 1(2) of this Act;

    (b)   designs which do not fulfil the requirements of sections 1B to 1D of this Act;

    (c)   designs to which a ground of refusal mentioned in Schedule A1 to this Act applies.

(2) A design ('the later design') shall be refused registration under this Act if it is not new or does not have individual character when compared with a design which –

    (a)   has been made available to the public on or after the relevant date; but

    (b)   is protected as from a date prior to the relevant date by virtue of registration under this Act or an application for such registration.

(3) In subsection (2) above 'the relevant date' means the date on which the application for the registration of the later design was made or is treated by virtue of section 3B(2), (3) or (5) or 14(2) of this Act as having been made.

Requirement of novelty and individual character.

1B.—(1) A design shall be protected by a right in a registered design to the extent that the design is new and has individual character.

(2) For the purposes of subsection (1) above, a design is new if no identical design or no design whose features differ only in immaterial details has been made available to the public before the relevant date.

(3) For the purposes of subsection (1) above, a design has individual character if the overall impression it produces on the informed user differs from the overall impression produced on such a user by any design which has been made available to the public before the relevant date.

(4) In determining the extent to which a design has individual character, the degree of freedom of the author in creating the design shall be taken into consideration.

(5) For the purposes of this section, a design has been made available to the public before the relevant date if –

    (a)   it has been published (whether following registration or otherwise), exhibited, used in trade or otherwise disclosed before that date; and

    (b)   the disclosure does not fall within subsection (6) below.

(6) A disclosure falls within this subsection if –

    (a)   it could not reasonably have become known before the relevant date in the normal course of business to persons carrying on business in the European Economic Area and specialising in the sector concerned;

    (b)   it was made to a person other than the designer, or any successor in title of his, under conditions of confidentiality (whether express or implied);

    (c)   it was made by the designer, or any successor in title of his, during the period of 12 months immediately preceding the relevant date;

    (d)   it was made by a person other than the designer, or any successor in title of his, during the period of 12 months immediately preceding the relevant date in consequence of information provided or other action taken by the designer or any successor in title of his; or

    (e)   it was made during the period of 12 months immediately preceding the relevant date as a consequence of an abuse in relation to the designer or any successor in title of his.

(7) In subsections (2), (3), (5) and (6) above 'the relevant date' means the date on which the application for the registration of the design was made or is treated by virtue of section 3B(2), (3) or (5) or 14(2) of this Act as having been made.

(8) For the purposes of this section, a design applied to or incorporated in a product which constitutes a component part of a complex product shall only be considered to be new and to have individual character –

    (a)   if the component part, once it has been incorporated into the complex product, remains visible during normal use of the complex product; and

    (b)   to the extent that those visible features of the component part are in themselves new and have individual character.

(9) In subsection (8) above 'normal use' means use by the end user; but does not include any maintenance, servicing or repair work in relation to the product.

Designs dictated by their technical function.
    1C.—(1) A right in a registered design shall not subsist in features of appearance of a product which are solely dictated by the product's technical function.

(2) A right in a registered design shall not subsist in features of appearance of a product which must necessarily be reproduced in their exact form and dimensions so as to permit the product in which the design is incorporated or to which it is applied to be mechanically connected to, or placed in, around or against, another product so that either product may perform its function.

(3) Subsection (2) above does not prevent a right in a registered design subsisting in a design serving the purpose of allowing multiple assembly or connection of mutually interchangeable products within a modular system.

Designs contrary to public policy or morality.
    1D. A right in a registered design shall not subsist in a design which is contrary to public policy or to accepted principles of morality.'

Designs registrable under the 1949 Act: emblems etc.
    3. Before Schedule 1 to the Registered Designs Act 1949 there shall be inserted –

'SCHEDULE A1

Grounds for refusal of registration in relation to emblems etc.

Grounds for refusal in relation to certain emblems etc.

1.—(1) A design shall be refused registration under this Act if it involves the use of –

    (a)   the Royal arms, or any of the principal armorial bearings of the Royal arms, or any insignia or device so nearly resembling the Royal arms or any such armorial bearing as to be likely to be mistaken for them or it;

    (b)   a representation of the Royal crown or any of the Royal flags;

    (c)   a representation of Her Majesty or any member of the Royal family, or any colourable imitation thereof; or

    (d)   words, letters or devices likely to lead persons to think that the applicant either has or recently has had Royal patronage or authorisation;

unless it appears to the registrar that consent for such use has been given by or on behalf of Her Majesty or (as the case may be) the relevant member of the Royal family.

(2) A design shall be refused registration under this Act if it involves the use of –

    (a)   the national flag of the United Kingdom (commonly known as the Union Jack); or

    (b)   the flag of England, Wales, Scotland, Northern Ireland or the Isle of Man,

and it appears to the registrar that the use would be misleading or grossly offensive.

(3) A design shall be refused registration under this Act if it involves the use of –

    (a)   arms to which a person is entitled by virtue of a grant of arms by the Crown; or

    (b)   insignia so nearly resembling such arms as to be likely to be mistaken for them;

unless it appears to the registrar that consent for such use has been given by or on behalf of the person concerned and the use is not in any way contrary to the law of arms.

(4) A design shall be refused registration under this Act if it involves the use of a controlled representation within the meaning of the Olympic Symbol etc. (Protection) Act 1995 unless it appears to the registrar that –

    (a)   the application is made by the person for the time being appointed under section 1(2) of the Olympic Symbol etc. (Protection) Act 1995 (power of Secretary of State to appoint a person as the proprietor of the Olympics association right); or

    (b)   consent for such use has been given by or on behalf of the person mentioned in paragraph (a) above.

Grounds for refusal in relation to emblems etc. of Paris Convention countries

2.—(1) A design shall be refused registration under this Act if it involves the use of the flag of a Paris Convention country unless –

    (a)   the authorisation of the competent authorities of that country has been given for the registration; or

    (b)   it appears to the registrar that the use of the flag in the manner proposed is permitted without such authorisation.

(2) A design shall be refused registration under this Act if it involves the use of the armorial bearings or any other state emblem of a Paris Convention country which is protected under the Paris Convention unless the authorisation of the competent authorities of that country has been given for the registration.

(3) A design shall be refused registration under this Act if –

    (a)   the design involves the use of an official sign or hallmark adopted by a Paris Convention country and indicating control and warranty;

    (b)   the sign or hallmark is protected under the Paris Convention; and

    (c)   the design could be applied to or incorporated in goods of the same, or a similar, kind as those in relation to which the sign or hallmark indicates control and warranty;

unless the authorisation of the competent authorities of that country has been given for the registration.

(4) The provisions of this paragraph as to national flags and other state emblems, and official signs or hallmarks, apply equally to anything which from a heraldic point of view imitates any such flag or other emblem, or sign or hallmark.

(5) Nothing in this paragraph prevents the registration of a design on the application of a national of a country who is authorised to make use of a state emblem, or official sign or hallmark, of that country, notwithstanding that it is similar to that of another country.

Grounds for refusal in relation to emblems etc. of certain international organisations

3.—(1) This paragraph applies to –

    (a)   the armorial bearings, flags or other emblems; and

    (b)   the abbreviations and names,

of international intergovernmental organisations of which one or more Paris Convention countries are members.

(2) A design shall be refused registration under this Act if it involves the use of any such emblem, abbreviation or name which is protected under the Paris Convention unless –

    (a)   the authorisation of the international organisation concerned has been given for the registration; or

    (b)   it appears to the registrar that the use of the emblem, abbreviation or name in the manner proposed –

      (i)   is not such as to suggest to the public that a connection exists between the organisation and the design; or

     (ii)   is not likely to mislead the public as to the existence of a connection between the user and the organisation.

(3) The provisions of this paragraph as to emblems of an international organisation apply equally to anything which from a heraldic point of view imitates any such emblem.

(4) Nothing in this paragraph affects the rights of a person whose *bona fide* use of the design in question began before 4th January 1962 (when the relevant provisions of the Paris Convention entered into force in relation to the United Kingdom).

Paragraphs 2 and 3: supplementary

4.—(1) For the purposes of paragraph 2 above state emblems of a Paris Convention country (other than the national flag), and official signs or hallmarks, shall be regarded as protected under the Paris Convention only if, or to the extent that –

    (a)   the country in question has notified the United Kingdom in accordance with Article 6ter(3) of the Convention that it desires to protect that emblem, sign or hallmark;

    (b)   the notification remains in force; and

    (c)   the United Kingdom has not objected to it in accordance with Article 6*ter*(4) or any such objection has been withdrawn.

(2) For the purposes of paragraph 3 above the emblems, abbreviations and names of an international organisation shall be regarded as protected under the Paris Convention only if, or to the extent that –

    (a)   the organisation in question has notified the United Kingdom in accordance with Article 6*ter*(3) of the Convention that it desires to protect that emblem, abbreviation or name;

    (b)   the notification remains in force; and

    (c)   the United Kingdom has not objected to it in accordance with Article 6*ter*(4) or any such objection has been withdrawn.

(3) Notification under Article 6*ter*(3) of the Paris Convention shall have effect only in relation to applications for the registration of designs made more than two months after the receipt of the notification.

Interpretation

5. In this Schedule –

'a Paris Convention country' means a country, other than the United Kingdom, which is a party to the Paris Convention; and

'the Paris Convention' means the Paris Convention for the Protection of Industrial Property of 20th March 1883.'

Registration of designs: general

4. For section 3 of the Registered Designs Act 1949[4] (proceedings for registration) there shall be substituted –

'Applications for registration.

3.—(1) An application for the registration of a design shall be made in the prescribed form and shall be filed at the Patent Office in the prescribed manner.

(2) An application for the registration of a design shall be made by the person claiming to be the proprietor of the design.

(3) An application for the registration of a design in which national unregistered design right subsists shall be made by the person claiming to be the design right owner.

(4) For the purpose of deciding whether, and to what extent, a design is new or has individual character, the registrar may make such searches (if any) as he thinks fit.

(5) An application for the registration of a design which, owing to any default or neglect on the part of the applicant, has not been completed so as to enable registration to be effected within such time as may be prescribed shall be deemed to be abandoned.

Determination of applications for registration.

3A.—(1) Subject as follows, the registrar shall not refuse an application for the registration of a design.

(2) If it appears to the registrar that an application for the registration of a design has not been made in accordance with any rules made under this Act, he may refuse the application.

(3) If it appears to the registrar that an application for the registration of a design has not been made in accordance with sections 3(2) and (3) and 14(1) of this Act, he shall refuse the application.

(4) If it appears to the registrar that any ground for refusal of registration mentioned in section 1A of this Act applies in relation to an application for the registration of a design, he shall refuse the application.

Modification of applications for registration.

3B.—(1) The registrar may, at any time before an application for the registration of a design is determined, permit the applicant to make such modifications of the application as the registrar thinks fit.

(2) Where an application for the registration of a design has been modified before it has been determined in such a way that the design has been altered significantly, the registrar may, for the purpose of deciding whether and to what extent the design is new or has individual character, direct that the application shall be treated as having been made on the date on which it was so modified.

(3) Where –

    (a)   an application for the registration of a design has disclosed more than one design and has been modified before it has been determined to exclude one or more designs from the application; and

    (b)   a subsequent application for the registration of a design so excluded has, within such period (if any) as has been prescribed for such applications, been made by the person who made the earlier application or his successor in title,

the registrar may, for the purpose of deciding whether and to what extent the design is new or has individual character, direct that the subsequent application shall be treated as having been made on the date on which the earlier application was, or is treated as having been, made.

(4) Where an application for the registration of a design has been refused on any ground mentioned in section 1A(1)(b) or (c) of this Act, the application may be modified by the applicant if it appears to the registrar that –

    (a)   the identity of the design is retained; and
    (b)   the modifications have been made in accordance with any rules made under this Act.

(5) An application modified under subsection (4) above shall be treated as the original application and, in particular, as made on the date on which the original application was made or is treated as having been made.

(6) Any modification under this section may, in particular, be effected by making a partial disclaimer in relation to the application.

Date of registration of designs.
    3C.—(1) Subject as follows, a design, when registered, shall be registered as of the date on which the application was made or is treated as having been made.

(2) Subsection (1) above shall not apply to an application which is treated as having been made on a particular date by section 14(2) of this Act or by virtue of the operation of section 3B(3) or (5) of this Act by reference to section 14(2) of this Act.

(3) A design, when registered, shall be registered as of –

    (a)   in the case of an application which is treated as having been made on a particular date by section 14(2) of this Act, the date on which the application was made;
    (b)   in the case of an application which is treated as having been made on a particular date by virtue of the operation of section 3B(3) of this Act by reference to section 14(2) of this Act, the date on which the earlier application was made;
    (c)   in the case of an application which is treated as having been made on a particular date by virtue of the operation of section 3B(5) of this Act by reference to section 14(2) of this Act, the date on which the original application was made.

Appeals in relation to applications for registration.
    3D. An appeal lies from any decision of the registrar under section 3A or 3B of this Act.'

Right given by registration under the 1949 Act
    5. For section 7 of the Registered Designs Act 1949[5] (right given by registration) there shall be substituted –

'Right given by registration.

7.—(1) The registration of a design under this Act gives the registered proprietor the exclusive right to use the design and any design which does not
produce on the informed user a different overall impression.

(2) For the purposes of subsection (1) above and section 7A of this Act any
reference to the use of a design includes a reference to –

(a)   the making, offering, putting on the market, importing, exporting
       or using of a product in which the design is incorporated or to
       which it is applied; or
(b)   stocking such a product for those purposes.

(3) In determining for the purposes of subsection (1) above whether a design
produces a different overall impression on the informed user, the degree of
freedom of the author in creating his design shall be taken into consideration.

(4) The right conferred by subsection (1) above is subject to any limitation
attaching to the registration in question (including, in particular, any partial disclaimer or any declaration by the registrar or a court of partial invalidity).

Infringements of rights in registered designs.

7A.—(1) Subject as follows, the right in a registered design is infringed by a
person who, without the consent of the registered proprietor, does anything
which by virtue of section 7 of this Act is the exclusive right of the registered
proprietor.

(2) The right in a registered design is not infringed by –

(a)   an act which is done privately and for purposes which are not
       commercial;
(b)   an act which is done for experimental purposes;
(c)   an act of reproduction for teaching purposes or for the purpose of
       making citations provided that the conditions mentioned in subsec-
       tion (3) below are satisfied;
(d)   the use of equipment on ships or aircraft which are registered in
       another country but which are temporarily in the United Kingdom;
(e)   the importation into the United Kingdom of spare parts or acces-
       sories for the purpose of repairing such ships or aircraft; or
(f)   the carrying out of repairs on such ships or aircraft.

(3) The conditions mentioned in this subsection are –

(a)   the act of reproduction is compatible with fair trade practice and
       does not unduly prejudice the normal exploitation of the design; and

(b)   mention is made of the source.

(4) The right in a registered design is not infringed by an act which relates to
a product in which any design protected by the registration is incorporated or to
which it is applied if the product has been put on the market in the European
Economic Area by the registered proprietor or with his consent.

(5) The right in a registered design of a component part which may be used
for the purpose of the repair of a complex product so as to restore its original
appearance is not infringed by the use for that purpose of any design protected
by the registration.

(6) No proceedings shall be taken in respect of an infringement of the right in a registered design committed before the date on which the certificate of registration of the design under this Act is granted.'

Removal of compulsory licence regimes

6.—(1) Section 10 of the Registered Designs Act 1949 (compulsory licence in respect of registered design) shall be omitted.

(2) In section 11A of that Act[6] (powers exercisable for protection of the public interest), in subsection (3) (power to ensure licences available as of right) –

    (a)   paragraph (b) and the word 'or' immediately preceding it shall be omitted; and

    (b)   the words from 'or may, instead' to the end of the subsection shall be omitted.

Cancellation and invalidation of registration

7. For section 11 of the Registered Designs Act 1949[7] (cancellation of registration) there shall be substituted –

'Cancellation of registration.

11. The registrar may, upon a request made in the prescribed manner by the registered proprietor, cancel the registration of a design.

Grounds for invalidity of registration.

11ZA.—(1) The registration of a design may be declared invalid on any of the grounds mentioned in section 1A of this Act.

(2) The registration of a design may be declared invalid on the ground of the registered proprietor not being the proprietor of the design and the proprietor of the design objecting.

(3) The registration of a design involving the use of an earlier distinctive sign may be declared invalid on the ground of an objection by the holder of rights to the sign which include the right to prohibit in the United Kingdom such use of the sign.

(4) The registration of a design constituting an unauthorised use of a work protected by the law of copyright in the United Kingdom may be declared invalid on the ground of an objection by the owner of the copyright.

(5) In this section and sections 11ZB, 11ZC and 11ZE of this Act (other than section 11ZE(1)) references to the registration of a design include references to the former registration of a design; and these sections shall apply, with necessary modifications, in relation to such former registrations.

Applications for declaration of invalidity.

11ZB.—(1) Any person interested may make an application to the registrar for a declaration of invalidity on the ground mentioned in section 1A(1)(a) or (b) of this Act.

(2) Any person concerned by the use in question may make an application to the registrar for a declaration of invalidity on the ground mentioned in section 1A(1)(c) of this Act.

(3) The relevant person may make an application to the registrar for a declaration of invalidity on the ground mentioned in section 1A(2) of this Act.

(4) In subsection (3) above 'the relevant person' means, in relation to an earlier design protected by virtue of registration under this Act or an application for such registration, the registered proprietor of the design or (as the case may be) the applicant.

(5) The person able to make an objection under subsection (2), (3) or (4) of section 11ZA of this Act may make an application to the registrar for a declaration of invalidity on the ground mentioned in that subsection.

(6) An application may be made under this section in relation to a design at any time after the design has been registered.

Determination of applications for declaration of invalidity.

11ZC.—(1) This section applies where an application has been made to the registrar for a declaration of invalidity in relation to a registration.

(2) If it appears to the registrar that the application has not been made in accordance with any rules made under this Act, he may refuse the application.

(3) If it appears to the registrar that the application has not been made in accordance with section 11ZB of this Act, he shall refuse the application.

(4) Subject to subsections (2) and (3) above, the registrar shall make a declaration of invalidity if it appears to him that the ground of invalidity specified in the application has been established in relation to the registration.

(5) Otherwise the registrar shall refuse the application.

(6) A declaration of invalidity may be a declaration of partial invalidity.

Modification of registration.

11ZD.—(1) Subsections (2) and (3) below apply where the registrar intends to declare the registration of a design invalid on any ground mentioned in section 1A(1)(b) or (c) or 11ZA(3) or (4) of this Act.

(2) The registrar shall inform the registered proprietor of that fact.

(3) The registered proprietor may make an application to the registrar for the registrar to make such modifications to the registration of the design as the registered proprietor specifies in his application.

(4) Such modifications may, in particular, include the inclusion on the register of a partial disclaimer by the registered proprietor.

(5) If it appears to the registrar that the application has not been made in accordance with any rules made under this Act, the registrar may refuse the application.

(6) If it appears to the registrar that the identity of the design is not retained or the modified registration would be invalid by virtue of section 11ZA of this Act, the registrar shall refuse the application.

(7) Otherwise the registrar shall make the specified modifications.

(8) A modification of a registration made under this section shall have effect, and be treated always to have had effect, from the grant of registration.

Effect of cancellation or invalidation of registration.

11ZE.—(1) A cancellation of registration under section 11 of this Act takes effect from the date of the registrar's decision or from such other date as the registrar may direct.

(2) Where the registrar declares the registration of a design invalid to any extent, the registration shall to that extent be treated as having been invalid from the date of registration or from such other date as the registrar may direct.

Appeals in relation to cancellation or invalidation.

11ZF. An appeal lies from any decision of the registrar under section 11 to 11ZE of this Act.'

Rectification of register

8.—(1) Section 20 of the Registered Designs Act 1949[8] (rectification of register) shall be amended as follows.

(2) In subsection (1) (applications for rectification) for the words 'any person aggrieved' there shall be substituted 'the relevant person'.

(3) After subsection (1) there shall be inserted –

'(1A) In subsection (1) above 'the relevant person' means –
- (a) in the case of an application invoking any ground referred to in section 1A(1)(c) of this Act, any person concerned by the use in question;
- (b) in the case of an application invoking the ground mentioned in section 1A(2) of this Act, the appropriate person;
- (c) in the case of an application invoking any ground mentioned in section 11ZA(2), (3) or (4) of this Act, the person able to make the objection;
- (d) in any other case, any person aggrieved.

(1B) In subsection (1A) above 'the appropriate person' means, in relation to an earlier design protected by virtue of registration under this Act or an application for such registration, the registered proprietor of the design or (as the case may be) the applicant.'

(4) After subsection (5) there shall be added –

'(6) Orders which may be made by the court under this section include, in particular, declarations of partial invalidity.'

Other modifications of enactments

9.—(1) The amendments specified in Schedule 1 (consequential amendments) shall have effect.

(2) The repeals specified in Schedule 2 shall have effect.

Transitional provisions: pending applications

10.—(1) This Regulation applies to applications for registration under the Registered Designs Act 1949 which have been made but not finally determined before the coming into force of these Regulations ('pending applications').

(2) The Act of 1949 as it has effect immediately before the coming into force of these Regulations shall continue to apply in relation to pending applications so far as it relates to the determination of such applications.

(3) Accordingly the amendments and repeals made by these Regulations shall not apply in relation to the determination of such applications.

Transitional provisions: transitional registrations

11.—(1) This Regulation applies to any registration under the Registered Designs Act 1949 which results from the determination of a pending application (within the meaning of Regulation 10).

(2) The Act of 1949 as it has effect immediately before the coming into force of these Regulations shall continue to apply in relation to registrations to which this Regulation applies ('transitional registrations') so far as the Act relates to the cancellation or invalidation of such registrations (other than cancellation by virtue of section 11(3) of that Act).

(3) Accordingly the amendments and repeals made by these Regulations shall, so far as they relate to the cancellation or invalidation of registrations, not apply in relation to transitional registrations.

(4) The amendments and repeals made by these Regulations shall otherwise (and subject to paragraphs (5) to (9) and Regulation 14) apply in relation to transitional registrations.

(5) In the application by virtue of paragraph (4) of the amendments made by Regulation 5, the fact that transitional registrations are in respect of any articles, or sets of articles, shall be disregarded.

(6) The amendments made by Regulation 4 shall not operate so as to determine the dates of registration of designs to which transitional registrations apply; and these dates shall be determined by reference to the Act of 1949 as it has effect immediately before the coming into force of these Regulations.

(7) Where –

(a) any such date of registration for the purposes of calculating the period for which the right in a registered design subsists, or any extension of that period, under section 8 of the Act of 1949 is determined by virtue of section 14(2) of that Act; and

(b) that date is earlier than the date which would otherwise have been the date of registration for those purposes;

the difference between the two dates shall be added to the first period of five years for which the right in the registered design is to subsist.

(8) Any reference in section 8 of the Act of 1949 to a period of five years shall, in the case of any such period which is extended by virtue of paragraph (7), be treated as a reference to the extended period.

(9) The repeal by these Regulations of the proviso in section 4(1) of the Act of 1949 and of the reference to it in section 8 of that Act shall not apply to the right in a design to which a transitional registration applies.

Transitional provisions: post-1989 registrations

12.—(1) This Regulation applies to –

(a) any registration under the Registered Designs Act 1949 which –

(i) has resulted from an application made on or after 1st August 1989 and before the coming into force of these Regulations; and

(ii) has given rise to a right in a registered design which is in force at the coming into force of these Regulations;

(b) any registration under the Act of 1949 which –

(i) has resulted from an application made on or after 1st August 1989 and before the coming into force of these Regulations; and

(ii) has given rise to a right in a registered design which is not in force at the coming into force of these Regulations but which is capable of being treated as never having ceased to be in force by virtue of section 8(4) of the Act of 1949 or of being restored by virtue of sections 8A and 8B of that Act; and

(c) any registration which subsequently ceases to fall within sub-paragraph (b) because the right in the registered design has been treated or restored as mentioned in paragraph (ii) of that sub-paragraph.

(2) The Act of 1949 as it has effect immediately before the coming into force of these Regulations shall continue to apply in relation to registrations to which this Regulation applies ('post-1989 registrations') so far as the Act relates to the cancellation or invalidation of such registrations (other than cancellation by virtue of section 11(3) of that Act and by reference to an expiry of copyright occurring on or after the coming into force of these Regulations).

(3) Accordingly the amendments and repeals made by these Regulations shall, so far as they relate to the cancellation or invalidation of registrations, not apply in relation to post-1989 registrations.

(4) The amendments and repeals made by these Regulations shall otherwise apply (subject to paragraphs (5) to (9) and Regulation 14) in relation to post-1989 registrations.

(5) In the application by virtue of paragraph (4) of the amendments made by Regulation 5, the fact that post-1989 registrations are in respect of any articles, or sets of articles, shall be disregarded.

(6) The amendments made by Regulation 4 shall not operate so as to alter the dates of registration of designs to which post-1989 registrations apply.

(7) Where –

(a) any such date of registration for the purposes of calculating the period for which the right in a registered design subsists, or any extension of that period, under section 8 of the Act of 1949 was determined by virtue of section 14(2) of that Act; and

(b) that date is earlier than the date which would otherwise have been the date of registration for those purposes;

the difference between the two dates shall be added to any period of five years which is current on the coming into force of these Regulations or, if no such period is current but a subsequent extension or restoration is effected under section 8, or sections 8A and 8B, of the Act of 1949, to the period resulting from that extension or restoration.

(8) Any reference in section 8 of the Act of 1949 to a period of five years shall, in the case of any such period which is extended by virtue of paragraph (7), be treated as a reference to the extended period.

(9) The repeal by these Regulations of the proviso in section 4(1) of the Act of 1949 and the reference to it in section 8 of that Act shall not apply to the right in a design to which a post-1989 registration applies.

Transitional provisions: pre-1989 registrations

13.—(1) This Regulation applies to –

(a) any registration under the Registered Designs Act 1949 which –
  (i) has resulted from an application made before 1st August 1989; and
  (ii) has given rise to a copyright in a registered design which is in force at the coming into force of these Regulations;

(b) any registration under the Act of 1949 which –
  (i) has resulted from an application made before 1st August 1989; and
  (ii) has given rise to a copyright in a registered design which is not in force at the coming into force of these Regulations but which would be capable of coming back into force by virtue of an extension of the period of copyright under section 8(2) of the Act of 1949 if that provision were amended as set out in paragraph (8); and

(c) any registration which subsequently ceases to fall within sub-paragraph (b) because the copyright in the registered design has come back into force by virtue of an extension of the period of copyright under section 8(2) of the Act of 1949 as amended by paragraph (8).

(2) Subject as follows, the amendments and repeals made by these Regulations shall not apply to any provision of the Act of 1949 which only has effect in relation to applications for registration made before 1st August 1989 or any registrations resulting from such applications.

(3) Any such provision and any other provision of the Act of 1949 as it has effect immediately before the coming into force of these Regulations in relation to registrations which fall within paragraph (1) ('pre-1989 registrations') shall continue to apply so far as it relates to the cancellation or invalidation of pre-1989 registrations (other than cancellation by virtue of section 11(3) of that Act and by reference to an expiry of copyright occurring on or after the coming into force of these Regulations).

(4) Accordingly the amendments and repeals made by these Regulations shall, so far as they relate to the cancellation or invalidation of registrations, not apply in relation to pre-1989 registrations.

(5) The amendments and repeals made by these Regulations shall otherwise apply (subject to paragraphs (2) and (9) to (12) and Regulation 14) in relation to pre-1989 registrations.

(6) Amendments and repeals corresponding to the amendments and repeals made by these Regulations (other than those relating to the cancellation or invalidation of registrations) shall be treated as having effect, with necessary modifications and subject to Regulation 14, in relation to any provision of the Act of 1949 which only has effect in relation to applications for registration made before 1st August 1989 or any registrations resulting from such applications.

(7) In the application by virtue of paragraph (6) of amendments corresponding to those made by Regulation 5, the fact that pre-1989 registrations are in respect of any articles, or sets of articles, shall be disregarded.

(8) In section 8(2) of the Act of 1949 as it has effect in relation to pre-1989 registrations (period of copyright) –

(a) after the words 'second period', where they appear for the second time, there shall be inserted 'and for a fourth period of five years from the expiration of the third period and for a fifth period of five years from the expiration of the fourth period';

(b) after the words 'second or third' there shall be inserted 'or fourth or fifth'; and

(c) after the words 'second period', where they appear for the third time, there shall be inserted 'or the third period or the fourth period'.

(9) The amendments made by Regulation 4 shall not operate so as to alter the dates of registration of designs to which pre-1989 registrations apply.

(10) Where –

(a) the date of registration for the purposes of calculating the period of copyright, or any extension of that period, under section 8(2) of the Act of 1949 as it has effect in relation to pre-1989 registrations was determined by virtue of section 14(2) of that Act; and

(b) that date is earlier than the date which would otherwise have been the date of registration for those purposes;

the difference between the two dates shall be added to any period of five years which is current on the coming into force of these Regulations or, if no such period is current but a subsequent extension is effected under section 8 of the Act of 1949 as amended by paragraph (8), to the period resulting from that extension.

(11) Any reference in section 8(2) of the Act of 1949 as amended by paragraph (8) to a period of five years shall, in the case of any such period which is extended by virtue of paragraph (10), be treated as a reference to the extended period.

(12) The repeal by these Regulations of the proviso in section 4(1) of the Act of 1949 shall not apply to the right in a design to which a pre-1989 registration applies.

Other transitional provisions
14.—(1) Any licence which –

(a) permits anything which would otherwise be an infringement under the Registered Designs Act 1949 of the right in a registered design or the copyright in a registered design; and

(b) was granted by the registered proprietor of the design, or under section 10 or 11A of the Act of 1949, before the coming into force of these Regulations,

shall continue in force, with necessary modifications, on or after the making of these Regulations.

(2) In determining the effect of any such licence on or after the coming into force of these Regulations, regard shall be had to the purpose for which the licence was granted; and, in particular, a licence granted for the full term or extent of the right in a registered design or the copyright in a registered design shall be treated as applying, subject to its other terms and conditions, to the full term or extent of that right as extended by virtue of these Regulations.

(3) The right in a registered design conferred by virtue of these Regulations in relation to registrations to which Regulation 11, 12 or 13 applies shall not enable the registered proprietor to prevent any person from continuing to carry out acts begun by him before the coming into force of these Regulations and which, at that time, the reg-

istered proprietor or, in the case of registrations to which Regulation 11 applies, a registered proprietor would have been unable to prevent.

(4) The right in a registered design conferred by virtue of these Regulations in relation to registrations to which Regulation 12 or 13 applies shall, in particular, not apply in relation to infringements committed in relation to those registrations before the coming into force of these Regulations.

(5) The repeals by these Regulations in section 5 of the Registered Designs Act 1949 shall not apply in relation to any evidence filed in support of an application made before the coming into force of these Regulations.

(6) The amendments and repeals made by these Regulations in section 22 of the Act of 1949 (other than the amendment to the proviso in subsection (2) of that section) shall not apply in relation to any registration which has resulted from an application made before the coming into force of these Regulations.

(7) The amendment to the proviso in section 22(2) of the Act of 1949 shall not apply where –

(a) the registration of the first-mentioned design resulted from an application made before the coming into force of these Regulations; and

(b) the application for the registration of the other design was also made before the coming into force of these Regulations.

(8) The amendments and repeals made by these Regulations in section 35 of the Act of 1949 shall not apply in relation to any offences committed before the coming into force of these Regulations.

(9) The repeal by these Regulations of provisions in section 44 of the Act of 1949 which relate to the meaning of a set of articles shall not apply so far as those provisions are required for the purposes of paragraph 6(2)(a) of Schedule 1 to the Copyright, Designs and Patents Act 1988.

(10) Any amendment or repeal by these Regulations of a provision in section 44 of the Act of 1949 or in any enactment other than the Act of 1949 shall not apply so far as that provision is required for the purposes of any other transitional provision made by these Regulations.

(11) The Act of 1949 as it has effect immediately before the coming into force of these Regulations shall continue to apply in relation to former registrations, whose registration resulted from an application made before the coming into force of these Regulations, so far as the Act relates to the cancellation or invalidation of such registrations.

(12) Paragraph (13) applies in relation to any registration to which Regulation 11, 12 or 13 applies which is in respect of any features of shape, configuration, pattern or ornament which do not fall within the new definition of 'design' inserted into section 1 of the Act of 1949 by Regulation 2 of these Regulations.

(13) The Act of 1949 shall, so far as it applies in relation to any such registration, apply as if the features concerned were included within the new definition of 'design' in that Act.

Melanie Johnson
Parliamentary Under-Secretary of State for Competition, Consumers and Markets
Department of Trade and Industry

8th December 2001

SCHEDULE 1
CONSEQUENTIAL AMENDMENTS

Chartered Associations (Protection of Names and Uniforms) Act 1926

1. In section 3 of the Chartered Associations (Protection of Names and Uniforms) Act 1926 (savings) –

    (a) for the word 'article', in the first place where it appears, there shall be substituted 'product';

    (b) for the words from 'in respect of ' to '1907', there shall be substituted 'where a design is applied to, or incorporated in, the product and the design is protected by virtue of registration under the Registered Designs Act 1949';

    (c) for the words 'such registered design', in both places where they appear, there shall be substituted 'the design'; and

    (d) for the words 'such article' there shall be substituted 'the product'.

Registered Designs Act 1949

2. In section 8B(6) of the Registered Designs Act 1949[9] (effect of order for restoration of right) –

    (a) for the words 'an article' there shall be substituted 'a product'; and

    (b) for the words 'the article' there shall be substituted 'the product'.

3. In section 9(1) of that Act[10] (exemption of innocent infringer from liability for damages) –

    (a) for the words 'an article' there shall be substituted 'a product'; and

    (b) for the words 'the article' there shall be substituted ', or incorporated in, the product'.

4.—(1) Section 14 of that Act[11] (registration of design where application for protection in convention country has been made) shall be amended as follows.

(2) In subsection (2) –

    (a) after the word 'whether' there shall be inserted '(and to what extent)'; and

    (b) after the word 'new' there shall be inserted 'or has individual character'.

(3) In subsection (3) for the words 'section 3(4)' there shall be substituted 'section 3B(2) or (3)'.

5. In section 15(2) of that Act (extension of time for applications under section 14 in certain cases) –

    (a) in paragraph (a), for the word 'articles' there shall be substituted 'products'; and

    (b) in paragraph (e) –
        (i) for the word 'articles' there shall be substituted 'products'; and
        (ii) after the word 'applied' there shall be inserted 'or in which it is incorporated'.

6.—(1) Section 19 (registration of assignments etc.)[12] of that Act shall be amended as follows.

(2) In subsection (3A) for the words 'design right', in both places where they appear, there shall be substituted 'national unregistered design right'.

(3) In subsection (3B) for the words 'design right', in the first and third places where they appear, there shall be substituted 'national unregistered design right'.

7.—(1) Section 22 of that Act[13] (inspection of registered designs) shall be amended as follows.

(2) In subsection (2) for the words from the beginning to 'no' there shall be substituted –

'Where –

(a) a design has been registered;
(b) a product to which the design was intended to be applied or in which it was intended to be incorporated was specified, in accordance with rules made under section 36 of this Act, in the application for the registration of the design; and
(c) the product so specified falls within any class prescribed for the purposes of this subsection,

no'.

(3) Also in subsection (2) –

(a) for the word 'articles' there shall be substituted 'products'; and
(b) for the words from 'it is the same' to 'trade' there shall be substituted ', by reference to the first-mentioned design, it is not new or does not have individual character'.

(4) In subsection (3) for the words from 'design' to 'class' there shall be substituted 'registered design and a specified product which falls within any class'.

8.—(1) Section 25 of that Act[14] (certificate of contested validity of registration) shall be amended as follows.

(2) In subsection (1) after the words 'the design is' there shall be inserted ', to any extent,'.

(3) In subsection (2) for the word 'cancellation' there shall be substituted 'invalidation'.

9. In section 30(3)(a) of that Act[15] (costs and security for costs) for the word 'cancellation' there shall be substituted 'invalidation'.

10.—(1) Section 35 of that Act[16] (fine for falsely representing a design as registered) shall be amended as follows.

(2) In subsection (1) –

(a) for the words 'any article' there shall be substituted ', or incorporated in, any product';
(b) the words 'in respect of that article' shall be omitted;
(c) for the words 'an article' there shall be substituted 'a product';
(d) for the words 'the article', in the first and second places where they appear, there shall be substituted ', or incorporated in, the product'; and
(e) the words 'in respect of the article' shall be omitted.

(3) In subsection (2) –

(a) for the words 'any article' there shall be substituted 'any product';
(b) after the word 'applied' there shall be inserted 'or in which it has been incorporated'; and
(c) for the words 'such article' there shall be substituted 'such product'.

11. In section 36(1A) of that Act[17] (general power of Secretary of State to make rules etc.), after paragraph (a), there shall be inserted –

'(ab) requiring applications for registration of designs to specify –
(i)   the products to which the designs are intended to be applied or in which they are intended to be incorporated;
(ii) the classification of the designs by reference to such test as may be prescribed;'.

12. In section 37(2) of that Act for the words from 'section', where it first appears, to 'Act', where it first appears, there shall be substituted 'section 15 of this Act'.

13. In section 43(2) of that Act (savings) for the word 'articles' there shall be substituted 'products'.

14.—(1) Section 44 of that Act (interpretation) shall be amended as follows.

(2) In subsection (1), in the definition of 'design'[18] for the words 'section 1(1)' there shall be substituted 'section 1(2)'.

(3) In subsection (1), at the appropriate places, there shall be inserted –

'"complex product" has the meaning assigned to it by section 1(3) of this Act;';

'national unregistered design right' means design right within the meaning of Part III of the Copyright, Designs and Patents Act 1988;';

'product' has the meaning assigned to it by section 1(3) of this Act;'.

(4) In subsection (4) for the words from 'section', where it first appears, to 'Act' there shall be substituted 'section 14 of this Act'.

15.—(1) Schedule 1 to that Act (use of registered designs for the services of the Crown) shall be amended as follows.

(2) In paragraph 1(6)[19] and (7), for the word 'articles', in each place where it appears, there shall be substituted 'products'.

(3) In paragraph 2(1)[20] for the words 'design right' there shall be substituted 'national unregistered design right'.

(4) In paragraph 2A(1) and (4)[21] –

(a) for the word 'articles' there shall be substituted 'products'; and
(b) after the word 'applied' there shall be inserted 'or in which it is incorporated'.

(5) In paragraph 3(2)(a) –

(a) after the word 'proceedings' there shall be inserted 'and the department are a relevant person within the meaning of section 20 of this Act';
(b) for the word 'cancellation' there shall be substituted 'invalidation'; and
(c) for the word 'cancelled' there shall be substituted 'declared invalid'.

(6) In paragraph 3(2)(b) –

    (a)   after the word 'case' there shall be inserted 'and provided that the department would be the relevant person within the meaning of section 20 of this Act if they had made an application on the grounds for invalidity being raised'; and

    (b)   for the word 'cancellation' there shall be substituted 'invalidation'.

Copyright, Designs and Patents Act 1988

16. In section 53(1)(b) of the Copyright, Designs and Patents Act 1988[22] (things done in reliance on registration of design) after the word 'cancellation' there shall be inserted 'or invalidation'.

SCHEDULE 2

REPEALS

Chapter	Short title	Extent of repeal
1949 c. 88.	The Registered Designs Act 1949.	In section 2(2), the words from ', or the' to 'any article,' and the words from 'or as', where they appear for a second time, to the end of the subsection.
		Section 4.
		In section 5, in subsection (2), paragraph (b) and the word 'and' immediately preceding it and, in subsection (3)(b), the words from ', or any' to 'above,'.
		Section 6.
		Section 8(5) and (6).
		Section 10.
		In section 11A(3), paragraph (b) and the word 'or' immediately preceding it, and the words from 'or may, instead' to the end of the subsection.
		Section 11A(4) and (5).
		Section 11B.
		Section 16.
		In section 22(1), paragraph (b) and the word 'and' immediately preceding it.
		In section 23(a), the words 'and, if so, in respect of what articles'.
		In section 30(3), paragraph (b).

Chapter	Short title	Extent of repeal
		In section 35(1), the words 'in respect of that article' and the words 'in respect of the article'.
		Section 43(1).
		In section 44, in subsection (1), the definitions of 'article', 'artistic work', 'corresponding design' and 'set of articles' and subsections (2) and (3).
		Section 48(5).
1988 c. 48.	The Copyright, Designs and Patents Act 1988.	Section 265. Section 268. In Schedule 3, paragraphs 1, 2, 3(4), 4, 6, 9 and 31(2) and (5).
1995 c. 21.	The Merchant Shipping Act 1995.	In Schedule 13, paragraph 26.
1995 c. 32.	The Olympic Symbol etc. (Protection) Act 1995.	Section 13(1).

EXPLANATORY NOTE

(This note is not part of the Regulations)

These regulations implement Directive 98/71/EC of the European Parliament and of the Council of 13th October 1998 on the legal protection of designs (O.J. No. L289, 28.10.1998, p.28) ('the Directive') which provides for harmonisation in the EC of the matters of registered design protection which most closely affect the functioning of the internal market. The Directive was extended to the European Economic Area by Decision No.21/2000 of the EEA Joint Committee.

The Registered Designs Act 1949 ('the Act') already provides a very similar protection to that required under the Directive. These regulations amend the Act insofar as its provisions do not comply with the requirements of the Directive. It also makes transitional provisions and consequential amendments to other Acts.

Regulations 2 to 8 implement the main requirements of the Directive. In particular they:

    (a)   extend the definition of 'design' and amend the requirements for a design to be protectable, including amending the test for novelty and introducing a test for 'individual character';

    (b)   amend the field of earlier disclosures against which a design is tested for novelty and individual character;

    (c)   allow the designer to apply for protection up to a year after he first discloses a design without his own disclosures counting against the registration;

(d) amend the period of protection to a maximum of 25 years from the filing date of the application (or date deemed as the filing date because of an amendment which changes the design or because an application has been 'divided out' from an application which contained more than one design), rather than from the date of filing any earlier 'priority' application as may be the case at present;

(e) amend the grounds on which the registrar may refuse an application or a third party may request a declaration of invalidity;

(f) amend the rights which are conferred by registration of a design, including types of use of the design which the right-holder can and cannot control;

(g) provide that the use of the design of a component part used for the purpose of the repair of a complex product so as to restore its original appearance shall not be an infringement of the rights in the design;

(h) make explicit the principle of 'exhaustion of rights', whereby a right-holder cannot continue to use these rights to control movement or use of a product after it has been put on the market in the EEA by him or with his consent.

Regulations 9 to 14 make consequential amendments to the Act and other Acts, together with transitional provisions for applications and registrations already existing when the regulations come into force, including the following:

(a) the validity of existing registrations, or registrations resulting from existing applications, will continue to be measured according to the Act as it applied to them immediately before these regulations came into force;

(b) amended rights in existing registrations cannot be used to prevent the continuation of actions begun by a third party prior to these regulations coming into force, which could not have been prevented before that time;

(c) the maximum period of protection for certain existing registrations which had been subject to a 15 year limit is extended to 25 years;

(d) the period of protection for existing registrations which depend on an earlier 'priority' application is extended so that the term expires on an anniversary of the filing date rather than the priority date (which may be up to six months earlier).

A regulatory impact assessment is available, copies of which have been placed in the libraries of both Houses of Parliament. Copies of the assessment are also available from the Intellectual Property Policy Directorate of the Patent Office, Room 3B38, Concept House, Cardiff Road, Newport NP10 8QQ.

Notes:

[1] S.I. 2000/1813.

[2] 1972 c. 68.

[3] 1949 c. 88. Section 1 as originally enacted was substituted by section 265 of the Copyright, Designs and Patents Act 1988 (c. 48) ('the 1988 Act') but not in relation to applications for registration made before 1st August 1989. Subsection (6) was added by section 13(1) of the Olympic Symbol etc. (Protection) Act 1995 (c. 32) in relation to applications for registration made on or after 20th September 1995.

[4] Section 3(2) to (7) was substituted by section 272 of, and paragraph 1 of Schedule 3 to, the 1988 Act.

[5] Section 7 as originally enacted was substituted by section 268 of the 1988 Act but not in relation to a design registered in pursuance of an application made before 1st August 1989.

[6] Section 11A was inserted by section 270 of the 1988 Act.

[7] Words in subsection (2) of section 11 were repealed by section 303(2) of, and Schedule 8 to, the 1988 Act. Subsections (3) to (5) of section 11 were substituted for subsection (2A) of that section (as inserted by section 44(3) of the Copyright Act 1956 (c. 74)) by section 272 of, and paragraph 6 of Schedule 3 to, the 1988 Act.

[8] Section 20(5) was added by section 272 of, and paragraph 11 of Schedule 3 to, the 1988 Act.

[9] Section 8B was inserted by section 269 of the 1988 Act.

[10] Section 9 was amended by section 272 of, and paragraph 5 of Schedule 3 to, the 1988 Act.

[11] Section 14(2) and (3) were substituted by section 272 of, and paragraph 7 of Schedule 3 to, the 1988 Act.

[12] Section 19(3A) and (3B) were inserted by section 272 of, and paragraph 10 of Schedule 3 to, the 1988 Act.

[13] Section 22(2) and (3) were amended by section 272 of, and paragraph 12 of Schedule 3 to, the 1988 Act.

[14] Section 25(2) was amended by section 272 of, and paragraph 14 of Schedule 3 to, the 1988 Act.

[15] Section 30 was substituted by section 272 of, and paragraph 19 of Schedule 3 to, the 1988 Act.

[16] Section 35 was amended by section 272 of, and paragraph 24 of Schedule 3 to, the 1988 Act but not, in the case of the amendment to section 35(1), in relation to offences committed before 1st August 1989.

[17] Section 36 was amended by section 272 of, and paragraph 26 of Schedule 3 to, the 1988 Act.

[18] The definition of 'design' was amended by section 272 of, and paragraph 31(7) of Schedule 3 to, the 1988 Act.

[19] Paragraph 1(6) was substituted by section 1(1) and (4) of the Defence Contracts Act 1958 (c. 38).

[20] The words 'design right' were inserted into paragraph 2(1) by section 272 of, and paragraph 37(2) of Schedule 3 to, the 1988 Act.

[21] Paragraph 2A was inserted by section 271 of the 1988 Act in relation to any Crown use of a registered design after 1st August 1989 even if the terms for such use were settled before that date.

[22] 1988 c. 48.

APPENDIX B2

The Registered Designs (Amendment) Rules 2001 (SI 2001/3950)

STATUTORY INSTRUMENTS

2001 No. 3950

DESIGNS

The **Registered Designs (Amendment) Rules** 2001

Made	*8th December 2001*
Laid before Parliament	*10th December 2001*
Coming into force	*9th December 2001*

The Secretary of State, in exercise of the powers conferred upon her by sections 3(1) and (5), 3B(3), 5(2), 11, 18(1), 22(2), 30(1), 36(1) and (1A), 39(1) and 44(1) of the **Registered Designs** Act 1949[1] and after consultation with the Council on Tribunals pursuant to section 8(1) of the Tribunals and Inquiries Act 1992[2], hereby makes the following **Rules** –

Citation and commencement

1. These **Rules** may be cited as the **Registered Designs (Amendment) Rules** 2001 and shall come into force on 9th December 2001.

Amendment of the Registered Designs Rules 1995

2. The **Registered Designs Rules** 1995[3] shall be **amended** as follows.

3. In **rule** 2 (interpretation), for the definitions of 'specimen' and 'textile article' there shall be substituted –

'"specimen" means a product to which a **design** is applied or in which it is incorporated;

"textile product" means textile and plastics piece goods, handkerchiefs, shawls and such other classes of products of a similar character as the registrar may from time to time decide; but does not include wallpaper and similar wall covering or lace goods;'

4. Rule 13 shall be omitted.

5. For **rule** 14 there shall be substituted –

'Product to which design is intended to be applied or in which it is intended to be incorporated

14.—(1) Every application shall specify the product to which the **design** is intended to be applied or in which it is intended to be incorporated.

(2) If any question arises as to whether –

(a) a **design** is intended to be applied to, or incorporated in, textile products, wallpaper or similar wall covering or lace; or

(b) a product to which a **design** is intended to be applied or in which it is intended to be incorporated is made substantially of lace; or

(c) a **design** intended to be applied to, or incorporated in, a textile product consists substantially of checks or stripes,

it shall be decided by the registrar.

(3) Nothing in paragraph (1) of this **rule** shall be taken to limit the scope of protection conferred by registration of a **design**.'

6.—(1) **Rule** 15 shall be **amended** as follows.

(2) For the heading there shall be substituted 'Partial disclaimers in relation to applications'.

(3) For paragraph (1) there shall be substituted –

'(1) An application may be accompanied by a partial disclaimer, in a form satisfactory to the registrar, indicating that the **design** is the appearance of a part only of a product or limiting the scope or extent of protection of the **design** to be conferred by registration.'

(4) In paragraph (2), for the word 'statement', where it first appears, there shall be substituted 'disclaimer' and the words 'and it shall be separate from any other statement or disclaimer' shall be omitted.

7. Rule 16 shall be omitted.

8. In **rule** 17, the words from the beginning to 'articles,' shall be omitted.

9. After **rule** 17 there shall be inserted –

'Descriptions explaining representations

17A. A brief description explaining the representations may appear on the front of the first sheet only of each representation or specimen (except where the registrar is satisfied that this is impracticable in which case it shall appear in a place and in a form satisfactory to the registrar) but any such description shall not be taken to limit the scope of protection conferred by registration of a **design**.'

10. Rule 18 shall be omitted.

11. In **rule** 19, the words ', whether to be applied to a single article or to a set of articles,' shall be omitted.

12. Rules 22 and 24 to 26 shall be omitted.

13. In **rule** 32, the words from 'provided always that' to the end of the **rule** shall be omitted.

14. Rules 34 and 35 shall be omitted.

15. In **rule** 36 –

(a)   for the words 'section 3(6)' there shall be substituted 'section 3(5)'; and
(b)   for the words '**rule** 34 above' there shall be substituted 'section 3B(3).'

16. After **rule** 36 there shall be inserted –

'MODIFICATION OF APPLICATIONS FOR REGISTRATION

Period prescribed for the purposes of section 3B(3)

36A. The period prescribed for the purposes of section 3B(3), which relates to the making of a subsequent application for the registration of a **design** excluded from an earlier application, shall be the shorter of –

(1) the period prescribed by **rule** 36 above for the completion of the earlier application (including any extension of time allowed under the said **rule** 36); and

(2) the period starting with the making of the earlier application and ending on the date on which the certificate of registration of the **design** which is the subject of the earlier application (as **amended**) is granted.'

17. The heading above **rules** 52 to 57 shall be **amended** as follows –

(a)   for the words 'Compulsory Licence under Section 10 or Cancellation' there shall be substituted 'Invalidation'; and
(b)   for the words 'Section 11(2) or (3)' there shall be substituted 'Section 11ZB'.

18. Paragraph (1) of **rule** 52 shall be **amended** as follows –

(a)   for the words 'the grant of a compulsory licence under section 10 or for the cancellation' there shall be substituted 'the invalidation'; and
(b)   for the words 'section 11(2) or (3)' there shall be substituted 'section 11ZB'.

19. In the heading above **rule** 58, for the words 'Section 11(1)' there shall be substituted 'Section 11'.

20. Rule 59 shall be omitted.

21. In paragraph (2) of **rule** 60, for the words 'the grant of a compulsory licence or for the cancellation' there shall be substituted 'the invalidation'.

22. In **rule** 68, the words 'and any such evidence as is mentioned in section 5(2)(b)' shall be omitted.

23. Rule 69 shall be **amended** as follows –

(a)   for the words 'to be applied to textile articles' there shall be substituted 'intended to be applied to, or incorporated in, textile products'; and
(b)   for the words 'to be applied to', in the second place where they appear, there shall be substituted 'intended to be applied to, or incorporated in'.

24. Rule 71 shall be **amended** as follows –

(a)   for the words 'an article' there shall be substituted ', or incorporated in, a product'; and

(b) for the words from 'as applied to that article' to 'applied to that or any other article' there shall be substituted 'appears to produce on the informed user the same overall impression as any **registered design**'.

25.—(1) **Rule** 76 shall be **amended** as follows.

(2) In paragraph (3), for the words from 'of time' to 'section 6(2)' there shall be substituted 'prescribed by **rule** 36A above'.

(3) In paragraph (4) –

(a) in sub-paragraph (b), the words '6(2) or' shall be omitted; and

(b) in sub-paragraphs (c) and (ii) for the words from 'of time' to '**rule** 34(1)(b) above' there shall be substituted 'prescribed by **rule** 36A above'.

26. Designs Forms 2A, 19A and 21 in Schedule 1 are replaced by **Designs** Forms 2A, 19A and 21 in the Schedule to these **Rules**.

Transitional provisions

27. The **amendments**, revocations and insertions made by **rules** 3 to 12, 14 to 16 and 25 of these **Rules** and the substitution of a new **Designs** Form 2A made by **rule** 26 of these **Rules** shall not apply in relation to any applications for registration under the **Registered Designs** Act 1949 which have been made but not finally determined before the coming into force of these **Rules** ('pending applications').

28.—(1) This **rule** applies to any registration under the **Registered Designs** Act 1949 which –

(a) results from the determination of a pending application (within the meaning of **rule** 27) ('transitional registration'); or

(b) has resulted from an application made before the coming into force of these **Rules** which has given rise to a right in a **registered design** which is in force at the coming into force of these **Rules** ('existing registration') including –

(i) any registration which has ceased to fall within sub-paragraph (a) of paragraph (1) of **rule** 29 below because the right in the **registered design** has been treated or restored as mentioned in sub-paragraph (ii) of that sub-paragraph; and

(ii) any registration which has ceased to fall within sub-paragraph (b) of paragraph (1) of **rule** 29 below because the copyright in the **registered design** has come back into force by virtue of an extension of the period of copyright under section 8(2) of the **Registered Designs** Act 1949 as **amended** by regulation 13(8) of the **Registered Designs** Regulations 2001[4].

(2) Subject to paragraph (3), the **amendments** and revocations made by **rules** 3, 13 to 14, 17 to 19, 21 and 23 of these **Rules** and the substitution of a new **Designs** Form 19A made by **rule** 26 of these **Rules** shall not apply in relation to transitional or existing registrations.

(3) The **amendments**, revocations and substitution mentioned in paragraph (2) above shall apply in relation to transitional and existing registrations in so far as such **amendments**, revocations and substitution relate to applications for the grant of a compulsory licence under section 10 of the **Registered Designs** Act 1949 or for cancellation of the registration of a **design** under section 11(3) of that Act (in each case as that Act has effect immediately before the coming into force of the **Registered**

Designs Regulations 2001) unless such cancellation is by reference to an expiry of copyright occurring before the coming into force of these **Rules**.

29.—(1) This **rule** applies to –

(a) any registration under the **Registered Designs** Act 1949 which –
   (i) has resulted from an application made on or after 1st August 1989 and before the coming into force of these **Rules**; and
   (ii) has given rise to a right in a **registered design** which is not in force at the coming into force of these **Rules** but which is capable of being treated as never having ceased to be in force by virtue of section 8(4) of the **Registered Designs** Act 1949 or of being restored by virtue of sections 8A and 8B of that Act;

(b) any registration under the **Registered Designs** Act 1949 which –
   (i) has resulted from an application made before 1st August 1989; and
   (ii) has given rise to a copyright in a **registered design** which is not in force at the coming into force of these **Rules** but which would be capable of coming back into force by virtue of an extension of the period of copyright under section 8(2) of the **Registered Designs** Act 1949 if that provision were **amended** as set out in regulation 13(8) of the **Registered Designs** Regulations 2001; and

(c) any former registration under the **Registered Designs** Act 1949 which resulted from an application made before the coming into force of these **Rules**.

(2) The **amendments** and revocations made by **rules** 14, 17 to 19 and 21 of these **Rules** and the substitution of a new **Designs** Form 19A made by **rule** 26 of these **Rules** shall not apply in relation to lapsed and former registrations as mentioned in paragraph (1) so far as the **amendments** and revocations relate to the cancellation or invalidation of any such registration (other than cancellation by virtue of section 11(3) of the **Registered Designs** Act 1949 as it has effect immediately before the coming into force of the **Registered Designs** Regulations 2001 unless such cancellation is by reference to an expiry of copyright occurring before the coming into force of these **Rules**).

30. The revocation made by **rule** 22 of these **Rules** shall not apply in relation to any evidence filed in support of an application made before the coming into force of these **Rules**.

Melanie Johnson,
Parliamentary Under-Secretary of State for Competition, Consumers and Markets
Department of Trade and Industry

8th December 2001

Designs Form 2A

Registered Designs Act 1949
(Rules 6, 12 and 14)

The Patent Office
Designs Registry

Application for registration
of a design
(See the notes on the back of this form)

Cardiff Road
Newport
South Wales
NP10 8QQ

1. Your reference

2. Full name, address and postcode of the or
   of each applicant
   (Names of individuals including all partners in a firm
   must be given in full. Underline the surname or family
   name. For a corporate body give its company name.)

   Designs ADP number *(if you know it)*

   If the applicant is a corporate body, give
   country/state of incorporation

3. Name of agent *(if you have one)*

   ìAddress for Serviceî in the United Kingdom to
   which all correspondence should be sent
   (including the postcode)

   Designs ADP number *(if you know it)*

4. Name the particular product(s) to which the design
   is intended to be applied, or in which it is intended
   to be incorporated
   (The listing of a product(s) shall not be taken to limit the scope of
   protection conferred by registration of the design.)

   Write the fee code T or O *(see note (e))*

5. Declaration of priority: Country   Date of filing
   (if any)   *(day / month / year)*

   Give the Convention country and filing date of
   any previous application made abroad from
   which priority is claimed under section 14

6. If 5 above applies, and the previous
   application was not made in the name*(s)* given
   at part 2, give details of the instrument *(for*
   example, deed of assignment) which gives the
   applicant the right to apply for registration.
   Include appropriate name*(s)* and date*(s)*.

   (If this information is not given at the time this form
   is filed you must supply it before the design is
   registered.)

Designs Form 2A

Designs Form 2A

---

7. Divisional application: Give the number and
   filing date of any relevant earlier application
   whose filing date is claimed under section 3B(3)

Number

Date of filing
(day / month / year)

---

8. Declaration

I/We apply to register the design shown in the accompanying
representations or specimens. I/We declare that the applicant*(s)*
claim*(s)* to be the owner*(s)* of the design and to be the owner of
any design right that exists in this design and that the owner
believes that the design is new and has individual character
subject to any partial disclaimer accompanying the application.
I/We also declare in respect of any entry at part 5 above that the
application made in the convention country upon which the
applicant relies is the first application made for registration of the
design in a convention country.

Signature*(s)*

Date

---

9. Name and daytime telephone number of
   person to contact in the United Kingdom

---

10. Checklist

Make sure you have enclosed:

ï representations or specimens of the design *(See note (c))*

ï any continuation sheets *(See note (d))*

ï the relevant fee *(See note (e))*

Notes

a) If you need help to fill in this form or you have any questions, please contact the Patent Office on 08459 500505.

b) Write your answers in capital letters using black ink or you may type them.

c) This form should be accompanied by two identical sets of representations (for example, drawings or photographs) or specimens of the design. A partial disclaimer, if appropriate, indicating that the design is the appearance of only part of the product for which protection is sought or limiting the scope or extent of the protection sought may appear on each representation or specimen. In the case of representations or specimens which consist of more than one sheet, the partial disclaimer need only appear on the first sheet. If it is impracticable for the partial disclaimer to appear on a specimen, it may be given on a separate sheet. Specimens may sometimes need to be replaced by representations. A brief description explaining the representations may appear on the front of the first sheet only of each representation or specimen. Any such description shall not be taken to limit the scope of protection conferred by registration of a design.

d) If there is not enough space for all the relevant details on any part of this form, please continue on a separate sheet of paper and write ìsee continuation sheetî in the relevant part. Any continuation sheet should be attached to this form.

e) A different fee is payable if the application relates to a design which is intended to be applied to, or incorporated in, a lace product or a textile product where the design consists mainly of checks and stripes (fee code T).

Otherwise the normal fee is payable (fee code O).

For details of the fees and ways to pay please contact the Designs Registry of the Patent Office.

f) Once you have filled in the form you must remember to sign and date it.

Designs Form 2A
(Revised 10/01)

Designs Form 19A

Registered Designs Act 1949
(Rules 52 and 58)

19A

The Patent Office
Designs Registry

Application for invalidation or
cancellation of registration
(See the notes on the back of this form)

Cardiff Road
Newport
South Wales
NP10 8QQ

1.   Your reference

2.   Registered design number

3.   Full name of the or of each registered
     proprietor

     Designs ADP number *(if you know it)*

4.   Full name, address and postcode of person
     making the application or request on this form
     (Leave blank if this is the same as given at part 3)

5.   Name of your agent *(if you have one)*

     ìAddress for serviceî in the United Kingdom
     to which all correspondence should be sent
     (including the postcode)

     Designs ADP number *(if you know it)*

6.   Explain the nature of your application

     Write the fee code A or B
     (See notes (c) and (f))

7.   Signature   Date

8.   Name and daytime telephone number of
     person to contact in the United Kingdom

Designs Form 19A

Designs Form 19A

Notes

a) If you need help to fill in this form or you have any questions, please contact the Patent Office on 08459 500505.

b) Write your answers in capital letters using black ink or you may type them.

c) You can use this form to apply for:

   i)   invalidation of the registration of a design which you do not own (fee code A).

   For i) you must send a statement setting out the grounds for invalidity of registration, the reason why you are able to raise those grounds (if appropriate) and any facts on which you rely.

   ii)   cancellation of the registration of a design which you do own (fee code B).

d) If there is not enough space for all the relevant details on any part of this form, please continue on a separate sheet of paper and write ìsee continuation sheetî in the relevant part. Any continuation sheet should be attached to this form.

(e) Where (c) i) applies, you must send two copies of this form and of the required statement.

(f) For details of the fees and ways to pay please contact the Designs Registry of the Patent Office.

g) Once you have filled in the form you must remember to sign and date it.

Designs Form 19A
(Revised 10/01)

Designs Form 21

Registered Designs Act 1949
(Rule 71)

Request for search among
registered designs

(See the notes on the back of this form)

The Patent Office
Designs Registry

Cardiff Road
Newport
South Wales
NP10 8QQ

1. Your reference

2. Full name, address and postcode to which the
    result of the search is to be sent

    Designs ADP number *(if you know it)*

3. Give the name of a product(s) to or in which the
    design shown in the attached representations
    (or specimens) has been applied or incorporated
    (or could reasonably be applied or incorporated)
    (See note (d))

4.

    Please tell me whether or not the design referred to in part 3
    appears to give the same overall impression as any registered
    design. Please send me a copy of the representation*(s)* of any
    such registered design and details of its entry in the register.

    Signature   Date

5. Name and daytime telephone number of
    person to contact in the United Kingdom

Designs Form 21

Designs Form 21

Notes

a) *If you need help to fill in this form or you have any questions, please contact the Patent Office on 08459 500505.*

b) *Write your answers in capital letters using black ink or you may type them.*

c) *You can only use this form to request a search for a single design.*

d) *Send the following with this form.*

 ï *two representations or specimens of the design; and*

 ï *the fee*

e) *For details of the fee and ways to pay please contact the Designs Registry of the Patent Office.*

f) *Once you have filled in the form you must remember to sign and date it.*

Designs Form 21
(Revised 10/01)

EXPLANATORY NOTE

*(This note is not part of the **Rules**)*

These **Rules amend** the **Registered Designs Rules** 1995 (S.I. 1995/2912 as **amended** by S.I. 1999/3196), consequent upon **amendments** made to the **Registered Designs** Act 1949 (c. 88) ('the 1949 Act') by the **Registered Designs** Regulations 2001 (S.I. 2001/3949). Those regulations implement Directive 98/71/EC of the European Parliament and of the Council of 13th October 1998 on the legal protection of **designs** (O.J. No. L289, 28.10.98, p. 28).

In particular, these **Rules** make the following changes to the **Registered Designs Rules** 1995 –

(a) they **amend rules** 2, 14, 17, 19, 69 and 71, revoke **rules** 13, 16 and 18 and insert a new rule 17A in order to change references to **designs** applied to articles to **designs** applied to, or incorporated in, products; to omit references to a single article and to a set of articles; and to reflect the new requirements of the 1949 Act for registration of a **design**;

(b) they **amend rule** 14 to provide for an application for registration of a **design** to specify the product to or in which the **design** is intended to be applied or incorporated rather than stating the article to which the **design** is to be applied since the protection conferred by registration will no longer be restricted to a specified article or set of articles;

(c) they **amend rule** 15 to provide for partial disclaimers limiting the scope or extent of protection to be conferred by registration in place of statements of novelty;

(d) they revoke **rules** 22 and 24 to 26 which provide for disclaimers, limitations and exclusions in relation to the registration of **designs** which are no longer applicable;

(e) they **amend rule** 32 to omit reference to a limitation on the duration of a right in a **registered design** which will no longer apply;

(f) they revoke rules 34 and 35 and insert a new **rule** 36A to reflect **amendments** to the 1949 Act affecting the assessment of novelty;

(g) they **amend rules** 52 and 60 and revoke **rule** 59 to omit references to compulsory licences and licences of right which are no longer available and to reflect new provisions in the 1949 Act for cancellation and invalidation of registrations;

(h) they **amend rule** 68 to omit reference to evidence which will no longer be filed in support of applications for registration; and

(i) they **amend rules** 36 and 76 and provide for new **Designs** Forms 2A, 19A and 21 consequent upon these **amendments**.

The remaining **rules** are unchanged.

Rules 27 to 30 make transitional provisions for applications and registrations already existing when these **Rules** come into force and for lapsed and former registrations at that time so far as the **Registered Designs Rules** 1995 apply to them.

A regulatory impact assessment is available, copies of which have been placed in the libraries of both Houses of Parliament. Copies of the assessment are also available from the Intellectual Property Policy Directorate, Concept House, Cardiff Road, Newport NP10 8QQ.

Notes:

[1] 1949 c. 88; sections 30(1) and 36(1A) of the 1949 Act were inserted by, and sections 3(5), 5(2), 22(2), 36(1) and 44(1) of that Act were **amended** by, the Copyright, **Designs** and Patents Act 1988 (c. 48), section 272 and Schedule 3, paragraphs 1, 3, 12, 19, 26 and 31; section 3B(3) was inserted by, and sections 3(1) and (5), 5(2), 11, 22(2), 36(1A) and 44 (1) were **amended** by, the **Registered Designs** Regulations 2001 (S.I. 2001/3949), regulations 4 and 7, Schedule 1, paragraphs 7, 11 and 14 and Schedule 2.

[2] 1992 c. 53.

[3] S.I. 1995/2912 as amended by S.I. 1999/3196.

[4] S.I. 2001/3949.

Registered Designs Act 1949

Registrable designs and proceedings for registration

1 Registration of designs

(1) A design may, subject to the following provisions of this Act, be registered under this Act on the making of an application for registration.

(2) In this Act 'design' means the appearance of the whole or a part of a product resulting from the features of, in particular, the lines, contours, colours, shape, texture or materials of the product or its ornamentation.

(3) In this Act –

'complex product' means a product which is composed of at least two replaceable component parts permitting disassembly and reassembly of the product; and

'product' means any industrial or handicraft item other than a computer program; and, in particular, includes packaging, get-up, graphic symbols, typographic type-faces and parts intended to be assembled into a complex product.

1A Substantive grounds for refusal of registration

(1) The following shall be refused registration under this Act –

    (a)   anything which does not fulfil the requirements of section 1(2) of this Act;
    (b)   designs which do not fulfil the requirements of sections 1B to 1D of this Act;
    (c)   designs to which a ground of refusal mentioned in Schedule A1 to this Act applies.

(2) A design ('the later design') shall be refused registration under this Act if it is not new or does not have individual character when compared with a design which –

    (a)   has been made available to the public on or after the relevant date; but
    (b)   is protected as from a date prior to the relevant date by virtue of registration under this Act or an application for such registration.

(3) In subsection (2) above 'the relevant date' means the date on which the application for the registration of the later design was made or is treated by virtue of section 3B(2), (3) or (5) or 14(2) of this Act as having been made.

1B Requirement of novelty and individual character

(1) A design shall be protected by a right in a registered design to the extent that the design is new and has individual character.

(2) For the purposes of subsection (1) above, a design is new if no identical design or no design whose features differ only in immaterial details has been made available to the public before the relevant date.

(3) For the purposes of subsection (1) above, a design has individual character if the overall impression it produces on the informed user differs from the overall impression produced on such a user by any design which has been made available to the public before the relevant date.

(4) In determining the extent to which a design has individual character, the degree of freedom of the author in creating the design shall be taken into consideration.

(5) For the purposes of this section, a design has been made available to the public before the relevant date if –

(a)   it has been published (whether following registration or otherwise), exhibited, used in trade or otherwise disclosed before that date; and
(b)   the disclosure does not fall within subsection (6) below.

(6) A disclosure falls within this subsection if –

(a)   it could not reasonably have become known before the relevant date in the normal course of business to persons carrying on business in the European Economic Area and specialising in the sector concerned;
(b)   it was made to a person other than the designer, or any successor in title of his, under conditions of confidentiality (whether express or implied);
(c)   it was made by the designer, or any successor in title of his, during the period of 12 months immediately preceding the relevant date;
(d)   it was made by a person other than the designer, or any successor in title of his, during the period of 12 months immediately preceding the relevant date in consequence of information provided or other action taken by the designer or any successor in title of his; or
(e)   it was made during the period of 12 months immediately preceding the relevant date as a consequence of an abuse in relation to the designer or any successor in title of his.

(7) In subsections (2), (3), (5) and (6) above 'the relevant date' means the date on which the application for the registration of the design was made or is treated by virtue of section 3B(2), (3) or (5) or 14(2) of this Act as having been made.

(8) For the purposes of this section, a design applied to or incorporated in a product which constitutes a component part of a complex product shall only be considered to be new and to have individual character –

(a)   if the component part, once it has been incorporated into the complex product, remains visible during normal use of the complex product; and
(b)   to the extent that those visible features of the component part are in themselves new and have individual character.

(9) In subsection (8) above 'normal use' means use by the end user; but does not include any maintenance, servicing or repair work in relation to the product.

1C Designs dictated by their technical function

(1) A right in a registered design shall not subsist in features of appearance of a product which are solely dictated by the product's technical function.

(2) A right in a registered design shall not subsist in features of appearance of a product which must necessarily be reproduced in their exact form and dimensions so as to permit the product in which the design is incorporated or to which it is applied to be mechanically connected to, or placed in, around or against, another product so that either product may perform its function.

(3) Subsection (2) above does not prevent a right in a registered design subsisting in a design serving the purpose of allowing multiple assembly or connection of mutually interchangeable products within a modular system.

1D Designs contrary to public policy or morality

A right in a registered design shall not subsist in a design which is contrary to public policy or to accepted principles of morality.

2 Proprietorship of designs

(1) The author of a design shall be treated for the purposes of this Act as the original proprietor of the design, subject to the following provisions.

(1A) Where a design is created in pursuance of a commission for money or money's worth, the person commissioning the design shall be treated as the original proprietor of the design.

(1B) Where, in a case not falling within subsection (1A), a design is created by an employee in the course of his employment, his employer shall be treated as the original proprietor of the design.

(2) Where a design becomes vested, whether by assignment, transmission or operation of law, in any person other than the original proprietor, either alone or jointly with the original proprietor, that other person, or as the case may be the original proprietor and that other person, shall be treated for the purposes of this Act as the proprietor of the design or as the proprietor of the design.

(3) In this Act the 'author' of a design means the person who creates it.

(4) In the case of a design generated by computer in circumstances such that there is no human author, the person by whom the arrangements necessary for the creation of the design are made shall be taken to be the author.

3 Applications for registration

(1) An application for the registration of a design shall be made in the prescribed form and shall be filed at the Patent Office in the prescribed manner.

(2) An application for the registration of a design shall be made by the person claiming to be the proprietor of the design.

(3) An application for the registration of a design in which national unregistered design right subsists shall be made by the person claiming to be the design right owner.

(4) For the purpose of deciding whether, and to what extent, a design is new or has individual character, the registrar may make such searches (if any) as he thinks fit.

(5) An application for the registration of a design which, owing to any default or neglect on the part of the applicant, has not been completed so as to enable registration to be effected within such time as may be prescribed shall be deemed to be abandoned.

3A Determination of applications for registration

(1) Subject as follows, the registrar shall not refuse an application for the registration of a design.

(2) If it appears to the registrar that an application for the registration of a design has not been made in accordance with any rules made under this Act, he may refuse the application.

(3) If it appears to the registrar that an application for the registration of a design has not been made in accordance with sections 3(2) and (3) and 14(1) of this Act, he shall refuse the application.

(4) If it appears to the registrar that any ground for refusal of registration mentioned in section 1A of this Act applies in relation to an application for the registration of a design, he shall refuse the application.

3B Modification of applications for registration

(1) The registrar may, at any time before an application for the registration of a design is determined, permit the applicant to make such modifications of the application as the registrar thinks fit.

(2) Where an application for the registration of a design has been modified before it has been determined in such a way that the design has been altered significantly, the registrar may, for the purpose of deciding whether and to what extent the design is new or has individual character, direct that the application shall be treated as having been made on the date on which it was so modified.

(3) Where –

    (a)   an application for the registration of a design has disclosed more than one design and has been modified before it has been determined to exclude one or more designs from the application; and

    (b)   a subsequent application for the registration of a design so excluded has, within such period (if any) as has been prescribed for such applications, been made by the person who made the earlier application or his successor in title,

the registrar may, for the purpose of deciding whether and to what extent the design is new or has individual character, direct that the subsequent application shall be treated as having been made on the date on which the earlier application was, or is treated as having been, made.

(4) Where an application for the registration of a design has been refused on any ground mentioned in section 1A(1)(b) or (c) of this Act, the application may be modified by the applicant if it appears to the registrar that –

(a)   the identity of the design is retained; and

(b)   the modifications have been made in accordance with any rules made under this Act.

(5) An application modified under subsection (4) above shall be treated as the original application and, in particular, as made on the date on which the original application was made or is treated as having been made.

(6) Any modification under this section may, in particular, be effected by making a partial disclaimer in relation to the application.

3C Date of registration of designs

(1) Subject as follows, a design, when registered, shall be registered as of the date on which the application was made or is treated as having been made.

(2) Subsection (1) above shall not apply to an application which is treated as having been made on a particular date by section 14(2) of this Act or by virtue of the operation of section 3B(3) or (5) of this Act by reference to section 14(2) of this Act.

(3) A design, when registered, shall be registered as of –

(a)   in the case of an application which is treated as having been made on a particular date by section 14(2) of this Act, the date on which the application was made;

(b)   in the case of an application which is treated as having been made on a particular date by virtue of the operation of section 3B(3) of this Act by reference to section 14(2) of this Act, the date on which the earlier application was made;

(c)   in the case of an application which is treated as having been made on a particular date by virtue of the operation of section 3B(5) of this Act by reference to section 14(2) of this Act, the date on which the original application was made.

3D Appeals in relation to applications for registration

An appeal lies from any decision of the registrar under section 3A or 3B of this Act.

4 Registration of same design in respect of other articles, etc

[*Repealed.*]

5 Provisions for secrecy of certain designs

(1) Where, either before or after the commencement of this Act, an application for the registration of a design has been made, and it appears to the registrar that the design is one of a class notified to him by the Secretary of State as relevant for defence purposes, he may give directions for prohibiting or restricting the publication of information with respect to the design, or the communication of such information to any person or class of persons specified in the directions.

(2) The Secretary of State shall by rules make provision for securing that where such directions are given –

(a) the representation or specimen of the design

shall not be open to public inspection at the Patent Office during the continuance in force of the directions.

(3) Where the registrar gives any such directions as aforesaid, he shall give notice of the application and of the directions to the Secretary of State, and thereupon the following provisions shall have effect, that is to say: –

    (a) the Secretary of State shall, upon receipt of such notice, consider whether the publication of the design would be prejudicial to the defence of the realm and unless a notice under paragraph (c) of this subsection has previously been given by that authority to the registrar, shall reconsider that question before the expiration of nine months from the date of filing of the application for registration of the design and at least once in every subsequent year;

    (b) for the purpose aforesaid, the Secretary of State may, at any time after the design has been registered or, with the consent of the applicant, at any time before the design has been registered, inspect the representation or specimen of the design filed in pursuance of the application;

    (c) if upon consideration of the design at any time it appears to the Secretary of State that the publication of the design would not, or would no longer, be prejudicial to the defence of the realm, he shall give notice to the registrar to that effect;

    (d) on the receipt of any such notice the registrar shall revoke the directions and may, subject to such conditions, if any, as he thinks fit, extend the time for doing anything required or authorised to be done by or under this Act in connection with the application or registration, whether or not that time has previously expired.

(4) No person resident in the United Kingdom shall, except under the authority of a written permit granted by or on behalf of the registrar, make or cause to be made any application outside the United Kingdom for the registration of a design of any class prescribed for the purposes of this subsection unless –

    (a) an application for registration of the same design has been made in the United Kingdom not less than six weeks before the application outside the United Kingdom; and

    (b) either no directions have been given under subsection (1) of this section in relation to the application in the United Kingdom or all such directions have been revoked:

Provided that this subsection shall not apply in relation to a design for which an application for protection has first been filed in a country outside the United Kingdom by a person resident outside the United Kingdom.

(5) [. . .]

6 Provisions as to confidential disclosure, etc

[*Repealed.*]

Effect of registration, etc

7 Right given by registration

(1) The registration of a design under this Act gives the registered proprietor the exclusive right to use the design and any design which does not produce on the informed user a different overall impression.

(2) For the purposes of subsection (1) above and section 7A of this Act any reference to the use of a design includes a reference to –

- (a) the making, offering, putting on the market, importing, exporting or using of a product in which the design is incorporated or to which it is applied; or
- (b) stocking such a product for those purposes.

(3) In determining for the purposes of subsection (1) above whether a design produces a different overall impression on the informed user, the degree of freedom of the author in creating his design shall be taken into consideration.

(4) The right conferred by subsection (1) above is subject to any limitation attaching to the registration in question (including, in particular, any partial disclaimer or any declaration by the registrar or a court of partial invalidity).

7A Infringements of rights in registered designs

(1) Subject as follows, the right in a registered design is infringed by a person who, without the consent of the registered proprietor, does anything which by virtue of section 7 of this Act is the exclusive right of the registered proprietor.

(2) The right in a registered design is not infringed by –

- (a) an act which is done privately and for purposes which are not commercial;
- (b) an act which is done for experimental purposes;
- (c) an act of reproduction for teaching purposes or for the purpose of making citations provided that the conditions mentioned in subsection (3) below are satisfied;
- (d) the use of equipment on ships or aircraft which are registered in another country but which are temporarily in the United Kingdom;
- (e) the importation into the United Kingdom of spare parts or accessories for the purpose of repairing such ships or aircraft; or
- (f) the carrying out of repairs on such ships or aircraft.

(3) The conditions mentioned in this subsection are –

- (a) the act of reproduction is compatible with fair trade practice and does not unduly prejudice the normal exploitation of the design; and
- (b) mention is made of the source.

(4) The right in a registered design is not infringed by an act which relates to a product in which any design protected by the registration is incorporated or to which it is applied if the product has been put on the market in the European Economic Area by the registered proprietor or with his consent.

(5) The right in a registered design of a component part which may be used for the purpose of the repair of a complex product so as to restore its original appearance is not infringed by the use for that purpose of any design protected by the registration.

(6) No proceedings shall be taken in respect of an infringement of the right in a registered design committed before the date on which the certificate of registration of the design under this Act is granted.

8 Duration of right in registered design

(1) The right in a registered design subsists in the first instance for a period of five years from the date of the registration of the design.

(2) The period for which the right subsists may be extended for a second, third, fourth and fifth period of five years, by applying to the registrar for an extension and paying the prescribed renewal fee.

(3) If the first, second, third or fourth period expires without such application and payment being made, the right shall cease to have effect; and the registrar shall, in accordance with rules made by the Secretary of State, notify the proprietor of that fact.

(4) If during the period of six months immediately following the end of that period an application for extension is made and the prescribed renewal fee and any prescribed additional fee is paid, the right shall be treated as if it had never expired, with the result that –

>(a) anything done under or in relation to the right during that further period shall be treated as valid,
>(b) an act which would have constituted an infringement of the right if it had not expired shall be treated as an infringement, and
>(c) an act which would have constituted use of the design for the services of the Crown if the right had not expired shall be treated as such use.

(5) [. . .]

(6) [. . .]

8A Restoration of lapsed right in design

(1) Where the right in a registered design has expired by reason of a failure to extend, in accordance with section 8(2) or (4), the period for which the right subsists, an application for the restoration of the right in the design may be made to the registrar within the prescribed period.

(2) The application may be made by the person who was the registered proprietor of the design or by any other person who would have been entitled to the right in the design if it had not expired; and where the design was held by two or more persons jointly, the application may, with the leave of the registrar, be made by one or more of them without joining the others.

(3) Notice of the application shall be published by the registrar in the prescribed manner.

(4) If the registrar is satisfied that the proprietor took reasonable care to see that the period for which the right subsisted was extended in accordance with section 8(2) or (4), he shall, on payment of any unpaid renewal fee and any prescribed additional fee, order the restoration of the right in the design.

(5) The order may be made subject to such conditions as the registrar thinks fit, and if the proprietor of the design does not comply with any condition the registrar may revoke the order and give such consequential directions as he thinks fit.

(6) Rules altering the period prescribed for the purposes of subsection (1) may contain such transitional provisions and savings as appear to the Secretary of State to be necessary or expedient.

8B Effect of order for restoration of right

(1) The effect of an order under section 8A for the restoration of the right in a registered design is as follows.

(2) Anything done under or in relation to the right during the period between expiry and restoration shall be treated as valid.

(3) Anything done during that period which would have constituted an infringement if the right had not expired shall be treated as an infringement –

    (a) if done at a time when it was possible for an application for extension to be made under section 8(4); or

    (b) if it was a continuation or repetition of an earlier infringing act.

(4) If, after it was no longer possible for such an application for extension to be made and before publication of notice of the application for restoration, a person –

    (a) began in good faith to do an act which would have constituted an infringement of the right in the design if it had not expired, or

    (b) made in good faith effective and serious preparations to do such an act,

he has the right to continue to do the act or, as the case may be, to do the act, notwithstanding the restoration of the right in the design; but this does not extend to granting a licence to another person to do the act.

(5) If the act was done, or the preparations were made, in the course of a business, the person entitled to the right conferred by subsection (4) may –

    (a) authorise the doing of that act by any partners of his for the time being in that business, and

    (b) assign that right, or transmit it on death (or in the case of a body corporate on its dissolution), to any person who acquires that part of the business in the course of which the act was done or the preparations were made.

(6) Where a product is disposed of to another in exercise of the rights conferred by subsection (4) or subsection (5), that other and any person claiming through him may deal with the product in the same way as if it had been disposed of by the registered proprietor of the design.

(7) The above provisions apply in relation to the use of a registered design for the services of the Crown as they apply in relation to infringement of the right in the design.

9 Exemption of innocent infringer from liability for damages

(1) In proceedings for the infringement of the right in a registered design damages shall not be awarded against a defendant who proves that at the date of the infringement he was not aware, and had no reasonable ground for supposing, that the design was registered; and a person shall not be deemed to have been aware or to have had reasonable grounds for supposing as aforesaid by reason only of the marking of a

product with the word 'registered' or any abbreviation thereof, or any word or words expressing or implying that the design applied to, or incorporated in, the product has been registered, unless the number of the design accompanied the word or words or the abbreviation in question.

(2) Nothing in this section shall affect the power of the court to grant an injuction in any proceedings for infringement of the right in a registered design.

10 Compulsory licence in respect of registered design

[*Repealed.*]

11 Cancellation of registration

The registrar may, upon a request made in the prescribed manner by the registered proprietor, cancel the registration of a design.

11ZA Grounds for invalidity of registration

(1) The registration of a design may be declared invalid on any of the grounds mentioned in section 1A of this Act.

(2) The registration of a design may be declared invalid on the ground of the registered proprietor not being the proprietor of the design and the proprietor of the design objecting.

(3) The registration of a design involving the use of an earlier distinctive sign may be declared invalid on the ground of an objection by the holder of rights to the sign which include the right to prohibit in the United Kingdom such use of the sign.

(4) The registration of a design constituting an unauthorised use of a work protected by the law of copyright in the United Kingdom may be declared invalid on the ground of an objection by the owner of the copyright.

(5) In this section and sections 11ZB, 11ZC and 11ZE of this Act (other than section 11ZE(1)) references to the registration of a design include references to the former registration of a design; and these sections shall apply, with necessary modifications, in relation to such former registrations.

11ZB Applications for declaration of invalidity

(1) Any person interested may make an application to the registrar for a declaration of invalidity on the ground mentioned in section 1A(1)(a) or (b) of this Act.

(2) Any person concerned by the use in question may make an application to the registrar for a declaration of invalidity on the ground mentioned in section 1A(1)(c) of this Act.

(3) The relevant person may make an application to the registrar for a declaration of invalidity on the ground mentioned in section 1A(2) of this Act.

(4) In subsection (3) above 'the relevant person' means, in relation to an earlier design protected by virtue of registration under this Act or an application for such registration, the registered proprietor of the design or (as the case may be) the applicant.

(5) The person able to make an objection under subsection (2), (3) or (4) of section 11ZA of this Act may make an application to the registrar for a declaration of invalidity on the ground mentioned in that subsection.

(6) An application may be made under this section in relation to a design at any time after the design has been registered.

11ZC Determination of applications for declaration of invalidity

(1) This section applies where an application has been made to the registrar for a declaration of invalidity in relation to a registration.

(2) If it appears to the registrar that the application has not been made in accordance with any rules made under this Act, he may refuse the application.

(3) If it appears to the registrar that the application has not been made in accordance with section 11ZB of this Act, he shall refuse the application.

(4) Subject to subsections (2) and (3) above, the registrar shall make a declaration of invalidity if it appears to him that the ground of invalidity specified in the application has been established in relation to the registration.

(5) Otherwise the registrar shall refuse the application.

(6) A declaration of invalidity may be a declaration of partial invalidity.

11ZD Modification of registration

(1) Subsections (2) and (3) below apply where the registrar intends to declare the registration of a design invalid on any ground mentioned in section 1A(1)(b) or (c) or 11ZA(3) or (4) of this Act.

(2) The registrar shall inform the registered proprietor of that fact.

(3) The registered proprietor may make an application to the registrar for the registrar to make such modifications to the registration of the design as the registered proprietor specifies in his application.

(4) Such modifications may, in particular, include the inclusion on the register of a partial disclaimer by the registered proprietor.

(5) If it appears to the registrar that the application has not been made in accordance with any rules made under this Act, the registrar may refuse the application.

(6) If it appears to the registrar that the identity of the design is not retained or the modified registration would be invalid by virtue of section 11ZA of this Act, the registrar shall refuse the application.

(7) Otherwise the registrar shall make the specified modifications.

(8) A modification of a registration made under this section shall have effect, and be treated always to have had effect, from the grant of registration.

11ZE Effect of cancellation or invalidation of registration

(1) A cancellation of registration under section 11 of this Act takes effect from the date of the registrar's decision or from such other date as the registrar may direct.

(2) Where the registrar declares the registration of a design invalid to any extent, the registration shall to that extent be treated as having been invalid from the date of registration or from such other date as the registrar may direct.

11ZF Appeals in relation to cancellation or invalidation

An appeal lies from any decision of the registrar under section 11 to 11ZE of this Act.

11A Powers exercisable for protection of the public interest

(1) Where a report of the Competition Commission has been laid before Parliament containing conclusions to the effect –

    (a) on a monopoly reference, that a monopoly situation exists and facts found by the Commission operate or may be expected to operate against the public interest,

    (b) on a merger reference, that a merger situation qualifying for investigation has been created and the creation of the situation, or particular elements in or consequences of it specified in the report, operate or may be expected to operate against the public interest,

    (c) on a competition reference, that a person was engaged in an anti-competitive practice which operated or may be expected to operate against the public interest, or

    (d) on a reference under section 11 of the Competition Act 1980 (reference of public bodies and certain other persons), that a person is pursuing a course of conduct which operates against the public interest,

the appropriate Minister or Ministers may apply to the registrar to take action under this section.

(2) Before making an application the appropriate Minister or Ministers shall publish, in such a manner as he or they think appropriate, a notice describing the nature of the proposed application and shall consider any representations which may be made within 30 days of such publication by persons whose interests appear to him or them to be affected.

(3) If on an application under this section it appears to the registrar that the matters specified in the Commission's report as being those which in the Commission's opinion operate or operated or may be expected to operate against the public interest include –

    (a) conditions in licences granted in respect of a registered design by its proprietor restricting the use of the design by the licensee or the right of the proprietor to grant other licences,

he may by order cancel or modify any such condition.

    (4) [. . .]

    (5) [. . .]

(6) An appeal lies from any order of the registrar under this section.

(7) In this section 'the appropriate Minister or Ministers' means the Minister or Ministers to whom the report of the Competition Commission was made.

11AB Powers exercisable following merger and market investigations

(1) Subsection (2) below applies where –

(a) section 41(2), 55(2), 66(6), 75(2), 83(2), 138(2), 147(2) or 160(2) of, or paragraph 5(2) or 10(2) of Schedule 7 to, the Enterprise Act 2002 (powers to take remedial action following merger or market investigations) applies;

(b) the Competition Commission or (as the case may be) the Secretary of State considers that it would be appropriate to make an application under this section for the purpose of remedying, mitigating or preventing a matter which cannot be dealt with under the enactment concerned; and

(c) the matter concerned involves conditions in licences granted in respect of a registered design by its proprietor restricting the use of the design by the licensee or the right of the proprietor to grant other licences.

(2) The Competition Commission or (as the case may be) the Secretary of State may apply to the registrar to take action under this section.

(3) Before making an application the Competition Commission or (as the case may be) the Secretary of State shall publish, in such manner as it or he thinks appropriate, a notice describing the nature of the proposed application and shall consider any representations which may be made within 30 days of such publication by persons whose interests appear to it or him to be affected.

(4) The registrar may, if it appears to him on an application under this section that the application is made in accordance with this section, by order cancel or modify any condition concerned of the kind mentioned in subsection (1)(c) above.

(5) An appeal lies from any order of the registrar under this section.

(6) References in this section to the Competition Commission shall, in cases where section 75(2) of the Enterprise Act 2002 applies, be read as references to the Office of Fair Trading.

(7) References in section 35, 36, 47, 63, 134 or 141 of the Enterprise Act 2002 (questions to be decided by the Competition Commission in its reports) to taking action under section 41(2), 55, 66, 138 or 147 shall include references to taking action under subsection (2) above.

(8) An order made by virtue of this section in consequence of action under subsection (2) above where an enactment mentioned in subsection (1)(a) above applies shall be treated, for the purposes of sections 91(3), 92(1)(a), 162(1) and 166(3) of the Enterprise Act 2002 (duties to register and keep under review enforcement orders etc), as if it were made under the relevant power in Part 3 or (as the case may be) 4 of that Act to make an enforcement order (within the meaning of the Part concerned).

[11B Undertaking to take licence of right in infringement proceedings

[*Repealed.*]

12 Use for services of Crown

The provisions of the First Schedule to this Act shall have effect with respect to the use of registered designs for the services of the Crown and the rights of third parties in respect of such use.

International Arrangements

13 Orders in Council as to convention countries

(1) His Majesty may, with a view to the fulfilment of a treaty, convention, arrangement or engagement, by Order in Council declare that any country specified in the Order is a convention country for the purposes of this Act:

Provided that a declaration may be made as aforesaid for the purposes either of all or of some only of the provisions of the Act, and a country in the case of which a declaration made for the purposes of some only of the provisions of this Act is in force shall be deemed to be a convention country for the purposes of those provisions only.

(2) His Majesty may by Order in Council direct that any of the Channel Islands, any colony . . . shall be deemed to be a convention country for the purposes of all or any of the provisions of this Act; and an Order made under this subsection may direct that any such provisions shall have effect, in relation to the territory in question, subject to such conditions or limitations, if any, as may be specified in the Order.

(3) For the purposes of subsection (1) of this section, every colony, protectorate, territory subject to the authority or under the suzerainty of another country, and territory administered by another country . . . under the trusteeship system of the United Nations, shall be deemed to be a country in the case of which a declaration may be made under that subsection.

14 Registration of design where application for protection in convention country has been made

(1) An application for registration of a design in respect of which protection has been applied for in a convention country may be made in accordance with the provisions of this Act by the person by whom the application for protection was made or his personal representative or assignee:

Provided that no application shall be made by virtue of this section after the expiration of six months from the date of the application for protection in a convention country or, where more than one such application for protection has been made, from the date of the first application.

(2) Where an application for registration of a design is made by virtue of this section, the application shall be treated, for the purpose of determining whether (and to what extent) that or any other design is new or has individual character, as made on the date of the application for protection in the convention country or, if more than one such application was made, on the date of the first such application.

(3) Subsection (2) shall not be construed as excluding the power to give directions under section 3B(2) or (3) of this Act in relation to an application made by virtue of this section.

(4) Where a person has applied for protection for a design by an application which –

    (a) in accordance with the terms of a treaty subsisting between two or more convention countries, is equivalent to an application duly made in any one of those convention countries; or

    (b) in accordance with the law of any convention country, is equivalent to an application duly made in that convention country,

he shall be deemed for the purposes of this section to have applied in that convention country.

15 Extension of time for applications under s. 14 in certain cases

(1) If the Secretary of State is satisfied that provision substantially equivalent to the provision to be made by or under this section has been or will be made under the law of any convention country, he may make rules empowering the registrar to extend the time for making applications under subsection (1) of section fourteen of this Act for registration of a design in respect of which protection has been applied for in that country in any case where the period specified in the proviso to that subsection expires during a period prescribed by the rules.

(2) Rules made under this section –
- (a) may, where any agreement or arrangement has been made between His Majesty's Government in the United Kingdom and the government of the convention country for the supply or mutual exchange of information or products, provide, either generally or in any class of case specified in the rules, that an extension of time shall not be granted under this section unless the design has been communicated in accordance with the agreement or arrangement;
- (b) may, either generally or in any class of case specified in the rules, fix the maximum extension which may be granted under this section;
- (c) may prescribe or allow any special procedure in connection with applications made by virtue of this section;
- (d) may empower the registrar to extend, in relation to any application made by virtue of this section, the time limited by or under the foregoing provisions of this Act for doing any act, subject to such conditions, if any, as may be imposed by or under the rules;
- (e) may provide for securing that the rights conferred by registration on an application made by virtue of this section shall be subject to such restrictions or conditions as may be specified by or under the rules and in particular to restrictions and conditions for the protection of persons (including persons acting on behalf of His Majesty) who, otherwise than as the result of a communication made in accordance with such an agreement or arrangement as is mentioned in paragraph (a) of this subsection, and before the date of the application in question or such later date as may be allowed by the rules, may have imported or made products to which the design is applied or in which it is incorporated or may have made an application for registration of the design.

16 Protection of designs communicated under international agreement

[*Repealed.*]

Register of designs, etc

17 Register of designs, etc

(1) The registrar shall maintain the register of designs, in which shall be entered –
- (a) the names and addresses of proprietors of registered designs;
- (b) notices of assignments and of transmissions of registered designs; and
- (c) such other matters as may be prescribed or as the registrar may think fit.

(2) No notice of any trust, whether express, implied or constructive, shall be entered in the register of designs, and the registrar shall not be affected by any such notice.

(3) The register need not be kept in documentary form.

(4) Subject to the provisions of this Act and to rules made by the Secretary of State under it, the public shall have a right to inspect the register at the Patent Office at all convenient times.

(5) Any person who applies for a certified copy of an entry in the register or a certified extract from the register shall be entitled to obtain such a copy or extract on payment of a fee prescribed in relation to certified copies and extracts; and rules made by the Secretary of State under this Act may provide that any person who applies for an uncertified copy or extract shall be entitled to such a copy or extract on payment of a fee prescribed in relation to uncertified copies and extracts.

(6) Applications under subsection (5) above or rules made by virtue of that subsection shall be made in such manner as may be prescribed.

(7) In relation to any portion of the register kept otherwise than in documentary form –

    (a) the right of inspection conferred by subsection (4) above is a right to inspect the material on the register; and

    (b) the right to a copy or extract conferred by subsection (5) above or rules is a right to a copy or extract in a form in which it can be taken away and in which it is visible and legible.

(8) Subject to subsection (11) below, the register shall be prima facie evidence of anything required or authorised by this Act to be entered in it and in Scotland shall be sufficient evidence of any such thing.

(9) A certificate purporting to be signed by the registrar and certifying that any entry which he is authorised by or under this Act to make has or has not been made, or that any other thing which he is so authorised to do has or has not been done, shall be prima facie evidence, and in Scotland shall be sufficient evidence, of the matters so certified.

(10) Each of the following –

    (a) a copy of an entry in the register or an extract from the register which is supplied under subsection (5) above;

    (b) a copy of any representation, specimen or document kept in the Patent Office or an extract from any such document,

which purports to be a certified copy or certified extract shall, subject to subsection (11) below, be admitted in evidence without further proof and without production of any original; and in Scotland such evidence shall be sufficient evidence.

(11) [. . .]

(12) In this section 'certified copy' and 'certified extract' mean a copy and extract certified by the registrar and sealed with the seal of the Patent Office.

18 Certificate of registration

(1) The registrar shall grant a certificate of registration in the prescribed form to the registered proprietor of a design when the design is registered.

(2) The registrar may, in a case where he is satisfied that the certificate of registration has been lost or destroyed, or in any other case in which he thinks it expedient, furnish one or more copies of the certificate.

19 Registration of assignments, etc

(1) Where any person becomes entitled by assignment, transmission or operation of law to a registered design or to a share in a registered design, or becomes entitled as mortgagee, licensee or otherwise to any other interest in a registered design, he shall apply to the registrar in the prescribed manner for the registration of his title as proprietor or co-proprietor or, as the case may be, of notice of his interest, in the register of designs.

(2) Without prejudice to the provisions of the foregoing subsection, an application for the registration of the title of any person becoming entitled by assignment to a registered design or a share in a registered design, or becoming entitled by virtue of a mortgage, licence or other instrument to any other interest in a registered design, may be made in the prescribed manner by the assignor, mortgagor, licensor or other party to that instrument, as the case may be.

(3) Where application is made under this section for the registration of the title of any person, the registrar shall, upon proof of title to his satisfaction –
- (a) where that person is entitled to a registered design or a share in a registered design, register him in the register of designs as proprietor or co-proprietor of the design, and enter in that register particulars of the instrument or event by which he derives title; or
- (b) where that person is entitled to any other interest in the registered design, enter in that register notice of his interest, with particulars of the instrument (if any) creating it.

(3A) Where national unregistered design right subsists in a registered design, the registrar shall not register an interest under subsection (3) unless he is satisfied that the person entitled to that interest is also entitled to a corresponding interest in the national unregistered design right.

(3B) Where national unregistered design right subsists in a registered design and the proprietor of the registered design is also the design right owner, an assignment of the national unregistered design right shall be taken to be also an assignment of the right in the registered design, unless a contrary intention appears.

(4) Subject to any rights vested in any other person of which notice is entered in the register of designs, the person or persons registered as proprietor of a registered design shall have power to assign, grant licences under, or otherwise deal with the design, and to give effectual receipts for any consideration for any such assignment, licence or dealing:

Provided that any equities in respect of the design may be enforced in like manner as in respect of any other personal property.

(5) Except for the purposes of an application to rectify the register under the following provisions of this Act, a document in respect of which no entry has been made in the register of designs under subsection (3) of this section shall not be admitted in any court as evidence of the title of any person to a registered design or share of or interest in a registered design unless the court otherwise directs.

20 Rectification of register

(1) The court may, on the application of the relevant person, order the register of designs to be rectified by the making of any entry therein or the variation or deletion of any entry therein.

(1A) In subsection (1) above 'the relevant person' means –

    (a) in the case of an application invoking any ground referred to in section 1A(1)(c) of this Act, any person concerned by the use in question;

    (b) in the case of an application invoking the ground mentioned in section 1A(2) of this Act, the appropriate person;

    (c) in the case of an application invoking any ground mentioned in section 11ZA(2), (3) or (4) of this Act, the person able to make the objection;

    (d) in any other case, any person aggrieved.

(1B) In subsection (1A) above 'the appropriate person' means, in relation to an earlier design protected by virtue of registration under this Act or an application for such registration, the registered proprietor of the design or (as the case may be) the applicant.

(2) In proceedings under this section the court may determine any question which it may be necessary or expedient to decide in connection with the rectification of the register.

(3) Notice of any application to the court under this section shall be given in the prescribed manner to the registrar, who shall be entitled to appear and be heard on the application, and shall appear if so directed by the court.

(4) Any order made by the court under this section shall direct that notice of the order shall be served on the registrar in the prescribed manner; and the registrar shall, on receipt of the notice, rectify the register accordingly.

(5) A rectification of the register under this section has effect as follows –

    (a) an entry made has effect from the date on which it should have been made,

    (b) an entry varied has effect as if it had originally been made in its varied form, and

    (c) an entry deleted shall be deemed never to have had effect,

unless, in any case, the court directs otherwise.

(6) Orders which may be made by the court under this section include, in particular, declarations of partial invalidity.

21 Power to correct clerical errors

(1) The registrar may, in accordance with the provisions of this section, correct any error in an application for the registration or in the representation of a design, or any error in the register of designs.

(2) A correction may be made in pursuance of this section either upon a request in writing made by any person interested and accompanied by the prescribed fee, or without such a request.

(3) Where the registrar proposes to make any such correction as aforesaid otherwise than in pursuance of a request made under this section, he shall give notice of the proposal to the registered proprietor or the applicant for registration of the design, as the case may be, and to any other person who appears to him to be concerned, and shall give them an opportunity to be heard before making the correction.

22 Inspection of registered designs

(1) Where a design has been registered under this Act, there shall be open to inspection at the Patent Office on and after the day on which the certificate of registration is issued –

(a) the representation or specimen of the design

This subsection has effect subject to the following provisions of this section and to any rules made under section 5(2) of this Act.

(2) Where –

(a) a design has been registered;
(b) a product to which the design was intended to be applied or in which it was intended to be incorporated was specified, in accordance with rules made under section 36 of this Act, in the application for the registration of the design; and
(c) the product so specified falls within any class prescribed for the purposes of this subsection,

No representation, specimen or evidence filed in pursuance of the application shall, until the expiration of such period after the day on which the certificate of registration is issued as may be prescribed in relation to products of that class, be open to inspection at the Patent Office except by the registered proprietor, a person authorised in writing by the registered proprietor, or a person authorised by the registrar or by the court:

Provided that where the registrar proposes to refuse an application for the registration of any other design on the ground that, by reference to the first-mentioned design, it is not new or does not have individual character the applicant shall be entitled to inspect the representation or specimen of the first-mentioned design filed in pursuance of the application for registration of that design.

(3) In the case of a registered design and a specified product which falls within any class prescribed for the purposes of the last foregoing subsection, the [representation, specimen or evidence] shall not, during the period prescribed as aforesaid, be inspected by any person by virtue of this section except in presence of the registrar or of an officer acting under him; and except in the case of an inspection authorised by the proviso to that subsection, the person making the inspection shall not be entitled to take a copy of the [representation, specimen or evidence] or any part thereof.

(4) Where an application for the registration of a design has been abandoned or refused, neither the application for registration nor any [representation, specimen or evidence] filed in pursuance thereof shall at any time be open to inspection at the Patent Office or be published by the registrar.

23 Information as to existence of right in registered design

On the request of a person furnishing such information as may enable the registrar to identify the design, and on payment of the prescribed fee, the registrar shall inform him –

(a) whether the design is registered, and
(b) whether any extension of the period of the right in the registered design has been granted

and shall state the date of registration and the name and address of the registered proprietor.

24 [*Repealed.*]

Legal proceedings and appeals

25 Certificate of contested validity of registration

(1) If in any proceedings before the court the validity of the registration of a design is contested, and it is found by the court that the design is, to any extent, validly registered, the court may certify that the validity of the registration of the design was contested in those proceedings.

(2) Where any such certificate has been granted, then if in any subsequent proceedings before the court for infringement of the [right in the registered design] or for invalidation of the registration of the design, a final order or judgment is made or given in favour of the registered proprietor, he shall, unless the court otherwise directs, be entitled to his costs as between solicitor and client:

Provided that this subsection shall not apply to the costs of any appeal in any such proceedings as aforesaid.

26 Remedy for groundless threats of infringement proceedings

(1) Where any person (whether entitled to or interested in a registered design or an application for registration of a design or not) by circulars, advertisements or otherwise threatens any other person with proceedings for infringement of the right in a registered design, any person aggrieved thereby may bring an action against him for any such relief as is mentioned in the next following subsection.

(2) Unless in any action brought by virtue of this section the defendant proves that the acts in respect of which proceedings were threatened constitute or, if done, would constitute, an infringement of the right in a registered design the registration of which is not shown by the plaintiff to be invalid, the plaintiff shall be entitled to the following relief, that is to say –
    (a) a declaration to the effect that the threats are unjustifiable;
    (b) an injunction against the continuance of the threats; and
    (c) such damages, if any, as he has sustained thereby.

(2A) Proceedings may not be brought under this section in respect of a threat to bring proceedings for an infringement alleged to consist of the making or importing of anything.

(3) For the avoidance of doubt it is hereby declared that a mere notification that a design is registered does not constitute a threat of proceedings within the meaning of this section.

27 The court

(1) In this Act 'the court' means –
    (a) in England and Wales the High Court or any patents county court having jurisdiction by virtue of an order under section 287 of the Copyright, Designs and Patents Act 1988,
    (b) in Scotland, the Court of Session, and
    (c) in Northern Ireland, the High Court.

(2) Provision may be made by rules of court with respect to proceedings in the High Court in England and Wales for references and applications under this Act to

be dealt with by such judge of that court as the Lord Chancellor may select for the purpose.

28 The Appeal Tribunal

(1) Any appeal from the registrar under this Act shall lie to the Appeal Tribunal.

(2) The Appeal Tribunal shall consist of –
- (a) one or more judges of the High Court nominated by the Lord Chancellor, and
- (b) one judge of the Court of Session nominated by the Lord President of that Court.

(2A) At any time when it consists of two or more judges, the jurisdiction of the Appeal Tribunal –
- (a) where in the case of any particular appeal the senior of those judges so directs, shall be exercised in relation to that appeal by both of the judges, or (if there are more than two) by two of them, sitting together, and
- (b) in relation to any appeal in respect of which no such direction is given, may be exercised by any one of the judges;

and, in the exercise of that jurisdiction, different appeals may be heard at the same time by different judges.

(3) The expenses of the Appeal Tribunal shall be defrayed and the fees to be taken therein may be fixed as if the Tribunal were a court of the High Court.

(4) The Appeal Tribunal may examine witnesses on oath and administer oaths for that purpose.

(5) Upon any appeal under this Act the Appeal Tribunal may by order award to any party such costs or expenses as the Tribunal may consider reasonable and direct how and by what parties the costs or expenses are to be paid; and any such order may be enforced –
- (a) in England and Wales or Northern Ireland, in the same way as an order of the High Court;
- (b) in Scotland, in the same way as a decree for expenses granted by the Court of Session.

(6) [. . .]

(7) Upon any appeal under this Act the Appeal Tribunal may exercise any power which could have been exercised by the registrar in the proceeding from which the appeal is brought.

(8) Subject to the foregoing provisions of this section the Appeal Tribunal may make rules for regulating all matters relating to proceedings before it under this Act including right of audience.

(8A) At any time when the Appeal Tribunal consists of two or more judges, the power to make rules under subsection (8) of this section shall be exercisable by the senior of those judges:

Provided that another of those judges may exercise that power if it appears to him that it is necessary for rules to be made and that the judge (or, if more than one, each of the judges) senior to him is for the time being prevented by illness, absence or otherwise from making them.

(9) An appeal to the Appeal Tribunal under this Act shall not be deemed to be a proceeding in the High Court.

(10) In this section 'the High Court' means the High Court in England and Wales; and for the purposes of this section the seniority of judges shall be reckoned by reference to the dates on which they were appointed judges of that court or the Court of Session.

Powers and duties of registrar

29 Exercise of discretionary powers of registrar

Without prejudice to any provisions of this Act requiring the registrar to hear any party to proceedings thereunder, or to give to any such party an opportunity to be heard, rules made by the Secretary of State under this Act shall require the registrar to give to any applicant for registration of a design an opportunity to be heard before exercising adversely to the applicant any discretion vested in the registrar by or under this Act.

30 Costs and security for costs

(1) Rules made by the Secretary of State under this Act may make provision empowering the registrar, in any proceedings before him under this Act –
    (a) to award any party such costs as he may consider reasonable, and
    (b) to direct how and by what parties they are to be paid.

(2) Any such order of the registrar may be enforced –
    (a) in England and Wales or Northern Ireland, in the same way as an order of the High Court;
    (b) in Scotland, in the same way as a decree for expenses granted by the Court of Session.

(3) Rules made by the Secretary of State under this Act may make provision empowering the registrar to require a person, in such cases as may be prescribed, to give security for the costs of –
    (a) an application for invalidation of the registration of a design,
    (b) [. . .]
    (c) an appeal from any decision of the registrar under this Act,

and enabling the application to appeal to be treated as abandoned in default of such security being given.

31 Evidence before registrar

Rules made by the Secretary of State under this Act may make provision –
    (a) as to the giving of evidence in proceedings before the registrar under this Act by affidavit or statutory declaration;
    (b) conferring on the registrar the powers of an official referee of the Supreme Court as regards the examination of witnesses on oath and the discovery and production of documents; and
    (c) applying in relation to the attendance of witnesses in proceedings before the registrar the rules applicable to the attendance of witnesses in proceedings before such a referee.

32 [*Repealed.*]

Offences

33 Offences under s.5

(1) If any person fails to comply with any direction given under section five of this Act or makes or causes to be made an application for the registration of a design in contravention of that section, he shall be guilty of an offence and liable –

    (a) on conviction on indictment to imprisonment for a term not exceeding two years or a fine, or both;

    (b) on summary conviction to imprisonment for a term not exceeding six months or a fine not exceeding the statutory maximum, or both.

(2) [. . .]

34 Falsification of register, etc

If any person makes or causes to be made a false entry in the register of designs, or a writing falsely purporting to be a copy of an entry in that register, or produces or tenders or causes to be produced or tendered in evidence any such writing, knowing the entry or writing to be false, he shall be guilty of an offence and liable –

    (a) on conviction on indictment to imprisonment for a term not exceeding two years or a fine, or both;

    (b) on summary conviction to imprisonment for a term not exceeding six months or a fine not exceeding the statutory maximum, or both.

35 Fine for falsely representing a design as registered

(1) If any person falsely represents that a design applied to, or incorporated in, any product sold by him is registered, he shall be liable on summary conviction to a fine not exceeding level 3 on the standard scale; and for the purposes of this provision a person who sells a product having stamped, engraved or impressed thereon or otherwise applied thereto the word 'registered', or any other word expressing or implying that the design applied to, or incorporated in, the product is registered, shall be deemed to represent that the design applied to, or incorporated in, the product is registered.

(2) If any person, after the right in a registered design has expired, marks any product to which the design has been applied or in which it has been incorporated with the word 'registered', or any word or words implying that there is a subsisting right in the design under this Act, or causes any such product to be so marked, he shall be liable on summary conviction to a fine not exceeding level 1 on the standard scale.

35A Offence by body corporate: liability of officers

(1) Where an offence under this Act committed by a body corporate is proved to have been committed with the consent or connivance of a director, manager, secretary or other similar officers of the body, or a person purporting to act in any such capacity, he as well as the body corporate is guilty of the offence and liable to be proceeded against and punished accordingly.

(2) In relation to a body corporate whose affairs are managed by its members 'director' means a member of the body corporate.

Rules, etc

36 General power of Secretary of State to make rules, etc

(1) Subject to the provisions of this Act, the Secretary of State may make such rules as he thinks expedient for regulating the business of the Patent Office in relation to designs and for regulating all matters by this Act placed under the direction or control of the registrar or the Secretary of State.

(1A) Rules may, in particular, make provision –

(a) prescribing the form of applications for registration of designs and of any representations or specimens of designs or other documents which may be filed at the Patent Office, and requiring copies to be furnished of any such representations, specimens or documents;

(ab) requiring applications for registration of designs to specify –
  (i) the products to which the designs are intended to be applied or in which they are intended to be incorporated;
  (ii) the classification of the designs by reference to such test as may be prescribed;

(b) regulating the procedure to be followed in connection with any application or request to the registrar or in connection with any proceeding before him, and authorising the rectification of irregularities of procedure;

(c) providing for the appointment of advisers to assist the registrar in proceedings before him;

(d) regulating the keeping of the register of designs;

(e) authorising the publication and sale of copies of representations of designs and other documents in the Patent Office;

(f) prescribing anything authorised or required by this Act to be prescribed by rules.

(1B) The remuneration of an adviser appointed to assist the registrar shall be determined by the Secretary of State with the consent of the Treasury and shall be defrayed out of money provided by Parliament.

(2) Rules made under this section may provide for the establishment of branch offices for designs and may authorise any document or thing required by or under this Act to be filed or done at the Patent Office to be filed or done at the branch office at Manchester or any other branch office established in pursuance of the rules.

37 Provisions as to rules and Orders

(1) [. . .]

(2) Any rules made by the Secretary of State in pursuance of section 15 of this Act, and any order made, direction given, or other action taken under the rules by the registrar, may be made, given or taken so as to have effect as respects things done or omitted to be done on or after such date, whether before or after the coming into operation of the rules or of this Act, as may be specified in the rules.

(3) Any power to make rules conferred by this Act on the Secretary of State or on the Appeal Tribunal shall be exercisable by statutory instrument; and the Statutory Instruments Act 1946 shall apply to a statutory instrument containing rules made by the Appeal Tribunal in like manner as if the rules had been made by a Minister of the Crown.

(4) Any statutory instrument containing rules made by the Secretary of State under this Act shall be subject to annulment in pursuance of a resolution of either House of Parliament.

(5) Any Order in Council made under this Act may be revoked or varied by a subsequent Order in Council.

38 [*Repealed.*]

39 Hours of business and excluded days

(1) Rules made by the Secretary of State under this Act may specify the hour at which the Patent Office shall be deemed to be closed on a day for the purposes of the transaction by the public of business under this Act or of any class of such business, and may specify days as excluded days for any such purposes.

(2) Any business done under this Act on any day after the hour specified as aforesaid in relation to business of that class, or on any day which is an excluded day in relation to business of that class, shall be deemed to have been done on the next following day not being an excluded day; and where the time for doing anything under this Act expires on an excluded day, that time shall be extended to the next following day not being an excluded day.

40 Fees

There shall be paid in respect of the registration of designs and applications therefore, and in respect of other matters relating to designs arising under this Act, such fees as may be prescribed by rules made by the Secretary of State with the consent of the Treasury.

41 Service of notices, etc, by post

Any notice required or authorised to be given by or under this Act, and any application or other document so authorised or required to be made or filed, may be given, made or filed by post.

42 Annual report of registrar

The Comptroller-General of Patents, Designs and Trade Marks shall, in his annual report with respect to the execution of the Patents Act 1977, include a report with respect to the execution of this Act as if it formed a part of or was included in that Act.

43 Savings

(1) [. . .]

(2) Nothing in this Act shall affect the right of the Crown or of any person deriving title directly or indirectly from the Crown to sell or use products forfeited under the laws relating to customs or excise.

44 Interpretation

(1) In this Act, except where the context otherwise requires, the following expressions have the meanings hereby respectively assigned by them, that is to say –

> 'Appeal Tribunal' means the Appeal Tribunal constituted and acting in accordance with section 28 of this Act as amended by the Administration of Justice Act 1969;
>
> 'assignee' includes the personal representative of a deceased assignee, and references to the assignee of any person include references to the assignee of the personal representative or assignee of that person;
>
> 'author' in relation to a design, has the meaning given by section 2(3) and (4);
>
> 'complex product' has the meaning assigned to it by section 1(3) of this Act;
>
> [. . .]
>
> 'the court' shall be construed in accordance with section 27 of this Act;
>
> 'design' has the meaning assigned to it by section 1(2) of this Act;
>
> 'employee', 'employment' and 'employer' refer to employment under a contract of service or of apprenticeship;
>
> [. . .]
>
> 'national unregistered design right' means design right within the meaning of Part III of the Copyright, Designs and Patents Act 1988;
>
> 'prescribed' means prescribed by rules made by the Secretary of State under this Act;
>
> 'product' has the meaning assigned to it by section 1(3) of this Act;
>
> 'proprietor' has the meaning assigned to it by section two of this Act;
>
> 'registered proprietor' means the person or persons for the time being entered in the register of designs as proprietor of the design;
>
> 'registrar' means the Comptroller-General of Patents Designs and Trade Marks;

(2) [. . .]

(3) [. . .]

(4) For the purposes of subsection (1) of section 14 of this Act, the expression 'personal representative', in relation to a deceased person, includes the legal representative of the deceased appointed in any country outside the United Kingdom.

45 Application to Scotland

In the application of this Act to Scotland –

> (1), (2) [. . .]
>
> (3) The expression 'injunction' means 'interdict' ; the expression 'arbitrator' means 'arbiter'; the expression 'plaintiff' means 'pursuer'; the expression 'defendant' means 'defender'.

46 Application to Northern Ireland

In the application of this Act to Northern Ireland –

> (1), (2) [. . .]
>
> (3) References to enactments include enactments comprised in Northern Ireland legislation:
>
> (3A) References to the Crown include the Crown in right of Her Majesty's Government in Northern Ireland:

(4) References to a Government department shall be construed as including references to a Northern Ireland department and in relation to a Northern Ireland department references to the Treasury shall be construed as references to the Department of Finance and Personnel:

(5) [. . .]

47 Application to Isle of Man

This Act extends to the Isle of Man, subject to any modifications contained in an Order made by Her Majesty in Council, and accordingly, subject to any such Order, references in this Act to the United Kingdom shall be construed as including the Isle of Man.

47A Territorial waters and the continental shelf

(1) For the purposes of this Act the territorial waters of the United Kingdom shall be treated as part of the United Kingdom.

(2) This Act applies to things done in the United Kingdom sector of the continental shelf on a structure or vessel which is present there for purposes directly connected with the exploration of the sea bed or subsoil or the exploitation of their natural resources as it applies to things done in the United Kingdom.

(3) The United Kingdom sector of the continental shelf means the areas designated by order under section 1(7) of the Continental Shelf Act 1964.

48 Repeals, savings, and transitional provisions

(1) [. . .]

(2) Subject to the provisions of this section, any Order in Council, rule, order, requirement, certificate, notice, decision, direction, authorisation, consent, application, request or thing made, issued, given or done under any enactment repealed by this Act shall, if in force at the commencement of this Act, and so far as it could have been made, issued, given or done under this Act, continue in force and have effect as if made, issued, given or done under the corresponding enactment of this Act.

(3) Any register kept under the Patents and Designs Act 1907, shall be deemed to form part of the corresponding register under this Act.

(4) Any design registered before the commmencement of this Act shall be deemed to be registered under this Act in respect of articles of the class in which it is registered.

(5) [. . .]

(6) Any document referring to any enactment repealed by this Act shall be construed as referring to the corresponding enactment of this Act.

(7) Nothing in the foregoing provisions of this section shall be taken as prejudicing the operation of section thirty-eight of the Interpretation Act 1889, (which relates to the effect of repeals).

49 Short title and commencement

(1) This Act may be cited as the Registered Designs Act 1949.

(2) This Act shall come into operation on the first day of January, nineteen hundred and fifty, immediately after the coming into operation of the Patents and Designs Act 1949.

SCHEDULES

SCHEDULE A1

Grounds for refusal of registration in relation to emblems etc.

1. *Grounds for refusal in relation to certain emblems etc.*

(1) A design shall be refused registration under this Act if it involves the use of –

(a) the Royal arms, or any of the principal armorial bearings of the Royal arms, or any insignia or device so nearly resembling the Royal arms or any such armorial bearing as to be likely to be mistaken for them or it;

(b) a representation of the Royal crown or any of the Royal flags;

(c) a representation of Her Majesty or any member of the Royal family, or any colourable imitation thereof; or

(d) words, letters or devices likely to lead persons to think that the applicant either has or recently has had Royal patronage or authorisation;

unless it appears to the registrar that consent for such use has been given by or on behalf of Her Majesty or (as the case may be) the relevant member of the Royal family.

(2) A design shall be refused registration under this Act if it involves the use of –

(a) the national flag of the United Kingdom (commonly known as the Union Jack); or

(b) the flag of England, Wales, Scotland, Northern Ireland or the Isle of Man,

and it appears to the registrar that the use would be misleading or grossly offensive.

(3) A design shall be refused registration under this Act if it involves the use of –

(a) arms to which a person is entitled by virtue of a grant of arms by the Crown; or

(b) insignia so nearly resembling such arms as to be likely to be mistaken for them;

unless it appears to the registrar that consent for such use has been given by or on behalf of the person concerned and the use is not in any way contrary to the law of arms.

(4) A design shall be refused registration under this Act if it involves the use of a controlled representation within the meaning of the Olympic Symbol etc. (Protection) Act 1995 unless it appears to the registrar that –

(a) the application is made by the person for the time being appointed under section 1(2) of the Olympic Symbol etc. (Protection) Act 1995 (power of Secretary of State to appoint a person as the proprietor of the Olympics association right); or

(b) consent for such use has been given by or on behalf of the person mentioned in paragraph (a) above.

2. *Grounds for refusal in relation to emblems etc. of Paris Convention countries*

(1) A design shall be refused registration under this Act if it involves the use of the flag of a Paris Convention country unless –

(a) the authorisation of the competent authorities of that country has been given for the registration; or

(b) it appears to the registrar that the use of the flag in the manner proposed is permitted without such authorisation.

(2) A design shall be refused registration under this Act if it involves the use of the armorial bearings or any other state emblem of a Paris Convention country which is protected under the Paris Convention unless the authorisation of the competent authorities of that country has been given for the registration.

(3) A design shall be refused registration under this Act if –

(a) the design involves the use of an official sign or hallmark adopted by a Paris Convention country and indicating control and warranty;

(b) the sign or hallmark is protected under the Paris Convention; and

(c) the design could be applied to or incorporated in goods of the same, or a similar, kind as those in relation to which the sign or hallmark indicates control and warranty;

unless the authorisation of the competent authorities of that country has been given for the registration.

(4) The provisions of this paragraph as to national flags and other state emblems, and official signs or hallmarks, apply equally to anything which from a heraldic point of view imitates any such flag or other emblem, or sign or hallmark.

(5) Nothing in this paragraph prevents the registration of a design on the application of a national of a country who is authorised to make use of a state emblem, or official sign or hallmark, of that country, notwithstanding that it is similar to that of another country.

3. *Grounds for refusal in relation to emblems etc. of certain international organisations*

(1) This paragraph applies to –

(a) the armorial bearings, flags or other emblems; and

(b) the abbreviations and names,

of international intergovernmental organisations of which one or more Paris Convention countries are members.

(2) A design shall be refused registration under this Act if it involves the use of any such emblem, abbreviation or name which is protected under the Paris Convention unless –

(a) the authorisation of the international organisation concerned has been given for the registration; or

(b) it appears to the registrar that the use of the emblem, abbreviation or name in the manner proposed –

(i) is not such as to suggest to the public that a connection exists between the organisation and the design; or

(ii) is not likely to mislead the public as to the existence of a connection between the user and the organisation.

(3) The provisions of this paragraph as to emblems of an international organisation apply equally to anything which from a heraldic point of view imitates any such emblem.

(4) Nothing in this paragraph affects the rights of a person whose *bona fide* use of the design in question began before 4th January 1962 (when the relevant provisions of the Paris Convention entered into force in relation to the United Kingdom).

4. *Paragraphs 2 and 3: supplementary*

(1) For the purposes of paragraph 2 above state emblems of a Paris Convention country (other than the national flag), and official signs or hallmarks, shall be regarded as protected under the Paris Convention only if, or to the extent that –

(a) the country in question has notified the United Kingdom in accordance with Article 6ter(3) of the Convention that it desires to protect that emblem, sign or hallmark;

(b) the notification remains in force; and

(c) the United Kingdom has not objected to it in accordance with Article 6*ter*(4) or any such objection has been withdrawn.

(2) For the purposes of paragraph 3 above the emblems, abbreviations and names of an international organisation shall be regarded as protected under the Paris Convention only if, or to the extent that –

(a) the organisation in question has notified the United Kingdom in accordance with Article 6*ter*(3) of the Convention that it desires to protect that emblem, abbreviation or name;

(b) the notification remains in force; and

(c) the United Kingdom has not objected to it in accordance with Article 6*ter*(4) or any such objection has been withdrawn.

(3) Notification under Article 6*ter*(3) of the Paris Convention shall have effect only in relation to applications for the registration of designs made more than two months after the receipt of the notification.

Interpretation

5. In this Schedule –

'a Paris Convention country' means a country, other than the United Kingdom, which is a party to the Paris Convention; and

'the Paris Convention' means the Paris Convention for the Protection of Industrial Property of 20th March 1883.'

FIRST SCHEDULE

Section 12

PROVISIONS AS TO THE USE OF REGISTERED DESIGNS FOR THE SERVICES OF THE CROWN AND AS TO THE RIGHTS OF THIRD PARTIES IN RESPECT OF SUCH USE

1 Use of registered designs for services of the Crown

(1) Notwithstanding anything in this Act, any Government department, and any person authorised in writing by a Government department, may use any registered design for the services of the Crown in accordance with the following provisions of this paragraph.

(2) If and so far as the design has before the date of registration thereof been duly recorded by or applied by or on behalf of a Government department otherwise than in consequence of the communication of the design directly or indirectly by the registered proprietor or any person from whom he derives title, any use of the design by virtue of this paragraph may be made free of any royalty or other payment to the registered proprietor.

(3) If and so far as the design has not been so recorded or applied as aforesaid, any use of the design made by virtue of this paragraph at any time after the date of registration thereof, or in consequence of any such communication as aforesaid, shall be made upon such terms as may be agreed upon, either before or after the use, between the Government department and the registered proprietor with the approval of the Treasury, or as may in default of agreement be determined by the court on a reference under paragraph 3 of this Schedule.

(4) The authority of a Government department in respect of a design may be given under this paragraph either before or after the design is registered and either before or after the acts in respect of which the authority is given are done, and may be given to any person whether or not he is authorised directly or indirectly by the registered proprietor to use the design.

(5) Where any use of a design is made by or with the authority of a Government department under this paragraph, then, unless it appears to the department that it would be contrary to the public interest so to do, the department shall notify the registered proprietor as soon as practicable after the use is begun, and furnish him with such information as to the extent of the use as he may from time to time require.

(6) For the purposes of this and the next following paragraph 'the services of the Crown' shall be deemed to include –

    (a) the supply to the government of any country outside the United Kingdom, in pursuance of an agreement or arrangement between Her Majesty's Government in the United Kingdom and the government of that country, of products required –

(i) for the defence of that country; or

(ii) for the defence of any other country whose government is party to any agreement or arrangement with Her Majesty's said Government in respect of defence matters;

(b) the supply to the United Nations, or to the government of any country belonging to that organisation, in pursuance of an agreement or arrangement between Her Majesty's Government and that organisation or government, of products required for any armed forces operating in pursuance of a resolution of that organisation or any organ of that organisation;

and the power of a Government department or a person authorised by a Government department under this paragraph to use a design shall include power to sell to any such government or to the said organisation any products the supply of which is authorised by this sub-paragraph, and to sell to any person any products made in the exercise of the powers conferred by this paragraph which are no longer required for the purpose for which they were made.

(7) The purchaser of any products sold in the exercise of powers conferred by this paragraph, and any person claiming through him, shall have power to deal with them in the same manner as if the rights in the registered design were held on behalf of His Majesty.

2 Rights of third parties in respect of Crown use

(1) In relation to any use of a registered design, or a design in respect of which an application for registration is pending, made for the services of the Crown –

(a) by a Government department or a person authorised by a Government department under the last foregoing paragraph; or

(b) by the registered proprietor or applicant for registration to the order of a Government department,

the provisions of any licence, assignment or agreement made, whether before or after the commencement of this Act, between the registered proprietor or applicant for registration or any person who derives title from him or from whom he derives title and any person other than a Government department shall be of no effect so far as those provisions restrict or regulate the use of the design, or any model, document or information relating thereto, or provide for the making of payments in respect of any such use, or calculated by reference thereto; and the reproduction or publication of any model or document in connection with the said use shall not be deemed to be an infringement of any copyright or national unregistered design right subsisting in the model or document.

(2) Where an exclusive licence granted otherwise than for royalties or other benefits determined by reference to the use of the design is in force under the registered design then –

(a) in relation to any use of the design which, but for the provisions of this and the last foregoing paragraph, would constitute an infringement of the rights of the licensee, sub-paragraph (3) of the last foregoing paragraph shall have effect as if for the reference to the registered proprietor there were substituted a reference to the licensee; and

(b) in relation to any use of the design by the licensee by virtue of an authority given under the last foregoing paragraph, that paragraph shall have effect as if the said sub-paragraph (3) were omitted.

(3) Subject to the provisions of the last foregoing sub-paragraph, where the registered design or the right to apply for or obtain registration of the design has been assigned to the registered proprietor in consideration of royalties or other benefits determined by reference to the use of the design, then –

(a) in relation to any use of the design by virtue of paragraph 1 of this Schedule, sub-paragraph (3) of that paragraph shall have effect as if the reference to the registered proprietor included a reference to the assignor, and any sum payable by virtue of that sub-paragraph shall be divided between the registered proprietor and the assignor in such proportion as may be agreed upon between them or as may in default of agreement be determined by the court on a reference under the next following paragraph; and

(b) in relation to any use of the design made for the services of the Crown by the registered proprietor to the order of a Government department, sub-paragraph (3) of paragraph 1 of this Schedule shall have effect as if that use were made by virtue of an authority given under that paragraph.

(4) Where, under sub-paragraph (3) of paragraph 1 of this Schedule, payments are required to be made by a Government department to a registered proprietor in respect of any use of a design, any person being the holder of an exclusive licence under the registered design (not being such a licence as is mentioned in sub-paragraph (2) of this paragraph) authorising him to make use of the design shall be entitled to recover from the registered proprietor such part (if any) of those payments as may be agreed upon between that person and the registered proprietor, or as may in default of agreement be determined by the court under the next following paragraph to be just having regard to any expenditure incurred by that person –

(a) in developing the said design; or

(b) in making payments to the registered proprietor, other than royalties or other payments determined by reference to the use of the design, in consideration of the licence;

and if, at any time before the amount of any such payment has been agreed upon between the Government department and the registered proprietor, that person gives notice, in writing of his interest to the department, any agreement as to the amount of that payment shall be of no effect unless it is made with his consent.

(5) In this paragraph 'exclusive licence' means a licence from a registered proprietor which confers on the licensee, or on the licensee and persons authorised by him, to the exclusion of all other persons (including the registered proprietor), any right in respect of the registered design.

2A Compensation for loss of profit

(1) Where Crown use is made of a registered design, the government department concerned shall pay –

(a) to the registered proprietor, or

(b) if there is an exclusive licence in force in respect of the design, to the exclusive licensee,

compensation for any loss resulting from his not being awarded a contract to supply the products to which the design is applied or in which it is incorporated.

(2) Compensation is payable only to the extent that such a contract could have been fulfilled from his existing manufacturing capacity; but is payable notwithstanding the existence of circumstances rendering him ineligible for the award of such a contract.

(3) In determining the loss, regard shall be had to the profit which would have been made on such a contract and to the extent to which any manufacturing capacity was underused.

(4) No compensation is payable in respect of any failure to secure contracts for the supply of products to which the design is applied or in which it is incorporated otherwise than for the services of the Crown.

(5) The amount payable under this paragraph shall, if not agreed between the registered proprietor or licensee and the government department concerned with the approval of the Treasury, be determined by the court on a reference under paragraph 3; and it is in addition to any amount payable under paragraph 1 or 2 of this Schedule.

(6) In this paragraph –

'Crown use', in relation to a design, means the doing of anything by virtue of paragraph 1 which would otherwise be an infringement of the right in the design; and

'the government department concerned', in relation to such use, means the government department by whom or on whose authority the act was done.

3 Reference of disputes as to Crown use

(1) Any dispute as to –

(a) the exercise by a Government department, or a person authorised by a Government department, of the powers conferred by paragraph 1 of this Schedule,

(b) terms for the use of a design for the services of the Crown under that paragraph,

(c) the right of any person to receive any part of a payment made under paragraph 1(3), or

(d) the right of any person to receive a payment under paragraph 2A,

may be referred to the court by either party to the dispute.

(2) In any proceedings under this paragraph to which a Government department are a party, the department may –

(a) if the registered proprietor is a party to the proceedings, and the department are a relevant person within the meaning of section 20 of this Act apply for invalidation of the registration of the design upon any ground upon which the registration of a design may be declared invalid on an application to the court under section twenty of this Act;

(b) in any case, and provided that the department would be the relevant person within the meaning of section 20 of this Act if they had made an application on the grounds for invalidity being raised put in issue the validity of the registration of the design without applying for its invalidation.

(3) If in such proceedings as aforesaid any question arises whether a design has been recorded or applied as mentioned in paragraph 1 of this Schedule, and the disclosure of any document recording the design, or of any evidence of the application

thereof, would in the opinion of the department be prejudicial to the public interest, the disclosure may be made confidentially to counsel for the other party or to an independent expert mutually agreed upon.

(4) In determining under this paragraph any dispute between a Government department and any person as to terms for the use of a design for the services of the Crown, the court shall have regard to any benefit or compensation which that person or any person from whom he derives title may have received, or may be entitled to receive, directly or indirectly from any Government department in respect of the design in question.

(5) In any proceedings under this paragraph the court may at any time order the whole proceedings or any question or issue of fact arising therein to be referred to a special or official referee or an arbitrator on such terms as the court may direct; and references to the court in the foregoing provisions of this paragraph shall be construed accordingly.

4 Special provisions as to Crown use during emergency

(1) During any period of emergency within the meaning of this paragraph, the powers exercisable in relation to a design by a Government department, or a person authorised by a Government department under paragraph 1 of this Schedule shall include power to use the design for any purpose which appears to the department necessary or expedient –

    (a) for the efficient prosecution of any war in which His Majesty may be engaged;

    (b) for the maintenance of supplies and services essential to the life of the community;

    (c) for securing a sufficiency of supplies and services essential to the well-being of the community;

    (d) for promoting the productivity of industry, commerce and agriculture;

    (e) for fostering and directing exports and reducing imports of any classes, from all or any countries and for redressing the balance of trade;

    (f) generally for ensuring that the whole resources of the community are available for use, and are used, in a manner best calculated to serve the interests of the community; or

    (g) for assisting the relief of suffering and the restoration and distribution of essential supplies and services in any part of His Majesty's dominions or any foreign countries that are in grave distress as the result of war;

and any reference in this Schedule to the services of the Crown shall be construed as including a reference to the purposes aforesaid.

(2) In this paragraph the expression 'period of emergency' means a period beginning on such date as may be declared by Order in Council to be the commencement, and ending on such date as may be so declared to be the termination, of a period of emergency for the purposes of this paragraph.

(3) No order in Council under this paragraph shall be submitted to Her Majesty unless a draft of it has been laid before and approved by a resolution of each House of Parliament.

SCHEDULE 2

[*Repealed.*]

The Berne Convention for the Protection of Literary and Artistic Works

Berne Convention (1886), completed at Paris (1896), revised at Berlin (1908), completed at Berne (1914), revised at Rome (1928), at Brussels (1948), at Stockholm (1967) and at Paris (1971), and amended in 1979 (Berne Union)

Status on 15 July 2003

State	Date on which State became party to the Convention	Latest Act of the Convention to which State is party and date on which State became party to that Act	
Albania	6 March 1994	Paris:	March 6, 1994
Algeria	19 April 1998	Paris:	April 19, 1998
Antigua and Barbuda	17 March 2000	Paris:	March 17, 2000
Argentina	10 June 1967	Paris,	Articles 1 to 21: February 19, 2000
		Paris,	Articles 22 to 38: October 8, 1980
Armenia	19 October 2000	Paris:	October 19, 2000
Australia	14 April 1928	Paris:	March 1, 1978
Austria	1 October 1920	Paris:	August 21, 1982
Azerbaijan	4 June 1999	Paris:	June 4, 1999
Bahamas	10 July 1973	Brussels:	July 10, 1973
		Paris,	Articles 22 to 38: January 8, 1977
Bahrain	2 March 1997	Paris:	March 2, 1997
Bangladesh	4 May 1999	Paris:	May 4, 1999
Barbados	30 July 1983	Paris:	July 30, 1983
Belarus	12 December 1997	Paris:	December 12, 1997
Belgium	5 December 1887	Paris:	September 29, 1999
Belize	17 June 2000	Paris:	June 17, 2000
Benin	3 January 1961	Paris:	March 12, 1975
Bolivia	4 November 1993	Paris:	November 4, 1993
Bosnia and Herzegovina	1 March 1992	Paris:	March 1, 1992
Botswana	15 April 1998	Paris:	April 15, 1998
Brazil	9 February 1922	Paris:	April 20, 1975
Bulgaria	5 December 1921	Paris:	December 4, 1974
Burkina Faso	19 August 1963	Paris:	January 24, 1976
Cameroon	21 September 1964	Paris,	Articles 1 to 21: October 10, 1974
			Articles 22 to 38: November 10, 1973

State	Date on which State became party to the Convention	Latest Act of the Convention to which State is party and date on which State became party to that Act	
Canada	10 April 1928	Paris:	June 26, 1998
Cape Verde	7 July 1997	Paris:	July 7, 1997
Central African Republic	3 September 1977	Paris:	September 3, 1977
Chad	25 November 1971	Brussels:	November 25, 1971
		Stockholm,	Articles 22 to 38: November 25, 1971
Chile	5 June 1970	Paris:	July 10, 1975
China	15 October 1992	Paris:	October 15, 1992
Colombia	7 March 1988	Paris:	March 7, 1988
Congo	8 May 1962	Paris:	December 5, 1975
Costa Rica	10 June 1978	Paris:	June 10, 1978
Côte d'Ivoire	1 January 1962	Paris,	Articles 1 to 21: October 10, 1974
		Paris,	Articles 22 to 38: May 4, 1974
Croatia	8 October 1991	Paris:	October 8, 1991
Cuba	20 February 1997	Paris:	February 20, 1997
Cyprus	24 February 1964	Paris:	July 27, 1983
Czech Republic	1 January 1993	Paris:	January 1, 1993
Democratic People's Republic of Korea	28 April 2003	Paris:	April 28, 2003
Democratic Republic of the Congo	8 October 1963	Paris:	January 31, 1975
Denmark	1 July 1903	Paris:	June 30, 1979
Djibouti	13 May 2002	Paris:	May 13, 2002
Dominica	7 August 1999	Paris:	August 7, 1999
Dominican Republic	24 December 1997	Paris:	December 24, 1997
Ecuador	9 October 1991	Paris:	October 9, 1991
Egypt	7 June 1977	Paris:	June 7, 1977
El Salvador	19 February 1994	Paris:	February 19, 1994
Equatorial Guinea	26 June 1997	Paris:	June 26, 1997
Estonia	26 October 1994	Paris:	October 26, 1994
Fiji	1 December 1971	Brussels:	December 1, 1971
		Stockholm,	Articles 22 to 38: March 15, 1972
Finland	1 April 1928	Paris:	November 1, 1986
France	5 December 1887	Paris,	Articles 1 to 21: October 10, 1974
		Paris,	Articles 22 to 38: December 15, 1972
Gabon	26 March 1962	Paris:	June 10, 1975
Gambia	7 March 1993	Paris:	March 7, 1993
Georgia	16 May 1995	Paris:	May 16, 1995
Germany	5 December 1887	Paris,	Articles 1 to 21: October 10, 1974
			Articles 22 to 38: January 22, 1974
Ghana	11 October 1991	Paris:	October 11, 1991
Greece	9 November 1920	Paris:	March 8, 1976
Grenada	22 September 1998	Paris:	September 22, 1998
Guatemala	28 July 1997	Paris:	July 28, 1997
Guinea	20 November 1980	Paris:	November 20, 1980
Guinea-Bissau	22 July 1991	Paris:	July 22, 1991
Guyana	25 October 1994	Paris:	October 25, 1994
Haiti	11 January 1996	Paris:	January 11, 1996
Holy See	12 September 1935	Paris:	April 24, 1975
Honduras	25 January 1990	Paris:	January 25, 1990
Hungary	14 February 1922	Paris,	Articles 1 to 21: October 10, 1974
		Paris,	Articles 22 to 38: December 15, 1972

State	Date on which State became party to the Convention	Latest Act of the Convention to which State is party and date on which State became party to that Act	
Iceland	7 September 1947	Paris,	Articles 1 to 21: August 25, 1999
		Paris,	Articles 22 to 38: December 28, 1984
India	1 April 1928	Paris,	Articles 1 to 21: May 6, 1984
		Paris,	Articles 22 to 38: January 10, 1975
Indonesia	5 September 1997	Paris:	September 5, 1997
Ireland	5 October 1927	Brussels:	July 5, 1959
		Stockholm,	Articles 22 to 38: December 21, 1970
Israel	24 March 1950	Brussels:	August 1, 1951
		Stockholm,	Articles 22 to 38: January 29 or February 26, 1970
Italy	5 December 1887	Paris:	November 14, 1979
Jamaica	1 January 1994	Paris:	January 1, 1994
Japan	15 July 1899	Paris:	April 24, 1975
Jordan	28 July 1999	Paris:	July 28, 1999
Kazakhstan	12 April 1999	Paris:	April 12, 1999
Kenya	11 June 1993	Paris:	June 11, 1993
Kyrgyzstan	8 July 1999	Paris:	July 8, 1999
Latvia	11 August 1995	Paris:	August 11, 1995
Lebanon	30 September 1947	Rome:	September 30, 1947
Lesotho	28 September 1989	Paris:	September 28, 1989
Liberia	8 March 1989	Paris:	March 8, 1989
Libyan Arab Jamahiriya	28 September 1976	Paris:	September 28, 1976
Liechtenstein	30 July 1931	Paris:	September 23, 1999
Lithuania	14 December 1994	Paris:	December 14, 1994
Luxembourg	20 June 1888	Paris:	April 20, 1975
Madagascar	1 January 1966	Brussels:	January 1, 1966
Malawi	12 October 1991	Paris:	October 12, 1991
Malaysia	1 October 1990	Paris:	October 1, 1990
Mali	19 March 1962	Paris:	December 5, 1977
Malta	21 September 1964	Rome:	September 21, 1964
		Paris,	Articles 22 to 38: December 12, 1977
Mauritania	6 February 1973	Paris:	September 21, 1976
Mauritius	10 May 1989	Paris:	May 10, 1989
Mexico	11 June 1967	Paris:	December 17, 1974
Micronesia (Federated States of)	7 October 2003	Paris:	October 7, 2003
Monaco	30 May 1889	Paris:	November 23, 1974
Mongolia	12 March 1998	Paris:	March 12, 1998
Morocco	16 June 1917	Paris:	May 17, 1987
Namibia	21 March 1990	Paris:	December 24, 1993
Netherlands	1 November 1912	Paris,	Articles 1 to 21: January 30, 1986
		Paris,	Articles 22 to 38: January 10, 1975
New Zealand	24 April 1928	Rome:	December 4, 1947
Nicaragua	23 August 2000	Paris:	August 23, 2000
Niger	2 May 1962	Paris:	May 21, 1975
Nigeria	14 September 1993	Paris:	September 14, 1993
Norway	13 April 1896	Paris,	Articles 1 to 21: October 11, 1995
		Paris,	Articles 22 to 38: June 13, 1974
Oman	14 July 1999	Paris:	July 14, 1999
Pakistan	5 July 1948	Rome:	July 5, 1948
		Stockholm,	Articles 22 to 38: January 29 or February 26, 1970

State	Date on which State became party to the Convention	Latest Act of the Convention to which State is party and date on which State became party to that Act	
Panama	8 June 1996	Paris:	June 8, 1996
Paraguay	2 January 1992	Paris:	January 2, 1992
Peru	20 August 1988	Paris:	August 20, 1988
Philippines	1 August 1951	Paris,	Articles 1 to 21: June 18, 1997
		Paris,	Articles 22 to 38: July 16, 1980
Poland	28 January 1920	Paris,	Articles 1 to 21: October 22, 1994
		Paris,	Articles 22 to 38: August 4, 1990
Portugal	29 March 1911	Paris:	January 12, 1979
Qatar	5 July 2000	Paris:	July 5, 2000
Republic of Korea	21 August 1996	Paris:	August 21, 1996
Republic of Moldova	2 November 1995	Paris:	November 2, 1995
Romania	1 January 1927	Paris:	September 9, 1998
Russian Federation	13 March 1995	Paris:	March 13, 1995
Rwanda	1 March 1984	Paris:	March 1, 1984
Saint Kitts and Nevis	9 April 1995	Paris:	April 9, 1995
Saint Lucia	24 August 1993	Paris:	August 24, 1993
Saint Vincent and the Grenadines	29 August 1995	Paris:	August 29, 1995
Senegal	25 August 1962	Paris:	August 12, 1975
Serbia and Montenegro	27 April 1992	Paris:	April 27, 1992

Universal Copyright Convention (revised Paris, 24 July 1971)

The Contracting States.

Moved by the desire to ensure in all countries copyright protection of literary, scientific and artistic works,

Convinced that a system of copyright protection appropriate to all nations of the world and expressed in a universal convention, additional to, and without impairing international systems already in force, will ensure respect for the rights of the individual and encourage the development of literature, the sciences and the arts,

Persuaded that such a universal copyright system will facilitate a wider dissemination of works of the human mind and increase international understanding,

Have resolved to revise the Universal Copyright Convention as signed at Geneva on 6 September 1952 (hereinafter called 'the 1952 Convention'), and consequently,

Have agreed as follows:

ARTICLE I

Each Contracting State undertakes to provide for the adequate and effective protection of the rights of authors and other copyright proprietors in literary, scientific and artistic works, including writings, musical, dramatic and cinematographic works, and paintings, engravings and sculpture.

ARTICLE II

1. Published works of nationals of any Contracting State and works first published in that State shall enjoy in each other Contracting State the same protection as that other State accords to works of its nationals first published in its own territory, as well as the protection specially granted by this Convention.

2. Unpublished works of nationals of each Contracting State shall enjoy in each other Contracting State the same protection as that other State accords to unpublished works of its own nationals, as well as the protection specially granted by this Convention.

3. For the purpose of this Convention any Contracting State may, by domestic legislation, assimilate to its own nationals any person domiciled in that State.

ARTICLE III

1. Any Contracting State which, under its domestic law, requires as a condition of copyright, compliance with formalities such as deposit, registration, notice, notarial certificates, payment of fees or manufacture or publication in that Contracting State, shall regard these requirements as satisfied with respect to all works protected in accordance with this Convention and first published outside its territory and the author of which is not one of its nationals, if from the time of the first publication all the copies of the work published with the authority of the author or other copyright proprietor bear the symbol © accompanied by the name of the copyright proprietor and the year of first publication placed in such manner and location as to give reasonable notice of claim of copyright.

2. The provisions of paragraph 1 shall not preclude any Contracting State from requiring formalities or other conditions for the acquisition and enjoyment of copyright in respect of works first published in its territory or works of its nationals wherever published.

3. The provisions of paragraph 1 shall not preclude any Contracting State from providing that a person seeking judicial relief must, in bringing the action, comply with procedural requirements, such as that the complainant must appear through domestic counsel or that the complainant must deposit with the court or an administrative office, or both, a copy of the work involved in the litigation; provided that failure to comply with such requirements shall not affect the validity of the copyright, nor shall any such requirement be imposed upon a national of another Contracting State if such requirement is not imposed on nationals of the State in which protection is claimed.

4. In each Contracting State there shall be legal means of protecting without formalities the unpublished works of nationals of other Contracting States.

5. If a Contracting State grants protection for more than one term of copyright and the first term is for a period longer than one of the minimum periods prescribed in Article IV, such State shall not be required to comply with the provisions of paragraph 1of this Article in respect of the second or any subsequent term of copyright.

ARTICLE IV

1. The duration of protection of a work shall be governed, in accordance with the provisions of Article II and this Article, by the law of the Contracting State in which protection is claimed.

2. (a) The term of protection for works protected under this Convention shall not be less than the life of the author and twenty-five years after his death. However, any Contracting State which, on the effective date of this Convention in that State, has limited this term for certain classes of works to a period computed from the first publication of the work, shall be entitled to maintain these exceptions and to extend them to other classes of works. For all these classes the term of protection shall not be less than twenty-five years from the date of first publication.

(b) Any Contracting State which, upon the effective date of this Convention in that State, does not compute the term of protection upon the basis of the life of the author, shall be entitled to compute the term of protection from the date of the first publication of the work or from its registration prior to publication, as the case may be, provided the term of protection shall not be less than twenty-five years from the date of first publication or from its registration prior to publication, as the case may be.

(c) If the legislation of a Contracting State grants two or more successive terms of protection, the duration of the first term shall not be less than one of the minimum periods specified in sub-paragraphs (a) and (b).

3. The provisions of paragraph 2 shall not apply to photographic works or to works of applied art; provided, however, that the term of protection in those Contracting States which protect photographic works, or works of applied art in so far as they are protected as artistic work, shall not be less than ten years for each of said classes of works.

4. (a) No Contracting State shall be obliged to grant protection to a work for a period longer than that fixed for the class of works to which the work in question belongs, in the case of unpublished works by the law of the Contracting State of which the author is a national, and in the case of published works by the law of the Contracting State in which the work has been first published.

(b) For the purposes of the application of sub-paragraph (a), if the law of any Contracting State grants two or more successive terms of protection, the period of protection of that State shall be considered to be the aggregate of those terms. However, if a specified work is not protected by such State during the second or any subsequent term for any reason, the other Contracting States shall not be obliged to protect it during the second or any subsequent term.

5. For the purposes of the application of paragraph 4, the work of a national of a Contracting State, first published in a non-Contracting State, shall be treated as though first published in the Contracting State of which the author is a national.

6. For the purposes of the application of paragraph 4, in case of simultaneous publication in two or more Contracting States, the work shall be treated as though first published in the State which affords the shortest term; any work published in two or more Contracting States within thirty days of its first publication shall be considered as having been published simultaneously in said Contracting States.

ARTICLE IV*bis*

1. The rights referred to in Article I shall include the basic rights ensuring the author's economic interests, including the exclusive right to authorize reproduction by any means, public performance and broadcasting. The provisions of this Article shall extend to works protected under this Convention either in their original form or in any form recognizably derived from the original.

2. However, any Contracting State may, by its domestic legislation, make exceptions that do not conflict with the spirit and provisions of this Convention, to the rights mentioned in paragraph 1 of this Article. Any State whose legislation so provides, shall nevertheless accord a reasonable degree of effective protection to each of the rights to which exception has been made.

ARTICLE V

1. The rights referred to in Article I shall include the exclusive right of the author to make, publish and authorize the making and publication of translations of works protected under this Convention.

2. However, any Contracting State may, by its domestic legislation, restrict the right of translation of writings, but only subject to the following provisions:

(a) If, after the expiration of a period of seven years from the date of the first publication of a writing, a translation of such writing has not been published in a language in general use in the Contracting State, by the owner of the right of translation or with his authorization, any national of such Contracting State may obtain a non-exclusive licence from the competent authority thereof to translate the work into that language and publish the work so translated.

(b) Such national shall in accordance with the procedure of the State concerned, establish either that he has requested, and been denied, authorization by the proprietor of the right to make and publish the translation, or that, after due diligence on his part, he was unable to find the owner of the right. A licence may also be granted on the same conditions if all previous editions of a translation in a language in general use in the Contracting State are out of print.

(c) If the owner of the right of translation cannot be found, then the applicant for a licence shall send copies of his application to the publisher whose name appears on the work and, if the nationality of the owner of the right of translation is known, to the diplomatic or consular representative of the State of which such owner is a national, or to the organization which may have been designated by the government of that State. The licence shall not be granted before the expiration of a period of two months from the date of the dispatch of the copies of the application.

(d) Due provision shall be made by domestic legislation to ensure to the owner of the right of translation a compensation which is just and conforms to international standards, to ensure payment and transmittal of such compensation, and to ensure a correct translation of the work.

(e) The original title and the name of the author of the work shall be printed on all copies of the published translation. The licence shall be valid only for publication of the translation in the territory of the Contracting State where it has been applied for. Copies so published may be imported and sold in another Contracting State if a language in general use in such other State is the same language as that into which the work has been so translated, and if the domestic law in such other State makes provision for such licences and does not prohibit such importation and sale. Where the foregoing conditions do not exist, the importation and sale of such copies in a Contracting State shall be governed by its domestic law and its agreements. The licence shall not be transferred by the licensee.

(f) The licence shall not be granted when the author has withdrawn from circulation all copies of the work.

ARTICLE V*bis*

1. Any Contracting State regarded as a developing country in conformity with the established practice of the General Assembly of the United Nations may, by a notification deposited with the Director-General of the United Nations Educational, Scientific and Cultural Organization (hereinafter called 'the Director-General') at the time of its ratification, acceptance or accession or thereafter, avail itself of any or all of the exceptions provided for in Articles V*ter* and V*quater*.

2. Any such notification shall be effective for ten years from the date of coming into force of this Convention, or for such part of that ten-year period as remains at the date of deposit of the notification, and may be renewed in whole or in part for further periods of ten years each if, not more than fifteen or less than three months before the expiration of the relevant ten-year period, the Contracting State deposits a further

notification with the Director-General. Initial notifications may also be made during these further periods of ten years in accordance with the provisions of this Article.

3. Notwithstanding the provisions of paragraph 2, a Contracting State that has ceased to be regarded as a developing country as referred to in paragraph 1 shall no longer be entitled to renew its notification made under the provisions of paragraph 1 or 2, and whether or not it formally withdraws the notification such State shall be pre-cluded from availing itself of the exceptions provided for in Articles V*ter* and V*quater* at the end of the current ten-year period, or at the end of three years after it has ceased to be regarded as a developing country, whichever period expires later.

4. Any copies of a work already made under the exceptions provided for in Articles V*ter* and V*quater* may continue to be distributed after the expiration of the period for which notifications under this Article were effective until their stock is exhausted.

5. Any Contracting State that has deposited a notification in accordance with Article XIII with respect to the application of this Convention to a particular country or ter-ritory, the situation of which can be regarded as analogous to that of the States referred to in paragraph 1 of this Article, may also deposit notifications and renew them in accordance with the provisions of this Article with respect to any such country or territory. During the effective period of such notifications, the provisions of Articles V*ter* and V*quater* may be applied with respect to such country or territory. The sending of copies from the country or territory to the Contracting State shall be considered as export within the meaning of Articles V*ter* and V*quater*.

ARTICLE V*ter*

1. (a) Any Contracting State to which Article V*bis* (1) applies may substitute for the period of seven years provided for in Article V (2) a period of three years or any longer period prescribed by its legislation. However, in the case of a translation into a language not in general use in one or more developed countries that are party to this Convention or only the 1952 Convention, the period shall be one year instead of three.

(b) A Contracting State to which Article V*bis* (1) applies may, with the unanimous agreement of the developed countries party to this Convention or only the 1952 Convention and in which the same language is in general use, substitute, in the case of translation into that language, for the period of three years provided for in sub-paragraph (a) another period as determined by such agreement but not shorter than one year. However, this sub-paragraph shall not apply where the language in question is English, French or Spanish. Notification of any such agreement shall be made to the Director-General.

(c) The licence may only be granted if the applicant, in accordance with the proce-dure of the State concerned, establishes either that he has requested, and been denied, authorization by the owner of the right of translation, or that, after due diligence on his part, he was unable to find the owner of the right. At the same time as he makes his request he shall inform either the International Copyright Information Centre established by the United Nations Educational, Scientific and Cultural Organization or any national or regional information centre which may have been designated in a notification to that effect deposited with the Director-General by the government of the State in which the publisher is believed to have his principal place of business.

(d) If the owner of the right of translation cannot be found, the applicant for a licence shall send, by registered airmail, copies of his application to the publisher whose name appears on the work and to any national or regional information centre as mentioned in sub-paragraph (c). If no such centre is notified he shall also send a copy to the international copyright information centre established by the United Nations Educational, Scientific and Cultural Organization.

2. (a) Licences obtainable after three years shall not be granted under this Article until a further period of six months has elapsed and licences obtainable after one year until a further period of nine months has elapsed. The further period shall begin either from the date of the request for permission to translate mentioned in paragraph 1(c) or, if the identity or address of the owner of the right of translation is not known, from the date of dispatch of the copies of the application for a licence mentioned in paragraph 1 (d).

(b) Licences shall not be granted if a translation has been published by the owner of the right of translation or with his authorization during the said period of six or nine months.

3. Any licence under this Article shall be granted only for the purpose of teaching, scholarship or research.

4. (a) Any licence granted under this Article shall not extend to the export of copies and shall be valid only for publication in the territory of the Contracting State where it has been applied for.

(b) Any copy published in accordance with a licence granted under this Article shall bear a notice in the appropriate language stating that the copy is available for distribution only in the Contracting State granting the licence. If the writing bears the notice specified in Article III (1) the copies shall bear the same notice.

(c) The prohibition of export provided for in sub-paragraph (a) shall not apply where a governmental or other public entity of a State which has granted a licence under this Article to translate a work into a language other than English, French or Spanish sends copies of a translation prepared under such licence to another country if:

(i)   the recipients are individuals who are nationals of the Contracting State granting the licence, or organizations grouping such individuals;

(ii) the copies are to be used only for the purpose of teaching, scholarship or research;

(iii) the sending of the copies and their subsequent distribution to recipients is without the object of commercial purpose; and

(iv) the country to which the copies have been sent has agreed with the Contracting State to allow the receipt, distribution or both and the Director-General has been notified of such agreement by any one of the governments which have concluded it.

5. Due provision shall be made at the national level to ensure:

(a) that the licence provides for just compensation that is consistent with standards of royalties normally operating in the case of licences freely negotiated between persons in the two countries concerned; and

(b) payment and transmittal of the compensation; however, should national currency regulations intervene, the competent authority shall make all efforts, by the use of international machinery, to ensure transmittal in internationally convertible currency or its equivalent.

6. Any licence granted by a Contracting State under this Article shall terminate if a translation of the work in the same language with substantially the same content as the edition in respect of which the licence was granted is published in the said State by the owner of the right of translation or with his authorization, at a price reasonably related to that normally charged in the same State for comparable works. Any

copies already made before the licence is terminated may continue to be distributed until their stock is exhausted.

7. For works which are composed mainly of illustrations a licence to translate the text and to reproduce the illustrations may be granted only if the conditions of Article V*quater* are also fulfilled.

8. (a) A licence to translate a work protected under this Convention, published in printed or analogous forms of reproduction, may also be granted to a broadcasting organization having its headquarters in a Contracting State to which Article V*bis* (1) applies, upon an application made in that State by the said organization under the following conditions:

    (i)   the translation is made from a copy made and acquired in accordance with the laws of the Contracting State;

    (ii)   the translation is for use only in broadcasts intended exclusively for teaching or for the dissemination of the results of specialized technical or scientific research to experts in a particular profession;

    (iii)   the translation is used exclusively for the purposes set out in condition (ii), through broadcasts lawfully made which are intended for recipients on the territory of the Contracting State, including broadcasts made through the medium of sound or visual recordings lawfully and exclusively made for the purpose of such broadcasts;

    (iv)   sound or visual recordings of the translation may be exchanged only between broadcasting organizations having their headquarters in the Contracting State granting the licence; and

    (v)   all uses made of the translation are without any commercial purpose.

(b) Provided all of the criteria and conditions set out in sub-paragraph (a) are met, a licence may also be granted to a broadcasting organization to translate any text incorporated in air audio-visual fixation which was itself prepared and published for the sole purpose of being used in connexion with systematic instructional activities.

(c) Subject to sub-paragraphs (a) and (b), the other provisions of this Article shall apply to the grant and exercise of the licence.

9. Subject to the provisions of this Article, the licence granted under this Article shall be governed by the provisions of Article V, and shall continue to be governed by the provisions of Article V and of this Article, even after the seven-year period provided for in Article V has expired. However, after the said period has expired, the licensee shall be free to request that the said licence be replaced by a new licence governed exclusively by the provisions of Article V.

ARTICLE V*quater*

1. Any Contracting State to which Article V*bis* (1) applies may adopt the following provisions:

(a) If, after the expiration of (i) the relevant period specified in sub-paragraph (c) commencing from the date of first publication of a particular edition of a literary, scientific or artistic work referred to in paragraph 3, or (ii) any longer period determined by national legislation of the State, copies of such edition have not been distributed in that State to the general public or in connexion with systematic instructional activities at a price reasonably related to that normally charged in the State for comparable works, by the owner of the right of reproduction or with his authorization, any national of such State may obtain a non-exclusive licence from the competent authority to publish such edition at that or a lower price for use in connexion with systematic instructional activities. The licence may only be granted if such national, in accordance with the procedure of the State concerned, establishes either that he has requested, and been denied, authorization by the proprietor of the right to publish such work, or that, after due diligence on his part, he was unable to find the owner of the right. At the same time as he makes his request he shall inform either the international copyright information centre established by the United Nations Educational, Scientific and Cultural Organization or any national or regional information centre referred to in sub-paragraph (d).

(b) A licence may also be granted on the same conditions if, for a period of six months, no authorized copies of the edition in question have been on sale in the State concerned to the general public or in connexion with systematic instructional activities at a price reasonably related to that normally charged in the State for comparable works.

(c) The period referred to in subparagraph (a) shall be five years except that:
    (i)   for works of the natural and physical sciences, including mathematics, and of technology, the period shall be three years;
    (ii)   for works of fiction, poetry, drama and music, and for art books, the period shall be seven years.

(d) If the owner of the right of reproduction cannot be found, the applicant for a licence shall send, by registered air mail, copies of his application to the publisher whose name appears on the work and to any national or regional information centre identified as such in a notification deposited with the Director-General by the State in which the publisher is believed to have his principal place of business. In the absence of any such notification, he shall also send a copy to the international copyright information centre established by the United Nations Educational, Scientific and Cultural Organization. The licence shall not be granted before the expiration of a period of three months from the date of dispatch of the copies of the application.

(e) Licences obtainable after three years shall not be granted under this Article:
    (i)   until a period of six months has elapsed from the date of the request for permission referred to in sub-paragraph (a) or, if the identity or address of the owner of the right of reproduction is unknown, from the date of the dispatch of the copies of the application for a licence referred to in sub-paragraph (d);
    (ii)   if any such distribution of copies of the edition as is mentioned in sub-paragraph (a) has taken place during that period.

(f) The name of the author and the title of the particular edition of the work shall be printed on all copies of the published reproduction. The licence shall not extend to the export of copies and shall be valid only for publication in the territory of the Contracting State where it has been applied for. The licence shall not be transferable by the licensee.

(g) Due provision shall be made by domestic legislation to ensure an accurate reproduction of the particular edition in question.

(h) A licence to reproduce and publish a translation of a work shall not be granted under this Article in the following cases:
    (i)   where the translation was not published by, the owner of the right of translation or with authorization;
    (ii)   where the translation is not in a language in general use in the State with power to grant the licence.

2. The exceptions provided for in paragraph 1 are subject to the following additional provisions:

(a) Any copy published in accordance with a licence granted under this Article shall bear a notice in the appropriate language stating that the copy is available for distribution only in the Contracting State to which the said licence applies. If the edition bears the notice specified in Article III (1), the copies shall bear the same notice.

(b) Due provision shall be made at the national level to ensure:

    (i)   that the licence provides for just compensation that is consistent with standards of royalties normally operating in the case of licences freely negotiated between persons in the two countries concerned; and

    (ii) payment and transmittal of the compensation; however, should national currency regulations intervene, the competent authority shall make all efforts, by the use of international machinery, to ensure transmittal in internationally convertible currency or its equivalent.

(c) Whenever copies of an edition of a work are distributed in the Contracting State to the general public or in connexion with systematic instructional activities, by the owner of the right of reproduction or with his authorization, at a price reasonably related to that normally charged in the State for comparable works, any licence granted under this Article shall terminate if such edition is in the same language and is substantially the same in content as the edition published under the licence. Any copies already made before the licence is terminated may continue to be distributed until their stock is exhausted.

(d) No licence shall be granted where the author has withdrawn from circulation all copies of the edition in question.

3. (a) Subject to sub-paragraph (b), the literary, scientific or artistic works to which this Article applies shall be limited to works published in printed or analogous forms of reproduction.

(b) The provisions of this Article shall also apply to reproduction in audio-visual form of lawfully made audio-visual fixations including any protected works incorporated therein and to the translation of any incorporated text into a language in general use in the State with power to grant the licence; always provided that the audio-visual fixations in question were prepared and published for the sole purpose of being used in connexion with systematic instructional activities.

ARTICLE VI

'Publication', as used in this Convention, means the reproduction in tangible form and the general distribution to the public of copies of a work from which it can be read or otherwise visually perceived.

ARTICLE VII

This Convention shall not apply to works or rights in works which, at the effective date of this Convention in a Contracting State where protection is claimed, are permanently in the public domain in the said Contracting State.

ARTICLE VIII

1. This Convention, which shall bear the date of 24 July 1971, shall be deposited with the Director-General and shall remain open for signature by all States party to the 1952 Convention for a period of 120 days after the date of this Convention. It shall be subject to ratification or acceptance by the signatory States.

2. Any State which has not signed this Convention may accede thereto.

3. Ratification, acceptance or accession shall be effected by the deposit of an instrument to that effect with the Director-General.

ARTICLE IX

1. This Convention shall come into force three months after the deposit of twelve instruments of ratification, acceptance or accession.

2. Subsequently, this Convention shall come into force in respect of each State three months after that State has deposited its instrument of ratification, acceptance or accession.

3. Accession to this Convention by a State not party to the 1952 Convention shall also constitute accession to that Convention; however, if its instrument of accession is deposited before this Convention comes into force, such State may make its accession to the 1952 Convention conditional upon the coming into force of this Convention. After the coming into force of this Convention, no State may accede solely to the 1952 Convention.

4. Relations between States party to this Convention and States that are party only to the 1952 Convention, shall be governed by the 1952 Convention. However, any State party only to the 1952 Convention may, by a notification deposited with the Director-General, declare that it will admit the application of the 1971 Convention to works of its nationals or works first published in its territory by all States party to this Convention.

ARTICLE X

1. Each Contracting State undertakes to adopt, in accordance with its Constitution, such measures as are necessary to ensure the application of this Convention.

2. It is understood that at the date this Convention comes into force in respect of any State, that State must be in a position under its domestic law to give effect to the terms of this Convention.

ARTICLE XI

1. An Intergovernmental Committee is hereby established with the following duties:

(a) to study the problems concerning the application and operation of the Universal Copyright Convention;
(b) to make preparation for periodic revisions of this Convention;
(c) to study any other problems concerning the international protection of copyright, in cooperation with the various interested international organizations, such as the United Nations Educational, Scientific and Cultural Organization, the International Union for the Protection of Literary and Artistic Works and the Organization of American States;
(d) to inform States party to the Universal Copyright Convention as to its activities.

2. The Committee shall consist of the representatives of eighteen States party to this Convention or only to the 1952 Convention.

3. The Committee shall be selected with due consideration to a fair balance of national interests on the basis of geographical location, population, languages and stage of development.

4. The Director-General of the United Nations Educational, Scientific and Cultural Organization, the Director-General of the World Intellectual Property Organization and the Secretary-General of the Organization of American States, or their representatives, may attend meetings of the Committee in an advisory capacity.

ARTICLE XII

The Intergovernmental Committee shall convene a conference for revision whenever it deems necessary, or at the request of at least ten States party to this Convention.

ARTICLE XIII

1. Any Contracting State may, at the time of deposit of its instrument of ratification, acceptance or accession, or at any time thereafter, declare by notification addressed to the Director-General that this Convention shall apply to all or any of the countries or territories for the international relations of which it is responsible and this Convention shall thereupon apply to the countries or territories named in such notification after the expiration of the term of three months provided for in Article IX. In the absence of such notification, this Convention shall not apply to any such country or territory.

2. However, nothing in this Article shall be understood as implying the recognition or tacit acceptance by a Contracting State of the factual situation concerning a country or territory to which this Convention is made applicable by another Contracting State in accordance with the provisions of this Article.

ARTICLE XIV

1. Any Contracting State may denounce this Convention in its own name or on behalf of all or any of the countries or territories with respect to which a notification has been given under Article XIII. The denunciation shall be made by notification addressed to the Director-General. Such denunciation shall also constitute denunciation of the 1952 Convention.

2. Such denunciation shall operate only in respect of the State or of the country or territory on whose behalf it was made and shall not take effect until twelve months after the date of receipt of the notification.

ARTICLE XV

A dispute between two or more Contracting States concerning the interpretation or application of this Convention, not settled by negotiation, shall, unless the States concerned agree on some other method of settlement, be brought before the International Court of Justice for determination by it.

ARTICLE XVI

1. This Convention shall be established in English, French and Spanish. The three texts shall be signed and shall be equally authoritative.

2. Official texts of this Convention shall be established by the Director-General, after consultation with the governments concerned, in Arabic, German, Italian and Portuguese.

3. Any Contracting State or group of Contracting States shall be entitled to have established by the Director-General other texts in the language of its choice by arrangement with the Director-General.

4. All such texts shall be annexed to the signed texts of this Convention.

ARTICLE XVII

1. This Convention shall not in any way affect the provisions of the Berne Convention for the Protection of Literary and Artistic Works or membership in the Union created by that Convention.

2. In application of the foregoing paragraph, a declaration has been annexed to the present Article. This declaration is an integral part of this Convention for the States bound by the Berne Convention on 1 January 1951, or which have or may become bound to it at a later date. The signature of this Convention by such States shall also constitute signature of the said declaration, and ratification, acceptance or accession by such States shall include the declaration, as well as this Convention.

ARTICLE XVIII

This Convention shall not abrogate multilateral or bilateral copyright conventions or arrangements that are or may be in effect exclusively between two or more American Republics. In the event of any difference either between the provisions of such existing conventions or arrangements and the provisions of this Convention, or between the provisions of this Convention and those of any new convention or arrangement which may be formulated between two or more American Republics after this Convention comes into force, the convention or arrangement most recently formulated shall prevail between the parties thereto. Rights in works acquired in any Contracting State under existing conventions or arrangements before the date this Convention comes into force in such State shall not be affected.

ARTICLE XIX

This Convention shall not abrogate multilateral or bilateral conventions or arrangements in effect between two or more Contracting States. In the event of any difference between the provisions of such existing conventions or arrangements and the provisions of this Convention, the provisions of this Convention shall prevail. Rights in works acquired in any Contracting State under existing conventions or arrangements before the date on which this Convention comes into force in such State shall not be affected. Nothing in this Article shall affect the provisions of Articles XVII and XVIII.

ARTICLE XX

Reservations to this Convention shall not be permitted.

ARTICLE XXI

1. The Director-General shall send duly certified copies of this Convention to the States interested and to the Secretary-General of the United Nations for registration by him.

2. He shall also inform all interested States of the ratifications, acceptances and accessions which have been deposited, the date on which this Convention comes into force, the notifications under this Convention and denunciations under Article XIV.

APPENDIX DECLARATION RELATING TO ARTICLE XVII

The States which are members of the International Union for the Protection of Literary and Artistic Works (hereinafter called 'the Berne Union') and which are signatories to this Convention,

Desiring to reinforce their mutual relations on the basis of the said Union and to avoid any conflict which might result from the coexistence of the Berne Convention and the Universal Copyright Convention,

Recognizing the temporary need of some States to adjust their level of copyright protection in accordance with their stage of cultural, social and economic development,

Have, by common agreement, accepted the terms of the following declaration:

(a) Except as provided by paragraph (b), works which, according to the Berne Convention, have as their country of origin a country which has withdrawn from the Berne Union after 1 January 1951, shall not be protected by the Universal Copyright Convention in the countries of the Berne Union;

(b) Where a Contracting State is regarded as a developing country in conformity with the established practice of the General Assembly of the United Nations, and has deposited with the Director-General of the United Nations Educational, Scientific and Cultural Organization, at the time of its withdrawal from the Berne Union, a notification to the effect that it regards itself as a developing country, the provisions of paragraph (a) shall not be applicable as long as such State may avail itself of the exceptions provided for by this Convention in accordance with Article V*bis*;

(c) The Universal Copyright Convention shall not be applicable to the relationships among countries of the Berne Union in so far as it relates to the protection of works having as their country of origin, within the meaning of the Berne Convention, a country of the Berne Union.

RESOLUTION CONCERNING ARTICLE XI

The Conference for Revision of the Universal Copyright Convention,

Having considered the problems relating to the intergovernmental Committee provided for in Article XI of this Convention, to which this resolution is annexed,

Resolves that:

1. At its inception, the Committee shall include representatives of the twelve States members of the Intergovernmental Committee established under Article XI of the 1952 Convention and the resolution annexed to it, and, in addition, representatives of the following States: Algeria, Australia, Japan, Mexico, Senegal and Yugoslavia.

2. Any States that are not party to the 1952 Convention and have not acceded to this Convention before the first ordinary session of the Committee following the entry into force of this Convention shall be replaced by other States to be selected by the Committee at its first ordinary session in conformity with the provisions of Article XI (2) and (3).

3. As soon as this Convention comes into force the Committee as provided for in paragraph 1 shall be deemed to be constituted in accordance with Article XI of this Convention.

4. A session of the Committee shall take place within one year after the coming into force of this Convention; thereafter the Committee shall meet in ordinary session at intervals of not more than two years.

5. The Committee shall elect its Chairman and two Vice-Chairmen. It shall establish its Rules of Procedure having regard to the following principles:

(a) The normal duration of the term of office of the members represented on the Committee shall be six years with one-third retiring every two years, it being however understood that, of the original terms of office, one-third shall expire at the end of the Committee's second ordinary session which will follow the entry into force of this Convention, a further third at the end of its third ordinary session, and the remaining third at the end of its fourth ordinary session.

(b) The rules governing the procedure whereby the Committee shall fill vacancies, the order in which terms of membership expire, eligibility for re-election, and election procedures, shall be based upon a balancing of the needs for continuity of membership and rotation of representation, as well as the considerations set out in Article XI (3).

Expresses the wish that the United Nations Educational, Scientific and Cultural Organization provide its Secretariat.

In faith whereof the undersigned, having deposited their respective full powers, have signed this Convention.

Done at Paris, this twenty-fourth day of July 1971, in a single copy.

PROTOCOL 1

Annexed to the Universal Copyright Convention as revised at Paris on 24 July 1971 concerning the application of that Convention to works of Stateless persons and refugees

The States party hereto, being also party to the Universal Copyright Convention as revised at Paris on 24 July 1971 (hereinafter called 'the 1971 Convention'),

Have accepted the following provisions:

1. Stateless persons and refugees who have their habitual residence in a State party to this Protocol shall, for the purposes of the 1971 Convention, be assimilated to the nationals of that State.

2. (a) This Protocol shall be signed and shall be subject to ratification or acceptance, or may be acceded to, as if the provisions of Article VIII of the 1971 Convention applied hereto.

(b) This Protocol shall enter into force in respect of each State, on the date of deposit of the instrument of ratification, acceptance or accession of the State concerned or on the date of entry into force of the 1971 Convention with respect to such State, whichever is the later.

(c) On the entry into force of this Protocol in respect of a State not party to Protocol 1 annexed to the 1952 Convention, the latter Protocol shall be deemed to enter into force in respect of such State.

In faith whereof the undersigned, being duly authorized thereto, have signed this Protocol.

Done at Paris this twenty-fourth day of July 1971, in the English, French and Spanish languages, the three texts being equally authoritative, in a single copy which shall be deposited with the Director-General of the United Nations Educational, Scientific and Cultural Organization. The Director-General shall send certified copies to the signatory States, and to the Secretary-General of the United Nations for registration.

PROTOCOL 2

Annexed to the Universal Copyright Convention as revised at Paris on 24 July 1971 concerning the application of that Convention to the works of certain international organizations

The States party hereto, being also party to the Universal Copyright Convention as revised at Paris on 24 July 1971 (hereinafter called 'the 1971 Convention'), have accepted the following provisions:

1. (a) The protection provided for in Article II (1) of the 1971 Convention shall apply to works published for the first time by the United Nations, by the Specialized Agencies in relationship therewith, or by the Organization of American States.

(b) Similarly, Article II (2) of the 1971 Convention shall apply to the said organization or agencies.

2. (a) This Protocol shall be signed and shall be subject to ratification or acceptance, or may be acceded to, as if the provisions of Article VIII of the 1971 Convention applied hereto.

(b) This Protocol shall enter into force for each State on the date of deposit of the instrument of ratification, acceptance or accession of the State concerned or on the date of entry into force of the 1971 Convention with respect to such State, whichever is the later.

In faith whereof the undersigned, being duly authorized thereto, have signed this Protocol.

Done at Paris, this twenty-fourth day of July 1971, in the English, French and Spanish languages, the three texts being equally authoritative, in a single copy which shall be deposited with the Director-General of the United Nations Educational, Scientific and Cultural Organization. The Director-General shall send certified copies to the signatory States, and to the Secretary-General of the United Nations for registration.

APPENDIX E

Application for registration of a design (UK)

Designs Form 2A

Registered Designs Act 1949
(Rules 6, 12 and 14)

The
Patent
Office

The Patent Office
Designs Registry

Cardiff Road
Newport
South Wales
NP10 8QQ

Application for registration
of a design
(See the notes on the back of this form)

1.	Your reference	*LSG / William Austin*
2.	Full name, address and postcode of the or of each applicant *(Names of individuals including all partners in a firm must be given in full. Underline the surname or family name. For a corporate body give its company name.)*	*William Austin* *1 Table Street* *Rivington*
	Designs ADP number *(if you know it)*	*RV10 6BF*
	If the applicant is a corporate body, give country/state of incorporation	
3.	Name of agent *(if you have one)*	*Briffa Solicitors*
	"Address for Service" in the United Kingdom to which all correspondence should be sent *(including the postcode)*	*Businesss Design Centre* *Upper Street* *London*
	Designs ADP number *(if you know it)*	*N1 0QH*
4.	Name the particular product(s) to which the design is intended to be applied, or in which it is intended to be incorporated *(The listing of a product(s) shall not be taken to limit the scope of protection conferred by registration of the design.)*	*TABLE*
	Write the fee code T or O *(see note (e))*	*O*

		Country	Date of filing *(day / month / year)*
5.	Declaration of priority: *(if any)* Give the Convention country and filing date of any previous application made abroad from which priority is claimed under section 14		

6. If 5 above applies, and the previous application was not made in the name *(s)* given at part 2, give details of the instrument *(for example, deed of assignment)* which gives the applicant the right to apply for registration. Include appropriate name *(s)* and date *(s)*.

(If this information is not given at the time this form is filed you must supply it before the design is registered.)

Designs Form 2A

Designs Form 2A

7. Divisional application: Give the number and filing date of any relevant earlier application whose filing date is claimed under section 3B(3)	Number	Date of filing *(day / month / year)*

8. Declaration

I/We apply to register the design shown in the accompanying representations or specimens. I/We declare that the applicant *(s)* claim *(s)* to be the owner *(s)* of the design and to be the owner of any design right that exists in this design and that the owner believes that the design is new and has individual character subject to any partial disclaimer accompanying the application. I/We also declare in respect of any entry at part 5 above that the application made in the convention country upon which the applicant relies is the first application made for registration of the design in a convention country.

Signature *(s)* ~~[signature]~~   Date **28 November 2003**

9. Name and daytime telephone number of person to contact in the United Kingdom

BRAFFA (LSG)   020 7288 6003

10. Checklist

Make sure you have enclosed:

- representations or specimens of the design *(See note (c))*

- any continuation sheets *(See note (d))*

- the relevant fee *(See note (e))*

Notes

a) *If you need help to fill in this form or you have any questions, please contact the Patent Office on 08459 500505.*

b) *Write your answers in capital letters using black ink or you may type them.*

c) *This form should be accompanied by two identical sets of representations (for example, drawings or photographs) or specimens of the design. A partial disclaimer, if appropriate, indicating that the design is the appearance of only part of the product for which protection is sought or limiting the scope or extent of the protection sought may appear on each representation or specimen. In the case of representations or specimens which consist of more than one sheet, the partial disclaimer need only appear on the first sheet. If it is impracticable for the partial disclaimer to appear on a specimen, it may be given on a separate sheet. Specimens may sometimes need to be replaced by representations. A brief description explaining the representations may appear on the front of the first sheet only of each representation or specimen. Any such description shall not be taken to limit the scope of protection conferred by registration of a design.*

d) *If there is not enough space for all the relevant details on any part of this form, please continue on a separate sheet of paper and write "see continuation sheet" in the relevant part. Any continuation sheet should be attached to this form.*

e) *A different fee is payable if the application relates to a design which is intended to be applied to, or incorporated in, a lace product or a textile product where the design consists mainly of checks and stripes (fee code T).*

   Otherwise the normal fee is payable (fee code O).

   For details of the fees and ways to pay please contact the Designs Registry of the Patent Office.

f) *Once you have filled in the form you must remember to sign and date it.*

Designs Form 2A
(Revised 10/01)

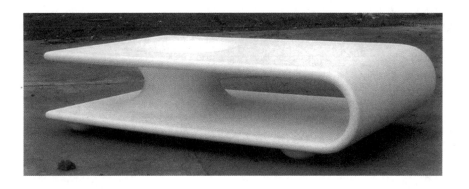

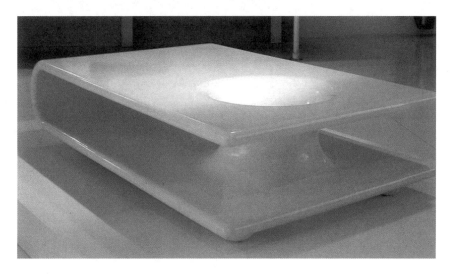

APPENDIX F

Application for registration of a Community Design (EC)

#DS001EN01V2A

★★★ R ★★★ OFFICE FOR HARMONIZATION IN THE INTERNAL MARKET (OHIM)

Avenida de Europa, 4
Apartado de Correos 77
E – 03080   Alicante

Tel. +34 – 965 138 800
Fax +34 – 965 131 344
information@oami.eu.int
http://oami.eu.int/

APPLICATION FOR REGISTERED COMMUNITY DESIGN

For receiving office	Date of receipt (DD/MM/YYYY) / /	Number of pages	Confirmation copy
For OHIM	/ /		

Application Type		Applicant/representative reference (not more than 20 characters)	
Multiple application	✔	Pyro Plastics (M)	
Number of designs	2	*Language	
Deferment[1]		Language of the application or ISO code	English
Specimen[2]		Second language	ES DE EN FR IT

Applicant[3] ID number		*Name MagManikin Limited	
Tel, fax, e-mail	+44(0)208 3456789	+44(0)208 3456788	customer.service@magmanikin.com
*Address			
Street and number	Biftolish Packer Centre		
City and postal code	North Road Halerart London N74 8AA		
Country	England		
Postal address			
Nationality and/or State of incorporation			

Representative[3] ID number		Name Briffa	
Tel, fax, e-mail	+44(0)20 7288 6003	+44(0)20 7288 6004	info@briffa.com
Address			
Street and number	Business Design Centre		
City and postal code	Upper Street Islington		
Country			
Postal address			

Fee check-list		TOTAL	*Payment of fees
Registration fee (1st design)		230 €	**Current account with OHIM**
for 2nd to 10th design	(115 € x . . .1)	115 €	☐ Current account of applicant/representative with OHIM
from 11th onwards	(50 € x . . .0)	0 €	account No
			☐ Do not use my current account with OHIM
Publication fee (1st design)	120 €	120 €	**Transfer to account of OHIM**
for 2nd to 10th design	(60 € x . .1)	60 €	☐ Transfer to account of OHIM Banco Bilbao Vizcaya Argentaria
from 11th onwards	(30 € x . .0)	0 €	0182-5596-90-0092222222 Swift code (BIC): BBVAESMM
			IBAN ES88 0182 5596 9000 9222 2222
Fee for deferment of publication (1st design) 40 €		0 €	☐ Transfer to account of OHIM La Caixa
for 2nd to 10th design	(20 € x . . .)	0 €	2100-2353-01-0700000888 Swift code (BIC): CAIXESBB
from 11th onwards	(10 € x . .0)	0 €	IBAN ES03 2100 2353 0107 0000 0888
TOTAL AMOUNT PAID		525 €	Date of transfer (DD/MM/YYYY) / /

Signature		
Date of signing (DD/MM/YYYY)	19 / 6 / 2003	☑ Payment by cheque made payable to the OHIM (attached)

Authority of the person signing		Name Alison Fortran
☑ Legal practitioner ☐ Professional representative		
☐ Applicant ☐ Employee representative	*Signature	A Fort

* Mandatory details
[1] Please tick the box if the application contains at least one design of which publication is deferred
[2] Please tick the box if the application contains at least one specimen of a two-dimensional design
[3] If more than one or if space provided is not sufficient, please continue on the attachment sheet

page number
1 of

#DS001EN02V2A

APPLICATION FOR REGISTERED COMMUNITY DESIGN
(continuation)
Reproduce this sheet in case of more than 1 design (use 1 sheet per design)

☐ Tick the box if the following data is the same for all designs contained in the application		
Design number `1` **out of total of** `2` **Applicant name** MagManikin Limited		

Indication of product(s)[1] ☑ Same indication of product for all designs		**Locarno classification**
Display and Sales Equipment		20.02
	☐ Tick the box if ornamentation	

Convention priority[2]		
	☐ Same priority for all designs	☐ Document attached
Country of first filing or ISO	England	
Date of first filing[3]	21 / 12 / 2002	
Filing number	1234567	

Exhibition priority[2]		
	☐ Same priority for all designs	☐ Document attached
Name of the exhibition		
Date and place[3]	/ /	
Date of first disclosure[3]	/ /	

Designer[2]		
	☐ Same designer for all designs	☐ Waiver
Name	Sydney Jones	
Address	723a Vancouver Boulevard West Vancouver ECV3I 9Z2 Canada	

Miscellaneous		
	☐ Request for deferment of publication	`6` Number of views
	☐ Design filed with a specimen[4]	

Brief description of the representation/specimen[5]

* *Mandatory details*

[1] *Indicate the usual generic name of the product(s) in which the design is intended to be incorporated or to which it is intended to be applied, preferably using the term(s) included in the EuroLocarno Database. If the space provided is not sufficient, please continue on the attachment sheet*

[2] *If more than one, please continue on the attachment sheet*

[3] *(DD/MM/YYYY)*

[4] *Filing with a specimen is only allowed in the case of deferment (see explanatory notes)*

[5] *Please continue on the attachment sheet if the space provided is not sufficient*

page number
☐ of ☐

REPRESENTATION/SPECIMEN SHEET

#DS001EN03V2A

Number of views	6	Design number(s)		out of total of		Applicant name MagManikin Limited

Please see photographs attached

Reproduce this sheet if space is not sufficient
A representation / specimen per design is mandatory

page number
of

FRONT VIEW

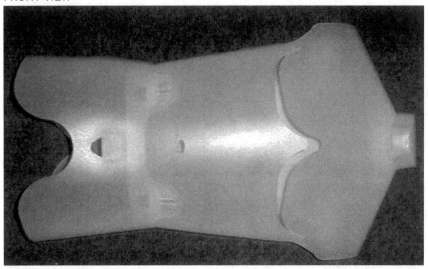

SIDE VIEW

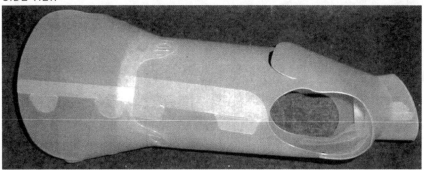

TOP VIEW

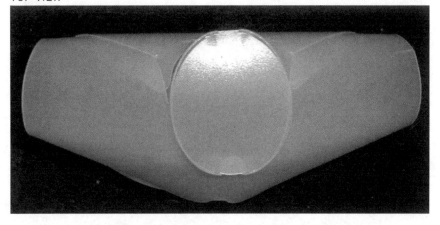

NOTE: Each photograph should appear on a separate page.

BACK VIEW

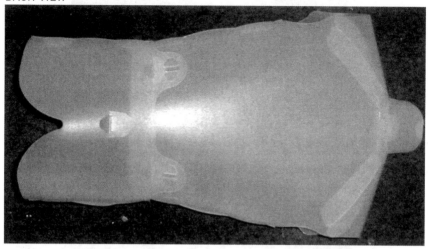

BENEATH VIEW

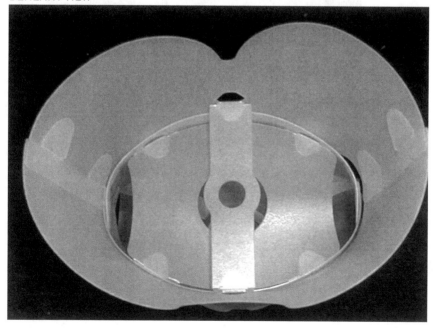

PERSPECTIVE VIEW

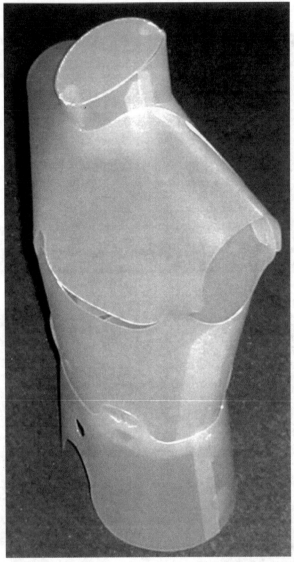

APPLICATION FOR REGISTERED COMMUNITY DESIGN
(continuation)

#DS001EN02V2A

Reproduce this sheet in case of more than 1 design (use 1 sheet per design)

Tick the box if the following data is the same for all designs contained in the application

Design number	2	out of total of	2	Applicant name	*Mag Manikin Limited*

*Indication of product(s)[1]	✓ Same indication of product for all designs	**Locarno classification**
Display and Sales Equipment		20.02
	☐ Tick the box if ornamentation	

Convention priority[2]		
	☐ Same priority for all designs	☐ Document attached
Country of first filing or ISO	England	
Date of first filing[3]	21 / 12 / 2002	
Filing number	1234568	

Exhibition priority[2]		
	☐ Same priority for all designs	☐ Document attached
Name of the exhibition		
Date and place[3]	/ /	
Date of first disclosure[3]	/ /	

Designer[2]		
	☐ Same designer for all designs	☐ Waiver
Name	Paul Ashley	
Address	28 Summer Grove Eastponds Bristol BS94 4PD	

Miscellaneous		
	☐ Request for deferment of publication	6 Number of views
	☐ Design filed with a specimen[4]	

Brief description of the representation/specimen[5]

* Mandatory details

[1] Indicate the usual generic name of the product(s) in which the design is intended to be incorporated or to which it is intended to be applied, preferably using the term(s) included in the EuroLocarno Database. If the space provided is not sufficient, please continue on the attachment sheet

[2] If more than one, please continue on the attachment sheet

[3] (DD/MM/YYYY)

[4] Filing with a specimen is only allowed in the case of deferment (see explanatory notes)

[5] Please continue on the attachment sheet if the space provided is not sufficient

page number
☐ of ☐

REPRESENTATION/SPECIMEN SHEET

#DS001EN03V2A

Number of views	6	Design number(s)		out of total of		Applicant name	MagManikin Limited

Please see photographs attached

Reproduce this sheet if space is not sufficient

A representation / specimen per design is mandatory

page number	
	of	

FRONT VIEW

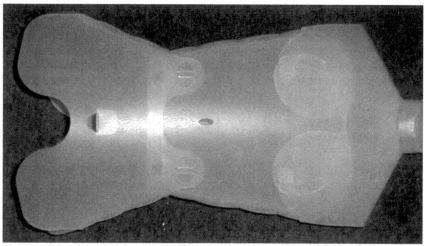

SIDE VIEW

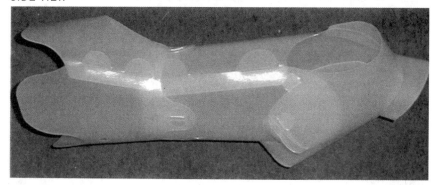

TOP VIEW

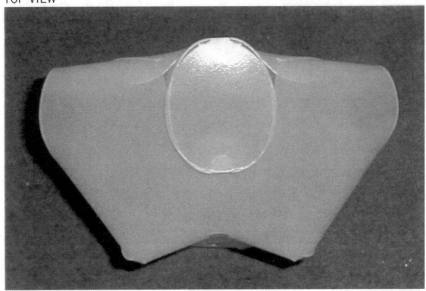

BACK VIEW

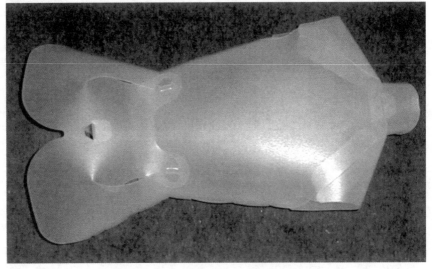

BENEATH VIEW

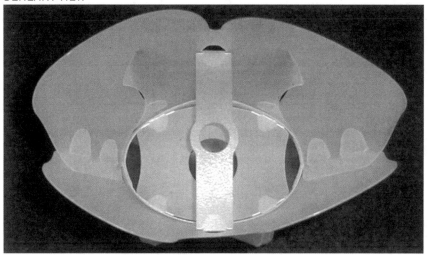

PERSPECTIVE VIEW

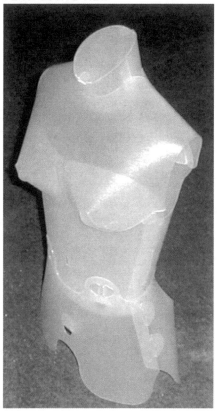

#DS001EN04V2A

ATTACHMENT SHEET

Applicant name MagManikin Limited

This sheet should be used for any additional information relating to :
additional applicant, additional representative, additional priority, additional designer, indication of product, brief description.

Please specify the field name(s) for each additional information

N/A

page number
of

Draft design licence

THIS AGREEMENT is made this   day of   2002

BETWEEN:

(1) Really Good Designing Company Ltd a company incorporated under the laws of England and Wales with registered number 1465177894 and whose registered office is located at Designer House, West Marsden, Gilbury GL19 7FU ('**Licensor**')

and

(2) Truly Excellent Licensing Company Ltd a company incorporated under the laws of England and Wales with registered number 16424976075 and whose registered office is located at 99–102 Rose St, North Effborough, Anshire AN4 2PD ('**Licensee**')

WHEREAS

(A) Licensor has expertise and reputation as a designer and would like to establish a manufacturing distribution network.
(B) Licensee has experience of designing and manufacturing the product and would like to take a licence from Licensor in order to establish a distribution network.

THE PARTIES AGREE AS FOLLOWS:

1. GRANT OF RIGHTS
   In consideration of the sums paid or to be paid in accordance with clauses 8, 9 and 10 below and subject to the terms and conditions under this Agreement, Licensor grants to Licensee an exclusive licence to manufacture, sell, reproduce and distribute the Designs and the Trademarks in order to produce the Licensed Products set out in the schedule attached. Licensor shall not sell the designs or Licensed Products to any third party during this Agreement.

2. LICENCE PERIOD
(a) This Agreement shall come into effect from the date of signature and shall continue for the period set out in the schedule attached ('the Term') subject to earlier termination under clause 14 below. The agreement year ('Agreement Year') shall run from the date of signature of this Agreement to the anniversary of that date in the following calendar year.
(b) In the event that this Agreement is not terminated according to the provisions in this Agreement in clause 14 the licence period shall automatically continue for a further year and shall continue in this manner until such time as it is properly terminated.

3. LICENCE TERRITORY
   The rights granted under this Agreement are restricted to the territories set out in the schedule attached ('the Territory').

4. ARTWORK, DESIGN AND COPYRIGHT
(a) Licensor shall provide to Licensee not less than fifteen (15) new designs of dresses for the September 2004 selling season and shall thereafter provide a number of designs to be mutually agreed in writing between the parties in readiness for the March and September selling seasons (the 'Designs'). The Designs shall comprise the full specification and paper pattern of the garment. All artwork, drawings, design, photographs, patterns or other copyright material involving the Designs whether created by Licensor or by Licensee (the 'New Designs') shall belong to

Licensor and any copyright created in the New Designs shall vest in and remain with Licensor absolutely.

(b) In the event that original designs or parts of original designs are created by Licensee, Licensee agrees to assign all copyright, design right and any other Intellectual Property rights to Licensor in accordance with clause 4(c).

(c) Accordingly and as consideration of the rights granted to Licensee under this Agreement, Licensee hereby assigns to Licensor with full title guarantee any existing and future Intellectual Property Rights which it creates in respect of the Designs or the New Designs.

(d) All Designs and New Designs shall be subject to the express approval of Licensor according to clause 5.

(e) The Designs, New Designs and all other artwork drawings, designs and other copyright materials, samples, off cuts, models and materials shall be returned to Licensor immediately upon expiration or termination of this Agreement.

5. APPROVAL OF DESIGNS AND SAMPLES

Licensee agrees that Licensor shall have the right of final approval of the appearance, quality, design and materials comprising the Licensed Products and that no manufacture, selling, distribution, advertising or marketing of the Licensed Products shall take place without the prior written approval of Licensor unless and until such approval has been obtained by Licensee. Licensee acknowledges that all designs, samples and marketing materials must reach Licensor's highest standards, set from time to time. In particular:

(a) Before commencing any of the rights granted under this Agreement, Licensee shall provide to Licensor for approval true and accurate samples of the Licensed Product and all packaging or advertising materials of whatever kind. The samples shall only be approved expressly by Licensor and shall be made exclusively by Licensee in its own factories according to the Designs and/or New Designs. There shall be no implied approval by default.

(b) Once the samples have been approved by Licensor, a sample collection shall be sent to each and every agent and distributor at the cost of Licensee by the sample delivery dates to be agreed in writing between the parties.

(c) The Licensed Products shall be marketed, advertised, distributed and sold at exhibitions (to be agreed in writing between the parties), via Licensee's agents, distributors and one dedicated salesperson employed on a full-time basis by Licensee.

(d) Licensee shall at all times ensure that the Licensed Products and the packaging, marketing and advertising thereof shall conform in image, style and approach to that of Licensor and shall seek Licensor's express approval for any packaging, marketing and advertising prior to using any such materials. Licensee shall consult with Licensor regarding its marketing policy and approach and the theme of any advertising campaign for the Licensed Products and its other products to ensure compliance with this clause.

(e) Licensee shall dedicate two full-time customer service representatives to Licensor and those person shall communicate to Licensee all feedback from customers and clients and Licensee shall in turn report that feedback to Licensor on a quarterly basis.

6. QUALITY CONTROL

(a) Licensee warrants that the Licensed Products, packaging and advertising materials manufactured, sold and distributed under this Agreement shall conform to the highest quality standards approved by Licensor in accordance with clause 5 above.

(b) Licensee acknowledges and agrees to permit Licensor to enter its premises to carry out random checks on the Licensed Products in production in order to verify the quality of the Licensed Products being produced. Such checks shall occur by prior written agreement between the parties and at Licensee's expense.

(c) In the event that any Licensed Products are returned due to inferior quality or workmanship then Licensee shall be responsible for compensation to the necessary party. Licensee shall at its own discretion either refund the price of the Licensed Product or replace it with a comparable product. Any royalty or other sums paid to Licensor in respect of the returned product shall not be refunded to Licensee.

(d) Licensor reserves the right to reject any Licensed Products and withhold payment in respect of any Licensed Products not reaching the required standard.

7. COPYRIGHT REGISTERED DESIGNS AND TRADE MARKS

(a) Licensee agrees that unless otherwise agreed in writing with Licensor all units of the Licensed Product and all advertising and publicity material relating thereto shall bear the credits and Copyright Notices and Trademarks specified in the schedule attached together with such other notices as Licensor may from time to time require including but not limited to registered design numbers.

(b) Licensor hereby grants Licensee the right to use the Trademarks in connection with this Agreement only in the form attached. Adaptation, amendment or unauthorised use of the Trademarks is strictly prohibited.

(c) Licensee acknowledges that ownership of all rights in the Trademarks, house or product style of the Licensed Products including goodwill therein vest in Licensor. Licensee shall not acquire any rights, title or interest of whatever nature in the Trademarks or goodwill as a result of its use under this Agreement.

(d) Licensee agrees to co-operate with Licensor in the filing of any application for registration of any trademarks and for recording Licensee as a user of the Trademarks or the registration of any design, utility or other Intellectual Property right relating to the Licensed Products or the Designs or the New Designs. Licensee shall do such act as is reasonably required for such applications.

(e) Licensee confirms that it has a UK registered trademark (number 1234567890) for the name Poshfrox.

(f) For the avoidance of doubt any goodwill and reputation generated through Licensee's use of the Trademarks shall accrue to the benefit of Licensor and not to Licensee.

(g) Licensee warrants that any copyright or New Designs or existing designs supplied by Licensee under this Agreement vests in Licensee (prior to the assignment to Licensor in clause 4c above) and Licensee undertakes that it shall within seven days of Licensor's request, supply to Licensor evidence of such right and enter into any confirmatory assignments which are requested by Licensor.

(h) Licensor shall indemnify and hold harmless Licensee against all costs (including legal costs) and damages and expenses awarded under final judgment by a court of competent jurisdiction arising out of any third party claim that the Licensed Products infringe a copyright, trade mark, or service mark or any other third party right in the Territory provided that Licensee

(i) allows Licensor conduct of the defence of such claim, including any settlement,

(ii) makes no prejudicial admission or statement,

(iii) notifies Licensor promptly of any claim, and

(iv) actively co-operates and assists Licensor in the defence of the claim.

(i) This indemnity will not apply if the infringement is the result of (a) Licensee modifying or misusing the Designs or Licensed Products, or (b) the failure of Licensee reasonably to use enhancements or modifications offered by Licensor to avoid infringement, or (c) any existing designs supplied by Licensee to Licensor for the purposes of this Agreement. This indemnity constitutes Licensee's sole and exclusive remedy and Licensor's entire liability with respect to any claims of infringement of third party rights of any kind.

(j) Licensee shall not co- or sub-brand the Licensed Products and the Trademarks and shall market and advertise the Licensed Products independently from all or any Licensee brands whether in existence at the date of this Agreement or which come into existence thereafter.

(k) Licensee shall be responsible for providing sufficient working capital to manage the distribution and manufacture of the Licensed Products throughout this Agreement. Thirteen per cent (13%) of the projected annual turnover shall be allocated to exhibitions, advertising and PR, which Licensor shall decide.

8. MINIMUM ROYALTY AND DESIGN FEES

(a) Licensee shall pay to Licensor a one-off Premium of £15,000 upon signing this Agreement. Licensee shall pay to Licensor a further £15,000 on the first anniversary of this Agreement. This Premium is non-refundable and is not an advance against Design Fees or Royalties.

(b) Licensee shall pay Licensor the minimum royalties set out in the Schedule attached (the 'Minimum Royalty'). The Minimum Royalty shall be paid to Licensor in equal monthly instalments by bank transfer from the date of this Agreement.

(c) Over and above the Minimum Royalty Licensee shall pay Licensor a royalty at the rates specified in the schedule attached (the 'Royalty') with respect to each unit of the Licensed Product.

(d) The Royalty shall be paid quarterly, the first quarter day being the date of signature of this Agreement and each quarter day being every three months thereafter.

(e) For each Design supplied under this Agreement by Licensor or which is created for the purposes of this Agreement Licensee will pay to Licensor by bank transfer within one month of its receipt £500 + VAT at the prevailing rate (the 'Design Fees') up to a total of £1 million + VAT at the prevailing rate per Design. Thereafter the fee for each Design supplied under this Agreement or which is created for the purposes of this Agreement will be £1000 + VAT at the prevailing rate. The Design Fees will be payable with 50% in advance of each and every Design being created and 50% on delivery of the each and every final Design by Licensor to Licensee.

9. PRICING LEVEL

The Licensed Producst shall retail at between £200 and £600 as more particularly described in the schedule.

10. ACCOUNTING, INSPECTION AND REPORTS

(a) Licensee shall deliver to Licensor on the quarter days set out above in clause 8 (d) a statement indicating the amount of the Licensed Product purchased from the manufacturer, the purchase price of the Licensed Product, the subsequent sales of the Licensed Product, the price that the Licensed Product was subsequently sold at and the total Royalty payable.

(b) At the same time Licensee shall deliver to Licensor a remittance for the full amount of the Royalty shown.

(c) Acceptance by Licensor of any payment pursuant to a statement shall not constitute a waiver of any breach of any term of this Agreement, nor shall acceptance of partial payment be deemed waiver of the outstanding balance.

(d) If Licensee fails to render a statement or pay the Royalty due to Licensor on the due dates, Licensor shall be entitled to charge interest on all sums outstanding with effect from the date when payment was due until the date of payment in full including all interest thereon at a rate of 4% above the base rate of [any bank] from time to time.

(e) In the event that Licensor disputes the statement supplied by Licensee, Licensor shall be entitled, upon reasonable notice, to inspect Licensee's books of accounts in order to verify the correct amount of Royalty payable. In the event that such statements are inaccurate by more than 5%, Licensor shall be entitled to terminate this Agreement immediately.

11. ADVERTISING AND PROMOTION

(a) Licensee shall be solely responsible for the cost and expense of all promotional and marketing expenditure with respect to the distribution of Licensed Products in the Territory over and above the 13% of the annual turnover of Licensor allocated for the purpose, including without limitation the cost of all sales representatives, direct mailing and advertising PROVIDED THAT Licensor shall have absolute approval over that promotion and marketing expenditure.

(b) Licensor and Licensee shall keep one another informed throughout the duration of this Agreement of all circumstances significant to the marketing and distribution of Licensed Products in the Territory and any changes relating to such circumstances.

12. AGENTS, ORDERS, DISTRIBUTION AND SALES CONDITIONS

(a) Licensee is authorised under this Agreement to appoint agents and sub-contractors in order to continue with its obligations under this Agreement PROVIDED THAT all agents and sub-contractors receive the full prior approval of Licensor in writing.

(b) Licensee agrees that it shall purchase materials for the Licensed Products only from parties who have been approved by Licensor.

(c) Licensee shall only distribute the Licensed Products to such third parties who have been approved by Licensor and who stock products of a comparable quality. Licensee shall not sell or in any way dispose of the Licensed Product to any person, firm or company for use either by itself or in association with any other product other than under the terms of this Agreement.

13. EXPIRY AND SELLING OFF CONDITIONS

If at the end of the Term or sooner termination of this Agreement Licensee shall have any stock of the Licensed Product or if Licensee shall have commenced an order for manufacture of the Licensed Product then Licensee shall (unless otherwise notified by Licensor) be entitled to sell the same and to complete the order for a period of 365 days PROVIDED THAT the terms of this Agreement shall apply to such sale (including the provisions relating to payment of Royalty). Licensor shall be entitled to licence the rights of the Licensed Products to any other third party in the Territory during the sell-off period.

14. TERMINATION

(a) Either Licensor or Licensee shall be entitled to terminate this Agreement in the event that the other party is in breach of any clause of this Agreement and having been given written notice of the same, has failed to remedy such breach within thirty (30) days.

(b) Either party may terminate this Agreement in the event that the other party becomes bankrupt or insolvent or shall enter into liquidation or any sort of agreement with its creditors. In the event this Agreement shall immediately terminate and cease to have effect.

(c) Licensor shall be entitled to terminate this Agreement at any time for convenience PROVIDED that any monies received in respect of the next forthcoming season shall be returned to Licensee.

(d) Licensor shall be entitled to terminate this Agreement in the event that Licensee is subject to a change of control or the purchase of the majority of its shares by a single entity or enters into any partnership agreement with any third party or where it enters in any arrangement with any third party that is in a similar business to Licensor without the prior approval of Licensor.

(e) In the event that Licensee does not notify Licensor in writing of its intention to terminate this Agreement at least six (6) months prior to the expiration of this Agreement, this Agreement will remain in force between the parties for a further twelve (12) months after the initial three year licence period at which point it shall cease and Licensee shall not be entitled to continue to sell, market or otherwise deal in Licensed Products.

15. CONSEQUENCES OF TERMINATION

(a) Termination of this Agreement shall be without prejudice to the rights and remedies of Licensor with respect to any antecedent breach by Licensee of any of its obligations under this Agreement or in respect of the payment of Royalties due prior to termination.

(b) Within seven days of termination of this Agreement for whatever reason, Licensee shall deliver to Licensor all stock, Designs, New Designs, or any other materials relating to the Licensed Products.

(c) Upon termination of this Agreement for whatever reason all sums due to Licensor under this Agreement shall be payable immediately in full.

(d) The provisions of clauses 4(c), 4(e), 8(b), 8(e), 12 and 14(c), shall survive termination of this Agreement.

16. PUBLIC AND PRODUCT LIABILITY

(a) Licensee shall obtain and maintain adequate public and product liability insurance in an amount of not less than the sum specified in the schedule attached naming Licensor as named insured as its interests may appear and providing protection against any and all claims, demands and causes of action arising out of any alleged defects in the Licensed Products. Evidence of such insurance shall be furnished by Licensee to Licensor promptly following signature of this Agreement and prior to the sale and distribution of the Licensed Products.

(b) Licensee shall promptly notify Licensor of all claims made to it and notified to its insurer and relating to the Licensed Products.

17. INDEMNITIES

(a) Licensee hereby indemnifies and agrees to hold harmless Licensor from any loss, liability, damages (where direct or consequential), expenses (including legal fees) arising out of any claims made against Licensor by a third party by reason of a breach of this Agreement by Licensee. Licensor shall give prompt written notice to Licensee in respect of such claim and shall assist Licensee in the conduct of the defence of any such action.

18. EXTENT AND LIMITATION OF RIGHTS

(a) Licensee shall not assign (whether in whole or in part) any of its obligations under this Agreement without Licensor's express written consent.

(b) Licensee is authorised to distribute to third parties of appropriate standing in order to establish a distribution network for the Licensed Products throughout the Territory **PROVIDED THAT** such third parties have been expressly authorised by Licensor and have entered into adequate protection of Licensor's rights.

(c) This Agreement is limited to the Licensed Products and nothing in this Agreement shall prevent Licensor from dealing with any of the rights and interests in the Designs and the New Designs or in its business generally which are not licensed under this Agreement for any other purpose or to any other third party.

19. GENERAL

(a) No waiver (whether express or implied) by either party of any breach by the other party of any of its obligations under this Agreement shall be deemed to constitute a waiver or consent to any subsequent or continuing breach by such party of any such obligations.

(b) Unless otherwise stated every notice and other communication given under this Agreement shall be sent by first class post addressed to the other party at the address above. Notice shall be deemed given two clear business days after posting.

(c) In the event of a party failing to perform any obligation under this Agreement (save the making of any payment due under or pursuant to this Agreement) as a result of strike, lock-out or other labour difficulties, fire, flood, act of God, embargo, act of war, act of terrorism, regulation or restriction of government or law or any other occurrence of circumstance beyond the reasonable control of the party, that party shall not be liable in damages or otherwise for failure to perform that obligation and such failure shall not be a ground for terminating this Agreement.

(d) Any and all information, data, sketches or drawings or any other material ('Confidential Information') that may be obtained by either party from any source as a result of this Agreement shall be considered strictly confidential. Furthermore, unless either party has given consent, neither party may at any time during this Agreement or at any time afterwards disclose such Confidential Information to any third party.

(e) Licensee shall, at its own expense, comply with all relevant local legal requirements in relation to the Licensed Products and in particular those relating to the storage, labelling, marketing and distribution of the Licensed Products in the Territory.

(f) This Agreement may not be varied or modified unless made in writing and executed under seal on behalf of both parties.

(g) This Agreement is to be governed by the laws of England and the parties submit to the non-exclusive jurisdiction of the English courts.

IN WITNESS of which the parties have caused this Agreement to be duly executed on the day and year first above written.

1)...

Acting as Director of
Really Good Designing Company Ltd

2)...

Acting as Director and Company Secretary of
Really Good Designing Company Ltd

Print Names

1)..

2)..

1)..
Acting as Director of
Truly Excellent Licensing Company Ltd

2)..
Acting as Director and Company Secretary of
Truly Excellent Licensing Company Ltd

Print Names

1)..

2)..

SCHEDULE

The Licensed Products

Ready to wear clothing made to the designs and marketed under the label PoshFrox each item to retail at approximately £200–£600 in the UK market.

Term

2 (two) years from the date of this Agreement

Territory

The World

Trademarks

The series of trade marks 'PoshFrox' obtained in UK as registered Trade Mark number 1234567890 (word and device) in class 25 attached to this Agreement at Annex 1. The Trademark DayFrox is not included in this Agreement.

Premium

£15,000 upon signature of this Agreement
£15,000 every 12 months thereof for the duration of this agreement

Minimum Royalty

£25,000 per annum

Royalty

10% of wholesale price

Copyright Notice

© Really Good Designing Company Limited 2003. All rights reserved. Any unauthorised copying, whether in whole or in part, use or amendment is strictly prohibited.

Insurance

Please see attached certificate

APPENDIX H

Non-disclosure agreement (NDA)

\<Client's Name\>
\<Client's Address\>

\<Date\>

Dear **\<insert name\>**

Further to our **\<meeting/telephone call\>** of **\<insert date\>** we enclose a copy of our draft proposal and designs of \<insert designs\> regarding the above project and we look forward to discussing it with you.

You will appreciate that a great deal of time and effort has been put into our proposal and in consideration of our disclosing it to you we would be grateful if you would agree the following:

1. To treat the contents of our proposal and all other information supplied to you orally, in documentary form, in machine-readable form or in the form of equipment, models or prototypes in respect of our proposal (the 'Information') as confidential. You are not obliged to treat as confidential any information which you can show is or was:

   (a) in the public domain otherwise than in breach of this agreement; or

   (b) in your possession with full rights to use it or disclose it to third parties (such information having been either independently developed by you or having been supplied to you by a third party without restriction on use or disclosure).

2. Not to permit or authorise the Information to be disclosed or used beyond the scope expressly permitted by this agreement including its copying or commercial exploitation in any way or release beyond your control.

3. To attach a copy of the enclosed notice to the front of all copies or reproductions of our proposal or part(s) thereof.

4. To restrict disclosure of the Information and copies or reproductions of the Information (or any part thereof) to the minimum number of persons required to enable you to assess the value of the Information to you.

5. To return all material and documents provided to you by us and all copies or reproductions thereof made by you if you decide not to pursue the development of our proposal. We may at any time request return of all such material and you will as soon as is practically possible comply with our request. After such decision or request you shall make no further use of the Information.

6. In consideration of the above we will of course keep any information about your business or clients confidential and we agree only to disclose any such information to those persons required to enable us to assess your needs.

7. These terms shall be governed by and construed under the laws of England and Wales.

Please acknowledge your agreement with the above terms by signing the enclosed copy of this letter.

We look forward to working with you.

Yours sincerely

....
<Insert name of Person Signing>

We hereby agree to abide by the above terms.

Signed:...

Full name:

Position:

Date:

STRICTLY CONFIDENTIAL

THE MATERIAL ATTACHED HERETO IS CONFIDENTIAL TO
<INSERT THE NAME OF YOUR BUSINESS> AND MAY BE READ
ONLY BY DULY AUTHORISED PERSONS. THE MATERIAL MAY
NOT BE REPRODUCED EITHER IN WHOLE OR IN PART WITHOUT
PERMISSION AND MAY NOT BE USED OR DISCLOSED WITHOUT
PERMISSION. NO COPIES OF THIS MATERIAL, WHETHER IN
WHOLE OR IN PART, MAY BE MADE WITHOUT ATTACHING A
COPY OF THIS NOTICE TO EACH SUCH COPY.

Freelancer agreement

[insert Artist's name]
[insert Artist's address]

11 July 2003

Dear **[insert name]**,

Re: [insert name of project]

On the basis that you have agreed to work for me and I have agreed to pay you for this work, the following sets out the terms on which we will do so and reflects our joint intentions. It also sets out our requirements regarding the rights in that work you do or create and the information which you may receive.

The Schedule attached sets out the main commercial details and the legal matters are dealt with in the letter. Together they make up our agreement. Please therefore sign and return the letter and the Schedule to me and I shall sign and return a copy to you.

We agree that:

Development
1. You will design and develop work for intended exploitation by me **[insert name and address]**. This work is detailed in the Schedule ('Work').

2. You will carry out the Work and deliver the same to me by or before the completion date detailed in the Schedule. You will advise me of the progress of the Work as and when this information is requested from you.

Payment
3. On delivery of the completed Work to me to my satisfaction and in accordance with my instructions to you, I will pay you a percentage share of the sums received by me in respect of the exploitation of the Work obtained from your work ('Sums' as detailed in the Schedule).

4. You shall be paid all Sums due hereunder quarterly, by direct bank transfer or cheque, within 30 days of the end of the quarter, interest accruing on any overdue payment at 3% above Bank of England base rate, compounded weekly.

5. You will be entitled to claim reasonable expenses as agreed from time to time with me in which event I will reimburse you for these within 30 days (or as soon as is reasonably practicable thereafter) against your invoice provided that copies of all receipts are provided.

6. With each of my payments to you, I will give you a copy of statements of account detailing all sums received by me in respect of the exploitation of the Work.

7. I shall keep full financial books and records relating to the Work for a reasonable time, which shall be made available to you or your authorised representative upon reasonable notice.

Rights

8. You warrant undertake and guarantee that the Work that you will supply to me will be your own original work and not copied wholly or substantially from any other work and if any part is not, then you have in place all relevant assignments necessary for the transfer and licence under this Agreement to be effective. For the sake of clarity, you also guarantee that you are and will be entitled to transfer and license all the rights in the Work including copyright, design right, patents, trade marks, patent rights, database right and similar rights whether registerable or not ('Intellectual Property Rights') and that you will not recreate any aspect of the Work or any material colourably similar to the Work or which may compete with the Work for any third party without our prior written consent.

9. You agree to indemnify and fully compensate me in the event that you breach clause 8 above.

10. In due consideration of your right to receive the Sums you assign to me (with full title guarantee) upon creation all Intellectual Property Rights in the Work. That includes the exclusive right to do and to authorise others to do any and all acts in relation to the Work throughout the World together with all rights of action in respect of any past or existing infringements of such Intellectual Property Rights like the right to claim damages in respect of any infringing works.

11. You also waive any so-called moral rights and therefore grant to me total and unlimited rights to use, modify and adapt the Work for all purposes and in any manner I think fit.

Confidential Information

12. You may in the course of our working relationship receive confidential information relating to my business or the business of my clients, including but not limited to information concerning my, or my client's products, marketing or business plans and details relating to financial arrangements with my clients and my relationship with any one client or clients generally.

13. You may only use any such confidential information for the purpose of carrying out Work under the terms of this agreement. Further, you must keep all such information confidential and not disclose it to any other person without my written consent. Insofar as any information is passed to you, whether it is contained on computer, paper, disk or other device, it shall be returned by you to me on completion of the project and at any time on demand and you shall not retain any copies of such information.

14. You undertake that you will not without my prior written permission solicit work directly from any of my clients in connection with the Work, this project or with any other project nor will you directly or indirectly induce or encourage any of my clients to move their business away from me for a period of 12 months after the completion of your Work with me. You further agree that this restriction is reasonable but if a court should hold that it is invalid but would be valid if either the period or the scope of the restriction were reduced then the restriction shall still apply but with such restriction(s) which are necessary to make it valid.

Quality

15. You warrant that you will perform your services in a professional and workman-like manner so that the Work is reasonably fit for any purpose disclosed to you and of a high standard of quality and workmanship.

16. You agree that while working for me you will be engaged on a freelance independent contractor basis and will not be my employee. Further, you agree that you have arranged or during the period of this Agreement will arrange to obtain Schedule D status and that you will be responsible for paying your own Income Tax and National Insurance contributions. Further, you agree to pay and indemnify me against all or any costs, taxes, claims or charges imposed by any taxation authority upon me in respect of my business relationship with you.

Term and Termination

17. This Agreement shall commence on the date hereof and shall continue for the Term (as described in the Schedule) or until the Work is completed or until either of us terminates by giving [insert] months' notice in writing to the other:

18. Either of us shall be entitled at any time to terminate this Agreement immediately by written notice if:
    18.1 the other commits any material breach of any term of this Agreement which (in the case of a breach capable of being remedied) shall not have been remedied within 14 days of a written request to remedy the same;
    18.2 the other shall be adjudged insolvent or bankrupt or shall be unable to pay its debts as they fall due or shall make assignment for the benefit of its creditors generally or have a receiver appointed for it or for any of its property or assets or if it shall discontinue or abandon or dispose of the whole or a substantial part of its business or shall have a petition presented or a resolution passed for its winding up or if notice is issued convening a meeting for the purpose of passing any such resolution.

Materials

19. You agree to retain and archive all original works created pursuant to this Agreement and which are created preparatory to or during the creation of the Work for me. You also agree to undertake additional services in relation to the Work on reasonable request and upon payment of reasonable additional fees.

20. You undertake that on completion of the Work for me, or earlier if this Agreement is terminated, you will, on request, pass to me all source materials created or developed in the performance of this Agreement, together with all documents of title, licences, software, animated images and audio, graphical and text materials.

General

21. You agree not to use any machinery on my premises without my permission and notwithstanding such consent you will not in any event load any of your own software onto my machinery or use your own computer discs on my machinery without consent.

22. Each party to this Agreement shall act in good faith towards the other.

23. This Agreement sets out the entire Agreement and replaces all other agreements between the parties relating to the subject matter of this Agreement and there are no representations or obligations other than those contained or referred to herein.

24. No failure to exercise and no delay in exercising on the part of either of the parties any right power or privilege hereunder shall operate as a waiver thereof

nor shall any single or partial exercise of any right power or privilege preclude any other or further exercise thereof or the exercise of any other right power or privilege. The rights and remedies provided in this Agreement are cumulative and not exclusive of any rights or remedies otherwise provided by law.

25. Nothing in this Agreement shall constitute a partnership or agency relationship between the parties hereto.

26. Nothing in this Agreement shall confer on any third party any benefit or the right to enforce any term of this Agreement.

27. This Agreement shall be construed in accordance with English Law and is subject to the exclusive Jurisdiction of the English Courts.

Yours faithfully

[Insert name of person paying freelancer]

I agree to the above terms:

Signed by _____

Date _____

SCHEDULE OF WORKS

ITEM	DETAILS
Work:	
Completion Date/ Term:	
Fees:	You will be paid [insert]

Signed by **[insert]** _____

Date _____

Signed by **[insert]** _____

Date _____

APPENDIX J

Directive 98/71/EC of the European Parliament and Council on the legal protection of designs

DIRECTIVE 98/71/EC OF THE EUROPEAN PARLIAMENT AND OF THE COUNCIL

of 13 October 1998

on the legal protection of designs

THE EUROPEAN PARLIAMENT AND THE COUNCIL OF THE EUROPEAN UNION,

Having regard to the Treaty establishing the European Community and in particular Article 100a thereof,

Having regard to the proposal by the Commission ([1]),

Having regard to the opinion of the Economic and Social Committee ([2]),

Acting in accordance with the procedure laid down in Article 189b of the Treaty ([3]), in the light of the joint text approved by the Conciliation Committee on 29 July 1998,

(1) Whereas the objectives of the Community, as laid down in the Treaty, include laying the foundations of an ever closer union among the peoples of Europe, fostering closer relations between Member States of the Community, and ensuring the economic and social progress of the Community countries by common action to eliminate the barriers which divide Europe; whereas to that end the Treaty provides for the establishment of an internal market characterised by the abolition of obstacles to the free movement of goods and also for the institution of a system ensuring that competition in the internal market is not distorted; whereas an approximation of the laws of the Member States on the legal protection of designs would further those objectives; (2) Whereas the differences in the legal protection of designs offered by the legislation of the Member States directly affect the establishment and functioning of the internal market as regards goods embodying designs; whereas such differences

---

([1]) OJ C 345, 23. 12. 1993, p. 14 and OJ C 142, 14. 5. 1996, p. 7.
([2]) OJ C 388, 31. 12. 1994, p. 9 and OJ C 110, 2. 5. 1995, p. 12.
([3]) Opinion of the European Parliament of 12 October 1995 (OJ C 287, 30. 10. 1995, p. 157), common position of the Council of 17 June 1997 (OJ C 237, 4. 8. 1997, p. 1), Decision of the European Parliament of 22 October 1997 (OJ C 339, 10. 11. 1997, p. 52). Decision of the European Parliament of 15 September 1998. Decision of the Council of 24 September 1998.

can distort competition within the internal market; (3) Whereas it is therefore necessary for the smooth functioning of the internal market to approximate the design protection laws of the Member States; (4) Whereas, in doing so, it is important to take into consideration the solutions and the advantages with which the Community design system will provide undertakings wishing to acquire design rights; (5) Whereas it is unnecessary to undertake a full-scale approximation of the design laws of the Member States, and it will be sufficient if approximation is limited to those national provisions of law which most directly affect the functioning of the internal market; whereas provisions on sanctions, remedies and enforcement should be left to national law; whereas the objectives of this limited approximation cannot be sufficiently achieved by the Member States acting alone; (6) Whereas Member States should accordingly remain free to fix the procedural provisions concerning registration, renewal and invalidation of design rights and provisions concerning the effects of such invalidity; (7) Whereas this Directive does not exclude the application to designs of national or Community legislation providing for protection other than that conferred by registration or publication as design, such as legislation relating to unregistered design rights, trade marks, patents and utility models, unfair competition or civil liability; (8) Whereas, in the absence of harmonisation of copyright law, it is important to establish the principle of cumulation of protection under specific registered design protection law and under copyright law, whilst leaving Member States free to establish the extent of copyright protection and the conditions under which such protection is conferred; (9) Whereas the attainment of the objectives of the internal market requires that the conditions for obtaining a registered design right be identical in all the Member States; whereas to that end it is necessary to give a unitary definition of the notion of design and of the requirements as to novelty and individual character with which registered design rights must comply; (10) Whereas it is essential, in order to facilitate the free movement of goods, to ensure in principle that registered design rights confer upon the right holder equivalent protection in all Member States; (11) Whereas protection is conferred by way of registration upon the right holder for those design features of a product, in whole or in part, which are shown visibly in an application and made available to the public by way of publication or consultation of the relevant file; (12) Whereas protection should not be extended to those component parts which are not visible during normal use of a product, or to those features of such part which are not visible when the part is mounted, or which would not, in themselves, fulfil the requirements as to novelty and individual character; whereas features of design which are excluded from protection for these reasons should not be taken into consideration for the purpose of assessing whether other features of the design fulfil the requirements for protection; (13) Whereas the assessment as to whether a design has individual character should be based on whether the overall impression produced on an informed user viewing the design clearly differs from that produced on him by the existing design corpus, taking into consideration the nature of the product to which the design is applied or in which it is incorporated, and in particular the industrial sector to which it belongs and the degree of freedom of the designer in developing the design; (14) Whereas technological innovation should not be hampered by granting design protection to features dictated solely by a technical function; whereas it is understood that this does not entail that a design must have an aesthetic quality; whereas, likewise, the interoperability of products of different makes should not be hindered by extending protection to the design of mechanical fittings; whereas features of a design which are excluded from protection for these reasons should not be taken into consideration for the purpose of assessing whether other features of the design fulfil the requirements for protection; (15) Whereas the mechanical fittings of modular products may nevertheless constitute an important element of the innovative characteristics of modular products and present a major marketing asset and therefore should be eligible for protection; (16) Whereas a design right shall not subsist in a design which is contrary to public policy or to accepted principles of morality; whereas this Directive does not constitute a harmonisation of national concepts of public policy or accepted principles of morality; (17) Whereas it is fundamental for the smooth functioning of the internal market to unify the term of protection afforded by registered design rights; (18) Whereas the provisions of this Directive are without prejudice to the application of the competition rules under Articles 85 and 86 of the Treaty; (19) Whereas the rapid adoption of this Directive has become a matter of urgency for a number of industrial sectors; whereas full-scale approximation of the laws of the Member States on the use of protected designs for the purpose of permitting the repair of a complex product so as to restore its original appearance, where the product incorporating the design or to which the design is applied constitutes a component part of a complex product upon whose appearance the protected design is dependent, cannot be introduced at the present stage; whereas the lack of full-scale approximation of the laws of the Member States on the use of protected designs for such repair of a complex product should not constitute an obstacle to the approximation of those other national provisions of design law which most directly affect the functioning of the internal market; whereas for this reason Member States should in the meantime maintain in force any provisions in conformity with the Treaty relating to the use of the design of a component part used for the purpose of the repair of a complex product so as to restore its original appearance, or, if they introduce any new provisions relating to such use, the purpose of these provisions should be only to liberalise the market in such parts; whereas those Member States which, on the date of entry into force of this Directive, do not provide for protection for designs of component parts are not required to introduce registration of designs for such parts; whereas three years after the implementation date the Commission should submit an analysis of the consequences of the provisions of this Directive for Community industry, for consumers, for competition and for the functioning of the internal market; whereas, in respect of component parts of complex products, the analysis should, in particular, consider harmonisation on the basis of possible options, including a remuneration system and a limited term of exclusivity; whereas, at the latest one year after the submission of its analysis, the Commission should, after consultation with the parties most affected, propose to the European Parliament and the Council any changes to this Directive needed to complete the internal market in respect of component parts of complex products, and any other changes which it considers necessary; (20) Whereas the transitional provision in Article 14 concerning the design of a component part used for the purpose of the repair of a complex product so as to restore its original appearance is in no case to be construed as constituting an obstacle to the free movement of a product which constitutes such a component part; (21) Whereas the substantive grounds for refusal of registration in those Member States which provide for substantive examination of applications prior to registration, and the substantive grounds for the invalidation of registered design rights in all the Member States, must be exhaustively enumerated,

HAVE ADOPTED THIS DIRECTIVE:

Article 1

Definitions

For the purpose of this Directive: (a) 'design' means the appearance of the whole or a part of a product resulting from the features of, in particular, the lines, contours, colours, shape, texture and/or materials of the product itself and/or its ornamentation; (b) 'product' means any industrial or handicraft item, including *inter alia* parts intended to be assembled into a complex product, packaging, get-up, graphic symbols and typographic typefaces, but excluding computer programs; (c) 'complex product' means a product which is composed of multiple components which can be replaced permitting disassembly and reassembly of the product.

Article 2

Scope of application

1. This Directive shall apply to: (a) design rights registered with the central industrial property offices of the Member States; (b) design rights registered at the Benelux Design Office; (c) design rights registered under international arrangements which have effect in a Member State; (d) applications for design rights referred to under (a), (b) and (c). 2. For the purpose of this Directive, design registration shall also comprise the publication following filing of the design with the industrial property office of a Member State in which such publication has the effect of bringing a design right into existence.

Article 3

Protection requirements

1. Member States shall protect designs by registration, and shall confer exclusive rights upon their holders in accordance with the provisions of this Directive. 2. A design shall be protected by a design right to the extent that it is new and has individual character. 3. A design applied to or incorporated in a product which constitutes a component part of a complex product shall only be considered to be new and to have individual character: (a) if the component part, once it has been incorporated into the complex product, remains visible during normal use of the latter, and (b) to the extent that those visible features of the component part fulfil in themselves the requirements as to novelty and individual character. 4. 'Normal use' within the meaning of paragraph (3)(a) shall mean use by the end user, excluding maintenance, servicing or repair work.

Article 4

Novelty

A design shall be considered new if no identical design has been made available to the public before the date of filing of the application for registration or, if priority is claimed, the date of priority. Designs shall be deemed to be identical if their features differ only in immaterial details.

Article 5

Individual character

1. A design shall be considered to have individual character if the overall impression it produces on the informed user differs from the overall impression produced on such a user by any design which has been made available to the public before the date of filing of the application for registration or, if priority is claimed, the date of priority. 2. In assessing individual character, the degree of freedom of the designer in developing the design shall be taken into consideration.

Article 6

Disclosure

1. For the purpose of applying Articles 4 and 5, a design shall be deemed to have been made available to the public if it has been published following registration or otherwise, or exhibited, used in trade or otherwise disclosed, except where these events could not reasonably have become known in the normal course of business to the circles specialised in the sector concerned, operating within the Community, before the date of filing of the application for registration or, if priority is claimed, the date of priority. The design shall not, however, be deemed to have been made available to the public for the sole reason that it has been disclosed to a third person under explicit or implicit conditions of confidentiality. 2. A disclosure shall not be taken into consideration for the purpose of applying Articles 4 and 5 if a design for which protection is claimed under a registered design right of a Member State has been made available to the public: (a) by the designer, his successor in title, or a third person as a result of information provided or action taken by the designer, or his successor in title; and (b) during the 12-month period preceding the date of filing of the application or, if priority is claimed, the date of priority. 3. Paragraph 2 shall also apply if the design has been made available to the public as a consequence of an abuse in relation to the designer or his successor in title.

Article 7

Designs dictated by their technical function and designs of interconnections

1. A design right shall not subsist in features of appearance of a product which are solely dictated by its technical function. 2. A design right shall not subsist in features of appearance of a product which must necessarily be reproduced in their exact form and dimensions in order to permit the product in which the design is incorporated or to which it is applied to be mechanically connected to or placed in, around or against another product so that either product may perform its function. 3. Notwithstanding paragraph 2, a design right shall, under the conditions set out in Articles 4 and 5, subsist in a design serving the purpose of allowing multiple assembly or connection of mutually interchangeable products within a modular system.

Article 8

Designs contrary to public policy or morality

A design right shall not subsist in a design which is contrary to public policy or to accepted principles of morality.

Article 9

Scope of protection

1. The scope of the protection conferred by a design right shall include any design which does not produce on the informed user a different overall impression. 2. In assessing the scope of protection, the degree of freedom of the designer in developing his design shall be taken into consideration.

Article 10

Term of protection

Upon registration, a design which meets the requirements of Article 3(2) shall be protected by a design right for one or more periods of five years from the date of filing of the application. The right holder may have the term of protection renewed for one or more periods of five years each, up to a total term of 25 years from the date of filing.

Article 11

Invalidity or refusal of registration

1. A design shall be refused registration, or, if the design has been registered, the design right shall be declared invalid: (a) if the design is not a design within the meaning of Article 1(a); or (b) if it does not fulfil the requirements of Articles 3 to 8; or (c) if the applicant for or the holder of the design right is not entitled to it under the law of the Member State concerned; or (d) if the design is in conflict with a prior design which has been made available to the public after the date of filing of the application or, if priority is claimed, the date of priority, and which is protected from a date prior to the said date by a registered Community design or an application for a registered Community design or by a design right of the Member State concerned, or by an application for such a right. 2. Any Member State may provide that a design shall be refused registration, or, if the design has been registered, that the design right shall be declared invalid: (a) if a distinctive sign is used in a subsequent design, and Community law or the law of the Member State concerned governing that sign confers on the right holder of the sign the right to prohibit such use; or (b) if the design constitutes an unauthorised use of a work protected under the copyright law of the Member State concerned; or (c) if the design constitutes an improper use of any of the items listed in Article 6b of the Paris Convention for the Protection of Industrial Property, or of badges, emblems and escutcheons other than those covered by Article 6b of the said Convention which are of particular public interest in the Member State concerned. 3. The ground provided for in paragraph 1(c) may be invoked solely by the person who is entitled to the design right under the law of the Member State concerned. 4. The grounds provided for in paragraph 1(d) and in paragraph 2(a) and (b) may be invoked solely by the applicant for or the holder of the con-

flicting right. 5. The ground provided for in paragraph 2(c) may be invoked solely by the person or entity concerned by the use. 6. Paragraphs 4 and 5 shall be without prejudice to the freedom of Member States to provide that the grounds provided for in paragraphs 1(d) and 2(c) may also be invoked by the appropriate authority of the Member State in question on its own initiative. 7. When a design has been refused registration or a design right has been declared invalid pursuant to paragraph 1(b) or to paragraph 2, the design may be registered or the design right maintained in an amended form, if in that form it complies with the requirements for protection and the identity of the design is retained. Registration or maintenance in an amended form may include registration accompanied by a partial disclaimer by the holder of the design right or entry in the design Register of a court decision declaring the partial invalidity of the design right. 8. Any Member State may provide that, by way of derogation from paragraphs 1 to 7, the grounds for refusal of registration or for invalidation in force in that State prior to the date on which the provisions necessary to comply with this Directive enter into force shall apply to design applications which have been made prior to that date and to resulting registrations. 9. A design right may be declared invalid even after it has lapsed or has been surrendered.

Article 12

Rights conferred by the design right

1. The registration of a design shall confer on its holder the exclusive right to use it and to prevent any third party not having his consent from using it. The aforementioned use shall cover, in particular, the making, offering, putting on the market, importing, exporting or using of a product in which the design is incorporated or to which it is applied, or stocking such a product for those purposes. 2. Where, under the law of a Member State, acts referred to in paragraph 1 could not be prevented before the date on which the provisions necessary to comply with this Directive entered into force, the rights conferred by the design right may not be invoked to prevent continuation of such acts by any person who had begun such acts prior to that date.

Article 13

Limitation of the rights conferred by the design right

1. The rights conferred by a design right upon registration shall not be exercised in respect of: (a) acts done privately and for non-commercial purposes; (b) acts done for experimental purposes; (c) acts of reproduction for the purposes of making citations or of teaching, provided that such acts are compatible with fair trade practice and do not unduly prejudice the normal exploitation of the design, and that mention is made of the source. 2. In addition, the rights conferred by a design right upon registration shall not be exercised in respect of: (a) the equipment on ships and aircraft registered in another country when these temporarily enter the territory of the Member State concerned; (b) the importation in the Member State concerned of spare parts and accessories for the purpose of repairing such craft; (c) the execution of repairs on such craft.

Article 14

Transitional provision

Until such time as amendments to this Directive are adopted on a proposal from the Commission in accordance with the provisions of Article 18, Member States shall maintain in force their existing legal provisions relating to the use of the design of a component part used for the purpose of the repair of a complex product so as to restore its original appearance and shall introduce changes to those provisions only if the purpose is to liberalise the market for such parts.

Article 15

Exhaustion of rights

The rights conferred by a design right upon registration shall not extend to acts relating to a product in which a design included within the scope of protection of the design right is incorporated or to which it is applied, when the product has been put on the market in the Community by the holder of the design right or with his consent.

Article 16

Relationship to other forms of protection

The provisions of this Directive shall be without prejudice to any provisions of Community law or of the law of the Member State concerned relating to unregistered design rights, trade marks or other distinctive signs, patents and utility models, typefaces, civil liability or unfair competition.

Article 17

Relationship to copyright

A design protected by a design right registered in or in respect of a Member State in accordance with this Directive shall also be eligible for protection under the law of copyright of that State as from the date on which the design was created or fixed in any form. The extent to which, and the conditions under which, such a protection is conferred, including the level of originality required, shall be determined by each Member State.

Article 18

Revision

Three years after the implementation date specified in Article 19, the Commission shall submit an analysis of the consequences of the provisions of this Directive for Community industry, in particular the industrial sectors which are most affected, particularly manufacturers of complex products and component parts, for consumers, for competition and for the functioning of the internal market. At the latest one year later the Commission shall propose to the European Parliament and the Council any changes to this Directive needed to complete the internal market in respect of component parts of complex products and any other changes which it considers necessary in light of its consultations with the parties most affected.

Article 19

Implementation

1. Member States shall bring into force the laws, regulations or administrative provisions necessary to comply with this Directive not later than 28 October 2001. When Member States adopt these provisions, they shall contain a reference to this Directive or shall be accompanied by such reference on the occasion of their official publication. The methods of making such reference shall be laid down by Member States. 2. Member States shall communicate to the Commission the provisions of national law which they adopt in the field governed by this Directive.

Article 20

Entry into force

This Directive shall enter into force on the 20th day following its publication in the *Official Journal of the European Communities*.

Article 21

Addressees

This Directive is addressed to the Member States.

Done at Luxembourg, 13 October 1998.

For the European Parliament	*For the Council*
The President	*The President*
J. M. GIL-ROBLES	C. EINEM

APPENDIX K

Council Regulation 6/2002 on Community designs

I

(Acts whose publication is obligatory)

COUNCIL REGULATION (EC) No 6/2002

of 12 December 2001

on Community designs

THE COUNCIL OF THE EUROPEAN UNION,

Having regard to the Treaty establishing the European Community, and in particular Article 308 thereof,

Having regard to the proposal from the Commission (¹),

Having regard to the opinion of the European Parliament (²),

Having regard to the opinion of the Economic and Social Committee (³),

Whereas:

(1) A unified system for obtaining a Community design to which uniform protection is given with uniform effect throughout the entire territory of the Community would further the objectives of the Community as laid down in the Treaty. (2) Only the Benelux countries have introduced a uniform design protection law. In all the other Member States the protection of designs is a matter for the relevant national law and is confined to the territory of the Member State concerned. Identical designs may be therefore protected differently in different Member States and for the benefit of different owners. This inevitably leads to conflicts in the course of trade between Member States. (3) The substantial differences between Member States' design laws prevent and distort Community-wide competition. In comparison with domestic trade in, and competition between, products incorporating a design, trade and competition within the Community are prevented and distorted by the large number of applications, offices, procedures, laws, nationally circumscribed exclusive rights and

---

(¹) OJ C 29, 31.1.1994, p. 20 and OJ C 248, 29.8.2000, p. 3.
(²) OJ C 67, 1.3.2001, p. 318.
(³) OJ C 110, 2.5.1995 and OJ C 75, 15.3.2000, p. 35.

the combined administrative expense with correspondingly high costs and fees for the applicant. Directive 98/71/EC of the European Parliament and of the Council of 13 October 1998 on the legal protection of designs ([4]) contributes to remedying this situation. (4) The effect of design protection being limited to the territory of the individual Member States whether or not their laws are approximated, leads to a possible division of the internal market with respect to products incorporating a design which is the subject of national rights held by different individuals, and hence constitutes an obstacle to the free movement of goods. (5) This calls for the creation of a Community design which is directly applicable in each Member State, because only in this way will it be possible to obtain, through one application made to the Office for Harmonisation in the Internal Market (Trade Marks and Design) in accordance with a single procedure under one law, one design right for one area encompassing all Member States. (6) Since the objectives of the proposed action, namely, the protection of one design right for one area encompassing all the Member States, cannot be sufficiently achieved by the Member States by reason of the scale and the effects of the creation of a Community design and a Community design authority and can therefore, and can therefore be better achieved at Community level, the Community may adopt measures, in accordance with the principle of subsidiarity as set out in Article 5 of the Treaty. In accordance with the principle of proportionality, as set out in that Article, this Regulation does not go beyond what is necessary in order to achieve those objectives. (7) Enhanced protection for industrial design not only promotes the contribution of individual designers to the sum of Community excellence in the field, but also encourages innovation and development of new products and investment in their production. (8) Consequently a more accessible design-protection system adapted to the needs of the internal market is essential for Community industries. (9) The substantive provisions of this Regulation on design law should be aligned with the respective provisions in Directive 98/71/EC. (10) Technological innovation should not be hampered by granting design protection to features dictated solely by a technical function. It is understood that this does not entail that a design must have an aesthetic quality. Likewise, the interoperability of products of different makes should not be hindered by extending protection to the design of mechanical fittings. Consequently, those features of a design which are excluded from protection for those reasons should not be taken into consideration for the purpose of assessing whether other features of the design fulfil the requirements for protection. (11) The mechanical fittings of modular products may nevertheless constitute an important element of the innovative characteristics of modular products and present a major marketing asset, and therefore should be eligible for protection. (12) Protection should not be extended to those component parts which are not visible during normal use of a product, nor to those features of such part which are not visible when the part is mounted, or which would not, in themselves, fulfil the requirements as to novelty and individual character. Therefore, those features of design which are excluded from protection for these reasons should not be taken into consideration for the purpose of assessing whether other features of the design fulfil the requirements for protection. (13) Full-scale approximation of the laws of the Member States on the use of protected designs for the purpose of permitting the repair of a complex product so as to restore its original appearance, where the design is applied to or incorporated in a product which constitutes a component part of a complex product upon whose appearance the protected design is dependent, could not be achieved through Directive 98/71/EC. Within the framework of the conciliation procedure on the said

---

([4]) OJ L 289, 28.10.1998, p. 28.

Directive, the Commission undertook to review the consequences of the provisions of that Directive three years after the deadline for transposition of the Directive in particular for the industrial sectors which are most affected. Under these circumstances, it is appropriate not to confer any protection as a Community design for a design which is applied to or incorporated in a product which constitutes a component part of a complex product upon whose appearance the design is dependent and which is used for the purpose of the repair of a complex product so as to restore its original appearance, until the Council has decided its policy on this issue on the basis of a Commission proposal. (14) The assessment as to whether a design has individual character should be based on whether the overall impression produced on an informed user viewing the design clearly differs from that produced on him by the existing design corpus, taking into consideration the nature of the product to which the design is applied or in which it is incorporated, and in particular the industrial sector to which it belongs and the degree of freedom of the designer in developing the design. (15) A Community design should, as far as possible, serve the needs of all sectors of industry in the Community. (16) Some of those sectors produce large numbers of designs for products frequently having a short market life where protection without the burden of registration formalities is an advantage and the duration of protection is of lesser significance. On the other hand, there are sectors of industry which value the advantages of registration for the greater legal certainty it provides and which require the possibility of a longer term of protection corresponding to the foreseeable market life of their products. (17) This calls for two forms of protection, one being a short-term unregistered design and the other being a longer term registered design. (18) A registered Community design requires the creation and maintenance of a register in which will be registered all those applications which comply with formal conditions and which have been accorded a date of filing. This registration system should in principle not be based upon substantive examination as to compliance with requirements for protection prior to registration, thereby keeping to a minimum the registration and other procedural burdens on applicants. (19) A Community design should not be upheld unless the design is new and unless it also possesses an individual character in comparison with other designs. (20) It is also necessary to allow the designer or his successor in title to test the products embodying the design in the market place before deciding whether the protection resulting from a registered Community design is desirable. To this end it is necessary to provide that disclosures of the design by the designer or his successor in title, or abusive disclosures during a period of 12 months prior to the date of the filing of the application for a registered Community design should not be prejudicial in assessing the novelty or the individual character of the design in question. (21) The exclusive nature of the right conferred by the registered Community design is consistent with its greater legal certainty. It is appropriate that the unregistered Community design should, however, constitute a right only to prevent copying. Protection could not therefore extend to design products which are the result of a design arrived at independently by a second designer. This right should also extend to trade in products embodying infringing designs. (22) The enforcement of these rights is to be left to national laws. It is necessary therefore to provide for some basic uniform sanctions in all Member States. These should make it possible, irrespective of the jurisdiction under which enforcement is sought, to stop the infringing acts. (23) Any third person who can establish that he has in good faith commenced use even for commercial purposes within the Community, or has made serious and effective preparations to that end, of a design included within the scope of protection of a registered Community design, which has not been copied from the latter, may be entitled to a limited exploitation of that design. (24) It is a fundamental objective of this Regulation that the procedure for obtaining a registered Community design should present the minimum cost and difficulty to applicants, so as to make it readily available to small and medium-sized enterprises as well as to individual designers. (25) Those sectors of industry producing large numbers of possibly short-lived designs over short periods of time of which only some may be eventually commercialised will find advantage in the unregistered Community design. Furthermore, there is also a need for these sectors to have easier recourse to the registered Community design. Therefore, the option of combining a number of designs in one multiple application would satisfy that need. However, the designs contained in a multiple application may be dealt with independently of each other for the purposes of enforcement of rights, licensing, rights in rem, levy of execution, insolvency proceedings, surrender, renewal, assignment, deferred publication or declaration of invalidity. (26) The normal publication following registration of a Community design could in some cases destroy or jeopardise the success of a commercial operation involving the design. The facility of a deferment of publication for a reasonable period affords a solution in such cases. (27) A procedure for hearing actions concerning validity of a registered Community design in a single place would bring savings in costs and time compared with procedures involving different national courts. (28) It is therefore necessary to provide safeguards including a right of appeal to a Board of Appeal, and ultimately to the Court of Justice. Such a procedure would assist the development of uniform interpretation of the requirements governing the validity of Community designs. (29) It is essential that the rights conferred by a Community design can be enforced in an efficient manner throughout the territory of the Community. (30) The litigation system should avoid as far as possible 'forum shopping'. It is therefore necessary to establish clear rules of international jurisdiction. (31) This Regulation does not preclude the application to designs protected by Community designs of the industrial property laws or other relevant laws of the Member States, such as those relating to design protection acquired by registration or those relating to unregistered designs, trade marks, patents and utility models, unfair competition or civil liability. (32) In the absence of the complete harmonisation of copyright law, it is important to establish the principle of cumulation of protection under the Community design and under copyright law, whilst leaving Member States free to establish the extent of copyright protection and the conditions under which such protection is conferred. (33) The measures necessary for the implementation of this Regulation should be adopted in accordance with Council Decision 1999/468/EC of 28 June 1999 laying down the procedures for the exercise of implementing powers conferred on the Commission ([1]),

HAS ADOPTED THIS REGULATION:

([1]) OJ L 184, 17.7.1999, p. 23.

TITLE I

GENERAL PROVISIONS

Article 1

Community design

1. A design which complies with the conditions contained in this Regulation is hereinafter referred to as a 'Community design'. 2. A design shall be protected: (a) by an 'unregistered Community design', if made available to the public in the manner provided for in this Regulation; (b) by a 'registered Community design', if registered in the manner provided for in this Regulation. 3. A Community design shall have a unitary character. It shall have equal effect throughout the Community. It shall not be registered, transferred or surrendered or be the subject of a decision declaring it invalid, nor shall its use be prohibited, save in respect of the whole Community. This principle and its implications shall apply unless otherwise provided in this Regulation.

Article 2

Office

The Office for Harmonisation in the Internal Market (Trade Marks and Designs), hereinafter referred to as 'the Office', instituted by Council Regulation (EC) No 40/94 of 20 December 1993 on the Community trade mark (¹), hereinafter referred to as the 'Regulation on the Community trade mark', shall carry out the tasks entrusted to it by this Regulation.

TITLE II

THE LAW RELATING TO DESIGNS

Section 1

Requirements for protection

Article 3

Definitions

For the purposes of this Regulation:

(a) 'design' means the appearance of the whole or a part of a product resulting from the features of, in particular, the lines, contours, colours, shape, texture and/or materials of the product itself and/or its ornamentation; (b) 'product' means any industrial or handicraft item, including *inter alia* parts intended to be assembled into a complex product, packaging, get-up, graphic symbols and typographic typefaces, but excluding computer programs; (c) 'complex product' means a product which is

---

(¹) OJ L 11, 14.1.1994, p. 1. Regulation as last amended by Regulation (EC) No 3288/94 (OJ L 349, 31.12.1994, p. 83).

composed of multiple components which can be replaced permitting disassembly and re-assembly of the product.

Article 4

Requirements for protection

1. A design shall be protected by a Community design to the extent that it is new and has individual character. 2. A design applied to or incorporated in a product which constitutes a component part of a complex product shall only be considered to be new and to have individual character: (a) if the component part, once it has been incorporated into the complex product, remains visible during normal use of the latter; and (b) to the extent that those visible features of the component part fulfil in themselves the requirements as to novelty and individual character. 3. 'Normal use' within the meaning of paragraph (2)(a) shall mean use by the end user, excluding maintenance, servicing or repair work.

Article 5

Novelty

1. A design shall be considered to be new if no identical design has been made available to the public: (a) in the case of an unregistered Community design, before the date on which the design for which protection is claimed has first been made available to the public; (b) in the case of a registered Community design, before the date of filing of the application for registration of the design for which protection is claimed, or, if priority is claimed, the date of priority. 2. Designs shall be deemed to be identical if their features differ only in immaterial details.

Article 6

Individual character

1. A design shall be considered to have individual character if the overall impression it produces on the informed user differs from the overall impression produced on such a user by any design which has been made available to the public: (a) in the case of an unregistered Community design, before the date on which the design for which protection is claimed has first been made available to the public; (b) in the case of a registered Community design, before the date of filing the application for registration or, if a priority is claimed, the date of priority. 2. In assessing individual character, the degree of freedom of the designer in developing the design shall be taken into consideration.

Article 7

Disclosure

1. For the purpose of applying Articles 5 and 6, a design shall be deemed to have been made available to the public if it has been published following registration or otherwise, or exhibited, used in trade or otherwise disclosed, before the date referred to in Articles 5(1)(a) and 6(1)(a) or in Articles 5(1)(b) and 6(1)(b), as the case may be, except where these events could not reasonably have become known in the normal course of business to the circles specialised in the sector concerned, operating within

the Community. The design shall not, however, be deemed to have been made available to the public for the sole reason that it has been disclosed to a third person under explicit or implicit conditions of confidentiality. 2. A disclosure shall not be taken into consideration for the purpose of applying Articles 5 and 6 and if a design for which protection is claimed under a registered Community design has been made available to the public: (a) by the designer, his successor in title, or a third person as a result of information provided or action taken by the designer or his successor in title; and (b) during the 12-month period preceding the date of filing of the application or, if a priority is claimed, the date of priority. 3. Paragraph 2 shall also apply if the design has been made available to the public as a consequence of an abuse in relation to the designer or his successor in title.

Article 8

Designs dictated by their technical function and designs of interconnections

1. A Community design shall not subsist in features of appearance of a product which are solely dictated by its technical function. 2. A Community design shall not subsist in features of appearance of a product which must necessarily be reproduced in their exact form and dimensions in order to permit the product in which the design is incorporated or to which it is applied to be mechanically connected to or placed in, around or against another product so that either product may perform its function. 3. Notwithstanding paragraph 2, a Community design shall under the conditions set out in Articles 5 and 6 subsist in a design serving the purpose of allowing the multiple assembly or connection of mutually interchangeable products within a modular system.

Article 9

Designs contrary to public policy or morality

A Community design shall not subsist in a design which is contrary to public policy or to accepted principles of morality.

Section 2

Scope and term of protection

Article 10

Scope of protection

1. The scope of the protection conferred by a Community design shall include any design which does not produce on the informed user a different overall impression. 2. In assessing the scope of protection, the degree of freedom of the designer in developing his design shall be taken into consideration.

Article 11

Commencement and term of protection of the unregistered Community design

1. A design which meets the requirements under Section 1 shall be protected by an unregistered Community design for a period of three years as from the date on which the design was first made available to the public within the Community. 2. For the purpose of paragraph 1, a design shall be deemed to have been made available to the public within the Community if it has been published, exhibited, used in trade or otherwise disclosed in such a way that, in the normal course of business, these events could reasonably have become known to the circles specialised in the sector concerned, operating within the Community. The design shall not, however, be deemed to have been made available to the public for the sole reason that it has been disclosed to a third person under explicit or implicit conditions of confidentiality.

Article 12

Commencement and term of protection of the registered Community design

Upon registration by the Office, a design which meets the requirements under Section 1 shall be protected by a registered Community design for a period of five years as from the date of the filing of the application. The right holder may have the term of protection renewed for one or more periods of five years each, up to a total term of 25 years from the date of filing.

Article 13

Renewal

1. Registration of the registered Community design shall be renewed at the request of the right holder or of any person expressly authorised by him, provided that the renewal fee has been paid. 2. The Office shall inform the right holder of the registered Community design and any person having a right entered in the register of Community designs, referred to in Article 72, hereafter referred to as the 'register' in respect of the registered Community design, of the expiry of the registration in good time before the said expiry. Failure to give such information shall not involve the responsibility of the Office. 3. The request for renewal shall be submitted and the renewal fee paid within a period of six months ending on the last day of the month in which protection ends. Failing this, the request may be submitted and the fee paid within a further period of six months from the day referred to in the first sentence, provided that an additional fee is paid within this further period. 4. Renewal shall take effect from the day following the date on which the existing registration expires. The renewal shall be entered in the register.

Section 3

Right to the Community design

Article 14

Right to the Community design

1. The right to the Community design shall vest in the designer or his successor in title. 2. If two or more persons have jointly developed a design, the right to the Community design shall vest in them jointly. 3. However, where a design is developed by an employee in the execution of his duties or following the instructions given by his employer, the right to the Community design shall vest in the employer, unless otherwise agreed or specified under national law.

Article 15

Claims relating to the entitlement to a Community design

1. If an unregistered Community design is disclosed or claimed by, or a registered Community design has been applied for or registered in the name of, a person who is not entitled to it under Article 14, the person entitled to it under that provision may, without prejudice to any other remedy which may be open to him, claim to become recognised as the legitimate holder of the Community design. 2. Where a person is jointly entitled to a Community design, that person may, in accordance with paragraph 1, claim to become recognised as joint holder. 3. Legal proceedings under paragraphs 1 or 2 shall be barred three years after the date of publication of a registered Community design or the date of disclosure of an unregistered Community design. This provision shall not apply if the person who is not entitled to the Community design was acting in bad faith at the time when such design was applied for or disclosed or was assigned to him. 4. In the case of a registered Community design, the following shall be entered in the register: (a) the mention that legal proceedings under paragraph 1 have been instituted; (b) the final decision or any other termination of the proceedings; (c) any change in the ownership of the registered Community design resulting from the final decision.

Article 16

Effects of a judgement on entitlement to a registered Community design

1. Where there is a complete change of ownership of a registered Community design as a result of legal proceedings under Article 15(1), licences and other rights shall lapse upon the entering in the register of the person entitled. 2. If, before the institution of the legal proceedings under Article 15(1) has been registered, the holder of the registered Community design or a licensee has exploited the design within the Community or made serious and effective preparations to do so, he may continue such exploitation provided that he requests within the period prescribed by the implementing regulation a non-exclusive licence from the new holder whose name is entered in the register. The licence shall be granted for a reasonable period and upon reasonable terms. 3. Paragraph 2 shall not apply if the holder of the registered Community design or the licensee was acting in bad faith at the time when he began to exploit the design or to make preparations to do so.

335

Article 17

Presumption in favour of the registered holder of the design

The person in whose name the registered Community design is registered or, prior to registration, the person in whose name the application is filed, shall be deemed to be the person entitled in any proceedings before the Office as well as in any other proceedings.

Article 18

Right of the designer to be cited

The designer shall have the right, in the same way as the applicant for or the holder of a registered Community design, to be cited as such before the Office and in the register. If the design is the result of teamwork, the citation of the team may replace the citation of the individual designers.

Section 4

Effects of the Community design

Article 19

Rights conferred by the Community design

1. A registered Community design shall confer on its holder the exclusive right to use it and to prevent any third party not having his consent from using it. The aforementioned use shall cover, in particular, the making, offering, putting on the market, importing, exporting or using of a product in which the design is incorporated or to which it is applied, or stocking such a product for those purposes. 2. An unregistered Community design shall, however, confer on its holder the right to prevent the acts referred to in paragraph 1 only if the contested use results from copying the protected design. The contested use shall not be deemed to result from copying the protected design if it results from an independent work of creation by a designer who may be reasonably thought not to be familiar with the design made available to the public by the holder. 3. Paragraph 2 shall also apply to a registered Community design subject to deferment of publication as long as the relevant entries in the register and the file have not been made available to the public in accordance with Article 50(4).

Article 20

Limitation of the rights conferred by a Community design

1. The rights conferred by a Community design shall not be exercised in respect of: (a) acts done privately and for non-commercial purposes; (b) acts done for experimental purposes; (c) acts of reproduction for the purpose of making citations or of teaching, provided that such acts are compatible with fair trade practice and do not unduly prejudice the normal exploitation of the design, and that mention is made of the source. 2. In addition, the rights conferred by a Community design shall not be exercised in respect of: (a) the equipment on ships and aircraft registered in a third country when these temporarily enter the territory of the Community; (b) the impor-

tation in the Community of spare parts and accessories for the purpose of repairing such craft; (c) the execution of repairs on such craft.

Article 21

Exhaustion of rights

The rights conferred by a Community design shall not extend to acts relating to a product in which a design included within the scope of protection of the Community design is incorporated or to which it is applied, when the product has been put on the market in the Community by the holder of the Community design or with his consent.

Article 22

Rights of prior use in respect of a registered Community design

1. A right of prior use shall exist for any third person who can establish that before the date of filing of the application, or, if a priority is claimed, before the date of priority, he has in good faith commenced use within the Community, or has made serious and effective preparations to that end, of a design included within the scope of protection of a registered Community design, which has not been copied from the latter. 2. The right of prior use shall entitle the third person to exploit the design for the purposes for which its use had been effected, or for which serious and effective preparations had been made, before the filing or priority date of the registered Community design. 3. The right of prior use shall not extend to granting a licence to another person to exploit the design. 4. The right of prior use cannot be transferred except, where the third person is a business, along with that part of the business in the course of which the act was done or the preparations were made.

Article 23

Government use

Any provision in the law of a Member State allowing use of national designs by or for the government may be applied to Community designs, but only to the extent that the use is necessary for essential defence or security needs.

Section 5

Invalidity

Article 24

Declaration of invalidity

1. A registered Community design shall be declared invalid on application to the Office in accordance with the procedure in Titles VI and VII or by a Community design court on the basis of a counterclaim in infringement proceedings. 2. A Community design may be declared invalid even after the Community design has lapsed or has been surrendered. 3. An unregistered Community design shall be declared invalid by a Community design court on application to such a court or on the basis of a counterclaim in infringement proceedings.

Article 25

Grounds for invalidity

1. A Community design may be declared invalid only in the following cases: (a) if the design does not correspond to the definition under Article 3(a); (b) if it does not fulfil the requirements of Articles 4 to 9; (c) if, by virtue of a court decision, the right holder is not entitled to the Community design under Article 14; (d) if the Community design is in conflict with a prior design which has been made available to the public after the date of filing of the application or, if a priority is claimed, the date of priority of the Community design, and which is protected from a date prior to the said date by a registered Community design or an application for such a design, or by a registered design right of a Member State, or by an application for such a right; (e) if a distinctive sign is used in a subsequent design, and Community law or the law of the Member State governing that sign confers on the right holder of the sign the right to prohibit such use; (f) if the design constitutes an unauthorised use of a work protected under the copyright law of a Member State; (g) if the design constitutes an improper use of any of the items listed in Article 6ter of the 'Paris Convention' for the Protection of Industrial Property hereafter referred to as the 'Paris Convention', or of badges, emblems and escutcheons other than those covered by the said Article 6ter and which are of particular public interest in a Member State. 2. The ground provided for in paragraph (1)(c) may be invoked solely by the person who is entitled to the Community design under Article 14. 3. The grounds provided for in paragraph (1)(d), (e) and (f) may be invoked solely by the applicant for or holder of the earlier right. 4. The ground provided for in paragraph (1)(g) may be invoked solely by the person or entity concerned by the use. 5. Paragraphs 3 and 4 shall be without prejudice to the freedom of Member States to provide that the grounds provided for in paragraphs 1(d) and (g) may also be invoked by the appropriate authority of the Member State in question on its own initiative. 6. A registered Community design which has been declared invalid pursuant to paragraph (1)(b), (e), (f) or (g) may be maintained in an amended form, if in that form it complies with the requirements for protection and the identity of the design is retained. 'Maintenance' in an amended form may include registration accompanied by a partial disclaimer by the holder of the registered Community design or entry in the register of a court decision or a decision by the Office declaring the partial invalidity of the registered Community design.

Article 26

Consequences of invalidity

1. A Community design shall be deemed not to have had, as from the outset, the effects specified in this Regulation, to the extent that it has been declared invalid. 2. Subject to the national provisions relating either to claims for compensation for damage caused by negligence or lack of good faith on the part of the holder of the Community design, or to unjust enrichment, the retroactive effect of invalidity of the Community design shall not affect: (a) any decision on infringement which has acquired the authority of a final decision and been enforced prior to the invalidity decision; (b) any contract concluded prior to the invalidity decision, in so far as it has been performed before the decision; however, repayment, to an extent justified by the circumstances, of sums paid under the relevant contract may be claimed on grounds of equity.

TITLE III

COMMUNITY DESIGNS AS OBJECTS OF PROPERTY

Article 27

Dealing with Community designs as national design rights

1. Unless Articles 28, 29, 30, 31 and 32 provide otherwise, a Community design as an object of property shall be dealt with in its entirety, and for the whole area of the Community, as a national design right of the Member State in which: (a) the holder has his seat or his domicile on the relevant date; or (b) where point (a) does not apply, the holder has an establishment on the relevant date. 2. In the case of a registered Community design, paragraph 1 shall apply according to the entries in the register. 3. In the case of joint holders, if two or more of them fulfil the condition under paragraph 1, the Member State referred to in that paragraph shall be determined: (a) in the case of an unregistered Community design, by reference to the relevant joint holder designated by them by common agreement; (b) in the case of a registered Community design, by reference to the first of the relevant joint holders in the order in which they are mentioned in the register. 4. Where paragraphs 1, 2 and 3 do not apply, the Member State referred to in paragraph 1 shall be the Member State in which the seat of the Office is situated.

Article 28

Transfer of the registered Community design

The transfer of a registered Community design shall be subject to the following provisions: (a) at the request of one of the parties, a transfer shall be entered in the register and published; (b) until such time as the transfer has been entered in the register, the successor in title may not invoke the rights arising from the registration of the Community design; (c) where there are time limits to be observed in dealings with the Office, the successor in title may make the corresponding statements to the Office once the request for registration of the transfer has been received by the Office; (d) all documents which by virtue of Article 66 require notification to the holder of the registered Community design shall be addressed by the Office to the person registered as holder or his representative, if one has been appointed.

Article 29

Rights in rem on a registered Community design

1. A registered Community design may be given as security or be the subject of rights *in rem*. 2. On request of one of the parties, the rights mentioned in paragraph 1 shall be entered in the register and published.

Article 30

Levy of execution

1. A registered Community design may be levied in execution. 2. As regards the procedure for levy of execution in respect of a registered Community design, the courts

339

and authorities of the Member State determined in accordance with Article 27 shall have exclusive jurisdiction. 3. On request of one of the parties, levy of execution shall be entered in the register and published.

Article 31

Insolvency proceedings

1. The only insolvency proceedings in which a Community design may be involved shall be those opened in the Member State within the territory of which the centre of a debtor's main interests is situated. 2. In the case of joint proprietorship of a Community design, paragraph 1 shall apply to the share of the joint proprietor. 3. Where a Community design is involved in insolvency proceedings, on request of the competent national authority an entry to this effect shall be made in the register and published in the Community Designs Bulletin referred to in Article 73(1).

Article 32

Licensing

1. A Community design may be licensed for the whole or part of the Community. A licence may be exclusive or non-exclusive. 2. Without prejudice to any legal proceedings based on the law of contract, the holder may invoke the rights conferred by the Community design against a licensee who contravenes any provision in his licensing contract with regard to its duration, the form in which the design may be used, the range of products for which the licence is granted and the quality of products manufactured by the licensee. 3. Without prejudice to the provisions of the licensing contract, the licensee may bring proceedings for infringement of a Community design only if the right holder consents thereto. However, the holder of an exclusive licence may bring such proceedings if the right holder in the Community design, having been given notice to do so, does not himself bring infringement proceedings within an appropriate period. 4. A licensee shall, for the purpose of obtaining compensation for damage suffered by him, be entitled to intervene in an infringement action brought by the right holder in a Community design. 5. In the case of a registered Community design, the grant or transfer of a licence in respect of such right shall, at the request of one of the parties, be entered in the register and published.

Article 33

Effects vis-à-vis third parties

1. The effects vis-à-vis third parties of the legal acts referred to in Articles 28, 29, 30 and 32 shall be governed by the law of the Member State determined in accordance with Article 27. 2. However, as regards registered Community designs, legal acts referred to in Articles 28, 29 and 32 shall only have effect vis-à-vis third parties in all the Member States after entry in the register. Nevertheless, such an act, before it is so entered, shall have effect vis-à-vis third parties who have acquired rights in the registered Community design after the date of that act but who knew of the act at the date on which the rights were acquired. 3. Paragraph 2 shall not apply to a person who acquires the registered Community design or a right concerning the registered Community design by way of transfer of the whole of the undertaking or by any other universal succession. 4. Until such time as common rules for the Member States in the field of insolvency enter into force, the effects vis-à-vis third parties of insol-

vency proceedings shall be governed by the law of the Member State in which such proceedings are first brought under the national law or the regulations applicable in this field.

Article 34

The application for a registered Community design as an object of property

1. An application for a registered Community design as an object of property shall be dealt with in its entirety, and for the whole area of the Community, as a national design right of the Member State determined in accordance with Article 27. 2. Articles 28, 29, 30, 31, 32 and 33 shall apply *mutatis mutandis* to applications for registered Community designs. Where the effect of one of these provisions is conditional upon an entry in the register, that formality shall be performed upon registration of the resulting registered Community design.

TITLE IV

APPLICATION FOR A REGISTERED COMMUNITY DESIGN

Section 1

Filing of applications and the conditions which govern them

Article 35

Filing and forwarding of applications

1. An application for a registered Community design shall be filed, at the option of the applicant: (a) at the Office; or (b) at the central industrial property office of a Member State; or (c) in the Benelux countries, at the Benelux Design Office. 2. Where the application is filed at the central industrial property office of a Member State or at the Benelux Design Office, that office shall take all steps to forward the application to the Office within two weeks after filing. It may charge the applicant a fee which shall not exceed the administrative costs of receiving and forwarding the application. 3. As soon as the Office has received an application which has been forwarded by a central industrial property office of a Member State or by the Benelux Design Office, it shall inform the applicant accordingly, indicating the date of its receipt at the Office. 4. No less than 10 years after the entry into force of this Regulation, the Commission shall draw up a report on the operation of the system of filing applications for registered Community designs, accompanied by any proposals for revision that it may deem appropriate.

Article 36

Conditions with which applications must comply

1. An application for a registered Community design shall contain: (a) a request for registration; (b) information identifying the applicant; (c) a representation of the design suitable for reproduction. However, if the object of the application is a two-dimensional design and the application contains a request for deferment of publication in accordance with Article 50, the representation of the design may be replaced

341

by a specimen. 2. The application shall further contain an indication of the products in which the design is intended to be incorporated or to which it is intended to be applied. 3. In addition, the application may contain: (a) a description explaining the representation or the specimen; (b) a request for deferment of publication of the registration in accordance with Article 50; (c) information identifying the representative if the applicant has appointed one; (d) the classification of the products in which the design is intended to be incorporated or to which it is intended to be applied according to class; (e) the citation of the designer or of the team of designers or a statement under the applicant's responsibility that the designer or the team of designers has waived the right to be cited. 4. The application shall be subject to the payment of the registration fee and the publication fee. Where a request for deferment under paragraph 3(b) is filed, the publication fee shall be replaced by the fee for deferment of publication. 5. The application shall comply with the conditions laid down in the implementing regulation. 6. The information contained in the elements mentioned in paragraph 2 and in paragraph 3(a) and (d) shall not affect the scope of protection of the design as such.

Article 37

Multiple applications

1. Several designs may be combined in one multiple application for registered Community designs. Except in cases of ornamentation, this possibility is subject to the condition that the products in which the designs are intended to be incorporated or to which they are intended to be applied all belong to the same class of the International Classification for Industrial Designs. 2. Besides the fees referred to in Article 36(4), the multiple application shall be subject to payment of an additional registration fee and an additional publication fee. Where the multiple application contains a request for deferment of publication, the additional publication fee shall be replaced by the additional fee for deferment of publication. The additional fees shall correspond to a percentage of the basic fees for each additional design. 3. The multiple application shall comply with the conditions of presentation laid down in the implementing regulation. 4. Each of the designs contained in a multiple application or registration may be dealt with separately from the others for the purpose of applying this Regulation. It may in particular, separately from the others, be enforced, licensed, be the subject of a right *in rem*, a levy of execution or insolvency proceedings, be surrendered, renewed or assigned, be the subject of deferred publication or be declared invalid. A multiple application or registration may be divided into separate applications or registrations only under the conditions set out in the implementing regulation.

Article 38

Date of filing

1. The date of filing of an application for a registered Community design shall be the date on which documents containing the information specified in Article 36(1) are filed with the Office by the applicant, or, if the application has been filed with the central industrial property office of a Member State or with the Benelux Design Office, with that office. 2. By derogation from paragraph 1, the date of filing of an application filed with the central industrial property office of a Member State or with the Benelux Design Office and reaching the Office more than two months after the

date on which documents containing the information specified in Article 36(1) have been filed shall be the date of receipt of such documents by the Office.

Article 39

Equivalence of Community filing with national filing

An application for a registered Community design which has been accorded a date of filing shall, in the Member States, be equivalent to a regular national filing, including where appropriate the priority claimed for the said application.

Article 40

Classification

For the purpose of this Regulation, use shall be made of the Annex to the Agreement establishing an International Classification for Industrial Designs, signed at Locarno on 8 October 1968.

Section 2

Priority

Article 41

Right of priority

1. A person who has duly filed an application for a design right or for a utility model in or for any State party to the Paris Convention for the Protection of Industrial Property, or to the Agreement establishing the World Trade Organisation, or his successors in title, shall enjoy, for the purpose of filing an application for a registered Community design in respect of the same design or utility model, a right of priority of six months from the date of filing of the first application. 2. Every filing that is equivalent to a regular national filing under the national law of the State where it was made or under bilateral or multilateral agreements shall be recognised as giving rise to a right of priority. 3. 'Regular national filing' means any filing that is sufficient to establish the date on which the application was filed, whatever may be the outcome of the application. 4. A subsequent application for a design which was the subject of a previous first application, and which is filed in or in respect of the same State, shall be considered as the first application for the purpose of determining priority, provided that, at the date of the filing of the subsequent application, the previous application has been withdrawn, abandoned or refused without being open to public inspection and without leaving any rights outstanding, and has not served as a basis for claiming priority. The previous application may not thereafter serve as a basis for claiming a right of priority. 5. If the first filing has been made in a State which is not a party to the Paris Convention, or to the Agreement establishing the World Trade Organisation, paragraphs 1 to 4 shall apply only in so far as that State, according to published findings, grants, on the basis of a filing made at the Office and subject to conditions equivalent to those laid down in this Regulation, a right of priority having equivalent effect.

Article 42

Claiming priority

An applicant for a registered Community design desiring to take advantage of the priority of a previous application shall file a declaration of priority and a copy of the previous application. If the language of the latter is not one of the languages of the Office, the Office may require a translation of the previous application in one of those languages.

Article 43

Effect of priority right

The effect of the right of priority shall be that the date of priority shall count as the date of the filing of the application for a registered Community design for the purpose of Articles 5, 6, 7, 22, 25(1)(d) and 50(1).

Article 44

Exhibition priority

1. If an applicant for a registered Community design has disclosed products in which the design is incorporated, or to which it is applied, at an official or officially recognised international exhibition falling within the terms of the Convention on International Exhibitions signed in Paris on 22 November 1928 and last revised on 30 November 1972, he may, if he files the application within a period of six months from the date of the first disclosure of such products, claim a right of priority from that date within the meaning of Article 43. 2. An applicant who wishes to claim priority pursuant to paragraph 1, under the conditions laid down in the implementing regulation, must file evidence that he has disclosed at an exhibition the products in or to which the design is incorporated or applied. 3. An exhibition priority granted in a Member State or in a third country does not extend the period of priority laid down in Article 41.

TITLE V

REGISTRATION PROCEDURE

Article 45

Examination as to formal requirements for filing

1. The Office shall examine whether the application complies with the requirements laid down in Article 36(1) for the accordance of a date of filing. 2. The Office shall examine whether: (a) the application complies with the other requirements laid down in Article 36(2), (3), (4) and (5) and, in the case of a multiple application, Article 37(1) and (2); (b) the application meets the formal requirements laid down in the implementing regulation for the implementation of Articles 36 and 37; (c) the requirements of Article 77(2) are satisfied; (d) the requirements concerning the claim to priority are satisfied, if a priority is claimed. 3. The conditions for the examination as to the formal requirements for filing shall be laid down in the implementing regulation.

Article 46

Remediable deficiencies

1. Where, in carrying out the examination under Article 45, the Office notes that there are deficiencies which may be corrected, the Office shall request the applicant to remedy them within the prescribed period. 2. If the deficiencies concern the requirements referred to in Article 36(1) and the applicant complies with the Office's request within the prescribed period, the Office shall accord as the date of filing the date on which the deficiencies are remedied. If the deficiencies are not remedied within the prescribed period, the application shall not be dealt with as an application for a registered Community design. 3. If the deficiencies concern the requirements, including the payment of fees, as referred to in Article 45(2)(a), (b) and (c) and the applicant complies with the Office's request within the prescribed period, the Office shall accord as the date of filing the date on which the application was originally filed. If the deficiencies or the default in payment are not remedied within the prescribed period, the Office shall refuse the application. 4. If the deficiencies concern the requirements referred to in Article 45(2)(d), failure to remedy them within the prescribed period shall result in the loss of the right of priority for the application.

Article 47

Grounds for non-registrability

1. If the Office, in carrying out the examination pursuant to Article 45, notices that the design for which protection is sought: (a) does not correspond to the definition under Article 3(a); or (b) is contrary to public policy or to accepted principles of morality, it shall refuse the application. 2. The application shall not be refused before the applicant has been allowed the opportunity of withdrawing or amending the application or of submitting his observations.

Article 48

Registration

If the requirements that an application for a registered Community design must satisfy have been fulfilled and to the extent that the application has not been refused by virtue of Article 47, the Office shall register the application in the Community design Register as a registered Community design. The registration shall bear the date of filing of the application referred to in Article 38.

Article 49

Publication

Upon registration, the Office shall publish the registered Community design in the Community Designs Bulletin as mentioned in Article 73(1). The contents of the publication shall be set out in the implementing regulation.

Article 50

Deferment of publication

1. The applicant for a registered Community design may request, when filing the application, that the publication of the registered Community design be deferred for a period of 30 months from the date of filing the application or, if a priority is claimed, from the date of priority. 2. Upon such request, where the conditions set out in Article 48 are satisfied, the registered Community design shall be registered, but neither the representation of the design nor any file relating to the application shall, subject to Article 74(2), be open to public inspection. 3. The Office shall publish in the Community Designs Bulletin a mention of the deferment of the publication of the registered Community design. The mention shall be accompanied by information identifying the right holder in the registered Community design, the date of filing the application and any other particulars prescribed by the implementing regulation. 4. At the expiry of the period of deferment, or at any earlier date on request by the right holder, the Office shall open to public inspection all the entries in the register and the file relating to the application and shall publish the registered Community design in the Community Designs Bulletin, provided that, within the time limit laid down in the implementing regulation: (a) the publication fee and, in the event of a multiple application, the additional publication fee are paid; (b) where use has been made of the option pursuant to Article 36(1)(c), the right holder has filed with the Office a representation of the design. If the right holder fails to comply with these requirements, the registered Community design shall be deemed from the outset not to have had the effects specified in this Regulation. 5. In the case of multiple applications, paragraph 4 need only be applied to some of the designs included therein. 6. The institution of legal proceedings on the basis of a registered Community design during the period of deferment of publication shall be subject to the condition that the information contained in the register and in the file relating to the application has been communicated to the person against whom the action is brought.

TITLE VI

SURRENDER AND INVALIDITY OF THE REGISTERED COMMUNITY DESIGN

Article 51

Surrender

1. The surrender of a registered Community design shall be declared to the Office in writing by the right holder. It shall not have effect until it has been entered in the register. 2. If a Community design which is subject to deferment of publication is surrendered it shall be deemed from the outset not to have had the effects specified in this Regulation. 3. A registered Community design may be partially surrendered provided that its amended form complies with the requirements for protection and the identity of the design is retained. 4. Surrender shall be registered only with the agreement of the proprietor of a right entered in the register. If a licence has been registered, surrender shall be entered in the register only if the right holder in the registered Community design proves that he has informed the licensee of his intention to surrender. This entry shall be made on expiry of the period prescribed by the implementing regulation. 5. If an action pursuant to Article 14 relating to the entitlement

to a registered Community design has been brought before a Community design court, the Office shall not enter the surrender in the register without the agreement of the claimant.

Article 52

Application for a declaration of invalidity

1. Subject to Article 25(2), (3), (4) and (5), any natural or legal person, as well as a public authority empowered to do so, may submit to the Office an application for a declaration of invalidity of a registered Community design. 2. The application shall be filed in a written reasoned statement. It shall not be deemed to have been filed until the fee for an application for a declaration of invalidity has been paid. 3. An application for a declaration of invalidity shall not be admissible if an application relating to the same subject matter and cause of action, and involving the same parties, has been adjudicated on by a Community design court and has acquired the authority of a final decision.

Article 53

Examination of the application

1. If the Office finds that the application for a declaration of invalidity is admissible, the Office shall examine whether the grounds for invalidity referred to in Article 25 prejudice the maintenance of the registered Community design. 2. In the examination of the application, which shall be conducted in accordance with the implementing regulation, the Office shall invite the parties, as often as necessary, to file observations, within a period to be fixed by the Office, on communications from the other parties or issued by itself. 3. The decision declaring the registered Community design invalid shall be entered in the register upon becoming final.

Article 54

Participation in the proceedings of the alleged infringer

1. In the event of an application for a declaration of invalidity of a registered Community design being filed, and as long as no final decision has been taken by the Office, any third party who proves that proceedings for infringement of the same design have been instituted against him may be joined as a party in the invalidity proceedings on request submitted within three months of the date on which the infringement proceedings were instituted. The same shall apply in respect of any third party who proves both that the right holder of the Community design has requested that he cease an alleged infringement of the design and that he has instituted proceedings for a court ruling that he is not infringing the Community design. 2. The request to be joined as a party shall be filed in a written reasoned statement. It shall not be deemed to have been filed until the invalidity fee, referred to in Article 52(2), has been paid. Thereafter the request shall, subject to any exceptions laid down in the implementing regulation, be treated as an application for a declaration of invalidity.

TITLE VII

APPEALS

Article 55

Decisions subject to appeal

1. An appeal shall lie from decisions of the examiners, the Administration of Trade Marks and Designs and Legal Division and Invalidity Divisions. It shall have suspensive effect. 2. A decision which does not terminate proceedings as regards one of the parties can only be appealed together with the final decision, unless the decision allows separate appeal.

Article 56

Persons entitled to appeal and to be parties to appeal proceedings

Any party to proceedings adversely affected by a decision may appeal. Any other parties to the proceedings shall be parties to the appeal proceedings as of right.

Article 57

Time limit and form of appeal

Notice of appeal must be filed in writing at the Office within two months after the date of notification of the decision appealed from. The notice shall be deemed to have been filed only when the fee for appeal has been paid. Within four months after the date of notification of the decision, a written statement setting out the grounds of appeal must be filed.

Article 58

Interlocutory revision

1. If the department whose decision is contested considers the appeal to be admissible and well founded, it shall rectify its decision. This shall not apply where the appellant is opposed by another party to the proceedings. 2. If the decision is not rectified within one month after receipt of the statement of grounds, the appeal shall be remitted to the Board of Appeal without delay and without comment as to its merits.

Article 59

Examination of appeals

1. If the appeal is admissible, the Board of Appeal shall examine whether the appeal is to be allowed. 2. In the examination of the appeal, the Board of Appeal shall invite the parties, as often as necessary, to file observations, within a period to be fixed by the Board of Appeal, on communications from the other parties or issued by itself.

Article 60

Decisions in respect of appeals

1. Following the examination as to the merits of the appeal, the Board of Appeal shall decide on the appeal. The Board of Appeal may either exercise any power within the competence of the department which was responsible for the decision appealed against or remit the case to that department for further prosecution. 2. If the Board of Appeal remits the case for further prosecution to the department whose decision was appealed, that department shall be bound by the *ratio decidendi* of the Board of Appeal, in so far as the facts are the same. 3. The decisions of the Boards of Appeal shall take effect only from the date of expiry of the period referred to in Article 61(5) or, if an action has been brought before the Court of Justice within that period, from the date of rejection of such action.

Article 61

Actions before the Court of Justice

1. Actions may be brought before the Court of Justice against decisions of the Boards of Appeal on appeals. 2. The action may be brought on grounds of lack of competence, infringement of an essential procedural requirement, infringement of the Treaty, of this Regulation or of any rule of law relating to their application or misuse of power. 3. The Court of Justice has jurisdiction to annul or to alter the contested decision. 4. The action shall be open to any party to proceedings before the Board of Appeal adversely affected by its decision. 5. The action shall be brought before the Court of Justice within two months of the date of notification of the decision of the Board of Appeal. 6. The Office shall be required to take the necessary measures to comply with the judgment of the Court of Justice.

TITLE VIII

PROCEDURE BEFORE THE OFFICE

Section 1

General provisions

Article 62

Statement of reasons on which decisions are based

Decisions of the Office shall state the reasons on which they are based. They shall be based only on reasons or evidence on which the parties concerned have had an opportunity to present their comments.

Article 63

Examination of the facts by the Office of its own motion

1. In proceedings before it the Office shall examine the facts of its own motion. However, in proceedings relating to a declaration of invalidity, the Office shall be

restricted in this examination to the facts, evidence and arguments provided by the parties and the relief sought. 2. The Office may disregard facts or evidence which are not submitted in due time by the parties concerned.

Article 64

Oral proceedings

1. If the Office considers that oral proceedings would be expedient, they shall be held either at the instance of the Office or at the request of any party to the proceedings. 2. Oral proceedings, including delivery of the decision, shall be public, unless the department before which the proceedings are taking place decides otherwise in cases where admission of the public could have serious and unjustified disadvantages, in particular for a party to the proceedings.

Article 65

Taking of evidence

1. In any proceedings before the Office the means of giving or obtaining evidence shall include the following: (a) hearing the parties; (b) requests for information; (c) the production of documents and items of evidence; (d) hearing witnesses; (e) opinions by experts; (f) statements in writing, sworn or affirmed or having a similar effect under the law of the State in which the statement is drawn up. 2. The relevant department of the Office may commission one of its members to examine the evidence adduced. 3. If the Office considers it necessary for a party, witness or expert to give evidence orally, it shall issue a summons to the person concerned to appear before it. 4. The parties shall be informed of the hearing of a witness or expert before the Office. They shall have the right to be present and to put questions to the witness or expert.

Article 66

Notification

The Office shall, as a matter of course, notify those concerned of decisions and summonses and of any notice or other communication from which a time limit is reckoned, or of which those concerned must be notified under other provisions of this Regulation or of the implementing regulation, or of which notification has been ordered by the President of the Office.

Article 67

Restitutio in integrum

1. The applicant for or holder of a registered Community design or any other party to proceedings before the Office who, in spite of all due care required by the circumstances having been taken, was unable to observe a time limit vis-à-vis the Office shall, upon application, have his rights re-established if the non-observance in question has the direct consequence, by virtue of the provisions of this Regulation, of causing the loss of any rights or means of redress. 2. The application must be filed in writing within two months of the removal of the cause of non-compliance with the time limit. The omitted act must be completed within this period. The application shall only be

admissible within the year immediately following the expiry of the unobserved time limit. In the case of non-submission of the request for renewal of registration or of non-payment of a renewal fee, the further period of six months provided for in the second sentence of Article 13(3) shall be deducted from the period of one year. 3. The application must state the grounds on which it is based and must set out the facts on which it relies. It shall not be deemed to be filed until the fee for the re-establishment of rights has been paid. 4. The department competent to decide on the omitted act shall decide upon the application. 5. The provisions of this Article shall not be applicable to the time limits referred to in paragraph 2 and Article 41(1). 6. Where the applicant for or holder of a registered Community design has his rights re-established, he may not invoke his rights vis-à-vis a third party who, in good faith, in the course of the period between the loss of rights in the application for or registration of the registered Community design and publication of the mention of re-establishment of those rights, has put on the market products in which a design included within the scope of protection of the registered Community design is incorporated or to which it is applied. 7. A third party who may avail himself of the provisions of paragraph 6 may bring third party proceedings against the decision re-establishing the rights of the applicant for or holder of the registered Community design within a period of two months as from the date of publication of the mention of re-establishment of those rights. 8. Nothing in this Article shall limit the right of a Member State to grant *restitutio in integrum* in respect of time limits provided for in this Regulation and to be complied with vis-à-vis the authorities of such State.

Article 68

Reference to general principles

In the absence of procedural provisions in this Regulation, the implementing regulation, the fees regulation or the rules of procedure of the Boards of Appeal, the Office shall take into account the principles of procedural law generally recognised in the Member States.

Article 69

Termination of financial obligations

1. Rights of the Office to the payment of fees shall be barred four years from the end of the calendar year in which the fee fell due. 2. Rights against the Office for the refunding of fees or sums of money paid in excess of a fee shall be barred after four years from the end of the calendar year in which the right arose. 3. The periods laid down in paragraphs 1 and 2 shall be interrupted, in the case covered by paragraph 1, by a request for payment of the fee and, in the case covered by paragraph 2, by a reasoned claim in writing. On interruption it shall begin again immediately and shall end at the latest six years after the end of the year in which it originally began, unless in the meantime judicial proceedings to enforce the right have begun. In this case the period shall end at the earliest one year after the judgment has acquired the authority of a final decision.

Section 2

Costs

Article 70

Apportionment of costs

1. The losing party in proceedings for a declaration of invalidity of a registered Community design or appeal proceedings shall bear the fees incurred by the other party as well as all costs incurred by him essential to the proceedings, including travel and subsistence and the remuneration of an agent, adviser or advocate, within the limits of scales set for each category of costs under the conditions laid down in the implementing regulation. 2. However, where each party succeeds on some and fails on other heads, or if reasons of equity so dictate, the Invalidity Division or Board of Appeal shall decide a different apportionment of costs. 3. A party who terminates the proceedings by surrendering the registered Community design or by not renewing its registration or by withdrawing the application for a declaration of invalidity or the appeal, shall bear the fees and the costs incurred by the other party as stipulated in paragraphs 1 and 2. 4. Where a case does not proceed to judgment, the costs shall be at the discretion of the Invalidity Division or Board of Appeal. 5. Where the parties conclude before the Invalidity Division or Board of Appeal a settlement of costs differing from that provided for in paragraphs 1, 2, 3 and 4, the body concerned shall take note of that agreement. 6. On request, the registry of the Invalidity Division or Board of Appeal shall fix the amount of the costs to be paid pursuant to the preceding paragraphs. The amount so determined may be reviewed by a decision of the Invalidity Division or Board of Appeal on a request filed within the period prescribed by the implementing regulation.

Article 71

Enforcement of decisions fixing the amount of costs

1. Any final decision of the Office fixing the amount of costs shall be enforceable. 2. Enforcement shall be governed by the rules of civil procedure in force in the State in the territory of which it is carried out. The order for its enforcement shall be appended to the decision, without any other formality than verification of the authenticity of the decision, by the national authority which the government of each Member State shall designate for this purpose and shall make known to the Office and to the Court of Justice. 3. When these formalities have been completed on application by the party concerned, the latter may proceed to enforcement in accordance with the national law, by bringing the matter directly before the competent authority. 4. Enforcement may be suspended only by a decision of the Court of Justice. However, the courts of the Member State concerned shall have jurisdiction over complaints that enforcement is being carried out in an irregular manner.

Section 3

Informing the public and the official authorities of the Member States

Article 72

Register of Community designs

The Office shall keep a register to be known as the register of Community designs, which shall contain those particulars of which the registration is provided for by this Regulation or by the implementing regulation. The register shall be open to public inspection, except to the extent that Article 50(2) provides otherwise.

Article 73

Periodical publications

1. This Office shall periodically publish a Community Designs Bulletin containing entries open to public inspection in the register as well as other particulars the publication of which is prescribed by this Regulation or by the implementing regulation. 2. Notices and information of a general character issued by the President of the Office, as well as any other information relevant to this Regulation or its implementation, shall be published in the Official Journal of the Office.

Article 74

Inspection of files

1. The files relating to applications for registered Community designs which have not yet been published or the files relating to registered Community designs which are subject to deferment of publication in accordance with Article 50 or which, being subject to such deferment, have been surrendered before or on the expiry of that period, shall not be made available for inspection without the consent of the applicant for or the right holder in the registered Community design. 2. Any person who can establish a legitimate interest may inspect a file without the consent of the applicant for or holder of the registered Community design prior to the publication or after the surrender of the latter in the case provided for in paragraph 1. This shall in particular apply if the interested person proves that the applicant for or the holder of the registered Community design has taken steps with a view to invoking against him the right under the registered Community design. 3. Subsequent to the publication of the registered Community design, the file may be inspected on request. 4. However, where a file is inspected pursuant to paragraph 2 or 3, certain documents in the file may be withheld from inspection in accordance with the provisions of the implementing regulation.

Article 75

Administrative cooperation

Unless otherwise provided in this Regulation or in national laws, the Office and the courts or authorities of the Member States shall on request give assistance to each other by communicating information or opening files for inspection. Where the Office opens files to inspection by courts, public prosecutors' offices or central industrial property offices, the inspection shall not be subject to the restrictions laid down in Article 74.

Article 76

Exchange of publications

1. The Office and the central industrial property offices of the Member States shall despatch to each other on request and for their own use one or more copies of their respective publications free of charge. 2. The Office may conclude agreements relating to the exchange or supply of publications.

Section 4

Representation

Article 77

General principles of representation

1. Subject to paragraph 2, no person shall be compelled to be represented before the Office. 2. Without prejudice to the second subparagraph of paragraph 3, natural or legal persons not having either their domicile or their principal place of business or a real and effective industrial or commercial establishment in the Community must be represented before the Office in accordance with Article 78(1) in all proceedings before the Office established by this Regulation, other than in filing an application for a registered Community design; the implementing regulation may permit other exceptions. 3. Natural or legal persons having their domicile or principal place of business or a real and effective industrial or commercial establishment in the Community may be represented before the Office by one of their employees, who must file with it a signed authorisation for inclusion in the files, the details of which are set out in the implementing regulation. An employee of a legal person to which this paragraph applies may also represent other legal persons which have economic connections with the first legal person, even if those other legal persons have neither their domicile nor their principal place of business nor a real and effective industrial or commercial establishment within the Community.

Article 78

Professional representation

1. Representation of natural or legal persons in proceedings before the Office under this Regulation may only be undertaken by: (a) any legal practitioner qualified in one of the Member States and having his place of business within the Community, to the extent that he is entitled, within the said State, to act as a representative in industrial property matters; or (b) any professional representatives whose name has been entered on the list of professional representatives referred to in Article 89(1)(b) of the Regulation on the Community trade mark; or (c) persons whose names are entered on the special list of professional representatives for design matters referred to in paragraph 4. 2. The persons referred to in paragraph 1(c) shall only be entitled to represent third persons in proceedings on design matters before the Office. 3. The imple-

menting regulation shall provide whether and under what conditions representatives must file with the Office a signed authorisation for insertion on the files. 4. Any natural person may be entered on the special list of professional representatives in design matters, if he fulfils the following conditions: (a) he must be a national of one of the Member States; (b) he must have his place of business or employment in the Community; (c) he must be entitled to represent natural or legal persons in design matters before the central industrial property office of a Member State or before the Benelux Design Office. Where, in that State, the entitlement to represent in design matters is not conditional upon the requirement of special professional qualifications, persons applying to be entered on the list must have habitually acted in design matters before the central industrial property office of the said State for at least five years. However, persons whose professional qualification to represent natural or legal persons in design matters before the central industrial property office of one of the Member States is officially recognised in accordance with the regulations laid by such State shall not be subject to the condition of having exercised the profession. 5. Entry on the list referred to in paragraph 4 shall be effected upon request, accompanied by a certificate furnished by the central industrial property office of the Member State concerned, which must indicate that the conditions laid down in the said paragraph are fulfilled. 6. The President of the Office may grant exemption from: (a) the requirement of paragraph 4(a) in special circumstances; (b) the requirement of paragraph 4(c), second sentence, if the applicant furnishes proof that he has acquired the requisite qualification in another way. 7. The conditions under which a person may be removed from the list shall be laid down in the implementing regulation.

TITLE IX

JURISDICTION AND PROCEDURE IN LEGAL ACTIONS RELATING TO COMMUNITY DESIGNS

Section 1

Jurisdiction and enforcement

Article 79

Application of the Convention on Jurisdiction and Enforcement

1. Unless otherwise specified in this Regulation, the Convention on Jurisdiction and the Enforcement of Judgements in Civil and Commercial Matters, signed in Brussels on 27 September 1968 (¹), hereinafter referred to as the 'Convention on Jurisdiction and Enforcement', shall apply to proceedings relating to Community designs and applications for registered Community designs, as well as to proceedings relating to actions on the basis of Community designs and national designs enjoying simultaneous protection. 2. The provisions of the Convention on Jurisdiction and Enforcement which are rendered applicable by the paragraph 1 shall have effect in respect of any Member State solely in the text which is in force in respect of that State at any given time. 3. In the event of proceedings in respect of the actions and claims referred to in Article 85: (a) Articles 2, 4, 5(1), (3), (4) and (5), 16(4) and 24 of the Convention on Jurisdiction and Enforcement shall not apply; (b) Articles 17 and 18 of that

---

(¹) OJ L 299, 31.12.1972, p. 32. Convention as amended by the Conventions on the Accession to that Convention of the States acceding to the European Communities.

Convention shall apply subject to the limitations in Article 82(4) of this Regulation; (c) the provisions of Title II of that Convention which are applicable to persons domiciled in a Member State shall also be applicable to persons who do not have a domicile in any Member State but have an establishment therein. 4. The provisions of the Convention on Jurisdiction and Enforcement shall not have effect in respect of any Member State for which that Convention has not yet entered into force. Until such entry into force, proceedings referred to in paragraph 1 shall be governed in such a Member State by any bilateral or multilateral convention governing its relationship with another Member State concerned, or, if no such convention exists, by its domestic law on jurisdiction, recognition and enforcement of decisions.

Section 2

Disputes concerning the infringement and validity of Community designs

Article 80

Community design courts

1. The Member States shall designate in their territories as limited a number as possible of national courts and tribunals of first and second instance (Community design courts) which shall perform the functions assigned to them by this Regulation. 2. Each Member State shall communicate to the Commission not later than 6 March 2005 a list of Community design courts, indicating their names and their territorial jurisdiction. 3. Any change made after communication of the list referred to in paragraph 2 in the number, names or territorial jurisdiction of the Community design courts shall be notified without delay by the Member State concerned to the Commission. 4. The information referred to in paragraphs 2 and 3 shall be notified by the Commission to the Member States and published in the *Official Journal of the European Communities*. 5. As long as a Member State has not communicated the list as stipulated in paragraph 2, jurisdiction for any proceedings resulting from an action covered by Article 81 for which the courts of that State have jurisdiction pursuant to Article 82 shall lie with that court of the State in question which would have jurisdiction *ratione loci* and *ratione materiae* in the case of proceedings relating to a national design right of that State.

Article 81

Jurisdiction over infringement and validity

The Community design courts shall have exclusive jurisdiction: (a) for infringement actions and – if they are permitted under national law – actions in respect of threatened infringement of Community designs; (b) for actions for declaration of non-infringement of Community designs, if they are permitted under national law; (c) for actions for a declaration of invalidity of an unregistered Community design; (d) for counterclaims for a declaration of invalidity of a Community design raised in connection with actions under (a).

Article 82

International jurisdiction

1. Subject to the provisions of this Regulation and to any provisions of the Convention on Jurisdiction and Enforcement applicable by virtue of Article 79, proceedings in respect of the actions and claims referred to in Article 81 shall be brought in the courts of the Member State in which the defendant is domiciled or, if he is not domiciled in any of the Member States, in any Member State in which he has an establishment. 2. If the defendant is neither domiciled nor has an establishment in any of the Member States, such proceedings shall be brought in the courts of the Member State in which the plaintiff is domiciled or, if he is not domiciled in any of the Member States, in any Member State in which he has an establishment. 3. If neither the defendant nor the plaintiff is so domiciled or has such an establishment, such proceedings shall be brought in the courts of the Member State where the Office has its seat. 4. Notwithstanding paragraphs 1, 2 and 3: (a) Article 17 of the Convention on Jurisdiction and Enforcement shall apply if the parties agree that a different Community design court shall have jurisdiction; (b) Article 18 of that Convention shall apply if the defendant enters an appearance before a different Community design court. 5. Proceedings in respect of the actions and claims referred to in Article 81(a) and (d) may also be brought in the courts of the Member State in which the act of infringement has been committed or threatened.

Article 83

Extent of jurisdiction on infringement

1. A Community design court whose jurisdiction is based on Article 82(1), (2) (3) or (4) shall have jurisdiction in respect of acts of infringement committed or threatened within the territory of any of the Member States. 2. A Community design court whose jurisdiction is based on Article 82(5) shall have jurisdiction only in respect of acts of infringement committed or threatened within the territory of the Member State in which that court is situated.

Article 84

Action or counterclaim for a declaration of invalidity of a Community design

1. An action or a counterclaim for a declaration of invalidity of a Community design may only be based on the grounds for invalidity mentioned in Article 25. 2. In the cases referred to in Article 25(2), (3), (4) and (5) the action or the counterclaim may be brought solely by the person entitled under those provisions. 3. If the counterclaim is brought in a legal action to which the right holder of the Community design is not already a party, he shall be informed thereof and may be joined as a party to the action in accordance with the conditions set out in the law of the Member State where the court is situated. 4. The validity of a Community design may not be put in issue in an action for a declaration of non-infringement.

Article 85

Presumption of validity – defence as to the merits

1. In proceedings in respect of an infringement action or an action for threatened infringement of a registered Community design, the Community design court shall treat the Community design as valid. Validity may be challenged only with a counter-claim for a declaration of invalidity. However, a plea relating to the invalidity of a Community design, submitted otherwise than by way of counterclaim, shall be admissible in so far as the defendant claims that the Community design could be declared invalid on account of an earlier national design right, within the meaning of Article 25(1)(d), belonging to him. 2. In proceedings in respect of an infringement action or an action for threatened infringement of an unregistered Community design, the Community design court shall treat the Community design as valid if the right holder produces proof that the conditions laid down in Article 11 have been met and indicates what constitutes the individual character of his Community design. However, the defendant may contest its validity by way of a plea or with a counterclaim for a declaration of invalidity.

Article 86

Judgements of invalidity

1. Where in a proceeding before a Community design court the Community design has been put in issue by way of a counterclaim for a declaration of invalidity: (a) if any of the grounds mentioned in Article 25 are found to prejudice the maintenance of the Community design, the court shall declare the Community design invalid; (b) if none of the grounds mentioned in Article 25 is found to prejudice the maintenance of the Community design, the court shall reject the counterclaim. 2. The Community design court with which a counterclaim for a declaration of invalidity of a registered Community design has been filed shall inform the Office of the date on which the counterclaim was filed. The latter shall record this fact in the register. 3. The Community design court hearing a counterclaim for a declaration of invalidity of a registered Community design may, on application by the right holder of the registered Community design and after hearing the other parties, stay the proceedings and request the defendant to submit an application for a declaration of invalidity to the Office within a time limit which the court shall determine. If the application is not made within the time limit, the proceedings shall continue; the counterclaim shall be deemed withdrawn. Article 91(3) shall apply. 4. Where a Community design court has given a judgment which has become final on a counterclaim for a declaration of invalidity of a registered Community design, a copy of the judgment shall be sent to the Office. Any party may request information about such transmission. The Office shall mention the judgment in the register in accordance with the provisions of the implementing regulation. 5. No counterclaim for a declaration of invalidity of a registered Community design may be made if an application relating to the same subject matter and cause of action, and involving the same parties, has already been determined by the Office in a decision which has become final.

Article 87

Effects of the judgement on invalidity

When it has become final, a judgment of a Community design court declaring a Community design invalid shall have in all the Member States the effects specified in Article 26.

Article 88

Applicable law

1. The Community design courts shall apply the provisions of this Regulation. 2. On all matters not covered by this Regulation, a Community design court shall apply its national law, including its private international law. 3. Unless otherwise provided in this Regulation, a Community design court shall apply the rules of procedure governing the same type of action relating to a national design right in the Member State where it is situated.

Article 89

Sanctions in actions for infringement

1. Where in an action for infringement or for threatened infringement a Community design court finds that the defendant has infringed or threatened to infringe a Community design, it shall, unless there are special reasons for not doing so, order the following measures: (a) an order prohibiting the defendant from proceeding with the acts which have infringed or would infringe the Community design; (b) an order to seize the infringing products; (c) an order to seize materials and implements predominantly used in order to manufacture the infringing goods, if their owner knew the effect for which such use was intended or if such effect would have been obvious in the circumstances; (d) any order imposing other sanctions appropriate under the circumstances which are provided by the law of the Member State in which the acts of infringement or threatened infringement are committed, including its private international law. 2. The Community design court shall take such measures in accordance with its national law as are aimed at ensuring that the orders referred to in paragraph 1 are complied with.

Article 90

Provisional measures, including protective measures

1. Application may be made to the courts of a Member State, including Community design courts, for such provisional measures, including protective measures, in respect of a Community design as may be available under the law of that State in respect of national design rights even if, under this Regulation, a Community design court of another Member State has jurisdiction as to the substance of the matter. 2. In proceedings relating to provisional measures, including protective measures, a plea otherwise than by way of counterclaim relating to the invalidity of a Community design submitted by the defendant shall be admissible. Article 85(2) shall, however, apply *mutatis mutandis*. 3. A Community design court whose jurisdiction is based on Article 82(1), (2), (3) or (4) shall have jurisdiction to grant provisional measures, including protective measures, which, subject to any necessary procedure for

recognition and enforcement pursuant to Title III of the Convention on Jurisdiction and Enforcement, are applicable in the territory of any Member State. No other court shall have such jurisdiction.

Article 91

Specific rules on related actions

1. A Community design court hearing an action referred to in Article 81, other than an action for a declaration of non-infringement, shall, unless there are special grounds for continuing the hearing, of its own motion after hearing the parties, or at the request of one of the parties and after hearing the other parties, stay the proceedings where the validity of the Community design is already in issue before another Community design court on account of a counterclaim or, in the case of a registered Community design, where an application for a declaration of invalidity has already been filed at the Office. 2. The Office, when hearing an application for a declaration of invalidity of a registered Community design, shall, unless there are special grounds for continuing the hearing, of its own motion after hearing the parties, or at the request of one of the parties and after hearing the other parties, stay the proceedings where the validity of the registered Community design is already in issue on account of a counterclaim before a Community design court. However, if one of the parties to the proceedings before the Community design court so requests, the court may, after hearing the other parties to these proceedings, stay the proceedings. The Office shall in this instance continue the proceedings pending before it. 3. Where the Community design court stays the proceedings it may order provisional measures, including protective measures, for the duration of the stay.

Article 92

Jurisdiction of Community design courts of second instance – further appeal

1. An appeal to the Community design courts of second instance shall lie from judgments of the Community design courts of first instance in respect of proceedings arising from the actions and claims referred to in Article 81. 2. The conditions under which an appeal may be lodged with a Community design court of second instance shall be determined by the national law of the Member State in which that court is located. 3. The national rules concerning further appeal shall be applicable in respect of judgments of Community design courts of second instance.

Section 3

Other disputes concerning Community designs

Article 93

Supplementary provisions on the jurisdiction of national courts other than Community design courts

1. Within the Member State whose courts have jurisdiction under Article 79(1) or (4), those courts shall have jurisdiction for actions relating to Community designs other than those referred to in Article 81 which would have jurisdiction *ratione loci* and *ratione materiae* in the case of actions relating to a national design right in that State.

2. Actions relating to a Community design, other than those referred to in Article 81, for which no court has jurisdiction pursuant to Article 79(1) and (4) and paragraph 1 of this Article may be heard before the courts of the Member State in which the Office has its seat.

Article 94

Obligation of the national court

A national court which is dealing with an action relating to a Community design other than the actions referred to in Article 81 shall treat the design as valid. Articles 85(2) and 90(2) shall, however, apply *mutatis mutandis.*

TITLE X

EFFECTS ON THE LAWS OF THE MEMBER STATES

Article 95

Parallel actions on the basis of Community designs and national design rights

1. Where actions for infringement or for threatened infringement involving the same cause of action and between the same parties are brought before the courts of different Member States, one seized on the basis of a Community design and the other seized on the basis of a national design right providing simultaneous protection, the court other than the court first seized shall of its own motion decline jurisdiction in favour of that court. The court which would be required to decline jurisdiction may stay its proceedings if the jurisdiction of the other court is contested. 2. The Community design court hearing an action for infringement or threatened infringement on the basis of a Community design shall reject the action if a final judgment on the merits has been given on the same cause of action and between the same parties on the basis of a design right providing simultaneous protection. 3. The court hearing an action for infringement or for threatened infringement on the basis of a national design right shall reject the action if a final judgment on the merits has been given on the same cause of action and between the same parties on the basis of a Community design providing simultaneous protection. 4. Paragraphs 1, 2 and 3 shall not apply in respect of provisional measures, including protective measures.

Article 96

Relationship to other forms of protection under national law

1. The provisions of this Regulation shall be without prejudice to any provisions of Community law or of the law of the Member States concerned relating to unregistered designs, trade marks or other distinctive signs, patents and utility models, typefaces, civil liability and unfair competition. 2. A design protected by a Community design shall also be eligible for protection under the law of copyright of Member States as from the date on which the design was created or fixed in any form. The extent to which, and the conditions under which, such a protection is conferred, including the level of originality required, shall be determined by each Member State.

TITLE XI

SUPPLEMENTARY PROVISIONS CONCERNING THE OFFICE

Section 1

General provisions

Article 97

General provision

Unless otherwise provided in this Title, Title XII of the Regulation on the Community trade mark shall apply to the Office with regard to its tasks under this Regulation.

Article 98

Language of proceedings

1. The application for a registered Community design shall be filed in one of the official languages of the Community. 2. The applicant must indicate a second language which shall be a language of the Office the use of which he accepts as a possible language of proceedings before the Office. If the application was filed in a language which is not one of the languages of the Office, the Office shall arrange to have the application translated into the language indicated by the applicant. 3. Where the applicant for a registered Community design is the sole party to proceedings before the Office, the language of proceedings shall be the language used for filing the application. If the application was made in a language other then the languages of the Office, the Office may send written communications to the applicant in the second language indicated by the applicant in his application. 4. In the case of invalidity proceedings, the language of proceedings shall be the language used for filing the application for a registered Community design if this is one of the languages of the Office. If the application was made in a language other than the languages of the Office, the language of proceedings shall be the second language indicated in the application. The application for a declaration of invalidity shall be filed in the language of proceedings. Where the language of proceedings is not the language used for filing the application for a registered Community design, the right holder of the Community design may file observations in the language of filing. The Office shall arrange to have those observations translated into the language of proceedings. The implementing regulation may provide that the translation expenses to be borne by the Office may not, subject to a derogation granted by the Office where justified by the complexity of the case, exceed an amount to be fixed for each category of proceedings on the basis of the average size of statements of case received by the Office. Expenditure in excess of this amount may be allocated to the losing party in accordance with Article 70. 5. Parties to invalidity proceedings may agree that a different official language of the Community is to be the language of the proceedings.

Article 99

Publication and register

1. All information the publication of which is prescribed by this Regulation or the implementing regulation shall be published in all the official languages of the Community. 2. All entries in the Register of Community designs shall be made in all the official languages of the Community. 3. In cases of doubt, the text in the language of the Office in which the application for a registered Community design was filed shall be authentic. If the application was filed in an official language of the Community other than one of the languages of the Office, the text in the second language indicated by the applicant shall be authentic.

Article 100

Supplementary powers of the President

In addition to the functions and powers conferred on the President of the Office by Article 119 of the Regulation on the Community trade mark, the President may place before the Commission any proposal to amend this Regulation, the implementing regulation, the fees regulation and any other rule to the extent that they apply to registered Community designs, after consulting the Administrative Board and, in the case of the fees regulation, the Budget Committee.

Article 101

Supplementary powers of the Administrative Board

In addition to the powers conferred on it by Article 121 *et seq* of the Regulation on the Community trade mark or by other provisions of this Regulation, the Administrative Board; (a) shall set the date for the first filing of applications for registered Community designs pursuant to Article 111(2); (b) shall be consulted before adoption of the guidelines for examination as to formal requirements, examination as to grounds for refusal of registration and invalidity proceedings in the Office and in the other cases provided for in this Regulation.

Section 2

Procedures

Article 102

Competence

For taking decisions in connection with the procedures laid down in this Regulation the following shall be competent: (a) examiners; (b) the Administration of Trade Marks and Designs and Legal Division; (c) Invalidity Divisions; (d) Boards of Appeal.

Article 103

Examiners

An examiner shall be responsible for taking decisions on behalf of the Office in relation to an application for a registered Community design.

Article 104

The Administration of Trade Marks and Designs and Legal Division

1. The Administration of Trade Marks and Legal Division provided for by Article 128 of the Regulation on the Community trade mark shall become the Administration of Trade Marks and Designs and Legal Division. 2. In addition to the powers conferred upon it by the Regulation on the Community trade mark, it shall be responsible for taking those decisions required by this Regulation which do not fall within the competence of an examiner or an Invalidity Division. It shall in particular be responsible for decisions in respect of entries in the register.

Article 105

Invalidity Divisions

1. An Invalidity Division shall be responsible for taking decisions in relation to applications for declarations of invalidity of registered Community designs. 2. An Invalidity Division shall consist of three members. At least one of the members must be legally qualified.

Article 106

Boards of Appeal

In addition to the powers conferred upon it by Article 131 of the Regulation on the Community trade mark, the Boards of Appeal instituted by that Regulation shall be responsible for deciding on appeals from decisions of the examiners, the Invalidity Divisions and from the decisions of the Administration of Trade Marks and Designs and Legal Division as regards their decisions concerning Community designs.

TITLE XII

FINAL PROVISIONS

Article 107

Implementing regulation

1. The rules implementing this Regulation shall be adopted in an implementing regulation. 2. In addition to the fees already provided for in this Regulation, fees shall be charged, in accordance with the detailed rules of application laid down in the implementing regulation and in a fees regulation, in the cases listed below: (a) late payment of the registration fee; (b) late payment of the publication fee; (c) late payment of the fee for deferment of publication; (d) late payment of additional fees

for multiple applications; (e) issue of a copy of the certificate of registration; (f) registration of the transfer of a registered Community design; (g) registration of a licence or another right in respect of a registered Community design; (h) cancellation of the registration of a licence or another right; (i) issue of an extract from the register; (j) inspection of the files; (k) issue of copies of file documents; (l) communication of information in a file; (m) review of the determination of the procedural costs to be refunded; (n) issue of certified copies of the application. 3. The implementing regulation and the fees regulation shall be adopted and amended in accordance with the procedure laid down in Article 109(2).

Article 108

Rules of procedure of the Boards of Appeal

The rules of procedure of the Boards of Appeal shall apply to appeals heard by those Boards under this Regulation, without prejudice to any necessary adjustment or additional provision, adopted in accordance with the procedure laid down in Article 109(2).

Article 109

Committee

1. The Commission shall be assisted by a Committee. 2. Where reference is made to this paragraph, Articles 5 and 7 of Decision 1999/468/EC shall apply. The period laid down in Article 5(6) of Decision 1999/468/EC shall be set at three months. 3. The Committee shall adopt its rules of procedure.

Article 110

Transitional provision

1. Until such time as amendments to this Regulation enter into force on a proposal from the Commission on this subject, protection as a Community design shall not exist for a design which constitutes a component part of a complex product used within the meaning of Article 19(1) for the purpose of the repair of that complex product so as to restore its original appearance. 2. The proposal from the Commission referred to in paragraph 1 shall be submitted together with, and take into consideration, any changes which the Commission shall propose on the same subject pursuant to Article 18 of Directive 98/71/EC.

Article 111

Entry into force

1. This Regulation shall enter into force on the 60th day following its publication in the *Official Journal of the European Communities*. 2. Applications for registered Community designs may be filed at the Office from the date fixed by the Administrative Board on the recommendation of the President of the Office. 3. Applications for registered Community designs filed within three months before the date referred to in paragraph 2 shall be deemed to have been filed on that date.

This Regulation shall be binding in its entirety and directly applicable in all Member States.

Done at Brussels, 12 December 2001.

For the Council
The President
M. AELVOET

Commission Regulation 2245/2002 implementing Council Regulation 6/2002 on Community Designs

COMMISSION REGULATION (EC) No 2245/2002

of 21 October 2002

implementing Council Regulation (EC) No 6/2002 on Community Designs

THE COMMISSION OF THE EUROPEAN COMMUNITIES,

Having regard to the Treaty establishing the European Community,

Having regard to Council Regulation (EC) No 6/2002 of 12 December 2001 on Community Designs (¹), and in particular Article 107(3) thereof,

Whereas:

(1) Regulation (EC) No 6/2002 creates a system enabling a design having effect throughout the Community to be obtained on the basis of an application to the Office for Harmonisation in the Internal Market (trade marks and designs) (hereinafter 'the Office'). (2) For this purpose, Regulation (EC) No 6/2002 contains the necessary provisions for a procedure leading to the registration of a Community Design, as well as for the administration of registered Community Designs, for appeals against decisions of the Office and for proceedings for the invalidation of a Community Design. (3) The present Regulation lays down the necessary measures for implementing the provisions of Regulation (EC) No 6/2002. (4) This Regulation should ensure the smooth and efficient operation of design proceedings before the Office. (5) The measures provided for in this Regulation are in accordance with the opinion of the Committee established under Article 109 of Regulation (EC) No 6/2002,

HAS ADOPTED THIS REGULATION:

(¹) OJ L 3, 5.1.2002, p. 1.

CHAPTER I

APPLICATION PROCEDURE

Article 1

Content of the application

1. The application for a registered Community Design shall contain: (a) a request for registration of the design as a registered Community Design; (b) the name, address and nationality of the applicant and the State in which the applicant is domiciled or in which it has its seat or establishment. Names of natural persons shall take the form of the family name and the given name(s). Names of legal entities shall be indicated by their official designation, which may be abbreviated in a customary manner; furthermore, the State whose law governs such entities shall be indicated. The telephone numbers as well as fax numbers and details of other data-communications links, such as electronic mail, may be given. Only one address shall, in principle, be indicated for each applicant; where several addresses are indicated, only the address mentioned first shall be taken into account, except where the applicant designates one of the addresses as an address for service. If the Office has given the applicant an identification number, it shall be sufficient to mention that number together with the name of the applicant; (c) a representation of the design in accordance with Article 4 of this Regulation or, if the application concerns a two-dimensional design and contains a request for deferment of publication in accordance with Article 50 of Regulation (EC) No 6/2002, a specimen in accordance with Article 5 of this Regulation; (d) an indication, in accordance with Article 3(3), of the products in which the design is intended to be incorporated or to which it is intended to be applied; (e) if the applicant has appointed a representative, the name of that representative and the address of his/her place of business in accordance with point (b); if the representative has more than one business address or if there are two or more representatives with different business addresses, the application shall indicate which address shall be used as an address for service; where no such indication is made, only the first-mentioned address shall be taken into account as an address for service. If there is more than one applicant, the application may indicate the appointment of one applicant or representative as common representative. If an appointed representative has been given an identification number by the Office, it shall be sufficient to mention that number together with the name of the representative; (f) if applicable, a declaration that priority of a previous application is claimed pursuant to Article 42 of Regulation (EC) No 6/2002, stating the date on which the previous application was filed and the country in which or for which it was filed; (g) if applicable, a declaration that exhibition priority is claimed pursuant to Article 44 of Regulation (EC) No 6/2002, stating the name of the exhibition and the date of the first disclosure of the products in which the design is incorporated or to which it is applied; (h) a specification of the language in which the application is filed, and of the second language pursuant to Article 98(2) of Regulation (EC) No 6/2002; (i) the signature of the applicant or his/her representative in accordance with Article 65.

2. The application may contain: (a) a single description per design not exceeding 100 words explaining the representation of the design or the specimen; the description must relate only to those features which appear in the reproductions of the design or the specimen; it shall not contain statements as to the purported novelty or individual character of the design or its technical value; (b) a request for deferment of publication of registration in accordance with Article 50(1) of Regulation (EC)

No 6/2002; (c) an indication of the 'Locarno classification' of the products contained in the application, that is to say, of the class or classes and the subclass or subclasses to which they belong in accordance with the Annex to the Agreement establishing an international classification for industrial designs, signed at Locarno on 8 October 1968 (hereinafter 'the Locarno Agreement'), referred to in Article 3 and subject to Article 2(2); (d) the citation of the designer or of the team of designers or a statement signed by the applicant to the effect that the designer or team of designers has waived the right to be cited under Article 36(3)(e) of Regulation (EC) No 6/2002.

Article 2

Multiple application

1. An application may be a multiple application requesting the registration of several designs. 2. When several designs other than ornamentation are combined in a multiple application, the application shall be divided if the products in which the designs are intended to be incorporated or to which they are intended to be applied belong to more than one class of the Locarno Classification. 3. For each design contained in the multiple application the applicant shall provide a representation of the design in accordance with Article 4 and the indication of the product in which the design is intended to be incorporated or to be applied. 4. The applicant shall number the designs contained in the multiple application consecutively, using arabic numerals.

Article 3

Classification and indication of products

1. Products shall be classified in accordance with Article 1 of the Locarno Agreement, as amended and in force at the date of filing of the design. 2. The classification of products shall serve exclusively administrative purposes. 3. The indication of products shall be worded in such a way as to indicate clearly the nature of the products and to enable each product to be classified in only one class of the Locarno classification, preferably using the terms appearing in the list of products set out therein. 4. The products shall be grouped according to the classes of the Locarno classification, each group being preceded by the number of the class to which that group of products belongs and presented in the order of the classes and subclasses under that classification.

Article 4

Representation of the design

1. The representation of the design shall consist in a graphic or photographic reproduction of the design, either in black and white or in colour. It shall meet the following requirements: (a) save where the application is filed by electronic means pursuant to Article 67, the representation must be filed on separate sheets of paper or reproduced on the page provided for that purpose in the form made available by the Office pursuant to Article 68; (b) in the case of separate sheets of paper, the design shall be reproduced on opaque white paper and either pasted or printed directly on it. Only one copy shall be filed and the sheets of paper shall not be folded or stapled; (c) the size of the separate sheet shall be DIN A4 size (29,7 cm × 21 cm) and the space used for the reproduction shall be no larger than 26,2 cm × 17 cm. A margin of at least 2,5 cm shall be left on the left-hand side; at the top of each sheet of paper the number of

views shall be indicated pursuant to paragraph 2 and, in the case of a multiple application, the consecutive number of the design; no explanatory text, wording or symbols, other than the indication 'top' or the name or address of the applicant, may be displayed thereon; (d) where the application is filed by electronic means, the graphic or photographic reproduction of the designs shall be in a data format determined by the President of the Office; the manner of identifying the different designs contained in a multiple application, or the different views, shall be determined by the President of the Office; (e) the design shall be reproduced on a neutral background and shall not be retouched with ink or correcting fluid. It shall be of a quality permitting all the details of the matter for which protection is sought to be clearly distinguished and permitting it to be reduced or enlarged to a size no greater than 8 cm by 16 cm per view for entry in the Register of Community Designs provided for in Article 72 of Regulation (EC) No 6/2002, hereinafter 'the Register', and for direct publishing in the *Community Designs Bulletin* referred to in Article 73 of that Regulation. 2. The representation may contain no more than seven different views of the design. Any one graphic or photographic reproduction may contain only one view. The applicant shall number each view using arabic numerals. The number shall consist of separate numerals separated by a point, the numeral to the left of the point indicating the number of the design, that to the right indicating the number of the view. In cases where more than seven views are provided, the Office may disregard for registration and publication any of the extra views. The Office shall take the views in the consecutive order in which the views are numbered by the applicant. 3. Where an application concerns a design that consists in a repeating surface pattern, the representation of the design shall show the complete pattern and a sufficient portion of the repeating surface. The size limits set out in paragraph 1(c) shall apply. 4. Where an application concerns a design consisting in a typographic typeface, the representation of the design shall consist in a string of all the letters of the alphabet, in both upper and lower case, and of all the arabic numerals, together with a text of five lines produced using that typeface, both letters and numerals being in the size pitch 16.

Article 5

Specimens

1. Where the application concerns a two-dimensional design and contains a request for a deferment of publication, in accordance with Article 50(1) of Regulation (EC) No 6/2002, the representation of the design may be replaced by a specimen pasted on a sheet of paper. Applications for which a specimen is submitted must be sent by a single mail or directly delivered to the office of filing. Both the application and the specimen shall be submitted at the same time. 2. The specimens shall not exceed 26,2 cm × 17 cm in size, 50 grams in weight or 3 mm in thickness. The specimen shall be capable of being stored, unfolded, alongside documents of the size prescribed in Article 4(1)(c). 3. Specimens that are perishable or dangerous to store shall not be filed. The specimen shall be filed in five copies; in the case of a multiple application, five copies of the specimen shall be filed for each design. 4. Where the design concerns a repeating surface pattern, the specimen shall show the complete pattern and a sufficient portion of the repeating surface in length and width. The limits set out in paragraph 2 shall apply.

Article 6

Fees for the application

1. The following fees shall be paid at the time when the application is submitted to the Office: (a) the registration fee; (b) the publication fee or a deferment fee if deferment of publication has been requested; (c) an additional registration fee in respect of each additional design included in a multiple application; (d) an additional publication fee in respect of each additional design included in a multiple application, or an additional deferment fee in respect of each additional design included in a multiple application if deferment of publication has been requested. 2. Where the application includes a request for deferment of publication of registration, the publication fee and any additional publication fee in respect of each additional design included in a multiple application shall be paid within the time limits specified in Article 15(4).

Article 7

Filing of the application

1. The Office shall mark the documents making up the application with the date of its receipt and the file number of the application. Each design contained in a multiple application shall be numbered by the Office in accordance with a system determined by the President. The Office shall issue to the applicant without delay a receipt which shall specify the file number, the representation, description or other identification of the design, the nature and the number of the documents and the date of their receipt. In the case of a multiple application, the receipt issued by the Office shall specify the first design and the number of designs filed. 2. If the application is filed with the central industrial property office of a Member State or at the Benelux Design Office in accordance with Article 35 of Regulation (EC) No 6/2002, the office of filing shall number each page of the application, using arabic numerals. The office of filing shall mark the documents making up the application with the date of receipt and the number of pages before forwarding the application to the Office. The office of filing shall issue to the applicant without delay a receipt specifying the nature and the number of the documents and the date of their receipt. 3. If the Office receives an application forwarded by the central industrial property office of a Member State or the Benelux Design Office, it shall mark the application with the date of receipt and the file number and shall issue to the applicant without delay a receipt in accordance with the third and fourth subparagraphs of paragraph 1, indicating the date of receipt at the Office.

Article 8

Claiming priority

1. Where the priority of one or more previous applications is claimed in the application pursuant to Article 42 of Regulation (EC) No 6/2002, the applicant shall indicate the file number of the previous application and file a copy of it within three months of the filing date referred to in Article 38 of that Regulation. The President of the Office shall determine the evidence to be provided by the applicant. 2. Where, subsequent to the filing of the application, the applicant wishes to claim the priority of one or more previous applications pursuant to Article 42 of Regulation (EC) No 6/2002, he/she shall submit, within one month of the filing date, the declaration of priority, stating the date on which and the country in or for which the previous application was

made. The applicant shall submit to the Office the indications and evidence referred to in paragraph 1 within three months of receipt of the declaration of priority.

Article 9

Exhibition priority

1. Where exhibition priority has been claimed in the application pursuant to Article 44 of Regulation (EC) No 6/2002, the applicant shall, together with the application or at the latest within three months of the filing date, file a certificate issued at the exhibition by the authority responsible for the protection of industrial property at the exhibition. That certificate shall declare that the design was incorporated in or applied to the product and disclosed at the exhibition, and shall state the opening date of the exhibition and, where the first disclosure of the product did not coincide with the opening date of the exhibition, the date of such first disclosure. The certificate shall be accompanied by an identification of the actual disclosure of the product, duly certified by that authority. 2. Where the applicant wishes to claim an exhibition priority subsequent to the filing of the application, the declaration of priority, indicating the name of the exhibition and the date of the first disclosure of the product in which the design was incorporated or to which it was applied, shall be submitted within one month of the filing date. The indications and evidence referred to in paragraph 1 shall be submitted to the Office within three months of receipt of the declaration of priority.

Article 10

Examination of requirements for a filing date and of formal requirements

1. The Office shall notify the applicant that a date of filing cannot be granted if the application does not contain: (a) a request for registration of the design as a registered Community Design; (b) information identifying the applicant; (c) a representation of the design pursuant to Article 4(1)(d) and (e) or, where applicable, a specimen. 2. If the deficiencies indicated in paragraph 1 are remedied within two months of receipt of the notification, the date on which all the deficiencies are remedied shall determine the date of filing. If the deficiencies are not remedied before the time limit expires, the application shall not be dealt with as a Community Design application. Any fees paid shall be refunded. 3. The Office shall call upon the applicant to remedy the deficiencies noted within a time limit specified by it where, although a date of filing has been granted, the examination reveals that: (a) the requirements set out in Articles 1, 2, 4 and 5 or the other formal requirements for applications laid down in the Regulation (EC) No 6/2002 or in this Regulation have not been complied with; (b) the full amount of the fees payable pursuant to Article 6(1), read in conjunction with Commission Regulation (EC) No 2246/2002 ([1]), has not been received by the Office; (c) where priority has been claimed pursuant to Articles 8 and 9, either in the application itself or within one month after the date of filing, the other requirements set out in those Articles have not been complied with; (d) in the case of a multiple application, the products in which the designs are intended to be incorporated or to which they are intended to be applied belong to more than one class of the Locarno classification. In particular, the Office shall call upon the applicant to pay the required fees within two months of the date of notification, together

---

([1]) See page 54 of this Official Journal.

with the late payment fees provided for in Article 107(2)(a) to (d) of Regulation (EC) No 6/2002 and as set out in Regulation (EC) No 2246/2002. In the case of the deficiency referred to in point (d) of the first subparagraph, the Office shall call upon the applicant to divide the multiple application in order to ensure compliance with the requirements under Article 2(2). It shall also call upon the applicant to pay the total amount of the fees for all the applications resulting from the separation of the multiple application, within such a time limit as it may specify. After the applicant has complied with the request to divide the application within the time limit set, the date of filing of the resulting application or applications shall be the date of filing granted to the multiple application initially filed. 4. If the deficiencies referred to in paragraph 3(a) and (d) are not remedied before the time limit expires, the Office shall reject the application. 5. If the fees payable pursuant to Article 6(1)(a) and (b) are not paid before the time limit expires, the Office shall reject the application. 6. If any additional fees payable pursuant to Article 6(1)(c) or (d) in respect of multiple applications are not paid or not paid in full before the time limit expires, the Office shall reject the application in respect of all the additional designs which are not covered by the amount paid. In the absence of any criteria for determining which designs are intended to be covered, the Office shall take the designs in the numerical order in which they are represented in accordance with Article 2(4). The Office shall reject the application in so far as it concerns designs for which additional fees have not been paid or have not been paid in full. 7. If the deficiencies referred to in paragraph 3(c) are not remedied before the time limit expires, the right of priority for the application shall be lost. 8. If any of the deficiencies referred to in paragraph 3 is not remedied before the time limit expires and such deficiency concerns only some of the designs contained in a multiple application, the Office shall reject the application, or the right of priority shall be lost, only in so far as those designs are concerned.

Article 11

Examination of grounds for non-registrability

1. Where, pursuant to Article 47 of Regulation (EC) No 6/2002, the Office finds, in the course of carrying out the examination under Article 10 of this Regulation, that the design for which protection is sought does not correspond to the definition of design provided in Article 3(a) of Regulation (EC) No 6/2002 or that the design is contrary to public policy or to accepted principles of morality, it shall inform the applicant that the design is non-registrable, specifying the ground for non-registrability. 2. The Office shall specify a time limit within which the applicant may submit his/her observations, withdraw the application or amend it by submitting an amended representation of the design, provided that the identity of the design is retained. 3. Where the applicant fails to overcome the grounds for non-registrability within the time limit, the Office shall refuse the application. If those grounds concern only some of the designs contained in a multiple application, the Office shall refuse the application only in so far as those designs are concerned.

Article 12

Withdrawal or correction of the application

1. The applicant may at any time withdraw a Community Design application or, in the case of a multiple application, withdraw some of the designs contained in the application. 2. Only the name and address of the applicant, errors of wording or of copying, or obvious mistakes may be corrected, at the request of the applicant and

provided that such correction does not change the representation of the design. 3. An application for the correction of the application pursuant to paragraph 2 shall contain: (a) the file number of the application; (b) the name and the address of the applicant in accordance with Article 1(1)(b); (c) where the applicant has appointed a representative, the name and the business address of the representative in accordance with Article 1(1)(e); (d) the indication of the element of the application to be corrected and that element in its corrected version. 4. If the requirements for the correction of the application are not fulfilled, the Office shall communicate the deficiency to the applicant. If the deficiency is not remedied within the time limits specified by the Office, the Office shall reject the application for correction. 5. A single application may be made for the correction of the same element in two or more applications submitted by the same applicant. 6. Paragraphs 2 to 5 shall apply *mutatis mutandis* to applications to correct the name or the business address of a representative appointed by the applicant.

CHAPTER II

REGISTRATION PROCEDURE

Article 13

Registration of the design

1. If the application satisfies the requirements referred to in Article 48 of Regulation (EC) No 6/2002, the design contained in that application and the particulars set out in Article 69(2) of this Regulation shall be recorded in the Register. 2. If the application contains a request for deferment of publication pursuant to Article 50 of Regulation (EC) No 6/2002, that fact and the date of expiry of the period of deferment shall be recorded. 3. The fees payable pursuant to Article 6(1) shall not be refunded even if the design applied for is not registered.

Article 14

Publication of the registration

1. The registration of the design shall be published in the *Community Designs Bulletin*. 2. Subject to paragraph 3, the publication of the registration shall contain: (a) the name and address of the holder of the Community Design (hereinafter 'the holder'); (b) where applicable, the name and business address of the representative appointed by the holder other than a representative falling within the first subparagraph of Article 77(3) of Regulation (EC) No 6/2002; if more than one representative has the same business address, only the name and business address of the first-named representative shall be published, the name being followed by the words 'et al'; if there are two or more representatives with different business addresses, only the address for service determined pursuant to Article 1(1)(e) of this Regulation shall be published; where an association of representatives is appointed pursuant to Article 62(9) only the name and business address of the association shall be published; (c) the representation of the design pursuant to Article 4; where the representation of the design is in colour, the publication shall be in colour; (d) where applicable, an indication that a description has been filed pursuant to Article 1(2)(a); (e) an indication of the products in which the design is intended to be incorporated or to which it is intended to be applied, preceded by the number of the relevant classes and subclasses of the Locarno

classification, and grouped accordingly; (f) where applicable, the name of the designer or the team of designers; (g) the date of filing and the file number and, in the case of a multiple application, the file number of each design; (h) where applicable, particulars of the claim of priority pursuant to Article 42 of Regulation (EC) No 6/2002; (i) where applicable, particulars of the claim of exhibition priority pursuant to Article 44 of Regulation (EC) No 6/2002; (j) the date and the registration number and the date of the publication of the registration; (k) the language in which the application was filed and the second language indicated by the applicant pursuant to Article 98(2) of Regulation (EC) No 6/2002. 3. If the application contains a request for deferment of publication pursuant to Article 50 of Regulation (EC) No 6/2002, a mention of the deferment shall be published in the *Community Designs Bulletin*, together with the name of the holder, the name of the representative, if any, the date of filing and registration, and the file number of the application. Neither the representation of the design nor any particulars identifying its appearance shall be published.

Article 15

Deferment of publication

1. Where the application contains a request for deferment of publication pursuant to Article 50 of Regulation (EC) No 6/2002, the holder shall, together with the request or at the latest three months before the 30-month deferment period expires: (a) pay the publication fee referred to in Article 6(1)(b); (b) in the case of a multiple registration, pay the additional publication fees, referred to in Article 6(1)(d); (c) in cases where a representation of the design has been replaced by a specimen in accordance with Article 5, file a representation of the design in accordance with Article 4. This applies to all the designs contained in a multiple application for which publication is requested; (d) in the case of a multiple registration, clearly indicate which of the designs contained therein is to be published or which of the designs are to be surrendered, or, if the period of deferment has not yet expired, for which designs deferment is to be continued. Where the holder requests publication before the expiry of the 30-month deferment period, he/she shall, at the latest three months before the requested date of publication, comply with the requirements set out in points (a) to (d) of the first paragraph. 2. If the holder fails to comply with the requirements set out in paragraph 1(c) or (d), the Office shall call upon him/her to remedy the deficiencies within a specified time limit which shall in no case expire after the 30-month deferment period. 3. If the holder fails to remedy the deficiencies referred to in paragraph 2 within the applicable time limit: (a) the registered Community Design shall be deemed from the outset not to have had the effects specified in Regulation (EC) No 6/2002; (b) where the holder has requested earlier publication as provided for under the second subparagraph of paragraph 1, the request shall be deemed not to have been filed. 4. If the holder fails to pay the fees referred to in paragraph 1(a) or (b), the Office shall call upon him/her to pay those fees together with the fees for late payment provided for in Article 107(2)(b) or (d) of Regulation (EC) No 6/2002 and as set out in Regulation (EC) No 2246/2002, within a specified time limit which shall in no case expire after the 30-month deferment period. If no payment has been made within that time limit, the Office shall notify the holder that the registered Community Design has from the outset not had the effects specified in Regulation (EC) No 6/2002. If, in respect of a multiple registration, a payment is made within that time limit but is insufficient to cover all the fees payable pursuant to paragraph 1(a) and (b), as well as the applicable fee for late payment, all the designs in respect of which the fees have not been paid shall be deemed from the outset not to have had the effects specified in

Regulation (EC) No 6/2002. Unless it is clear which designs the amount paid is intended to cover, and in the absence of other criteria for determining which designs are intended to be covered, the Office shall take the designs in the numerical order in which they are represented in accordance with Article 2(4). All designs for which the additional publication fee has not been paid or has not been paid in full, together with the applicable fee for late payment, shall be deemed from the outset not to have had the effects specified in Regulation (EC) No 6/2002.

Article 16

Publication after the period for deferment

1. Where the holder has complied with the requirements laid down in Article 15, the Office shall, at the expiry of the period for deferment or in the case of a request for earlier publication, as soon as is technically possible: (a) publish the registered Community Design in the *Community Designs Bulletin*, with the indications set out in Article 14(2), together with an indication of the fact that the application contained a request for deferment of publication pursuant to Article 50 of Regulation (EC) No 6/2002 and, where applicable, that a specimen was filed in accordance with Article 5 of this Regulation; (b) make available for public inspection any file relating to the design; (c) open to public inspection all the entries in the Register, including any entries withheld from inspection pursuant to Article 73. 2. Where Article 15(4) applies, the actions referred to in paragraph 1 of this Article shall not take place in respect of those designs contained in the multiple registration which are deemed from the outset not to have had the effects specified in Regulation (EC) No 6/2002.

Article 17

Certificate of registration

1. After publication, the Office shall issue to the holder a certificate of registration which shall contain the entries in the Register provided for in Article 69(2) and a statement to the effect that those entries have been recorded in the Register. 2. The holder may request that certified or uncertified copies of the certificate of registration be supplied to him/her upon payment of a fee.

Article 18

Maintenance of the design in an amended form

1. Where, pursuant to Article 25(6) of Regulation (EC) No 6/2002, the registered Community Design is maintained in an amended form, the Community Design in its amended form shall be entered in the Register and published in the *Community Designs Bulletin*. 2. Maintenance of a design in an amended form may include a partial disclaimer, not exceeding 100 words, by the holder or an entry in the Register of Community Designs of a court decision or a decision by the Office declaring the partial invalidity of the design right.

Article 19

Change of the name or address of the holder or of his/her registered representative

1. A change of the name or address of the holder which is not the consequence of a transfer of the registered design shall, at the request of the holder, be recorded in the Register. 2. An application for a change of the name or address of the holder shall contain: (a) the registration number of the design; (b) the name and the address of the holder as recorded in the Register. If the holder has been given an identification number by the Office, it shall be sufficient to indicate that number together with the name of the holder; (c) the indication of the name and address of the holder, as changed, in accordance with Article 1(1)(b); (d) where the holder has appointed a representative, the name and business address of the representative, in accordance with Article 1(1)(e). 3. The application referred to in paragraph 2 shall not be subject to payment of a fee. 4. A single application may be made for a change of the name or address in respect of two or more registrations of the same holder. 5. If the requirements set out in paragraphs 1 and 2 are not fulfilled, the Office shall communicate the deficiency to the applicant. If the deficiency is not remedied within the time limits specified by the Office, the Office shall reject the application. 6. Paragraphs 1 to 5 shall apply *mutatis mutandis* to a change of the name or address of the registered representative. 7. Paragraphs 1 to 6 shall apply *mutatis mutandis* to applications for Community Designs. The change shall be recorded in the files kept by the Office concerning the Community Design application.

Article 20

Correction of mistakes and errors in the Register and in the publication of the registration

Where the registration of a design or the publication of the registration contains a mistake or error attributable to the Office, the Office shall correct the error or mistake of its own motion or at the request of the holder. Where such a request is made by the holder, Article 19 shall apply *mutatis mutandis*. The request shall not be subject to payment of a fee. The Office shall publish the corrections made pursuant to this Article.

CHAPTER III

RENEWAL OF REGISTRATION

Article 21

Notification of expiry of registration

At least six months before expiry of the registration, the Office shall inform the holder, and any person having a right entered in the Register, including a licence, in respect of the Community Design, that the registration is approaching expiry. Failure to give notification shall not affect the expiry of the registration.

Article 22

Renewal of registration

1. An application for renewal of registration shall contain: (a) where the application is filed by the holder, his/her name and address in accordance with Article 1(1)(b); (b) where the application is filed by a person expressly authorised to do so by the holder, the name and address of that person and evidence that he/she is authorised to file the application; (c) where the applicant has appointed a representative, the name and business address of the representative in accordance with Article 1(1)(e); (d) the registration number; (e) where applicable, an indication that renewal is requested for all the designs covered by a multiple registration or, if the renewal is not requested for all such designs, an indication of those designs for which renewal is requested. 2. The fees payable pursuant to Article 13 of Regulation (EC) No 6/2002 for the renewal of a registration shall consist of: (a) a renewal fee, which, in cases where several designs are covered by a multiple registration, shall be proportionate to the number of designs covered by the renewal; (b) where applicable, the additional fee for late payment of the renewal fee or late submission of the request for renewal, pursuant to Article 13 of Regulation (EC) No 6/2002, as specified in Regulation (EC) No 2246/2002. 3. Where the application for renewal is filed within the time limits provided for in Article 13(3) of Regulation (EC) No 6/2002, but the other conditions for renewal provided for in Article 13 thereof and in this Regulation are not satisfied, the Office shall inform the applicant of the deficiencies. If the application is filed by a person whom the holder has expressly authorised to do so, the holder of the design shall receive a copy of the notification. 4. Where an application for renewal is not submitted or is submitted after expiry of the time limit provided for in the second sentence of Article 13(3) of Regulation (EC) No 6/2002, or if the fees are not paid or are paid only after expiry of the relevant time limit, or if the deficiencies are not remedied within the time limit specified by the Office, the Office shall determine that the registration has expired and shall notify accordingly the holder and, where appropriate, the applicant for renewal and the person recorded in the Register as having rights in the design. In the case of a multiple registration, where the fees paid are insufficient to cover all the designs for which renewal is requested, such a determination shall be made only after the Office has established which designs the amount paid is intended to cover. In the absence of other criteria for determining which designs are intended to be covered, the Office shall take the designs in the numerical order in which they are represented in accordance with Article 2(4). The Office shall determine that the registration has expired with regard to all designs for which the renewal fees have not been paid or have not been paid in full. 5. Where the determination made pursuant to paragraph 4 has become final, the Office shall cancel the design from the Register with effect from the day following the day on which the existing registration expired. 6. Where the renewal fees provided for in paragraph 2 have been paid but the registration is not renewed, those fees shall be refunded.

CHAPTER IV

TRANSFER, LICENCES AND OTHER RIGHTS, CHANGES

Article 23

Transfer

1. An application for registration of a transfer pursuant to Article 28 of Regulation (EC) No 6/2002 shall contain: (a) the registration number of the Community Design; (b) particulars of the new holder in accordance with Article 1(1)(b); (c) where not all of the designs covered by a multiple registration are included in the transfer, particulars of the registered designs to which the transfer relates; (d) documents duly establishing the transfer. 2. The application may contain, where applicable, the name and business address of the representative of the new holder, to be set out in accordance with Article 1(1)(e). 3. The application shall not be deemed to have been filed until the required fee has been paid. If the fee is not paid or is not paid in full, the Office shall notify the applicant accordingly. 4. The following shall constitute sufficient proof of transfer under paragraph 1(d): (a) the application for registration of the transfer is signed by the registered holder or his/her representative and by the successor in title or his/her representative; or (b) the application, if submitted by the successor in title, is accompanied by a declaration, signed by the registered holder or his/her representative, that he/she agrees to the registration of the successor in title; or (c) the application is accompanied by a completed transfer form or document, signed by the registered holder or his/her representative and by the successor in title or his/her representative. 5. Where the conditions applicable to the registration of a transfer are not fulfilled, the Office shall notify the applicant of the deficiencies. If the deficiencies are not remedied within the time limit specified by the Office, it shall reject the application for registration of the transfer. 6. A single application for registration of a transfer may be submitted for two or more registered Community Designs, provided that the registered holder and the successor in title are the same in each case. 7. Paragraphs 1 to 6 shall apply *mutatis mutandis* to the transfer of applications for registered Community Designs. The transfer shall be recorded in the files kept by the Office concerning the Community Design application.

Article 24

Registration of licences and other rights

1. Article 23(1)(a), (b) and (c) and Article 23(2), (3), (5) and (6) shall apply *mutatis mutandis* to the registration of the grant or transfer of a licence, to registration of the creation or transfer of a right *in rem* in respect of a registered Community Design, and to registration of enforcement measures. However, where a registered Community Design is involved in insolvency proceedings, the request of the competent national authority for an entry in the Register to this effect shall not be subject to payment of a fee. In the case of a multiple registration, each registered Community Design may, separately from the others, be licensed, the subject of a right *in rem*, levy of execution or insolvency proceedings. 2. Where the registered Community Design is licensed for only a part of the Community, or for a limited period of time, the application for registration of the licence shall indicate the part of the Community or the period of time for which the licence is granted. 3. Where the conditions applicable to registration of licences and other rights, set out in Articles 29, 30 or 32 of Regulation (EC)

No 6/2002, in paragraph 1 of this Article, and in the other applicable Articles of this Regulation are not fulfilled, the Office shall notify the applicant of the deficiencies. If the deficiencies are not remedied within a time limit specified by the Office, it shall reject the application for registration. 4. Paragraphs 1, 2 and 3 shall apply *mutatis mutandis* to licences and other rights concerning applications for registered Community Designs. Licences, rights *in rem* and enforcement measures shall be recorded in the files kept by the Office concerning the Community Design application. 5. The request for a non-exclusive licence pursuant to Article 16(2) of Regulation (EC) No 6/2002 shall be made within three months of the date of the entry in the Register of the newly entitled holder.

Article 25

Special provisions for the registration of a licence

1. A licence in respect of a registered Community Design shall be recorded in the Register as an exclusive licence if the holder of the design or the licensee so requests. 2. A licence in respect of a registered Community Design shall be recorded in the Register as a sub-licence where it is granted by a licensee whose licence is recorded in the Register. 3. A licence in respect of a registered Community Design shall be recorded in the Register as a territorially limited licence if it is granted for a part of the Community. 4. A licence in respect of a registered Community Design shall be recorded in the Register as a temporary licence if it is granted for a limited period of time.

Article 26

Cancellation or modification of the registration of licences and other rights

1. A registration effected under Article 24 shall be cancelled upon application by one of the persons concerned. 2. The application shall contain: (a) the registration number of the registered Community Design, or in the case of a multiple registration, the number of each design; and (b) particulars of the right whose registration is to be cancelled. 3. Application for cancellation of the registration of a licence or other right shall not be deemed to have been filed until the required fee has been paid. If the fee is not paid or is not paid in full, the Office shall notify the applicant accordingly. A request from a competent national authority for cancellation of an entry where a registered Community Design is involved in insolvency proceedings shall not be subject to payment of a fee. 4. The application shall be accompanied by documents showing that the registered right no longer exists or by a statement by the licensee or the holder of another right to the effect that he/she consents to cancellation of the registration. 5. Where the requirements for cancellation of the registration are not satisfied, the Office shall notify the applicant of the deficiencies. If the deficiencies are not remedied within the time limit specified by the Office, it shall reject the application for cancellation of the registration. 6. Paragraphs 1, 2, 4 and 5 shall apply *mutatis mutandis* to a request for modification of a registration effected pursuant to Article 24. 7. Paragraphs 1 to 6 shall apply *mutatis mutandis* to entries made in the files pursuant to Article 24(4).

CHAPTER V

SURRENDER AND INVALIDITY

Article 27

Surrender

A declaration of surrender pursuant to Article 51 of Regulation (EC) No 6/2002 shall contain: (a) the registration number of the registered Community Design; (b) the name and address of the holder in accordance with Article 1(1)(b); (c) where a representative has been appointed, the name and business address of the representative in accordance with Article 1(1)(e); (d) where surrender is declared only for some of the designs contained in a multiple registration, an indication of the designs for which the surrender is declared or the designs which are to remain registered; (e) where, pursuant to Article 51(3) of Regulation (EC) No 6/2002, the registered Community Design is partially surrendered, a representation of the amended design in accordance with Article 4 of this Regulation. 2. Where a right of a third party relating to the registered Community Design is entered in the Register, it shall be sufficient proof of his/her agreement to the surrender that a declaration of consent to the surrender is signed by the holder of that right or his/her representative. Where a licence has been registered, surrender of the design shall be registered three months after the date on which the holder satisfies the Office that he/she has informed the licensee of his/her intention to surrender it. If the holder proves to the Office before the expiry of that period that the licensee has given his/her consent, the surrender shall be registered forthwith. 3. Where a claim relating to the entitlement to a registered Community Design has been brought before a court pursuant to Article 15 of Regulation (EC) No 6/2002, a declaration of consent to the surrender, signed by the claimant or his/her representative, shall be sufficient proof of his/her agreement to the surrender. 4. If the requirements governing surrender are not fulfilled, the Office shall communicate the deficiencies to the declarant. If the deficiencies are not remedied within the time limit specified by the Office, the Office shall reject the entry of the surrender in the Register.

Article 28

Application for a declaration of invalidity

1. An application to the Office for a declaration of invalidity pursuant to Article 52 of Regulation (EC) No 6/2002 shall contain: (a) as concerns the registered Community Design for which the declaration of invalidity is sought: (i) its registration number; (ii) the name and address of its holder; (b) as regards the grounds on which the application is based: (i) a statement of the grounds on which the application for a declaration of invalidity is based; (ii) additionally, in the case of an application pursuant to Article 25(1)(d) of Regulation (EC) No 6/2002, the representation and particulars identifying the prior design on which the application for a declaration of invalidity is based and showing that the applicant is entitled to invoke the earlier design as a ground for invalidity pursuant to Article 25(3) of that Regulation; (iii) additionally, in the case of an application pursuant to Article 25(1)(e) or (f) of Regulation (EC) No 6/2002, the representation and particulars identifying the distinctive sign or the work protected by copyright on which the application for a declaration of invalidity is based and particulars showing that the applicant is the holder of the earlier right pursuant to Article 25(3) of that Regulation; (iv) additionally, in the case of an

application pursuant to Article 25(1)(g) of the Regulation (EC) No 6/2002, the representation and particulars of the relevant item as referred to in that Article and particulars showing that the application is filed by the person or entity concerned by the improper use pursuant to Article 25(4) of that Regulation; (v) where the ground for invalidity is that the registered Community Design does not fulfil the requirements set out in Article 5 or 6 of Regulation (EC) No 6/2002, the indication and the reproduction of the prior designs that could form an obstacle to the novelty or individual character of the registered Community Design, as well as documents proving the existence of those earlier designs; (vi) an indication of the facts, evidence and arguments submitted in support of those grounds; (c) as concerns the applicant: (i) his/her name and address in accordance with Article 1(1)(b); (ii) if the applicant has appointed a representative, the name and the business address of the representative, in accordance with Article 1(1)(e); (iii) additionally, in the case of an application pursuant to Article 25(1)(c) of Regulation (EC) No 6/2002, particulars showing that the application is made by a person or by persons duly entitled pursuant to Article 25(2) of that Regulation. 2. The application shall be subject to the fee referred to in Article 52(2) of Regulation (EC) No 6/2002. 3. The Office shall inform the holder that an application for declaration of invalidity has been filed.

Article 29

Languages used in invalidity proceedings

1. The application for a declaration of invalidity shall be filed in the language of proceedings pursuant to Article 98(4) of Regulation (EC) No 6/2002. 2. Where the language of proceedings is not the language used for filing the application and the holder has filed his/her observations in the language of filing, the Office shall arrange to have those observations translated into the language of proceedings. 3. Three years after the date fixed in accordance with Article 111(2) of Regulation (EC) No 6/2002, the Commission will submit to the Committee mentioned in Article 109 of Regulation (EC) No 6/2002 a report on the application of paragraph 2 of this Article and, if appropriate, proposals for fixing a limit for the expenses borne by the Office in this respect as provided for in the fourth subparagraph of Article 98(4) of Regulation (EC) No 6/2002. 4. The Commission may decide to submit the report and possible proposals referred to in paragraph 3 at an earlier date, and the Committee shall discuss them as a matter of priority if the facilities in paragraph 2 lead to disproportionate expenditure. 5. Where the evidence in support of the application is not filed in the language of the invalidity proceedings, the applicant shall file a translation of that evidence into that language within two months of the filing of such evidence. 6. Where the applicant for a declaration of invalidity or the holder informs the Office, within two months of receipt by the holder of the communication referred to in Article 31(1) of this Regulation, that they have agreed on a different language of proceedings pursuant to Article 98(5) of Regulation (EC) No 6/2002, the applicant shall, where the application was not filed in that language, file a translation of the application in that language within one month of the said date.

Article 30

Rejection of the application for declaration of invalidity as inadmissible

1. If the Office finds that the application for declaration of invalidity does not comply with Article 52 of Regulation (EC) No 6/2002, Article 28(1) of this Regulation or any other provision of Regulation (EC) No 6/2002 or this Regulation, it shall inform the

applicant accordingly and shall call upon him/her to remedy the deficiencies within such time limit as it may specify. If the deficiencies are not remedied within the specified time limit, the Office shall reject the application as inadmissible. 2. Where the Office finds that the required fees have not been paid, it shall inform the applicant accordingly and shall inform him/her that the application will be deemed not to have been filed if the required fees are not paid within a specified time limit. If the required fees are paid after the expiry of the time limit specified, they shall be refunded to the applicant. 3. Any decision to reject an application for a declaration of invalidity pursuant to paragraph 1 shall be communicated to the applicant. Where, pursuant to paragraph 2, an application is deemed not to have been filed, the applicant shall be informed accordingly.

Article 31

Examination of the application for a declaration of invalidity

1. If the Office does not reject the application for declaration of invalidity in accordance with Article 30, it shall communicate such application to the holder and shall request him/her to file his/her observations within such time limits as it may specify. 2. If the holder files no observations, the Office may base its decision concerning invalidity on the evidence before it. 3. Any observations filed by the holder shall be communicated to the applicant, who may be called upon by the Office to reply within specified time limits. 4. All communications pursuant to Article 53(2) of Regulation (EC) No 6/2002 and all observations filed in that respect shall be sent to the parties concerned. 5. The Office may call upon the parties to make a friendly settlement.

Article 32

Multiple applications for a declaration of invalidity

1. Where a number of applications for a declaration of invalidity have been filed relating to the same registered Community Design, the Office may deal with them in one set of proceedings. The Office may subsequently decide no longer to deal with them in that way. 2. If a preliminary examination of one or more applications reveals that the registered Community Design may be invalid, the Office may suspend the other invalidity proceedings. The Office shall inform the remaining applicants of any relevant decisions taken during such proceedings as are continued. 3. Once a decision declaring the invalidity of the design has become final, the applications in respect of which the proceedings have been suspended in accordance with paragraph 2 shall be deemed to have been disposed of and the applicants concerned shall be informed accordingly. Such disposition shall be considered to constitute a case which has not proceeded to judgment for the purposes of Article 70(4) of Regulation (EC) No 6/2002. 4. The Office shall refund 50 % of the invalidity fee referred to in Article 52(2) of Regulation (EC) No 6/2002 paid by each applicant whose application is deemed to have been disposed of in accordance with paragraphs 1, 2 and 3 of this Article.

Article 33

Participation of an alleged infringer

Where, pursuant to Article 54 of Regulation (EC) No 6/2002, an alleged infringer seeks to join the proceedings, he/she shall be subject to the relevant provisions of

Articles 28, 29 and 30 of this Regulation, and shall in particular file a reasoned statement and pay the fee referred to in Article 52(2) of Regulation (EC) No 6/2002.

CHAPTER VI

APPEALS

Article 34

Content of the notice of appeal

1. The notice of appeal shall contain: (a) the name and address of the appellant in accordance with Article 1(1)(b); (b) where the appellant has appointed a representative, the name and the business address of the representative in accordance with Article 1(1)(e); (c) a statement identifying the decision which is contested and the extent to which amendment or cancellation of the decision is requested. 2. The notice of appeal shall be filed in the language of the proceedings in which the decision subject to the appeal was taken.

Article 35

Rejection of the appeal as inadmissible

1. If the appeal does not comply with Articles 55, 56 and 57 of Regulation (EC) No 6/2002 and Article 34(1)(c) and (2) of this Regulation, the Board of Appeal shall reject it as inadmissible, unless each deficiency has been remedied before the relevant time limit laid down in Article 57 of Regulation (EC) No 6/2002 has expired. 2. If the Board of Appeal finds that the appeal does not comply with other provisions of Regulation (EC) No 6/2002 or other provisions of this Regulation, in particular with Article 34(1)(a) and (b), it shall inform the appellant accordingly and shall request him/her to remedy the deficiencies noted within such time limit as it may specify. If the deficiencies are not remedied in good time, the Board of Appeal shall reject the appeal as inadmissible. 3. If the fee for appeal has been paid after expiry of the time limits for the filing of an appeal pursuant to Article 57 of Regulation (EC) No 6/2002, the appeal shall be deemed not to have been filed and the appeal fee shall be refunded to the appellant.

Article 36

Examination of appeals

1. Save as otherwise provided, the provisions relating to proceedings before the department which has made the decision against which the appeal is brought shall be applicable to appeal proceedings *mutatis mutandis*. 2. The Board of Appeal's decision shall contain: (a) a statement that it is delivered by the Board; (b) the date when the decision was taken; (c) the names of the Chairman and the other members of the Board of Appeal taking part; (d) the name of the competent employee of the registry; (e) the names of the parties and of their representatives; (f) a statement of the issues to be decided; (g) a summary of the facts; (h) the reasons; (i) the order of the Board of Appeal, including, where necessary, a decision on costs. 3. The decision shall be signed by the Chairman and the other members of the Board of Appeal and by the employee of the registry of the Board of Appeal.

Article 37

Reimbursement of appeal fees

The reimbursement of appeal fees shall be ordered in the event of interlocutory revision or where the Board of Appeal deems an appeal to be allowable, if such reimbursement is equitable by reason of a substantial procedural violation. In the event of interlocutory revision, reimbursement shall be ordered by the department whose decision has been impugned, and in other cases by the Board of Appeal.

CHAPTER VII

DECISIONS AND COMMUNICATIONS OF THE OFFICE

Article 38

Form of decisions

1. Decisions of the Office shall be in writing and shall state the reasons on which they are based. Where oral proceedings are held before the Office, the decision may be given orally. Subsequently, the decision in writing shall be notified to the parties. 2. Decisions of the Office which are open to appeal shall be accompanied by a written communication indicating that notice of appeal must be filed in writing at the Office within two months of the date of notification of the decision from which appeal is to be made. The communications shall also draw the attention of the parties to the provisions laid down in Articles 55, 56 and 57 of Regulation (EC) No 6/2002. The parties may not plead any failure to communicate the availability of such appeal proceedings.

Article 39

Correction of errors in decisions

In decisions of the Office, only linguistic errors, errors of transcription and obvious mistakes may be corrected. They shall be corrected by the department which took the decision, acting of its own motion or at the request of an interested party.

Article 40

Noting of loss of rights

1. If the Office finds that the loss of any rights results from Regulation (EC) No 6/2002 or this Regulation without any decision having been taken, it shall communicate this to the person concerned in accordance with Article 66 of Regulation (EC) No 6/2002, and shall draw his/her attention to the legal remedies set out in paragraph 2 of this Article. 2. If the person concerned considers that the finding of the Office is inaccurate, he/she may, within two months of notification of the communication referred to in paragraph 1, apply for a decision on the matter by the Office. Such decision shall be given only if the Office disagrees with the person requesting it; otherwise the Office shall amend its finding and inform the person requesting the decision.

Article 41

Signature, name, seal

1. Any decision, communication or notice from the Office shall indicate the department or division of the Office as well as the name or the names of the official or officials responsible. They shall be signed by the official or officials, or, instead of a signature, carry a printed or stamped seal of the Office. 2. The President of the Office may determine that other means of identifying the department or division of the Office and the name of the official or officials responsible or an identification other than a seal may be used where decisions, communications or notices are transmitted by fax or any other technical means of communication.

CHAPTER VIII

ORAL PROCEEDINGS AND TAKING OF EVIDENCE

Article 42

Summons to oral proceedings

1. The parties shall be summoned to oral proceedings provided for in Article 64 of Regulation (EC) No 6/2002 and their attention shall be drawn to paragraph 3 of this Article. At least one month's notice of the summons shall be given unless the parties agree to a shorter time limit. 2. When issuing the summons, the Office shall draw attention to the points which in its opinion need to be discussed in order for the decision to be taken. 3. If a party who has been duly summoned to oral proceedings before the Office does not appear as summoned, the proceedings may continue without him/her.

Article 43

Taking of evidence by the Office

1. Where the Office considers it necessary to hear the oral evidence of parties, of witnesses or of experts or to carry out an inspection, it shall take a decision to that end, stating the means by which it intends to obtain evidence, the relevant facts to be proved and the date, time and place of the hearing or inspection. If oral evidence from witnesses and experts is requested by a party, the decision of the Office shall determine the period of time within which the party filing the request must make known to the Office the names and addresses of the witnesses and experts whom the party wishes to be heard. 2. The period of notice given in the summons of a party, witness or expert to give evidence shall be at least one month, unless they agree to a shorter time limit. The summons shall contain: (a) an extract from the decision mentioned in the first subparagraph of paragraph 1, indicating in particular the date, time and place of the hearing ordered and stating the facts regarding which the parties, witnesses and experts are to be heard; (b) the names of the parties to proceedings and particulars of the rights which the witnesses or experts may invoke pursuant to Article 45(2) to (5).

Article 44

Commissioning of experts

1. The Office shall decide in what form the report made by an expert whom it appoints shall be submitted. 2. The terms of reference of the expert shall include: (a) a precise description of his/her task; (b) the time limit laid down for the submission of the expert's report; (c) the names of the parties to the proceedings; (d) particulars of the claims which the expert may invoke pursuant to Article 45(2), (3) and (4). 3. A copy of any written report shall be submitted to the parties. 4. The parties may object to an expert on grounds of incompetence or on the same grounds as those on which · objection may be made to an examiner or to a member of a Division or Board of Appeal pursuant to Article 132(1) and (3) of Council Regulation (EC) No 40/94 ([1]). The department of the Office concerned shall rule on the objection.

Article 45

Costs of taking of evidence

1. The taking of evidence by the Office may be made conditional upon deposit with it, by the party who has requested the evidence to be taken, of a sum which shall be fixed by reference to an estimate of the costs. 2. Witnesses and experts who are summoned by and appear before the Office shall be entitled to reimbursement of reasonable expenses for travel and subsistence. An advance for those expenses may be granted to them by the Office. The first sentence shall apply also to witnesses and experts who appear before the Office without being summoned by it and who are heard as witnesses or experts. 3. Witnesses entitled to reimbursement under paragraph 2 shall also be entitled to appropriate compensation for loss of earnings, and experts shall be entitled to fees for their services. Those payments shall be made to the witnesses and experts after they have fulfilled their duties or tasks, where such witnesses and experts have been summoned by the Office on its own initiative. 4. The amounts and the advances for expenses to be paid pursuant to paragraphs 1, 2 and 3 shall be determined by the President of the Office and shall be published in the Official Journal of the Office. The amounts shall be calculated on the same basis as the compensation and salaries received by officials in grades A 4 to A 8 as laid down in the Staff Regulations of officials of the European Communities and in Annex VII thereto. 5. Final liability for the amounts due or paid pursuant to paragraphs 1 to 4 shall lie with: (a) the Office where the Office, on its own initiative, considered it necessary to hear the oral evidence of witnesses or experts; or (b) the party concerned where that party requested the giving of oral evidence by witnesses or experts, subject to the decision on apportionment and fixing of costs pursuant to Articles 70 and 71 of Regulation (EC) No 6/2002 and Article 79 of this Regulation. The party referred to in point (b) of the first subparagraph shall reimburse the Office for any advances duly paid.

---

(1) OJ L 11, 14.1.1994, p. 1.

Article 46

Minutes of oral proceedings and of evidence

1. Minutes of oral proceedings or the taking of evidence shall be drawn up, containing the essentials of the oral proceedings or of the taking of evidence, the relevant statements made by the parties, the testimony of the parties, witnesses or experts and the result of any inspection. 2. The minutes of the testimony of a witness, expert or party shall be read out or submitted to him/her so that he/she may examine them. It shall be noted in the minutes that this formality has been carried out and that the person who gave the testimony approved the minutes. Where his/her approval is not given, his/her objections shall be noted. 3. The minutes shall be signed by the employee who drew them up and by the employee who conducted the oral proceedings or taking of evidence. 4. The parties shall be provided with a copy of the minutes. 5. Upon request, the Office shall make available to the parties transcripts of recordings of the oral proceedings, in typescript or in any other machine-readable form. The release of transcripts of those recordings shall be subject to the payment of the costs incurred by the Office in making such transcript. The amount to be charged shall be determined by the President of the Office.

CHAPTER IX

NOTIFICATIONS

Article 47

General provisions on notifications

1. In proceedings before the Office, any notifications to be made by the Office shall take the form of the original document, of a copy thereof certified by, or bearing the seal of, the Office or of a computer print-out bearing such seal. Copies of documents emanating from the parties themselves shall not require such certification. 2. Notifications shall be made: (a) by post in accordance with Article 48; (b) by hand delivery in accordance with Article 49; (c) by deposit in a post box at the Office in accordance with Article 50; (d) by fax and other technical means in accordance with Article 51; (e) by public notification in accordance with Article 52.

Article 48

Notification by post

1. Decisions subject to a time limit for appeal, summonses and other documents as determined by the President of the Office shall be notified by registered letter with acknowledgement of delivery. Decisions and communications subject to another time limit shall be notified by registered letter, unless the President of the Office determines otherwise. All other communications shall be ordinary mail. 2. Notifications to addressees having neither their domicile nor their principal place of business nor an establishment in the Community and who have not appointed a representative in accordance with Article 77(2) of Regulation (EC) No 6/2002 shall be effected by posting the document requiring notification by ordinary mail to the last address of the addressee known to the Office. Notification shall be deemed to have been effected when the posting has taken place. 3. Where notification is effected by registered letter, whether or not with acknowledgement of delivery, it shall be deemed to be delivered

to the addressee on the 10th day following that of its posting, unless the letter has failed to reach the addressee or has reached him/her at a later date. In the event of any dispute, it shall be for the Office to establish that the letter has reached its destination or to establish the date on which it was delivered to the addressee, as the case may be. 4. Notification by registered letter, with or without acknowledgement of delivery, shall be deemed to have been effected even if the addressee refuses to accept the letter. 5. To the extent that notification by post is not covered by paragraphs 1 to 4, the law of the State on the territory of which notification is made shall apply.

Article 49

Notification by hand delivery

Notification may be effected on the premises of the Office by hand delivery of the document to the addressee, who shall on delivery acknowledge its receipt.

Article 50

Notification by deposit in a post box at the Office

Notification may also be effected to addressees who have been provided with a post box at the Office, by depositing the document therein. A written notification of deposit shall be inserted in the files. The date of deposit shall be recorded on the document. Notification shall be deemed to have taken place on the fifth day following deposit of the document in the post box at the Office.

Article 51

Notification by fax and other technical means

Notification by fax shall be effected by transmitting either the original or a copy, as provided for in Article 47(1), of the document to be notified. The details of such transmission shall be determined by the President of the Office. 2. Details of notification by other technical means of communication shall be determined by the President of the Office.

Article 52

Public notification

1. If the address of the addressee cannot be established, or if notification in accordance with Article 48(1) has proved to be impossible even after a second attempt by the Office, notification shall be effected by public notice. Such notice shall be published at least in the *Community Designs Bulletin*. 2. The President of the Office shall determine how the public notice is to be given and shall fix the beginning of the time limit of one month on the expiry of which the document shall be deemed to have been notified.

Article 53

Notification to representatives

1. If a representative has been appointed or where the applicant first named in a common application is considered to be the common representative pursuant to Article 61(1), notifications shall be addressed to that appointed or common representative. 2. If several representatives have been appointed for a single interested party, notification to any one of them shall be sufficient, unless a specific address for service has been indicated in accordance with Article 1(1)(e). 3. If several interested parties have appointed a common representative, notification of a single document to the common representative shall be sufficient.

Article 54

Irregularities in notification

Where a document has reached the addressee, if the Office is unable to prove that it has been duly notified or if provisions relating to its notification have not been observed, the document shall be deemed to have been notified on the date established by the Office as the date of receipt.

Article 55

Notification of documents in the case of several parties

Documents emanating from parties which contain substantive proposals, or a declaration of withdrawal of a substantive proposal, shall be notified to the other parties as a matter of course. Notification may be dispensed with where the document contains no new pleadings and the matter is ready for decision.

CHAPTER X

TIME LIMITS

Article 56

Calculation of time limits

1. Time limits shall be laid down in terms of full years, months, weeks or days. 2. The beginning of any time limit shall be calculated starting on the day following the day on which the relevant event occurred, the event being either a procedural step or the expiry of another time limit. Where that procedural step is a notification, the event considered shall be the receipt of the document notified, unless otherwise provided. 3. Where a time limit is expressed as one year or a certain number of years, it shall expire in the relevant subsequent year in the month having the same name and on the day having the same number as the month and the day on which the relevant event occurred. Where the relevant month has no day with the same number the time limit shall expire on the last day of that month. 4. Where a time limit is expressed as one month or a certain number of months, it shall expire in the relevant subsequent month on the day which has the same number as the day on which the relevant event occurred. Where the day on which the relevant event occurred was the last day of a

month or where the relevant subsequent month has no day with the same number the time limit shall expire on the last day of that month. 5. Where a time limit is expressed as one week or a certain number of weeks, it shall expire in the relevant subsequent week on the day having the same name as the day on which the relevant event occurred.

Article 57

Duration of time limits

1. Where Regulation (EC) No 6/2002 or this Regulation provide for a time limit to be specified by the Office, such time limit shall, when the party concerned has its domicile or its principal place of business or an establishment within the Community, be not less than one month, or, when those conditions are not fulfilled, not less than two months, and no more than six months. The Office may, when this is appropriate under the circumstances, grant an extension of a time limit specified if such extension is requested by the party concerned and the request is submitted before the original time limit expires. 2. Where there are two or more parties, the Office may make the extension of a time limit subject to the agreement of the other parties.

Article 58

Expiry of time limits in special cases

1. If a time limit expires on a day on which the Office is not open for receipt of documents or on which, for reasons other than those referred to in paragraph 2, ordinary mail is not delivered in the locality in which the Office is located, the time limit shall extend until the first day thereafter on which the Office is open for receipt of documents and on which ordinary mail is delivered. The days on which the Office is not open for receipt of documents shall be determined by the President of the Office before the commencement of each calendar year. 2. If a time limit expires on a day on which there is a general interruption or subsequent dislocation in the delivery of mail in a Member State or between a Member State and the Office, the time limit shall extend until the first day following the end of the period of interruption or dislocation, for parties having their residence or registered office in the State concerned or who have appointed representatives with a place of business in that State. In the event of the Member State concerned being the State in which the Office is located, the first subparagraph shall apply to all parties. The period referred to in the first subparagraph shall be as determined by the President of the Office. 3. Paragraphs 1 and 2 shall apply *mutatis mutandis* to the time limits provided for in Regulation (EC) No 6/2002 or this Regulation in the case of transactions to be carried out with the competent authority within the meaning of Article 35(1)(b) and (c) of Regulation (EC) No 6/2002. 4. If an exceptional occurrence such as natural disaster or strike interrupts or dislocates the proper functioning of the Office so that any communication from the Office to parties concerning the expiry of a time limit is delayed, acts to be completed within such a time limit may still be validly completed within one month of the notification of the delayed communication. The date of commencement and the end of any such interruption or dislocation shall be as determined by the President of the Office.

CHAPTER XI

INTERRUPTION OF PROCEEDINGS AND WAIVING OF ENFORCED RECOVERY PROCEDURES

Article 59

Interruption of proceedings

1. Proceedings before the Office shall be interrupted: (a) in the event of the death or legal incapacity of the applicant for or holder of a registered Community Design or of the person authorised by national law to act on his/her behalf; (b) in the event that the applicant for or holder of a registered Community Design is, as a result of some action taken against his/her property, prevented for legal reasons from continuing the proceedings before the Office; (c) in the event of the death or legal incapacity of the representative of an applicant for or holder of a registered Community Design or of his/her being prevented for legal reasons resulting from action taken against his/her property from continuing the proceedings before the Office. To the extent that the events referred to in point (a) of the first subparagraph do not affect the authorisation of a representative appointed under Article 78 of Regulation (EC) No 6/2002, proceedings shall be interrupted only on application by such representative. 2. When, in the cases referred to in points (a) and (b) of the first subparagraph of paragraph 1, the Office has been informed of the identity of the person authorised to continue the proceedings before the Office, the Office shall communicate to such person and to any interested third parties that the proceedings shall be resumed as from a date to be fixed by the Office. 3. In the case referred to in paragraph 1(c), the proceedings shall be resumed when the Office has been informed of the appointment of a new representative of the applicant or when the Office has notified to the other parties the communication of the appointment of a new representative of the holder of the design. If, three months after the beginning of the interruption of the proceedings, the Office has not been informed of the appointment of a new representative, it shall communicate that fact to the applicant for or holder of the registered Community Design: (a) where Article 77(2) of Regulation (EC) No 6/2002 is applicable, that the Community Design application will be deemed to be withdrawn if the information is not submitted within two months after that communication is notified; or (b) where Article 77(2) of Regulation (EC) No 6/2002 is not applicable, that the proceedings will be resumed with the applicant for or holder as from the date on which that communication is notified. 4. The time limits, other than the time limit for paying the renewal fees, in force as regards the applicant for or holder of the Community Design at the date of interruption of the proceedings, shall begin again as from the day on which the proceedings are resumed.

Article 60

Waiving of enforced recovery procedures

The President of the Office may waive action for the enforced recovery of any sum due where the sum to be recovered is minimal or where such recovery is too uncertain.

CHAPTER XII

REPRESENTATION

Article 61

Appointment of a common representative

1. If there is more than one applicant and the application for a registered Community Design does not name a common representative, the applicant first named in the application shall be considered to be the common representative. However, if one of the applicants is obliged to appoint a professional representative, such representative shall be considered to be the common representative unless the applicant named first in the application has also appointed a professional representative. The first and second subparagraphs shall apply *mutatis mutandis* to third parties acting in common in applying for a declaration of invalidity, and to joint holders of a registered Community Design. 2. If, during the course of proceedings, transfer is made to more than one person, and such persons have not appointed a common representative, paragraph 1 shall apply. If such application is not possible, the Office shall require such persons to appoint a common representative within two months. If this request is not complied with, the Office shall appoint the common representative.

Article 62

Authorisations

1. Legal practitioners and professional representatives entered on the lists maintained by the Office pursuant to Article 78(1)(b) or (c) of Regulation (EC) No 6/2002 may file with the Office a signed authorisation for inclusion in the files. Such authorisation shall be filed if the Office expressly requires it or, where there are several parties to the proceedings in which the representative acts before the Office, one of the parties expressly request it. 2. Employees acting on behalf of natural or legal persons pursuant to Article 77(3) of Regulation (EC) No 6/2002 shall file with the Office a signed authorisation for insertion in the files. 3. The authorisation may be filed in any of the official languages of the Community. It may cover one or more applications or registered Community Designs or may be in the form of a general authorisation allowing the representative to act in respect of all proceedings before the Office to which the person who has issued it is a party. 4. Where, pursuant to paragraphs 1 or 2, an authorisation has to be filed, the Office shall specify a time limit within which such authorisation shall be filed. If the authorisation is not filed in due time, proceedings shall be continued with the represented person. Any procedural steps other than the filing of the application taken by the representative shall be deemed not to have been taken if the represented person does not approve them. The application of Article 77(2) of Regulation (EC) No 6/2002 shall remain unaffected. 5. Paragraphs 1, 2 and 3 shall apply *mutatis mutandis* to a document withdrawing an authorisation. 6. Any representative who has ceased to be authorised shall continue to be regarded as the representative until the termination of his/her authorisation has been communicated to the Office. 7. Subject to any provisions to the contrary contained therein, an authorisation shall not terminate vis-à-vis the Office upon the death of the person who gave it. 8. Where several representatives are appointed by the same party, they may, notwithstanding any provisions to the contrary in their authorisations, act either

collectively or individually. 9. The authorisation of an association of representatives shall be deemed to be an authorisation of any representative who can establish that he/she practises within that association.

Article 63

Representation

Any notification or other communication addressed by the Office to the duly authorised representative shall have the same effect as if it had been addressed to the represented person. Any communication addressed to the Office by the duly authorised representative shall have the same effect as if it originated from the represented person.

Article 64

Amendment of the special list of professional representatives for design matters

1. The entry of a professional representative in the special list of professional representatives for design matters, as referred to in Article 78(4) of Regulation (EC) No 6/2002, shall be deleted at his/her request. 2. The entry of a professional representative shall be deleted automatically: (a) in the event of the death or legal incapacity of the professional representative; (b) where the professional representative is no longer a national of a Member State, unless the President of the Office has granted an exemption pursuant to Article 78(6)(a) of Regulation (EC) No 6/2002; (c) where the professional representative no longer has his/her place of business or employment in the Community; (d) where the professional representative no longer possesses the entitlement referred to in the first sentence of Article 78(4)(c) of Regulation (EC) No 6/2002. 3. The entry of a professional representative shall be suspended of the Office's own motion where his/her entitlement to represent natural or legal persons before the Benelux Design Office or the central industrial property office of the Member State as referred to in the first sentence of Article 78(4)(c) of Regulation (EC) No 6/2002 has been suspended. 4. A person whose entry has been deleted shall, upon request pursuant to Article 78(5) of Regulation (EC) No 6/2002, be reinstated in the list of professional representatives if the conditions for deletion no longer exist. 5. The Benelux Design Office and the central industrial property offices of the Member States concerned shall, where they are aware thereof, promptly inform the Office of any relevant events referred to in paragraphs 2 and 3. 6. The amendments of the special list of professional representatives for design matters shall be published in the Official Journal of the Office.

CHAPTER XIII

WRITTEN COMMUNICATIONS AND FORMS

Article 65

Communication in writing or by other means

1. Subject to paragraph 2, applications for the registration of a Community Design as well as any other application or declaration provided for in Regulation (EC) No 6/2002 and all other communications addressed to the Office shall be submitted as

follows: (a) by submitting a signed original of the document in question to the Office, by post, personal delivery, or by any other means; annexes to documents submitted need not be signed; (b) by transmitting a signed original by fax in accordance with Article 66; or (c) by transmitting the contents of the communication by electronic means in accordance with Article 67. 2. Where the applicant avails himself of the possibility provided for in Article 36(1)(c) of Regulation (EC) No 6/2002 of filing a specimen of the design, the application and the specimen shall be submitted to the Office by a single mail in the form prescribed in paragraph 1(a) of this Article. If the application and the specimen, or specimens in the case of a multiple application, are not submitted by a single mail the Office shall not give a filing date until the last item has been received pursuant to Article 10(1) of this Regulation.

Article 66

Communication by fax

1. Where an application for registration of a Community Design is submitted by fax and the application contains a reproduction of the design pursuant to Article 4(1) which does not satisfy the requirements of that Article, the required reproduction suitable for registration and publication shall be submitted to the Office in accordance with Article 65(1)(a). Where the reproduction is received by the Office within a time limit of one month from the date of the receipt of the fax, the application shall be deemed to have been received by the Office on the date on which the fax was received. Where the reproduction is received by the Office after the expiry of that time limit, the application shall be deemed to have been received by the Office on the date on which the reproduction was received. 2. Where a communication received by fax is incomplete or illegible, or where the Office has reasonable doubts as to the accuracy of the transmission, the Office shall inform the sender accordingly and shall call upon him/her, within a time limit to be specified by the Office, to retransmit the original by fax or to submit the original in accordance with Article 65(1)(a). Where that request is complied with within the time limit specified, the date of the receipt of the retransmission or of the original shall be deemed to be the date of the receipt of the original communication, provided that where the deficiency concerns the granting of a filing date for an application to register a Community Design, the provisions on the filing date shall apply. Where the request is not complied with within the time limit specified, the communication shall be deemed not to have been received. 3. Any communication submitted to the Office by fax shall be considered to be duly signed if the reproduction of the signature appears on the printout produced by the fax. 4. The President of the Office may determine additional requirements for communication by fax, such as the equipment to be used, technical details of communication, and methods of identifying the sender.

Article 67

Communication by electronic means

1. Applications for registration of a Community Design may be submitted by electronic means, including the representation of the design, and notwithstanding Article 65(2) in the case of filing a specimen. The conditions shall be laid down by the President of the Office. 2. The President of the Office shall determine the requirements for communication by electronic means, such as the equipment to be used, technical details of communication, and methods of identifying the sender. 3. Where a communication is sent by electronic means, Article 66(2) shall apply *mutatis mutandis*.

4. Where a communication is sent to the Office by electronic means, the indication of the name of the sender shall be deemed to be equivalent to the signature.

Article 68

Forms

1. The Office shall make available free of charge forms for the purpose of: (a) filing an application for a registered Community Design; (b) applying for the correction of an application or a registration; (c) applying for the registration of a transfer and the transfer form and transfer document referred to in Article 23(4); (d) applying for the registration of a licence; (e) applying for renewal of registration of a registered Community Design; (f) applying for a declaration of invalidity of a registered Community Design; (g) applying for *restitutio in integrum*; (h) taking an appeal; (i) authorising a representative, in the form of an individual authorisation and in the form of a general authorisation. 2. The Office may make other forms available free of charge. 3. The Office shall make available the forms referred to in paragraphs 1 and 2 in all the official languages of the Community. 4. The Office shall place the forms at the disposal of the Benelux Design Office and of the Member States' central industrial property offices free of charge. 5. The Office may also make available the forms in machine-readable form. 6. Parties to proceedings before the Office should use the forms provided by the Office, or copies of those forms, or forms with the same content and format as those forms, such as forms generated by means of electronic data processing. 7. Forms shall be completed in such a manner as to permit an automated input of the content into a computer, such as by character recognition or scanning.

CHAPTER XIV

INFORMATION TO THE PUBLIC

Article 69

Register of Community Designs

1. The Register may be maintained in the form of an electronic database. 2. The Register shall contain the following entries: (a) the date of filing the application; (b) the file number of the application and the file number of each individual design included in a multiple application; (c) the date of the publication of the registration; (d) the name, the address and the nationality of the applicant and the State in which he/she is domiciled or has his/her seat or establishment; (e) the name and business address of the representative, other than an employee acting as representative in accordance with the first subparagraph of Article 77(3) of Regulation (EC) No 6/2002; where there is more than one representative, only the name and business address of the first named representative, the name being followed by the words 'et al', shall be recorded; where an association of representatives is appointed, only the name and address of the association shall be recorded; (f) the representation of the design; (g) an indication of the products by their names, preceded by the numbers of the classes and subclasses of the Locarno classification, and grouped accordingly; (h) particulars of claims of priority pursuant to Article 42 of Regulation (EC) No 6/2002; (i) particulars of claims of exhibition priority pursuant to Article 44 of Regulation (EC) No 6/2002; (j) where applicable, the citation of the designer or of the team of designers pursuant to Article 18 of Regulation (EC) No 6/2002, or a statement that

the designer or the team of designers has waived the right to be cited; (k) the language in which the application was filed and the second language which the applicant has indicated in his/her application, pursuant to Article 98(2) of Regulation (EC) No 6/2002; (l) the date of registration of the design in the Register and the registration number; (m) a mention of any request for deferment of publication pursuant to Article 50(3) of Regulation (EC) No 6/2002, specifying the date of expiry of the period of deferment; (n) a mention that a specimen was filed pursuant to Article 5; (o) a mention that a description was filed pursuant to Article 1(2)(a). 3. In addition to the entries set out in paragraph 2 the Register shall contain the following entries, each accompanied by the date of recording such entry: (a) changes in the name, the address or the nationality of the holder or in the State in which he/she is domiciled or has his/her seat or establishment; (b) changes in the name or business address of the representative, other than a representative falling within the first subparagraph of Article 77(3) of Regulation (EC) No 6/2002; (c) when a new representative is appointed, the name and business address of that representative; (d) a mention that a multiple application or registration has been divided into separate applications or registrations pursuant to Article 37(4) of Regulation (EC) No 6/2002; (e) the notice of an amendment to the design pursuant to Article 25(6) of Regulation (EC) No 6/2002, including, if applicable, a reference to the disclaimer made or the court decision or the decision by the Office declaring the partial invalidity of the design right, as well as corrections of mistakes and errors pursuant to Article 20 of this Regulation; (f) a mention that entitlement proceedings have been instituted under Article 15(1) of Regulation (EC) No 6/2002 in respect of a registered Community Design; (g) the final decision or other termination of proceedings pursuant to Article 15(4)(b) of Regulation (EC) No 6/2002 concerning entitlement proceedings; (h) a change of ownership pursuant to Article 15(4)(c) of Regulation (EC) No 6/2002; (i) transfers pursuant to Article 28 of Regulation (EC) No 6/2002; (j) the creation or transfer of a right *in rem* pursuant to Article 29 of Regulation (EC) No 6/2002 and the nature of the right *in rem*; (k) levy of execution pursuant to Article 30 of Regulation (EC) No 6/2002 and insolvency proceedings pursuant to Article 31 of that Regulation; (l) the grant or transfer of a licence pursuant to Article 16(2) or Article 32 of Regulation (EC) No 6/2002 and, where applicable, the type of licence pursuant to Article 25 of this Regulation; (m) renewal of the registration pursuant to Article 13 of Regulation (EC) No 6/2002 and the date from which it takes effect; (n) a record of the determination of the expiry of the registration; (o) a declaration of total or partial surrender by the holder pursuant to Article 51(1) and (3) of Regulation (EC) No 6/2002; (p) the date of submission of an application or of the filing of a counterclaim for a declaration of invalidity pursuant, respectively, to Article 52 or Article 86(2) of Regulation (EC) No 6/2002; (q) the date and content of the decision on the application or counterclaim for declaration of invalidity or any other termination of proceedings pursuant, respectively, to Article 53 or Article 86(4) of Regulation (EC) No 6/2002; (r) a mention pursuant to Article 50(4) of Regulation (EC) No 6/2002 that the registered Community Design is deemed from the outset not to have had the effects specified in that Regulation; (s) the cancellation of the representative recorded pursuant to paragraph 2(e); (t) the modification or cancellation from the Register of the items referred to in points (j), (k) and (l). 4. The President of the Office may determine that items other than those referred to in paragraphs 2 and 3 shall be entered in the Register. 5. The holder shall be notified of any change in the Register. 6. Subject to Article 73, the Office shall provide certified or uncertified extracts from the Register on request, on payment of a fee.

CHAPTER XV

COMMUNITY DESIGNS BULLETIN AND DATA BASE

Article 70

Community Designs Bulletin

1. The Office shall determine the frequency of the publication of the *Community Designs Bulletin* and the manner in which such publication shall take place. 2. Without prejudice to the provisions of Article 50(2) of Regulation (EC) No 6/2002 and subject to Articles 14 and 16 of this Regulation relating to deferment of publication, the *Community Designs Bulletin* shall contain publications of registration and of entries made in the Register as well as other particulars relating to registrations of designs whose publication is prescribed by Regulation (EC) No 6/2002 or by this Regulation. 3. Where particulars whose publication is prescribed in Regulation (EC) No 6/2002 or in this Regulation are published in the *Community Designs Bulletin*, the date of issue shown on the Bulletin shall be taken as the date of publication of the particulars. 4. The information the publication of which is prescribed in Articles 14 and 16 shall, where appropriate, be published in all the official languages of the Community.

Article 71

Database

1. The Office shall maintain an electronic database with the particulars of applications for registration of Community Designs and entries in the Register. The Office may, subject to the restrictions prescribed by Article 50(2) and (3) of Regulation (EC) No 6/2002, make available the contents of that database for direct access or on CD-ROM or in any other machine-readable form. 2. The President of the Office shall determine the conditions of access to the database and the manner in which the contents of this database may be made available in machine-readable form, including the charges for those acts.

CHAPTER XVI

INSPECTION OF FILES AND KEEPING OF FILES

Article 72

Parts of the file excluded from inspection

The parts of the file which shall be excluded from inspection pursuant to Article 74(4) of Regulation (EC) No 6/2002 shall be: (a) documents relating to exclusion or objection pursuant to Article 132 of Regulation (EC) No 40/94, the provisions of that Article being considered for this purpose as applying *mutatis mutandis* to registered Community Designs and to applications for these; (b) draft decisions and opinions, and all other internal documents used for the preparation of decisions and opinions; (c) parts of the file which the party concerned showed a special interest in keeping confidential before the application for inspection of the files was made, unless inspection of such part of the file is justified by overriding legitimate interests of the party seeking inspection.

Article 73

Inspection of the Register of Community Designs

Where the registration is subject to a deferment of publication pursuant to Article 50(1) of Regulation (EC) No 6/2002: (a) access to the Register to persons other than the holder shall be limited to the name of the holder, the name of any representative, the date of filing and registration, the file number of the application and the mention that publication is deferred; (b) the certified or uncertified extracts from the Register shall contain only the name of the holder, the name of any representative, the date of filing and registration, the file number of the application and the mention that publication is deferred, except where the request has been made by the holder or his/her representative.

Article 74

Procedures for the inspection of files

1. Inspection of the files of registered Community Designs shall either be of the original document, or of copies thereof, or of technical means of storage if the files are so stored. The request for inspection of the files shall not be deemed to have been made until the required fee has been paid. The means of inspection shall be determined by the President of the Office. 2. Where inspection of the files relates to an application for a registered Community Design or to a registered Community Design which is subject to deferment of publication, which, being subject to such deferment, has been surrendered before or on the expiry of that period or which, pursuant to Article 50(4) of Regulation (EC) No 6/2002, is deemed from the outset not to have had the effects specified in that Regulation, the request shall contain an indication and evidence to the effect that: (a) the applicant for or holder of the Community Design has consented to the inspection; or (b) the person requesting the inspection has established a legitimate interest in the inspection of the file, in particular where the applicant for or holder of the Community Design has stated that after the design has been registered he/she will invoke the rights under it against the person requesting the inspection. 3. Inspection of the files shall take place on the premises of the Office. 4. On request, inspection of the files shall be effected by means of issuing copies of file documents. Such copies shall incur fees. 5. The Office shall issue on request certified or uncertified copies of the application for a registered Community Design or of those file documents of which copies may be issued pursuant to paragraph 4 upon payment of a fee.

Article 75

Communication of information contained in the files

Subject to the restrictions provided for in Article 74 of Regulation (EC) No 6/2002 and Articles 72 and 73 of this Regulation, the Office may, upon request, communicate information from any file of a Community Design applied for or of a registered Community Design, subject to payment of a fee. However, the Office may require the applicant to inspect the file *in situ*, should it deem that to be appropriate in view of the quantity of information to be supplied.

Article 76

Keeping of files

1. The Office shall keep the files relating to Community Design applications and to registered Community Designs for at least five years from the end of the year in which: (a) the application is rejected or withdrawn; (b) the registration of the registered Community Design expires definitively; (c) the complete surrender of the registered Community Design is registered pursuant to Article 51 of Regulation (EC) No 6/2002; (d) the registered Community Design is definitively removed from the Register; (e) the registered Community Design is deemed not to have had the effects specified in Regulation (EC) No 6/2002 pursuant to Article 50(4) thereof. 2. The President of the Office shall determine the form in which the files shall be kept.

CHAPTER XVII

ADMINISTRATIVE COOPERATION

Article 77

Exchange of information and communications between the Office and the authorities of the Member States

1. The Office and the central industrial property offices of the Member States and the Benelux Design Office shall, upon request, communicate to each other relevant information about the filing of applications for registered Community Designs, Benelux designs or national registered designs and about proceedings relating to such applications and the designs registered as a result thereof. Such communications shall not be subject to the restrictions provided for in Article 74 of Regulation (EC) No 6/2002. 2. Communications between the Office and the courts or authorities of the Member States which arise out of the application of Regulation (EC) No 6/2002 or this Regulation shall be effected directly between those authorities. Such communication may also be effected through the central industrial property offices of the Member States or the Benelux Design Office. 3. Expenditure in respect of communications pursuant to paragraphs 1 and 2 shall be chargeable to the authority making the communications, which shall be exempt from fees.

Article 78

Inspection of files by or via courts or authorities of the Member States

1. Inspection of files relating to Community Designs applied for or registered Community Designs by courts or authorities of the Member States shall if so requested be of the original documents or of copies thereof. Article 74 shall not apply. 2. Courts or public prosecutors' offices of the Member States may, in the course of proceedings before them, open files or copies thereof transmitted by the Office to inspection by third parties. Such inspection shall be subject to Article 74 of Regulation (EC) No 6/2002. 3. The Office shall not charge any fee for inspections pursuant to paragraphs 1 and 2. 4. The Office shall, at the time of transmission of the files or copies thereof to the courts or public prosecutors' offices of the Member States, indicate the restrictions to which the inspection of files relating to Community

Designs applied for or registered Community Designs is subject pursuant to Article 74 of Regulation (EC) No 6/2002 and Article 72 of this Regulation.

CHAPTER XVIII

COSTS

Article 79

Apportionment and fixing of costs

1. Apportionment of costs pursuant to Article 70(1) and (2) of Regulation (EC) No 6/2002 shall be dealt with in the decision on the application for a declaration of invalidity of a registered Community Design, or in the decision on the appeal. 2. Apportionment of costs pursuant to Article 70(3) and (4) of Regulation (EC) No 6/2002 shall be dealt with in a decision on costs by the Invalidity Division or the Board of Appeal. 3. A bill of costs, with supporting evidence, shall be attached to the request for the fixing of costs provided for in the first sentence of Article 70(6) of Regulation (EC) No 6/2002. The request shall be admissible only if the decision in respect of which the fixing of costs is required has become final. Costs may be fixed once their credibility is established. 4. The request provided for in the second sentence of Article 70(6) of Regulation (EC) No 6/2002 for a review of the decision of the registry on the fixing of costs, stating the reasons on which it is based, must be filed at the Office within one month of the date of notification of the awarding of costs. It shall not be deemed to be filed until the fee for reviewing the amount of the costs has been paid. 5. The Invalidity Division or the Board of Appeal, as the case may be, shall take a decision on the request referred to in paragraph 4 without oral proceedings. 6. The fees to be borne by the losing party pursuant to Article 70(1) of Regulation (EC) No 6/2002 shall be limited to the fees incurred by the other party for the application for a declaration of invalidity and/or for the appeal. 7. Costs essential to the proceedings and actually incurred by the successful party shall be borne by the losing party in accordance with Article 70(1) of Regulation (EC) No 6/2002 on the basis of the following maximum rates: (a) travel expenses of one party for the outward and return journey between the place of residence or the place of business and the place where oral proceedings are held or where evidence is taken, as follows: (i) the cost of the first-class rail fare including usual transport supplements where the total distance by rail does not exceed 800 km; (ii) the cost of the tourist-class air fare where the total distance by rail exceeds 800 km or the route includes a sea crossing; (b) subsistence expenses of one party equal to the daily subsistence allowance for officials in grades A 4 to A 8 as laid down in Article 13 of Annex VII to the Staff Regulations of officials of the European Communities; (c) travel expenses of representatives within the meaning of Article 78(1) of Regulation (EC) No 6/2002 and of witnesses and of experts, at the rates provided for in point (a); (d) subsistence expenses of representatives within the meaning of Article 78(1) of Regulation (EC) No 6/2002 and of witnesses and experts, at the rates referred to in point (b); (e) costs entailed in the taking of evidence in the form of examination of witnesses, opinions by experts or inspection, up to EUR 300 per proceedings; (f) costs of representation, within the meaning of Article 78(1) of Regulation (EC) No 6/2002: (i) of the applicant in proceedings relating to invalidity of a registered Community Design up to EUR 400; (ii) of the holder in proceedings relating to invalidity of a registered Community Design up to EUR 400; (iii) of the appellant in appeal proceedings up to EUR 500; (iv) of the defendant in appeal proceedings up to EUR 500; (g) where the successful

party is represented by more than one representative within the meaning of Article 78(1) of the Regulation (EC) No 6/2002, the losing party shall bear the costs referred to in points (c), (d) and (f) for one such person only; (h) the losing party shall not be obliged to reimburse the successful party for any costs, expenses and fees other than those referred to in points (a) to (g). Where the taking of evidence in any of the proceedings referred to in point (f) of the first subparagraph involves the examination of witnesses, opinions by experts or inspection, an additional amount shall be granted for representation costs of up to EUR 600 per proceedings.

CHAPTER XIX

LANGUAGES

Article 80

Applications and declarations

Without prejudice to Article 98(4) of Regulation (EC) No 6/2002: (a) any application or declaration relating to an application for a registered Community Design may be filed in the language used for filing the application or in the second language indicated by the applicant in his/her application; (b) any application or declaration other than an application for declaration of invalidity pursuant to Article 52 of Regulation (EC) No 6/2002, or declaration of surrender pursuant to Article 51 of that Regulation relating to a registered Community Design may be filed in one of the languages of the Office; (c) when any of the forms provided by the Office pursuant to Article 68 is used, such forms may be used in any of the official languages of the Community, provided that the form is completed in one of the languages of the Office, as far as textual elements are concerned.

Article 81

Written proceedings

1. Without prejudice to Article 98(3) and (5) of Regulation (EC) No 6/2002 and save as otherwise provided in this Regulation, in written proceedings before the Office a party may use any language of the Office. If the language chosen is not the language of the proceedings, the party shall supply a translation into that language within one month of the date of the submission of the original document. Where the applicant for a registered Community Design is the sole party to proceedings before the Office and the language used for the filing of the application for the registered Community Design is not one of the languages of the Office, the translation may also be filed in the second language indicated by the applicant in his/her application. 2. Save as otherwise provided in this Regulation, documents to be used in proceedings before the Office may be filed in an official language of the Community. Where the language of such documents is not the language of the proceedings the Office may require that a translation be supplied, within a time limit specified by it, in that language or, at the choice of the party to the proceeding, in any language of the Office.

Article 82

Oral proceedings

1. Any party to oral proceedings before the Office may, in place of the language of proceedings, use one of the other official languages of the Community, on condition that he/she makes provision for interpretation into the language of proceedings. Where the oral proceedings are held in a proceeding concerning the application for registration of a design the applicant may use either the language of the application or the second language indicated by him/her. 2. In oral proceedings concerning the application for registration of a design, the staff of the Office may use either the language of the application or the second language indicated by the applicant. In all other oral proceedings, the staff of the Office may use, in place of the language of the proceedings, one of the other languages of the Office, on condition that the party or parties to the proceedings agree(s) to such use. 3. With regard to the taking of evidence, any party to be heard, witness or expert who is unable to express himself/herself adequately in the language of proceedings, may use any of the official languages of the Community. Where the taking of evidence is decided upon following a request by a party to the proceedings, parties to be heard, witnesses or experts who express themselves in languages other than the language of proceedings may be heard only if the party who made the request makes provision for interpretation into that language. In proceedings concerning the application for registration of a design, in place of the language of the application, the second language indicated by the applicant may be used. In any proceedings with only one party, the Office may at the request of the party concerned permit derogation from the provisions in this paragraph. 4. If the parties and the Office so agree, any official language of the Community may be used in oral proceedings. 5. The Office shall, if necessary, make provision at its own expense for interpretation into the language of proceedings, or, where appropriate, into its other languages, unless this interpretation is the responsibility of one of the parties to the proceedings. 6. Statements by staff of the Office, by parties to the proceedings and by witnesses and experts, made in one of the languages of the Office during oral proceedings shall be entered in the minutes in the language employed. Statements made in any other language shall be entered in the language of proceedings. Corrections to the application for or the registration of a Community Design shall be entered in the minutes in the language of proceedings.

Article 83

Certification of translations

1. When a translation of any document is to be filed, the Office may require the filing, within a time limit to be specified by it, of a certificate that the translation corresponds to the original text. Where the certificate relates to the translation of a previous application pursuant to Article 42 of Regulation (EC) No 6/2002, such time limit shall not be less than three months after the date of filing of the application. Where the certificate is not filed within that time limit, the document shall be deemed not to have been received. 2. The President of the Office may determine the manner in which translations are certified.

Article 84

Legal authenticity of translations

In the absence of evidence to the contrary, the Office may assume that a translation corresponds to the relevant original text.

CHAPTER XX

RECIPROCITY, TRANSITION PERIOD AND ENTRY INTO FORCE

Article 85

Publication of reciprocity

1. If necessary, the President of the Office shall request the Commission to enquire whether a State which is not party to the Paris Convention for the Protection of Industrial Property or to the Agreement establishing the World Trade Organisation grants reciprocal treatment within the meaning of Article 41(5) Regulation (EC) No 6/2002. 2. If the Commission determines that reciprocal treatment in accordance with paragraph 1 is granted, it shall publish a communication to that effect in the *Official Journal of the European Communities*. 3. Article 41(5) of Regulation (EC) No 6/2002 shall apply from the date of publication in the *Official Journal of the European Communities* of the communication referred to in paragraph 2, unless the communication states an earlier date from which it is applicable. Article 41(5) of Regulation (EC) No 6/2002 shall cease to be applicable from the date of publication in the *Official Journal of the European Communities* of a communication of the Commission stating that reciprocal treatment is no longer granted, unless the communication states an earlier date from which it is applicable. 4. Communications referred to in paragraphs 2 and 3 shall also be published in the Official Journal of the Office.

Article 86

Transition period

1. Any application for registration of a Community Design filed no more than three months before the date fixed pursuant to Article 111(2) of Regulation (EC) No 6/2002 shall be marked by the Office with the filing date determined pursuant to that provision and with the actual date of receipt of the application. 2. With regard to the application, the priority period of six months provided for in Articles 41 and 44 of Regulation (EC) No 6/2002 shall be calculated from the date fixed pursuant to Article 111(2) of that Regulation. 3. The Office may issue a receipt to the applicant prior to the date fixed pursuant to Article 111(2) of Regulation (EC) No 6/2002. 4. The Office may examine the applications prior to the date fixed pursuant to Article 111(2) of Regulation (EC) No 6/2002 and communicate with the applicant with a view to remedying any deficiencies prior to that date. Any decisions with regard to such applications may be taken only after that date. 5. Where the date of receipt of an application for the registration of a Community Design by the Office, by the central industrial property office of a Member State or by the Benelux Design Office is before the commencement of the three-month period specified in Article 111(3) of Regulation (EC) No 6/2002 the application shall be deemed not to have been filed. The applicant shall be informed accordingly and the application shall be sent back to him/her.

Article 87

Entry into force

This Regulation shall enter into force on the seventh day following its publication in the *Official Journal of the European Communities*.

This Regulation shall be binding in its entirety and directly applicable in all Member States.

Done at Brussels, 21 October 2002.

For the Commission

Frederik BOLKESTEIN

Member of the Commission

Glossary

Berne Convention Convention administered by WIPO, which grants copyright protection to work created by UK national or residents

Community Design Registered and unregistered design rights as introduced by the European Design Directive

Community registrations Registrations for Community registered designs

Copyright, Designs and Patents Act 1988 (CDPA 1988) Main statute governing UK copyright law, as amended to reflect the European Directives including the European Design Directive

Designs Registry Registry within the UK Patent Office which administers affairs relating to UK registered designs

EEA European Economic Area

EC Treaty Treaty of Rome 1957

European Design Directive Directive establishing Community Design adopted 13 October 1998

Member State A country which is a Member State of the European Economic Area

Office for Harmonisation in the Internal Market (OHIM) Office in Alicante, Spain to which applications for Community Registered Designs and Community Trade Marks are made

registered Community Design Pan-European registered design right introduced by the European Design Directive, effective December 2002

registered design UK registered design under the Registered Designs Act 1949 as amended by the Registered Designs (Amendment) Regulations 2001

Registered Designs Act 1949 The current UK legislation governing registered designs as amended by the Registered Designs (Amendment) Regulations 2001

Registered Designs (Amendment) Regulations 2001 Regulations amending the provisions in respect of registered designs in the UK, as governed by the Registered Designs Act 1949 as amended

Regulations European Design Regulations as implemented by Council Regulations (EC) No.6/2002 of 12 December 2001.

Trade-Related Terms of Intellectual Property Rights (TRIPS) Part of the WIPO Agreement, administered by WIPO

United Nations Educational, Scientific and Cultural Organisation (UNESCO) Organisation which administers the UCC

United States Patent and Trade Mark Office (USPTO)

Universal Copyright Convention (UCC) Convention administered by UNESCO giving UK national copyright protection in countries which are members of the UCC

unregistered Community Design Pan-European unregistered design right introduced by the European Design Directive, effective March 2003

unregistered design right UK unregistered design right introduced under the Copyright, Designs and Patents Act 1988

World Intellectual Property Organisation (WIPO) Organisation which administers the Berne Convention

Index

Drafting Confidentiality Agreements

Mark Anderson

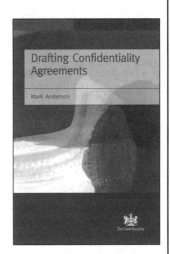

Confidentiality agreements are an important feature of a wide variety of business negotiations. This book gives practical assistance to lawyers and commercial managers who need to draft or negotiate a confidentiality agreement. It includes a summary of the law of confidence as it affects commercial relationships.

The book is divided into three parts:

- a practical explanation of how English law protects confidential information in a business context
- a discussion of commercial practice in relation to confidentiality agreements, including commentary on the terms of such agreements
- a selection of precedents for confidentiality agreements.

The practical nature of the book is enhanced by arguments for and against particular provisions, points to watch out for in confidentiality agreements and model wording for a range of different situations.

The book is accompanied by a free CD-ROM containing easily customised precedents for a variety of situations.

1 85328 871 3   May 2003   128 pages   £39.95

Available from Marston Book Services:
Tel. 01235 465 656.

The Law Society

Enterprise Act 2002

The New Law of Mergers, Monopolies and Cartels

Tim Frazer, Susan Hinchliffe and *Kyla George*

The Enterprise Act 2002 has radically changed the UK's competition law regime. This book provides you with a clear, comprehensive and immediate guide to the new merger control and market investigation procedures and the sanctions against cartel activities.

Key features include:

- detailed guidance on the practical impact of these sweeping changes and the new powers of the competition authorities
- explanation of how the new rules interact with the existing competition rules under the Competition Act 1998
- relevant sections and schedules of the Enterprise Act 2002 are reproduced in full.

This time-saving book brings together all of the UK competition rules in one single, concise reference work. It is ideal for senior managers and commercial lawyers who need to be thoroughly briefed on the new systems and penalties from a very early stage.

1 85328 896 9   February 2003   528 pages   £49.95

Available from Marston Book Services:
Tel. 01235 465 656.

The Law Society